The
HAPPINESS
of the
BRITISH WORKING
CLASS

The
HAPPINESS
of the
BRITISH
WORKING CLASS

JAMIE L. BRONSTEIN

STANFORD UNIVERSITY PRESS
Stanford, California

Stanford University Press
Stanford, California

© 2023 by Jamie Lara Bronstein. All rights reserved.

This book has been partially underwritten by the Peter Stansky Publication Fund in British Studies. For more information on the fund, please see www.sup.org/stanskyfund.

No part of this book may be reproduced or transmitted in any form or by any means, electronic or mechanical, including photocopying and recording, or in any information storage or retrieval system without the prior written permission of Stanford University Press.

Printed in the United States of America on acid-free, archival-quality paper

Library of Congress Cataloging-in-Publication Data
Names: Bronstein, Jamie L., 1968- author.
Title: The happiness of the British working class / Jamie L. Bronstein.
Description: Stanford, California : Stanford University Press, 2023. | Includes bibliographical references and index.
Identifiers: LCCN 2022022193 (print) | LCCN 2022022194 (ebook) | ISBN 9781503630499 (cloth) | ISBN 9781503633841 (paperback) | ISBN 9781503633858 (epub)
Subjects: LCSH: English literature—19th century—History and criticism. | Working class authors—Great Britain—History—19th century. | Happiness in literature. | Working class in literature. | Autobiography.
Classification: LCC PR468.H37 (print) | LCC PR468.H37 (ebook) | DDC 820.9/35—dc23/eng/20221102
LC record available at https://lccn.loc.gov/2022022193
LC ebook record available at https://lccn.loc.gov/2022022194

Cover design: Rob Ehle
Cover painting: Edmund Aylburton Willis, *An Idyllic Day*, Bedford Art Gallery
Typeset by Elliott Beard in Sabon LT Pro 10/13

For Mike and Evan

CONTENTS

	Acknowledgments	ix
	Introduction	1
ONE	Interrogating Autobiographies	11
TWO	The Simple Pleasures of Childhood	27
THREE	Work and Flow	42
FOUR	Life Is with People	65
FIVE	The Natural World	92
SIX	Self-Cultivation	106
SEVEN	The Way of Duty	124
EIGHT	Absent Happiness	148
NINE	Sadness, Fear, and Anger	159
TEN	The Past and the Present Converse	185
	Conclusion	209
	Notes	213
	Bibliography	255
	Index	281

ACKNOWLEDGMENTS

VERY FEW PROJECTS THAT TAKE a decade to research and write can come to fruition without the significant help of other people, and I would like to take a moment to acknowledge their contributions.

Faculty members at New Mexico State University can take a free course every semester as a benefit, so in 2008, I started taking undergraduate courses in the philosophy department. In 2013, I enrolled in my philosophy colleague Mark Walker's class, entitled "Should We Want to Be Happy?" This was my introduction to the philosophical literature on happiness, and we really dug in every week, reading and arguing in small groups. The class even set up a "Socrates booth" outside the student center, where, dressed in togas, we accosted passersby as though we were in the agora. We asked them about their conception of happiness; in return, each of them earned a chocolate bar.

The class inspired me to think about valorizations and definitions of happiness or well-being over time, and to reflect on my research field of nineteenth-century Britain, and the "standard of living" debate. Could working people undergoing the dislocations that accompanied industrialization have been happy, and if so, what was the nature of their happiness? Subsequent conversations and classes with my philosophy colleagues Lori Keleher, Jean-Paul Vessel, and Tim Cleveland have helped to hone my thoughts about the concept of happiness and the structure of philosophical argumentation, contributing greatly to this work. Peter Hutcheson of

Texas State University also provided helpful comments on an early version of chapter 1.

Once I understood that it might be possible to use working-class autobiographies to learn something about happiness in the nineteenth century, I obtained a copy of the 1984 annotated bibliography *The Autobiography of the Working Class* and began working my way through every autobiography I could obtain, either physically or digitally. I thank the interlibrary loan librarians at the NMSU library for their assiduousness. I also appreciate the help I received from Special Collections at the Brunel University Library; Sunderland Local Studies Center; Wake Forest University Library; Bristol Public Library; Coventry Local History Centre; Glasgow Public Library; Newport Reference Library; Islington Local History Library; and Stoke-on-Trent Archives. A mini-grant and a subsequent travel grant from the NMSU College of Arts and Sciences funded trips to collections in New York, New Jersey, and London. Thanks also to David Vincent for his online help. While in the British Library I met Florence Boos, whose scholarship on working-class women writers intersects with mine, and to whom I am grateful for our conversations.

As the stories told by working-class autobiographers began to cohere thematically, early iterations of some of the chapters here were presented at meetings of the Western Conference on British Studies. I am indebted to my WCBS colleagues for their help and support, particularly Richard Follett, Lynn Mackay, Greg Smith, Marjorie Levine-Clark, and Christopher Frank. Peter Stansky, who advised my PhD dissertation in the 1990s, continued to be an encouraging mentor and friend as I pursued this project. The comments and suggestions of anonymous reviewers for Stanford University Press helped me to deepen the historiography of the chapters. I extend my deep gratitude to my friend Danny Wade, who read the entire manuscript with a transcriptionist's careful eye. Finally, thanks to Mike and Evan Zigmond, for all your love, support, and laughs.

The
HAPPINESS
of the
BRITISH
WORKING CLASS

Introduction

LOOKING BACK ON HIS LIFE AT the age of eighty, William Hutton, who had risen from poverty to become a bookbinder, papermaker, landowner, and writer, considered the question of happiness at length, under the heading "What is a happy life?":

> Suppose a man endeavours after health, and his endeavours are blessed with such success that, by a proper use of his animal powers, he can, at fourscore, walk thirty miles a day. Suppose him, by assiduity and temperance, to have attained a complete independence, that he can reside in a house to his wish, with a garden for use and amusement, is blessed with a son and daughter of the most affectionate kind, who attentively watch his little wants with a view to supply them; add as an appendage to this little family a pair of old and faithful horses who are strangers to the lash, and whose value increases with the years. Still add to a taste for reading, the benefits arising from a library of choice Authors. Would you pronounce this a *happy man*? That man is myself. Though my morning was lowering, my evening is sunshine.[1]

John Britton, who started life as a wine-bottler's apprentice before becoming a writer, penned a similar gloss on happiness, considering his penchant for finding nature and art delightful, loving to read, and having "an affectionate and amiable wife, the esteem of many good and estimable men, and an intimacy, I hope friendship, with several eminent and distinguished personages."[2]

Of what did happiness consist for British working people in the nineteenth century? That is the central question addressed in this study. The question may seem puzzling, since it implies that human emotions are not simply biological facts but also mental constructs based on common physiological experiences. A person may experience a negatively inflected state of high physical arousal, and yet whether she perceives or describes that experience as anger or fear or disgust depends at least in part on the social context in which the event occurs.[3] But is happiness an emotion, or is it something else? Philosophers have made a cottage industry out of assessing competing views on this question. Some argue that happiness is reducible to sensory pleasure (hedonism); others that we are happy when our desires are satisfied; others that happiness is an attitudinal disposition; and still others that there is some objective standard of human flourishing against which a particular person's well-being can be measured.[4] Still others endorse "whole life satisfaction" as a definition of happiness: that we are happy if we judge that our lives have gone well.

Hutton and Britton, looking back on their lives from the perspective of old age, each made a cognitive judgment that they had lived happy lives, comparing their experiences against a list of criteria that each thought necessary or sufficient for happiness. But this long-term retrospective assessment was not the only way in which working-class autobiographers described happiness. As this book will show, they also recounted positive dispositions of character; experiences that brought laughter; transient states of intense joy or rapture that made them weep happy tears; activities or states of affairs that made them feel contentment or lose track of time in a pleasurable way. They described happiness in ways that might include any or all these reactions to good states of affairs. In all these ways, they behaved as though they considered happiness to be an emotional state that was phenomenologically consistent, persistent, central, and had the ability to drive behavior.[5] But not all of them even considered maximization of happiness as the key to the good life. Some thought social, political, or religious change, pursued as a duty, to be life's goal. Others experienced extreme poverty, disability, or illness and did not focus on happiness in their autobiographies; their writings help to delineate the shortcomings of Victorian society. This book explores the happiness of working-class people in an era of intense social and economic change, through the prism of 363 working-class autobiographies of Britons born between 1750 and 1870.[6]

As Darrin McMahon pointed out in 2014, happiness has received less focus from historians of the emotions than have fear, anger, grief, and shame.[7] Moreover, the histories of happiness that do exist tend to focus on happiness as expressed in normative literature, rather than exploring the phenomenology of happiness conveyed through firsthand narratives.[8] Scholars have been quite creative about mining sources for the history of the emotions, looking variously at artistic productions, folklore, normative sources like conduct manuals, funeral and burial practices, and wills. But studies exploring and contextualizing the emotional histories of ordinary working people are rare.[9] This study, focused on a discrete time, place, and social class, should serve as a partial corrective.

Some historians, heavily influenced by neuropsychologists, see emotions as primarily biological, prior to rational judgment, and universal. Others see emotions as "cogmotions"—attempts intellectually to grapple with or translate emotional judgments.[10] But most historians of the emotions believe that the experience of certain emotions is historically and culturally contingent: that people perceive, name, act out, and display their feelings (or "moods" or "passions") through cultural and chronological frames. Although its origins have been credited to the work of Lucien Febvre and Norbert Elias in the early twentieth century, the modern field of emotions history began to flourish in the 1980s with the work of Peter and Carol Stearns. They developed "emotionology," focusing on the emotional proscriptions and prescriptions specified by the normative texts of specific times and places: conduct books, popular magazines, children's' literature, sermons, etc.[11] Normative literature can be combined with the external perception of emotional display. Thus, Christina Kotchemidova has argued that the rules of emotional display in the nineteenth-century United States called for conversational candor and the expression of positive affect; travelers from England found Americans to be unusual in this respect.[12]

A slightly different historiographical trajectory, initiated by William Reddy, proposes that entire nations at various times have had "emotional regimes," or structures of expectation about emotional experience and display. For Reddy, these regimes have coexisted alongside "emotional refuges," which provide more emotional liberty.[13] A third trajectory, identified with Barbara Rosenwein, argues that emotional expression has always coexisted alongside emotional restraint, and that people move among multiple "emotional communities."[14] As a longtime student of labor- and working-class history, I approached the topic with the belief that nineteenth-century British working people shared a culture and thus most likely shared an emotional community or communities.

This project is a social and cultural history of happiness as it was lived by working people in industrializing Britain, drawn from a careful examination of their own words. Which activities, experiences, and relationships made them content, satisfied, or joyful? How can we know what working people thought about their own happiness? Their narratives about their whole lives are replete with descriptions of emotional experience. I learned, through wide reading, that while many working-class Britons may have participated in shared emotional communities, not all did; that geography, upward mobility, gender, religious belief, political commitments, and lack of basic economic resources all influenced the way in which they defined and experienced their emotional lives.

Nineteenth-century Britain is a prime historical setting for an exploration of working-class happiness. The expansion of literacy, the availability of printing, and the notion that working people's lives might have some inherent value or interest led to a profusion of autobiographical writing. Emotions in general, and happiness in particular, were the subject of a larger cultural discourse in that time and place.[15] British thinkers and policymakers in the nineteenth century argued about the nature of the good life, and some of their ideas are still cornerstones of the philosophical literature on happiness.[16] The English philosopher Jeremy Bentham proposed that happiness was a function of pleasure. He argued that the utility of any experience—its ratio of pleasure to pain—could be mathematically calculated. About pleasure Bentham was notoriously nonjudgmental, quipping that pushpin (a game) was as good as poetry. He maintained that individual utilities could be added together and generalized into policies intended to produce societal happiness, and that the goal of social policy should be to maximize the greatest good for the greatest number. Bentham's protégé, John Stuart Mill, disagreed, claiming that, particularly when designing national policies, the "higher pleasures" of art, education, and culture were superior to the "lower pleasures" of satiating animal desires. While most working-class autobiographers had not read Bentham or Mill, they had views on these questions.[17]

Furthermore, the prescriptive literature on happiness was influenced by class. For those who could afford it, the eighteenth century had ushered in an era of happiness through consumption: more comfortably appointed houses, toys for children, pleasure gardens, attractive public spaces, exotic food.[18] In the nineteenth century, the recipe for contentment shifted from consumption to consanguinity. Men belonging to a growing middle class were urged to cultivate familial happiness by expressing affection and willingness to compromise; the most coveted happiness being a low-key, stoic satisfaction and contentment.[19] Novels and domestic manuals intended for middle-class women emphasized a social version of happiness within the family. Women were directed to perform or oversee household tasks thoughtfully, set a good moral example, provide a ready ear, and counteract the competitive and masculine world of the market. Aristocratic women were directed to host others within their circle, pursue charitable outreach to the local community, hone their accomplishments in music, drawing, embroidery, or amateur theatricals, participate in sports and games, and pass the time in conversation with a small group of similarly situated women.[20] Upwardly mobile working people might aim to pattern their lives after these normative scripts, but, as this book will show, working-class people also created their own.

Asking questions about happiness in the early nineteenth century not only broadens our knowledge about the valuation and the nature of happiness in the past but can also create a dialogue with the interdisciplinary field of "happiness studies" that has matured since the 1990s. The existence of the field of happiness studies, with its own journals, tells us much about our own social priorities.[21] Books about how to be happier have flown off the shelves. Scholars have found correlations between happiness and a host of positive outcomes, including better health and happier marriages.[22] But it is relatively rare for these social-scientific investigations to incorporate (or even acknowledge) historical studies. Writing in 1999, Mihály Csíkszentmihályi complained that comparative studies about happiness through time were lacking. In 2018, historians Barbara Rosenwein and Riccardo Cristiani still lamented historians' exclusion from the modern scientific research on emotions.[23]

Mining working-class autobiographies from the nineteenth century can inform the modern social science literature on happiness by showing how the modern literature itself is historically contingent. To give just one example: the economist Richard Easterlin and his co-authors argued that wealth and happiness are not always correlated in the modern West; that once a certain rather low level of comfort has been reached, people adapt to that level of comfort, want more, and feel "relative deprivation" compared with others in their society who have more; they are on a "hedonic treadmill."[24] Working-class autobiographies, in contrast, put little emphasis on materialism as a cornerstone of happiness. In a preface to the autobiography of Joseph Gutteridge, William Jolly noted that "amid the growing luxury of our age and the overestimate of mere surroundings as necessary to happiness, it is of inestimable service to humanity to be, from time to time, recalled to the true pleasures of plain living and high thinking."[25] There is a lot to unpack here. Was Gutteridge adapting to social and economic constraints when he recalled his nonmaterialistic happiness? Was Jolly reacting to the beginnings of the "hedonic treadmill" by proposing an older set of norms? As chapter 10 shows, the nineteenth century has some valuable lessons for the twenty-first.[26]

This book consists of a chapter that evaluates the sources, eight chapters that explore happiness thematically, and a cross-disciplinary final chapter directed at the field of happiness studies. Chapter 1, "Interrogating Autobiographies," considers some potential drawbacks about using life writing as a source for the history of the emotions. It investigates the questions of verifying authorship, the motivations of working-class autobiographers, and the influences of genre conventions and audience expectations on included and excluded topics. Complicating things even further is the possibility that talking about or writing about how we are feeling—as life-writers do—has the potential to alter those feelings. Statements made about emotions experienced in the past pose additional challenges.[27] Although due to differential levels of literacy the autobiographies are not representative either by geographical region of the British Isles or by gender, this chapter argues for the importance of the sources as some of the only evidence we have about the inner lives of nineteenth-century working people.

The thematic chapters of the book invite the reader to dive into the social and emotional worlds of British working people born before 1870. Each of these chapters explores happiness as it relates to a topic in British social or cultural history that in turn has its own deep historiography. While I am thus indebted to the expertise of many scholars, my contribution here is to expand our knowledge of what it felt like to be a member of the British working class by linking writers' positive emotional experiences and assessments to these topics. To borrow a phrase from Sarah Ahmed, "Happiness might play a crucial role in shaping our near sphere, the world that takes shape around us, as a world of familiar things."[28] Investigating happiness enlightens for us the "near sphere" of working people, building a rich social and cultural history out of the autobiographers' own words.

Chapter 2, "The Simple Pleasures of Childhood," chronicles the ways in which autobiographers, largely writing in adulthood or old age, felt nostalgia for the period in their lives in which they were freest from economic and familial responsibilities. Almost all autobiographers elaborated on the primary pleasures of childhood, including shelter and warmth, parental or grandparental presence, comforting foods, and a few playthings. Some facets of working-class childhood emerged unexpectedly and repeatedly. For example, for children who were put to work at an early age, contributing to the family economy could evoke joy and pride. Nonetheless, Sundays were joyful days, promising physical freedom, the opportunity for sleep, and the intellectual stimulation of Sunday school.

The industrial transformation of nineteenth-century Britain occurred unevenly by region and chronology. Thus, occupations of autobiographers in the study range widely: from soldier or sailor to farmworker to miner to metalworker to domestic servant. As chapter 3, "Work and Flow," demonstrates, some working people (notably, not factory workers) found their occupations or avocations so satisfying that time slipped away without their noticing, producing what psychologist Mihály Csíkszentmihályi terms a "flow state." Workers also associated happiness in the workplace with factors like the opportunity for innovation and creativity (sometimes pursued through projects outside of work hours), autonomy, a feeling of respect in the workplace, and like-minded co-workers (some workers preferred a playful workplace, with practical jokes; others, being surrounded by sober and focused co-workers).

Chapter 4, "Life Is with People," delves into the importance of social ties. Starting with the most intimate relationships and moving outward, it explores happiness in the context of romantic relationships and marriage. It was very common for autobiographers to document the joyful atmosphere of the newlywed household and to credit their happiness to long-standing marital relationships (although interestingly, second marriages tended to be much less happy). But they also depended on wider networks of friends and family, and in a historical moment in which leave-taking for work or emigration was common, scenes of grief-stricken parting and joyful reunion recur. Working people—particularly men—were expanding their social horizons from extended-family members and drinking companions to encompass the friendships they formed with co-workers, co-religionists, and like-minded strivers. Finally, celebrations like holiday weeks, fairs, and races provided opportunities to feel a sense of connection to a wider community; individual commemorations of important national events stood out to writers even decades later.

Chapter 5, "The Natural World," shows that many working-class autobiographers cared deeply about the environment; the attempts by rational recreationists to draw them out into the countryside overlapped rather than conflicted with workers' desires. Autobiographers sought the outdoors for leisure, exercise, solitude, and quiet. (Interestingly, there are few descriptions of trespassing, ball-playing in inappropriate areas, or loud picnicking.) They were apt to see the appeal of rugged, sublime, and pastoral landscapes. They found the countryside full of resources outside the constraints of the market: fish, berries, birds' nests, and components that could be made into simple toys; and they wrote about the enjoyment produced by growing vegetables and flowers. The psychological transports produced by nature undermine the argument that workers experienced higher wages and increased opportunities for consumption as completely positive developments, given the relationship between industrialization and the destruction of the environment.

Chapter 6, "Self-Cultivation," explores the relationship between happiness and intellectual development. Bentham may have equated the pleasure of poetry with the pleasure of the game of pushpin, but working-class autobiographers (likely influenced by normative expectations about respectability) had much more to say about the former than the latter. This chapter shows that many found delight in avidly reading whatever material they could get their hands on through networks of book-borrowing and intellectual patronage. They experienced the joys of self-directed research, becoming collectors and classifiers, amateur botanists and geologists. A few gained access to musical instruments, sometimes using them as leverage for upward mobility. All (except for those who dictated their autobiographies to others) were authors, but many were also poets who burst with pride when their works were published for the first time.

For some writers more oriented toward the Aristotelian concept of eudaimonia, happiness was not the measure of a life well lived, as chapter 7, "The Way of Duty," shows. Rather, such a life entailed accomplishment, or at least a steadfast commitment toward improving humankind. This axiology was common among Chartists, trade unionists, and Socialists, but also among temperance lecturers and Methodist preachers, suggesting that neither class position nor ideology solely dictated membership in an emotional community. This chapter also illustrates the relationship between happiness and religious belief. In an age of evangelical emphasis on sinfulness, for many autobiographers the transformation to professed belief was associated with joy, relief, and a kind of fatalism as they handed over responsibilities to God. Chapter 8, "Absent Happiness," considers those autobiographers whose life writing made no mention, or almost no mention, of happiness. Ill health or extreme poverty prevented individuals from achieving their life goals or engaging in self-reflection about the good life.

Chapter 9, "Sadness, Fear, and Anger," reflects on some of the more negative emotions expressed in working-class autobiographies. It explores working-class autobiographers' expressions of grief at the loss of loved ones, particularly their partners and children, and the tension between men's tears, which were shed in private, and their later willingness to write about having shed tears in private. It shows that autobiographers associated fear with childhood or rusticity, and used anecdotes about fear for comic relief. Finally, it demonstrates that working-class autobiographers wrote less about anger than about other emotions, tentatively suggesting that for most writers, changing mores around the uncontrolled expression of anger or the use of interpersonal violence shaped what was socially acceptable to divulge.

Finally, chapter 10, "The Past and the Present Converse," reviews hypotheses about subjective well-being posed by modern philosophers and social scientists, and the way in which my research about happiness among nineteenth-century working people supports or challenges these. Many British working-class autobiographers described being happier in childhood and old age than in midlife, when family concerns and economic stresses were at their height. This is a characteristic of modern life review that contemporary scholars call the "U-shaped happiness curve." In contrast, very few working-class autobiographers discussed feeling pressure or unhappiness caused by comparing their own social standing with that of their neighbors. While much of the modern philosophical literature focuses on cheerful moods as a sign of substantive well-being, I show that working-class autobiographers distrusted moods, describing them as part of a complex of whipsawing emotions sometimes associated with insanity or religious enthusiasm taken to an extreme.

By the end of each autobiography I read for this project, I felt as though I had been allowed a privileged glimpse into the life of a long-dead person through his or her own unique voice, conveyed variously by the rhythm of the writing, the lightness of humor and depth of seriousness, the joy in successes and struggle with hardships. The result of reading working-class autobiographies through the prism of happiness is a wide-ranging reflection on the industrial-era working-class experience: on family, friends, work, interaction with the natural world, science and creativity, political causes and religious commitments, physical and economic struggles.

ONE

Interrogating Autobiographies

PEOPLE WHO LABORED FOR A LIVING, or who were raised in working-class households with significant economic disadvantages, generated more than one type of writing. In some ways, other kinds of literature that workers produced, including letters to the editors of various publications, speeches given at meetings, poetry, and songs, were more likely to be emotionally expressive than were their autobiographies. This study uses working-class autobiography rather than those other sources, because autobiographies most resemble the firsthand accounts of emotional experience used by modern scholars researching the emotions.[1] But how well do working-class autobiographies hold up as a source to produce knowledge about happiness in particular? To what extent can we trust them? How might authors have been shaped by such considerations as genre norms and audience expectations? What motivated individual authors? This chapter engages those questions.

Although working-class autobiographies were long lightly explored in contrast with other kinds of sources that touch on the welfare of British working people during the period of industrialization, some historians have recently made extensive use of them, including Jane Humphries, Regenia Gagnier, Nan Hackett, David Vincent, Julie-Marie Strange, Patrick Joyce, and John Burnett. Emma Griffin in particular has made these autobiographies the cornerstone of her work, looking at them not just as qualitative but also as quantitative evidence concerning such questions as the trajectory of the nineteenth century, the emotional health of the working-class family, and the existence of hunger during the Industrial Revolution.[2] In addition, a major public-history project has sorted autobiographies from John Burnett's collection at Brunel University into a database searchable by keyword, thus making it easier for historians to perform "distant reading" as well as close reading of these documents.[3] The increasingly widespread use of autobiographies testifies to the understanding that this set of first-person narratives in particular provides evidence of a type that exists nowhere else—evidence in someone's own words about how it felt to be a person living during a period of social and economic transformation.

Of course, autobiographies have peculiar epistemic properties that have to be taken into account. Are they veridical documents? Not all documents purporting to be working-class autobiographies were in fact so, but, because they defy widespread patterns, patently inauthentic autobiographies stand out. Some were entirely fictional. In 1867, the Reverend George Huntington published *The Autobiography of John Brown, Cordwainer*, presenting himself as the editor rather than the author of the document. But many aspects of "Brown's" autobiography are unusual. The "author" describes his upbringing in the (imaginary) Yorkshire village of "Elmington," with a particular focus on events within the parish church. The supposed author writes almost nothing about his home or family life, or the experience of the leather work that would have occupied a cordwainer's days. At the age of twenty-one, the "author" goes by Parliamentary train to the fictional Lancashire town of "Aston," where he again is completely preoccupied by popular religiosity and the extent to which the Church of England excluded working people from worship by demanding pew rent and placing a premium on dress clothes.[4] By an amazing coincidence, the "editor" of the autobiography (Huntington) was born in Elloughton, Yorkshire, and then moved to Salford in Lancashire, where he worked with colliers as a church rector.[5] The obvious conclusion is that Huntington himself wrote the *Autobiography*.

But sometimes, the desire to narrate having lived a life of basic dignity led autobiographers to dissemble, as in the case of John Rowlands. Born out of wedlock to a mother who deserted him, Rowlands was raised in a workhouse, educated in a paupers' school, and shuffled around among uncaring relatives. He recalled not only being unhappy but also having his unhappiness compounded by the shame and poor treatment that his status elicited from other people. Only emigration, and the possibility of starting over, offered him the prospect of dignity. Rowlands described the first real moment of joy he had felt as a young man, when he disembarked from the ship on which he worked to enter New Orleans the first time. "I was nearly overwhelmed with blissful feeling that rises from emancipation. I was free!—and I was happy, yes, actually happy, for I was free—at last the boy was free!"[6]

Rowlands described being hired by Henry Hope Stanley, a wealthy New Orleans trader who recognized Rowlands as a worthy person and bought him clothes and a trunk. Rowlands said Stanley tutored him academically and in manners, and gave him increasingly responsible positions in his business.[7] Rowlands even reported that his mentor had adopted him as his son:

> To have an unbreathed, unformed wish plucked out of the silence, and fashioned into a fact as real as though my dead father had been restored to life and claimed me, was a marvel so great that I seemed to be divided into two individuals—one strenuously denying that such a thing could be, and the other arraying all the proofs of the fact.[8]

In tribute to the man who had plucked him out of misery, Rowlands changed his own name to Henry Morton Stanley. Unfortunately for this inspiring tale, Henry Morton Stanley's biographer has established convincingly that not only did Henry Hope Stanley *not* adopt the younger man, but that the two most likely never met.[9] Stanley himself confessed that "the knowledge that every moment makes me older, the fluctuations to which the spirit is subject, hour to hour, forever remind me that happiness is not to be secured in the world, except for brief periods." For Stanley, to be happy involved "to be without sorrow, fear, anxiety, doubt," and to forget what reminded him of unhappiness.[10] These feelings no doubt explain his decision to rewrite his early life.[11] But Stanley's autobiography and that of "John Brown" are unusual. In general, working-class autobiographers did not fictionalize the names of people, places, or events in their own lives, and many of their stories of occupation, location, and family composition can be successfully checked against census records.

Scholars have identified other autobiographies as collaborative efforts based on real lives. One of the most fascinating collaborative working-class autobiographies written in the nineteenth century was that of "Elizabeth (Betty) Dobbs," a joint project of a charwoman and the American actress who interviewed her. Florence Boos has identified the life story in *The Autobiography of a Charwoman* as that of Martha Grimes, even though some parts seem to have been fictionalized by its narrator, and other parts by its scribe. *The Autobiography of a Charwoman* describes Grimes's life in a chaotic household, her mother's drunkenness, and her stepmother's abusiveness. It correctly documents the birth of Grimes's first child out of wedlock, and her subsequent marriages and the births of other children. Chronologies are slightly scrambled, and audience expectations are considered; for example, the *Autobiography*'s narrator is seduced by a single employer, while the actual Martha Grimes more controversially bore the illegitimate child of a married man.[12] Another collaboration, between Francis West and the disabled textile worker Jonathan Saville, was shaped by West's priorities. Saville's life served in part as proof of God's providence, given that Saville survived an abusive childhood in mining, spinning, and warping before becoming a lay preacher. Saville's memoir switches back and forth between first and third person, making West's commentaries clearly perceptible.[13]

While a few autobiographies are either fictional or collaborative, the vast majority of working-class autobiographies written by people born before 1870 were intended to communicate something real about the material world.[14] With very few exceptions, nineteenth-century working-class autobiography was motivated by a sincere desire to leave an accurate historical record; moreover, in contrast with diaristic writing, it tends to present a coherent version of the self.[15] It is easy to cross-check writers' assertions against historical events, and I have even found it possible to use historical records to identify anonymous memoirs on the basis of internal evidence. It is also occasionally possible to compare the self-reported emotional states of an autobiographer with evidence of how he or she seemed to other people, although when self-reports conflict with external reports, all one can really do is examine both. Robert Blatchford, the British Socialist and founder of the immensely influential *Clarion* newspaper, described himself as a very happy person. He remembered having a buoyant temperament as a young man, so much so that even time spent "on the tramp" without any money became an adventure. As he crossed the country from Yorkshire to London, he fell in love with the English countryside and with English women, who, one after another, took him in and provided for him. "Yes, it was a delightful holiday, and the ingredients of the feast were youth, novelty, adventure, hope, and fine weather. That was fifty-nine years ago, and it would remain with me as a fragrant and sunny memory if I lived to be five hundred."[16] Blatchford professed that his cheerful temperament made him a favorite throughout his life: "I was treated with a queer sort of tender esteem and affection, resembling the regard which grown-ups show to a favoured and favourite youngster."[17]

Blatchford's public assessment of his demeanor conflicts with descriptions by his biographers, who had the additional evidence of personal letters or direct acquaintance. Laurence Thompson described Blatchford as having had fits of nervous depression, often following illness, with a demonstrably combative personality and intermittently gruff, impatient, and brooding.[18] Albert Lyons, who was friends with Blatchford, admired him greatly but also noted his fits of depression.[19] Blatchford himself made a comment that explains the distance between his inner life and his external emotional display: "When a man writes he says what he believes and feels. His utterance is himself—as he *would* be. But it is the spirit of the man you have. But in his *life* you have the body and the soul together. The spirit, or mind, speaks nobly—is the man as he *would* be. The body and mind together are the man he *can* be."[20] Blatchford aspired to be happy, noting that happiness was the meaning of life. "Have I not told you a hundred times that the people want cheering more than they want improving? Is not the first line of my creed, 'The object of life is to be happy'? People do not live to work. They work to live."[21] Blatchford's memoir may not tell us how happy he was personally, but it does show that he considered happiness to be an intrinsic value around which he constructed his autobiographical persona. These sorts of epistemic problems explain why most historians working with these documents look at many autobiographies.

Another potential issue with working-class autobiographies is the inability of historians to fully immerse themselves in the authors' world. As the music historian Vic Gammon has noted, both the writer and the contemporaneous reader of these documents brought to the experience minds full of cultural references, oral traditions, songs, and memories to which modern historians have very limited access.[22] But it is worth making the effort to reconstruct as much of that shared cultural meaning as possible.

After having established that most autobiographies strive to be truthful testimonies, other questions naturally arise: What motivated the production of these documents? How are the documents inflected by those motivations? To a great extent, the autobiographies consulted for this project fall into a category that Richard Coe terms "memoir" because the author attempts to recount what happened in ways that can be verified by outside sources. Unlike the largely twentieth-century, middle-class writers whose works Coe explores, these working-class deponents did not necessarily describe themselves as psychologically unique, although they sometimes wrote memoirs because they had unusual occupations or experiences from which they thought readers might benefit.[23] "I am not an exceptional man," the miller James Edwin Saunders wrote, "but I sometimes think I have had an exceptional opportunity of learning the lessons that life is meant to teach, and that my trust is to pass on the simple message of a simple man's life."[24] The vast majority of working-class autobiographers not only asserted particular reasons for having written but also explicitly aimed their narratives at a named audience. George Parkinson, who spent the first decades of his life underground as a Durham miner before becoming a Methodist preacher, was typical of working-class autobiographers in his expressed reason for writing. "During the later years of a long and busy life I have been much pressed by a wide circle of friends to write its story," he explained.[25] Robert Dottie said that although he had often been asked to write his memoirs, "it has never presented itself to my mind conclusively that I could 'dish up' anything concerning my humble self of sufficient interest to justify its glorification in type."[26]

Other authors cited slightly different motivations. David Barr wrote his autobiography so that "the narrative may prove an encouragement and stimulus to some lad to struggle with poverty and difficulties in his effort to clamber up the difficult and rugged steeps of life."[27] William Tayler wrote his memoir in order to improve his handwriting.[28] Some autobiographers wrote because they found the process of remembering and writing to be enjoyable.[29] Joseph Donaldson, who submitted his autobiography anonymously for publication in 1823, noted that even if his autobiography turned out to be a failure as a literary document, "many an hour I have whiled away in writing it . . . might have otherwise passed over me heavily enough. The pleasures of memory, I think, in many cases, are even superior to those of hope."[30] John Harris, a Cornish miner and poet, "sat down to write about myself, and to enjoy some of the delight of which the Scotch poet speaks, in rambling in thought over long-forsaken tracts, and pleasantly musing through the dim aisles of the past."[31] Carolyn Steedman, who edited the memoir of soldier John Pearman, notes that although Pearman did not edit his memoir in a way that suggested he meant it to be read, it is impossible to write something without imagining an audience for it.[32]

Many early autobiographies were written with an instrumental purpose, such as to give cover to charitable contributions or to intervene in a political movement.[33] Samuel Parsons (born 1762) provides an example of the former. He was a strolling player in various theatrical companies in and around York, but by 1822 had found himself without a means of support. He published by subscription a book of songs and poems with a brief account of his life attached. The unnamed author of the volume's preface remarked that the quality of the writing was marginal, but that "Poor Parsons is suffering under the pains of indigence, and with a family to support... the claims of humanity are beyond those of any other claim whatsoever."[34]

Another autobiography clearly intended to raise funds is that of Edward Finlay, a peripatetic Irishman born around the turn of the nineteenth century. Finlay spent time in Manchester, Liverpool, and Glasgow. Although his hands were disabled from a fire, he was a very fast wire-chain maker, who would knit chains and wire puzzles in public while crying "Penny-a-yard!" In 1854, Finlay was arrested for begging—apparently one of many times that he fell afoul of the law—but during those stints when he steered clear of jail he managed to collect enough money to have his autobiography privately printed. His memoir recounts one horrible event after another: penury, the birth and death of many infants, a paralyzing stroke late in pregnancy that left his wife unable to support herself; and directs prayers at men and women who might read his narrative and feel charitable.[35]

Robert Blincoe's autobiography resembles the rich corpus of firsthand narratives penned by formerly enslaved people in the United States. These narratives had particular goals and were unapologetically collaborative efforts between an educated, socially accepted interlocutor and a marginalized person who had experienced ill treatment. Blincoe's contemporaries understood his autobiography to be a political document, and included it as evidence while lobbying for restrictions on factory hours.[36] The autobiographies of Mary Prince, who had been born a slave in Jamaica, and Elizabeth Storie, who sought redress for medical malpractice that ruined her life, were also instrumental narratives meant to create change.[37] The *Extraordinary Confessions of a Female Pickpocket* had an arresting title to sell copies, but also was published as an argument that female factory operatives found themselves in sexual thrall to their immediate factory superiors.[38]

How do the genre conventions of autobiography impact the way historians can use these documents? Expectations of genre—of narrative, language, form—shaped what autobiographers felt comfortable discussing and omitting for an imagined audience or even under editorial pressure.[39] Editors pushed authors to omit information about bodies, families, and strong emotions like grief.[40] Students of autobiography have identified stock formats into which autobiographers integrated their own details:

the conversion narrative, for example, which compares and contrasts life before and after some great life conversion (not necessarily a religious conversion); or the jeremiad, the autobiography as a detail of individual suffering. Some autobiographies were written to "set the record straight" or settle scores.[41] David Vincent points to the religious conversion narrative, the oral tradition, and slightly later, the story of a political struggle as genres toward which workers gravitated.[42] Jane Rendall, who looked at fifteen autobiographies written by working-class women, identified additional categories like the repentance narrative, the petition, and the life cycle of the family economy.[43] By 1851, some of the characteristics of working-class autobiography were clear enough for the writer Charles Kingsley self-consciously to frame his novel *Alton Locke* as a fictional addition to the genre.[44]

Some authors were self-consciously literary, choosing the style of the picaresque (particularly common with soldiers' and sailors' narratives) or relating their experiences with humor.[45] Others, like the traveling showman George Sanger, clearly created a stage persona—Sanger began his memoir with anticipatory "patter" of the kind he used every day as a carnival barker.[46] Some autobiographies recount the struggles of particular groups—Chartists (activists in the 1830s and 1840s who sought universal male suffrage and other political reforms) or trade unionists, for example—refracted through the prism of one participant's experiences. Some autobiographers viewed their own experiences as representative of larger groups: farm laborers, or potters, or miners. Nineteenth-century working-class autobiographers, unlike those who wrote about their lives in the late twentieth century, did not see themselves as primarily taking part in a common project of reconstructing or showing nostalgia for a world that they had lost. Their autobiographies therefore tend to be idiosyncratic.[47]

Does the pressure exerted by genre expectations negate the value of working-class autobiographies? In her book *Subjectivities,* the scholar Regenia Gagnier argued that middle-class readership expectations produced a hegemonic cultural discourse of upward mobility and the "self-made man," and noted that working-class autobiographies tended to fail as literary documents when they followed this model.[48] We can see the impact of that pressure on James Dunn's *From Coal-Mine Upwards,* whose preface notes: "No man can raise himself in the social scale, especially if his early life be passed under great disadvantages, unless he has marked qualities such as determination, pluck, patience, and principle."[49] While Gagnier rightly noted that many working people's lives did not fit easily into this type of narrative, the products of the conflict between expectations and reality yield interesting results from the perspective of the history of emotions. For example, Mary Loughran reflected on the way in which her brother Patrick's life-changing and disabling accident had impacted her own life-course; she gave up the idea of having a home of her own—and had to say no to a promising relationship—to take care of him. "I have been urged to end my story in the usual way but how can I? When I believe I have never really cared enough for anyone to give up my freedom. But I suddenly realized I could care."[50] Similarly, the pseudonymous "Jacques," whose work life included periods as a flax-dresser (one who prepares flax to be spun into thread), a tanner, a railroad navvy (manual laborer), and a bank clerk, periods of drinking and sobriety, and periods of the most severe destitution and separation from his family, acknowledged that "my life, if not absolutely wasted, has been unimproved and fruitless; the present is still a struggle with unpropitious circumstances; the future pregnant with anticipations of disaster, loneliness, and sorrow." Jacques's memoir may have been a failed contribution to the narrative of upward mobility, but "it contains a faithful reflex of his feelings in the various trying situations in which he has been placed; and what can only be chiefly known to himself, and for which he alone can conscientiously vouch—and he does vouch—is its entire veracity."[51]

The content of autobiography was influenced not just by literary conventions but also by larger social conventions. Psychologists studying "declarative subjective well-being"—any self-report of well-being that a person makes to an audience—note that audience expectations condition the types of things that people are willing to report; in a way, the target audience for that report imposes goals on people. One goal may be managing others' impressions or building a persona; another may be expressing the type of emotion that is socially sanctioned. Sometimes reporters manage to delude themselves as well as their audiences, and authors in the nineteenth century understood this.[52] As John Wilson, who rose from working in a coal pit to serving as a labor leader and MP, acknowledged in the introduction to his autobiography, "There is in us all a desire to show ourselves off as well as we can, and thus magnify our virtues and strong points and lessen the vices and weak places . . . We want the power to 'see oursels as others see us . . .' "[53]

The category of "larger social conventions" includes norms of emotional display; these varied by gender, age, and even geography. Autobiographies by working women born before 1870 are rare. As Emma Griffin has noted, not until late twentieth-century local history and oral history projects specifically sought out women writers did the number of female autobiographers substantially increase, and even then, their narratives tend to be shorter and less confident.[54] But the few that exist for the earlier period show more expression of feelings than do most memoirs by men. Deborah Smith, born in 1858, was in her early fifties when she had a revelation from God that she should write her autobiography. "From that moment my whole life was different. Old things passed away, and life became new, and I realized that I had been born again, filled with spirit and with power. What a feeling of joy and peace which passeth human understanding!"[55] She still had to work to support her family; her writing was done in the stolen hours. "I would have given up much for this work; it gave me the greatest satisfaction, and in this way some of my happiest hours were spent."[56] Smith described in detail the feelings of loss at the death of her husband and her young son. "Our inner life is very rarely revealed to others," she wrote.[57]

Ellen Johnston, a factory worker from Glasgow, was persecuted and perhaps sexually abused by her stepfather, but forced to mask her distress in public. "I often smiled when my heart was weeping—the gilded mask of false merriment made me often appear happy in company when I was only playing the dissembler."[58] Her stepfather's persecution lasted for three years, during which period she ran away five times. By the age of sixteen she was pregnant, and "I never loved life more dearly and longed for the hour when I would have something to love me," before giving birth to a daughter.[59] Johnston began to supplement her factory work with poetry, which led to the publication of her memoir. Notably, she was pressured to censor her feelings twice: during the abuse, and then in a second, revised version of her autobiography, published two years after the first. In the second, she omitted any mention of her stepfather's advances, her pregnancy, or even the birth of her child.

Another female autobiographer, Louise Jermy, introduced her emotional life to her readers from her childhood fears onward.[60] Compared with the memoirs written by men, Jermy's is more explicit about the stresses within her family, and the ways in which they made her life miserable. Jermy's mother having died, her father married a woman with whom he went on to have several more children. Because the large family needed to move into a house and was financially struggling, the father bought the stepmother a mangle to wring out laundry, and the lion's share of the hard work mangling clothing fell to young Louise. In addition to contracting tubercular hip disease during this period, Louise was physically abused by her stepmother, and relied on her older sister to ward off serious injury.[61]

Jermy had a brief glimpse of happiness when, after finishing her dressmaking apprenticeship at the age of seventeen, she was sent for two weeks to a convalescent home. There, she and other women sang hymns and prepared meals, and she taught a class of Sunday school children. "It was a very beautiful place and I was very, very happy, so happy that I dreaded going home, and when the time was over and I found myself at home again, I had the biggest lump in my throat you can imagine." When her stepmother prevented her from continuing as a dressmaker with the rationale that it didn't pay enough, Jermy deferred to her stepmother's wishes and took successive jobs in domestic service. But even these jobs, as physically demanding and painful for her as they were, provided autonomy and relative happiness in contrast with the constant battle with her stepmother. A visit to a friend of her grandmother's gave her an opportunity to "be loved and petted, waited on, fussed over . . . To live in an atmosphere of love and kindliness, for even such a short time, seemed to open my eyes and heart, too, to what home life should be, and I saw clearly how terribly I had been cheated of everything that goes to make life beautiful."[62] To a much greater extent than the memoirs of most male autobiographers, Jermy's was a chronicle of the way in which relationships with others made her feel.

Autobiographer Ann Candler's major life preoccupation was trying to provide for a growing family though her soldier husband was almost never at home. He would intermittently appear, use her income to go on drinking binges, reconcile with his wife long enough to conceive another child, and then leave—a pattern for which she blamed herself. Still Candler, who wrote while imprisoned in the Tottingstone House of Industry (a workhouse), was primarily focused on her emotional ties with other members of her family. "Of nine children two remain near me, to afford me substantial happiness and satisfaction as a parent; but my uncertainty about the others, and solicitude for their welfare, are too often painful in the extreme."[63]

Without a husband or children and able to support herself through her writing, Mary Ann Hearn (aka Marianne Farningham) structured her life around her religious work. She found joy not only in writing for the *Sunday School Times* but also through having her own personal space. In midlife, she acquired a cottage in Wales: "Here have gracious summertimes almost renewed my youth, and caused my heart to sing for joy. How much I wish everybody could have such a haven as I!"[64] With no immediate family upon which to spend her earnings, Hearn was able to travel to the Holy Land and to Rome, where she found the "delicious air" to be "positively intoxicating." "I could have wished myself a boy, that I might throw up my hat and dance for joy," she wrote.[65] These memoirs help to delineate the gendered norms of emotional expression.

Emotional display rules could also vary by culture.[66] Katie Barclay has argued that in Ireland's law courts, it was acceptable and even expected for jurists and lawyers to display tears.[67] Some autobiographers asserted that Scotsmen were particularly encouraged to hide their emotions. David Kirkwood, a Glasgow mechanical engineer who led the Clydeside revolts and then entered Parliament, noted that his countrymen "were ashamed of their own emotions. In a crowd, they would wallow in sentiment. They would become almost tearful as they sang of 'My ain kind dearie O,' but they would think shame to speak tenderly to their wives and children in public.'"[68] Andrew Carnegie agreed that in general Scots were reserved in emotional expression. Thus, on the rare occasion that his father shed a tear out of pride at his son's accomplishments, the event stayed with him "and warmed my heart for years and years." Carnegie went on to reflect "how reserved the Scot is! Where he feels most he expresses least. Quite right! There are holy depths which it is sacrilege to disturb. Silence is more eloquent than words."[69]

Victorian autobiographers sometimes signaled to their readers that they were omitting intimate details. As an anonymous blacksmith who contributed his autobiography to the *Commonwealth* newspaper put it, "Had the object of the author of this sketch been to have given a full history of himself as a *man*, including his inner life as well as his outer, his 'autobiography' would have appeared in a different form. But as his object was to give a sketch of his struggles with life as a *working man*, he has omitted what may perhaps appear to many the more interesting portions."[70] John Wilson left out of his autobiography "many events in my life which are best forgotten . . . they would have been neither creditable nor profitable, and therefore of no service, which should be the aim of all, either in living our life or in describing it."[71] In addition to this self-censorship, David Vincent has argued that working-class autobiographies were impacted by the poverty of language; that working people lacked the language to talk about emotions in detail, and thus were reduced to clichés or describing their feelings as ineffable.[72] George Parkinson recounted the horrific mine explosion that killed many of his workmates, nearly suffocated him, and led to his final departure from the pit. "Though sixty years have passed since then, the feelings of that moment, with the indescribable sense of relief then experienced, are, as I write this story, again realized with a vividness and excitement of feeling beyond the power of expression, either by voice or pen, and must perforce remain among the things which cannot be told."[73] Clearly, autobiographies will not tell us everything, but this is true of any historical primary source.

Are autobiographies tainted by the process by which humans encode and then recall memories? Modern social scientists assert that the process of remembering changes memories; that recent happy events are usually granted more weight in assessments of well-being, particularly if remembered vividly, because the memory itself will elicit a re-experiencing of the happy mood.[74] People with happy dispositions "tend to remember favorable events, whereas unhappy people tend to remember unfavorable ones."[75] While some working-class autobiographers described more episodes of happiness and contentment than others, suggesting their authors had happier dispositions, in the majority of the working-class autobiographies writers focused on happiness in childhood, suggesting that how recently events occurred does not always have a straightforward impact on the stories that writers tell.[76] Moreover, nineteenth-century autobiographers, having experienced the act of remembering and writing, understood and admitted that their recollections were fallible. As Henry Snell, a farm boy who rose to the House of Lords, wrote, "Incidents taken from the record of a man's changing thoughts, activities and aims, his alternating enthusiasms and depressions, his troubled searchings and sorrowful renunciations, more nearly represent the hasty snapshot of an hour than the balanced portrait of a life, and the story of every man, whose mind is influenced by increased knowledge and experience, is full of inconsistencies."[77]

It might be objected that deriving evidence about happiness from working-class autobiographers skews our picture of the nineteenth-century lived experience, since those autobiographers do not represent every possible occupation or status, and are not fully representative of the population of Great Britain geographically, occupationally, by gender, or by household size.[78] Autobiographies were disproportionately written by literate men and by those educated in Scotland; while about two thirds of men and half of women were literate in England in 1840, in Scotland, the literacy rate (measured by the percentage of people who signed marriage registers) was closer to 90 percent.[79] While those who worked on farms as children are well represented, education in rural England was hit-or-miss, and instruction in English hampered education for native Welsh speakers.[80]

In addition to imbalances of gender and region, the corpus of working-class autobiographies may reflect imbalances of status. Modern researchers on happiness in developing countries suggest that where income information is unavailable, educational attainments can serve as a proxy for income: wealthier people are more likely to be literate.[81] If this generalization also applies to the nineteenth century, the poorest people, by extension the least-educated people, and the least likely to leave autobiographical evidence, may also have been the least happy (I expand on this idea in chapter 8). But even if few of the poorest Britons were directly represented through their own words, social norms permeate societies.[82] Working people who wrote autobiographies were aware of, witnessed, and sometimes wrote about the experiences of others in their neighborhoods. "Lower class people certainly write less, but the greater uniformity of life imposed by poverty warrants wider generalization from each single work," the historian Alfred Kelly argues.[83] Nan Hackett goes even further, contending that since they tend to be minimally introspective and without many literary flourishes, working-class autobiographies speak for a class rather than an individual.[84] While she probably overstates the case, it is unquestionably true that these are valuable sources, and that their collective value outweighs the caveats I have outlined.

Working-class autobiographies have been rarely used as sources for the history of emotions. John Burnett, the modern scholar most responsible for collecting working-class autobiographies and for originally grappling with the genre, used individual autobiographies as source material to depict working people's occupational and educational lives in *Useful Toil* and *Destiny Obscure*. Through wide reading, he noted that working-class autobiographies tend to travel along common lines, with much emphasis on education and childhood, detailed descriptions of house interiors and childhood games and school and work experiences, but little detail provided about personal relationships, especially intimate relationships.[85] While working people did not normally provide much emotional description about their lives in the documents they left for posterity, Burnett saw change over time: autobiographies became more sophisticated and more introspective in the late nineteenth century and into the twentieth. In contrast, autobiographies produced by those born in the 1700s tend to be chronological listings of occupations or events, without the self-reflectiveness or interiority of later works.[86]

David Vincent used working-class autobiographies to study working-class reactions to the deaths of loved ones.[87] Julie-Marie Strange plumbed the autobiographies for evidence about working-class fatherhood, arguing that while some fathers were distant, and young children spent more time with their mothers, in general the breadwinner role had an emotional content, and working men often deeply cared about their children's welfare. She also used these autobiographies to deeply explore death and grief.[88] Emma Griffin, who has used the autobiographies both quantitatively and qualitatively, has argued that the materially poorest lives may also have been the most emotionally impoverished. While around 40 percent of working-class autobiographers "described happy hopes, loving mothers, and contented childhoods," other writers were either neutral, did not mention their mothers, or described their mothers' housekeeping skills as a sort of stand-in for love. She concludes their childhoods may have been relatively lacking in love, due to male desertion of the family, overworked mothers, and domestic violence.[89]

These projects have only scratched the surface of what is possible. In her book *Help Me to Find My People: The African American Search for Family Lost in Slavery*, Heather A. Williams intensively uses autobiographies written by Black Americans during and after the existence of slavery in the United States, along with interviews conducted in the 1930s under the auspices of the Federal Writers Project. A combination of close reading, knowledge of the larger context, and an attempt to really understand and empathize with their stories results in a history that compassionately brings to the fore the trauma of family separation. Many of the same objections that I answer in this chapter have already been raised about the narratives of enslaved people: lack of geographic representativeness, the impact of old age in coloring views of a life in retrospect, the impact of self-censorship in front of an audience. And yet, as Williams points out, we can only gain access to the experiences of the enslaved by reading their words.[90] Echoing Williams's sentiments, in *An Everyday Life of the English Working Class*, Carolyn Steedman noted that most of the sources used to describe the experiences of working-class people were elicited by Parliamentary Commissioners and journalists, and that these people asked "the kind of question that is only ever put to subaltern subjects."[91] Working-class autobiographies, in contrast, reflect whatever it is that these subjects wanted others to know about them.

As this chapter has shown, working-class autobiographies may pose epistemic challenges for the researcher. The questions of authenticity, intended audience, and motivation for writing are obvious; the omissions and silences conditioned by genre expectations are perhaps less obvious. While autobiographies read in a sufficient quantity may justify drawing larger conclusions about emotional display rules and taboo topics, the individuals whose autobiographies seem to transgress those rules are some of the most enlightening. The existing corpus of working-class autobiographies is heavily weighted toward literate men in England and Scotland, but as this chapter has shown, autobiographies written by women contained more emotional expressiveness. Despite all these caveats, autobiographies are rich source material for the interpretation of nineteenth-century working-class lives, and indispensable for anyone attempting to write about emotions.

TWO

The Simple Pleasures of Childhood

ALMOST ALL WORKING-CLASS AUTOBIOGRAPHERS began their autobiographies by recounting some of their earliest memories, making working-class autobiography one of the most reliable sources of documentation for childhood experiences.[1] As this chapter will show, despite the hardships wreaked by economic dislocation or family tragedy, the majority of working-class autobiographers remembered at least parts of their childhoods fondly. This was a tendency that these autobiographers shared with writers of other social classes; the study of memory and nostalgia has revealed that memories associated with heightened emotions are more easily recalled. These fond memories of childhood are also evidence of larger social changes dating from the late eighteenth century that prioritized protecting childhood as a separate stage of life dedicated to innocence.[2]

In contrast with middle-class autobiographers, however, for working-class autobiographers born before 1870, the concepts of "home" and "family" and even "childhood" came under pressure from deaths in the family, job-related relocations, and the necessity of entering the workforce at an early age.[3] Rather, as this chapter will demonstrate, working-class autobiographers fondly remembered bonds formed with immediate or extended family members; exposure to the wider culture through the stories, songs, and imitation of older people; opportunities for outdoor play, even in the absence of playthings; and paeans to special foods. Older children remembered being prepared for or entering the workforce, and the physical or emotional toll on their bodies being offset by pride in their new roles in helping to support the family.

Although these autobiographers were looking back to a period before the working classes had reaped the economic gains of industrialization, they tended to express nostalgia; but this was more often a nostalgia for lost parents and the innocent childhood self than for a lost world. John Younger, born in 1785, noted in his autobiography that "there may be a pleasure, to a mind jaded and harassed amid the toils and trammels of life, to throw back an occasional glance over the sunny hours and flowery fields of our simplest delights, when the opening roses of life were enjoyed in their freshness, their prickles yet undiscovered." Younger's first memories were a series of associations dating from infancy: a song that reached him in his cradle, his mother's warm hands, the sights and sounds of moths and swallows.[4] As the historian Anna Davin has noted, in contrast with wealthy households that had nurseries, space limitations in working-class households often meant that infants slept alongside their mothers and were carried around until they could walk.[5]

Other autobiographers were able to remember similar experiences as very young children. Born in 1745, Thomas Holcroft remembered "being played with by my parents, and of the extreme pleasure it gave me."[6] His parents were so solicitous of him that even being sent out to beg for food from house to house on their behalf made him happy.[7] Christopher Thomson recalled his mother holding him on her lap and singing a song about a cuckoo. "The joy of that morning was stereotyped upon my memory, and I read it anew each year, when the specked herald proclaims her spring-tide mission. I become a boy again, and look back with fondness to that May morning, and hear my mother's chaunt."[8] Charles Shaw of Tunstall, who started work at the age of seven and was consigned to a workhouse before he was ten, had joyful memories of being at dame school (similar to a preschool), because the teacher set the children's chairs outside near a busy street and the children could watch their mothers passing by doing errands.[9]

"Childhood . . . is the one really blissful period in existence," Thomas Lipton reflected. "It matters not whether the bairn be born of low estate or cradled in the lap of luxury; there is something in the early years that has little to do with environment but which insists on every child having its fair share of happiness." While this is no doubt wishful thinking, in Lipton's opinion poor children were often happier than wealthy ones, since their early relationships were more likely to be with parents and extended families than with governesses or servants.[10] The Chartist poet Thomas Cooper fondly remembered instances of sensory and interpersonal pleasure from his childhood: the songs and stories of his father; being held by the hand; hearing a church organ playing; and eating bread spread with fresh cream.[11]

George Parkinson, who went to work in the mines at the age of six, described such close family relationships. "My father and mother were practical people, living in the present, the joy of their lives being found in ministering to the needs of those around them in every possible way." His grandmother lived in the same village, and some of the happiest hours of his young childhood were spent playing by her fireside.[12] John Harris also felt doted upon by his grandparents, and his early pleasant memories are notable for the many sensory details he conjured simultaneously. His grandmother brought back sweets from the store and cooked potato cakes for him in the ashes, and "as I ate the crisp cake, and listened to the music of the crackling furze and heath under the pot, the click of her needles as she sat by the hot embers, and her enchaining story as wild as our own hills, I felt sure that I had the dearest, kindest, grandmother in all the world."[13] Elizabeth Oakley, the seventh of ten children of a Norfolk bootmaker, accounted her childhood happy due to her "dear and tender mother" and her mother's brother, who was the "kindest of Uncles and the best of friends." These pleasant relationships helped to offset the influence of an abusive father.[14]

Although rarely treated with grand gestures of affection, working-class children received love and material support.[15] Love expressed in a low-key emotional register was still love, and it was possible for some children to receive that love and support from surrogate parent figures and then remember happy childhoods.[16] Jane Humphries and Alannah Tomkins have provided several examples of working-class memoirists who expressed gratitude for care received in poorhouses or workhouses, even as they tended to be scantily fed, overly regimented, deprived of novelty, and surfeited with corporal discipline.[17] Of course, as Tomkins notes, the distance of decades and the need to wring positive meanings from life trajectories may in part explain this.[18] Henry Price, the illegitimate son of a church organist, who was sent to live in the poorhouse by his mother, had positive memories of his childhood. "Taken altogether these Poor Houses were very good homes. We were all Happy there, well-fed, nurs'd and doctor'd, went in and out just as we pleased, dress'd like others. Fields and gardens all round us, we fattened our own pigs, made our own Bread, Brewed our own beer." Because when he entered the house he was placed with the children and old men, he had especially good memories of the songs that the old soldiers used to sing. Price contrasted this experience with circumstances brought about by the New Poor Law, when the inmates were forced to wear uniforms, segregated into a panopticon-shaped workhouse, and, worst of all, fed a scanty diet. "There were times when I felt very lonely and forsaken and had a good cry."[19] Jonathan Saville, born in 1759, lost his mother when he was three years old, after which time he was apprenticed to some colliers whose abuse and neglect resulted in a bone break to his thigh that never healed. His experience changed for the better when he was sent to Horton workhouse, where a kindly overseer nursed him back to health and taught him to walk with crutches.[20] George Lloyd lost his mother to childbirth and his father to desertion, then, transferred from one guardian to another, became homeless. When he finally found work as a collier's helper and lodged with the man's kindly family, he was ecstatic. His new friends advanced him the money for a suit, some shoes, and even to have his photograph taken. "Mr. Bowen [the tailor] said 'you will get a fit next week.' I thought to myself, I am nearly having one now at this sudden stroke of luck," Lloyd remembered.[21]

Parents, parent-figures, and grandparents initiated children into a wider family culture through their songs and stories. The sailor Joshua Marsden "well remembers, when he was a but a little boy, nothing gave him more pleasure than the recital of incidents in his father's life; he sat with eager delight listening to many a relation and anecdote, which in long winter nights . . . his father used to tell."[22] Frederick Rolfe, the self-proclaimed "King of the Norfolk Poachers," "was never so happy as when I was listening to [my grandfather's] tales of smuggling and other Outlaw tricks, it used to warm my heart to hear them."[23] Mary Loughran, writing under the pseudonym Maureen Hamish, moved from Ireland to Scotland to be a domestic servant and ended up living for a time with her grandfather. She remembered walking to Mass with him and home again every Sunday, with great pleasure because he was so familiar with the surroundings and told such interesting stories. "He used to entertain me with tales of his boyhood and of the time when he ran away with my grandmother because he loved her" and their parents objected. She asked for that same story to be retold over and over.[24]

In turn, these family cultures were embedded in a wider regional culture. Joseph Robson, born in Newcastle, was raised by his grandparents, and credited his grandmother with providing him "the inspirations of the Scottish muse" that later characterized his published poetry: "How often have I sat at her feet, when a boy, and listened with delight to the songs and ballads of her native Caledonia."[25] The Scottish comedian Harry Lauder was permanently affected by his mother's Highland stories, which not only delighted him in childhood but made every rendition of Highland classics he performed later onstage doubly pleasant, first in the ecstasy of the moment and then for the memory.[26] William Hammond, who later moved to Glasgow and became a handloom weaver, had fond memories of his native Ireland, particularly "an old woman named Sally Ferguson, one of the best story-tellers in Tyrone." Sally's recitals "kept the noisiest boy among us keenly interested," telling tales and singing songs and warning children about the Banshee.[27] Similarly, Duncan Campbell liked to listen to the old people of his village. "I was without a brother, and although I had plenty of boy cousins, and enjoyed boyish pranks and school play and scrapes, I felt lonely at times, and liked nothing better than to sit at the feet of the 'Gray Egyptians' and listen attentively to their talk. They were full of stories of the olden times, which hugely delighted me."[28]

Worlds of Discovery

Because working-class children generally had no nurseries to be confined to, their world of discovery could include a parent's workplace. Henry Jones's memories of his family's happiness were linked to the playful relationship between his mother and his father; he recounted her pranks, such as sewing the father's suspenders to his trousers, making it impossible for him to take off his clothes at the end of the day.[29] Jones's fondness for his father was so great that he decided to become a shoemaker. His early days in the workshop combined talk about the day's events, sung snatches of popular songs, lunchtime walks down by the river, and his father's storytelling. He called these, collectively, the "joys of the workshop."[30] Mary Smith's mother died when she was two years old, so her father often brought her to his shoemaking shop. Smith "was delighted with the quietude of the place," and listened to her father and the other workers having deep philosophical discussions that were punctuated with the beating of the leather on the lapstone. Later, when she was sent to school, he would collect her and give her a piggyback ride home, "his head bare, and his happy face bright with childish talk to his little 'wench'."[31]

Overcrowded housing pushed both boys and girls outdoors for their play.[32] Thomas Burt, who entered a coal pit at the age of ten, remembered his early childhood as a particularly happy time, filled with "marble-playing, kite-flying, and other childish games."[33] His favorite activities included swimming and taking long walks with his maternal grandfather, who "had a great liking for children, and was full of little plans and devices to interest and amuse them."[34] David Kirkwood was similarly enthusiastic about the walks in the country that he had taken with his father, who "would walk me till I was fit to drop. Even as a child, I preferred walking with my father to playing with other children. We were monarchs of the world."[35]

Childhood represented physical freedom, since so many childhood activities took place outdoors. Alexander Murison, later a professor of linguistics, remembered his childhood as a "delightful time" despite the lack of mental stimulation from books. Not only was there plenty to eat, but also his surroundings were beautiful: "Out of school, it was a charming world; brown under the plough and the barrow, yellow with waving corn, green with the lush grass, white under the sheet of snow, sunshine, rain, snow—singing of birds, lowing of cattle, wimplings of the burns, rushing and howling of wind—all alike enjoyable in turn." Murison also appreciated the freedom to switch between tasks, alternately helping his mother with errands, working in his father's wright shop as it struck his fancy, fishing, dancing, and singing.[36] Similarly, Alf Ireson of Oundle remembered his life in the village as "full of romance. The free open country provides fun and mischief for boys and girls alike." The children enjoyed their walks to school through the countryside, saw soldiers marching, observed fox hunts, and spent summers bathing in the river.

Ireson's happiest times were spent with the local ratcatcher: "To have a day with this aged man was my boyish delight. In those days I loved to kill."[37] As this anecdote suggests, activities that adults defined as work could be construed by children as play. Edward Anderson tended sheep for his father as a boy, noting, "I knew no care but for my father's flock ... with pleasure then I spent the summer's day."[38] When he was only about eight years old, Joseph Severn, whose father was a silk-winder, charged him with minding his baby brother on Saturday afternoons. He devised a method of tying his brother to his back, and he and his friends spent the time stealing eggs from birds' nests and fruit from orchards. Those afternoons he described as "the happiest days of my childhood," since the longer he and his brother stayed away from home, the less silk-winding Joseph was expected to help with.[39] States of affairs that agitated adults were merely exciting to children; Joseph Terry, who grew up aboard a coal barge, found it a tremendous adventure, only reflecting later about the panic his mother had experienced trying to ensure that none of her children fell overboard.[40] These experiences contrast with those of upper-class children, who were generally subject to more restrictions about outdoor play, insulated from village children, and warned not to get their clothing dirty.[41]

Autobiographers recalled being satisfied with little. Although Elizabeth Campbell was sent to her first position as a servant at the age of seven, she took pleasure in recalling her childhood surroundings, the books she had been allowed to read, and the strict discipline of her father and stepmother.[42] F. H. Spencer, who later became a government inspector of schools, remembered having "a happy, free, interesting boyhood, had always clothes (of a kind) to wear, lived on the simplest food (lots of bread and homemade jam, especially rhubarb jam), and never went hungry nor very cold." His pastimes included attending Band of Hope meetings, stealing turnips, and playing stickball.[43]

Imagination could compensate for the lack of store-bought playthings. Working-class children turned household castoffs into toys. One of Samuel Bamford's only childhood playthings was a tin can, out of which he ate bread and milk, and which he liked so much that he took it to bed at night.[44] James Edwin Saunders found an old spinning wheel in an attic that he called "the joy of my boyish life . . . I turned it by hand, turned it by foot, turned it with a stick and turned it with a string . . . after its discovery [I] was never in need of a companion again."[45] Thomas Jones of Rhymney described himself and his friends going home "wild with joy" after damming a stream with coal dust, making a pond for their paper boats, and then letting loose the floodgates, "dooming our paper boats to instant destruction." He and his friends also traded marbles, bowled hoops, spun tops, blew soap bubbles, played duckstones (similar to horseshoes or bocce), and dropped stones into wells.[46] Janet Bathgate's cat, garden, dolls, and baby brother figured largely in her happy Scottish rural childhood, although her happy days were shortened when she was sent into domestic service at the age of seven, and expected to work steadily from five in the morning until ten at night.[47]

Some autobiographers remembered moments of particular visual or aural beauty. Jacob Holkinson recalled walking with his father between the Leith Water and the mill stream, and on another occasion accompanying his parents on an excursion to Inchkeith lighthouse. He remembered the "blue bosom of the Firth was all studded over with boats and vessels, whose snowy sails spread wing-like to catch the breeze, whilst overhead the sky presented one wild field of glowing azure . . . So strongly was my infant mind impressed with the beauty of the scene, that I can recall, even now, the delightful feelings it produced."[48] John Harris thought about autumn walks with his father: "We climbed our hill together, he leading me by the hand. Gaining its summit we paused, and looked upward. The firmament was covered with stars, shining in silvery splendor through the clear air . . . my infantile vision was riveted upon the scene, while the sparkling constellations flung their effulgence across the void."[49] Joseph Gutteridge's fondest childhood memories included listening to his father and his uncles playing music. "I would sit almost entranced while they played the pieces of music then most in vogue—quick and slow marches, set pieces, and oftentimes compositions of their own."[50] Similarly, Samuel Gompers, who was born in London, remembered being taken to concerts by his grandfather. "In those happy hours I lived in another world and quivered with the beauty of tone and melody or grew tense when the music dropped in minor or developed in some grand effect. Grandfather introduced me to a world that brought a lifetime of pleasure."[51]

Many working-class autobiographers remembered the foods of their childhood with special relish.[52] Jane Humphries emphasizes, in her study of working-class children and labor, that many children were hungry a lot of the time, which helps to explain autobiographers' focus on food.[53] Emma Griffin pushes her examination further to quantify mentions of hunger in autobiographies, noting that of the 341 deponents in her sample, about a third recalled having gone hungry at some time, with the majority of those describing hunger belonging to rural occupations. Griffin's major contribution to the question is her argument that industrialization per se was not responsible for creating hungry children, but that families solved the problem of insufficient food by focusing purchased calories on male breadwinners, forcing children, women, and by extension, gestating fetuses, to be underfed. In turn, Griffin's argument contributes to her wider contention that the negative short-run impact of industrialization in Britain has been assumed rather than substantiated.[54]

While the economic data are hard to pin down, the phenomenology surrounding food is clearer. Food contributed to children's happiness in ways that, decades later, they recalled experiencing. An anonymous London orphan, apprenticed by the parish to work in a textile mill in 1815, recounted being constantly hungry. Fed a scanty diet of oatcakes and oatmeal, he supplemented his diet whenever he could with turnips stolen from a farmer's field. When he could stand it no longer, he ran away, managing to reach London by begging along the journey. In London, parish officials eager to absolve themselves of the responsibility for his care apprenticed him again, but his second apprenticeship featured slightly better food, including a can of ale and a piece of unbuttered cake on Christmas. "To have seen us walking up and down flourishing the flour-cake in one hand, and the can of ale in the other, would have made anyone think we were the happiest mortals in the world. We felt ourselves, for once, as big as the king."[55] Will Dagley, a farm laborer whose memories were rendered mostly in dialect, recounted that at one of the places where he worked, the woods were full of pheasants and partridges, "and a jolly time [we] had . . . plenty to eat and plenty to drink." During the winters, when pigs were killed, all of the workpeople had meat. "Theeur was plenty uv ivverything and I spent some a the happiest times of mi life theeur."[56] Alexander Somerville remembered his mother giving him new butter on gray bread made out of barley and beans, "and off I would go, eating it as I went with a relish and a gladness of heart which would hardly have been higher if I had thought there was no butter so good as ours, and no mother in the world like mine."[57] For Ben Brierley, currant bread was a huge treat: "Ye children of the present day who have your milk and buns, and a field to play in, and have not to carry small loads of timber over hard highways for three or four hours without a bite, after an indifferent breakfast . . . try to realize for yourself the hardship, that was supposed to be pleasure, which we had to endure in the 'good old times' when William the Fourth was king."[58] And William Henry Lax admitted that even in old age, "a sweet apple brings me to the apex of happiness!"[59]

Happiness, Nostalgia, and Child Labor

In retrospect, much of the joy of childhood emanated from childhood innocence and the novelty of experience, remembered after decades of adult aggravations. The poet John Clare looked back at his childhood when "a week scarcely came without a promise of some fresh delight."[60] In adulthood, the calendar was marked off with celebrations like Valentine's Day and the first of May, but the joy of doing things for the first time was missing: "There is nothing of that new and refreshing sunshine upon the picture now . . . it shines from the heavens upon real matter of fact existences and weary occupations."[61] Clare also fondly remembered his first friend, Richard Turnill, whose companionship he called an "image of happiness" before Turnill died at an early age.[62] Henry White, son of a rural laborer, recalled after a space of sixty years:

> Well do I remember those early days of my boyhood, when all seemed to go smoothly along with the running stream; no care, no sorrow of any kind to mar the pleasures of the day, or to interfere with the innocent amusements enjoyed, as a rule, by children of

that tender age; living, as it were, only for the day, like many of our beautiful butterflies—sporting in the sunshine only for a few hours—happy, happy child; no care, no thoughts for the morrow."[63]

For White, this period ended at age ten, when he began long and painful workdays in the fields, first scaring crows, then reaping and plowing.

The nostalgia for the freedom of childhood points back at the difficulty of being impulsive or living in the moment as a Victorian working-class adult, when anything—a workplace injury, a protracted illness, a downturn in trade, the unexpected addition of an additional mouth to feed—fell squarely on individual families, and, particularly, on fathers. John Younger remembered part of his childhood happiness residing in not needing to plan for anything other than his own amusement. "I understood nothing of the machinery that moved the affections of men!"[64] Thomas Martin Wheeler described the passage from childhood to adulthood by apostrophizing time itself: "Oh, who does not look back with delight on boyish days, when life was all enchantment, when, let the kaleidoscope be ever so varied, its colours were always bright, and each new combination more varied than the last? Time, what boyish dreams of fairy land hast thou destroyed, what rosy bowers hast thou turned to dungeon cells."[65] Mary Ann Smith waxed similarly poetic: "O happy time of childhood! When small troubles enhance future pleasures—pleasures which are the abiding joy of a long life! Before the jealousies and envies of life begin, all is new and untried."[66] The Chartist tailor Robert Lowery spoke for many of his contemporaries when he noted that childhood in retrospect seemed like the moment of greatest happiness because children had little responsibility: "The bounding blood and animal spirits give a zest to material life, when we only see the beautiful and joyous, and a kind providence veils from us the shades and dark shadows which lie in the onward pathway that age and experience alone can enable us to perceive."[67]

The simple pleasures of childhood, such as they were, ended with the ritual of entering into paid work. Jane Humphries has emphasized that child labor was integral to the industrial expansion of the nineteenth century; not just in the textile industry, in which the boom in handloom weaving expanded the child workforce, but also in agriculture, coal mining, piecework, and the assembly of articles like pins and nails.[68] As we have seen, some girls were sent into service as early as age seven. By the age of twelve, most working-class boys had secured some kind of employment. Children entered the workforce in large numbers in part through something like a prisoner's-dilemma scenario: if all adults had been able to withhold their children's labor, the prevailing wage for adult labor might have risen; but most working-class families, particularly single parent households, did not generally have the luxury to make such an objection. Regulation of child labor was absent or insufficient, depending on the field, and technological developments increased the demand for children to undertake individual steps in larger mechanized processes. Finally, the entry of large numbers of children in the workforce enabled employers to lower the prevailing wage rate, in a kind of vicious cycle.[69]

While girls' assumption of adult responsibilities began within the household at an early age, many male autobiographers described entry into the workforce as a major rite of passage and a point of pride.[70] Their stories illustrate both the expectation that male family members contribute economically, and the fact that the pressure of poverty influenced what working-class children were supposed to find enjoyable. Thomas Lipton's parents' small shop had been failing economically, so at age ten he found work elsewhere as a shop assistant. While his long workdays prevented childhood play, Lipton was full of pride and happiness when he was able to turn his pay over to his mother for the first time.[71] After serving as a messenger boy and working in a textile factory, he finally secured a job as a cabin boy on a steamer; a job that made him completely happy, since it involved both an advance of wages and the opportunity to work with the sailors and ships that had long fascinated him.[72]

Working-class children largely understood the unwritten wage contract: that their scanty earnings were part of the family budget, and should be handed directly to their mothers.[73] Being able to fulfill that contract was a source of pride and pleasure, a means of tightening the family's emotional bonds, and so commonly written about that it became a trope.[74] George Sanger was thrilled when, at about the age of six, he was allowed to join the family's traveling peepshow as a barker.[75] Joseph Severn was delighted with his first earnings as a farmworker at the age of eleven, since "I had the happy feeling of knowing that I had been able to help my parents to the extent of earning my own food and sixpence a day during the time." One of his first purchases was a half-ounce of tobacco, which he proudly gave to his father.[76] George Edwards grew up in a household so impoverished that his family subsisted on stolen turnips. Because he only owned one change of clothes, he had to go to bed early on Saturday nights so that his mother could mend and wash them. When he got his first job scaring crows at the age of six, he came home "as proud as a duke," reassuring his mother that she no longer needed to worry about not being able to feed them (and had no idea why she burst into tears).[77] Peter Featherstone reported that "one of my greatest surprises, and highest joy was when my Master giving me my Indenture, put upon it a five pound note."[78]

William Arnold, who had been working since the age of six, asked to work on his own account before he was fifteen, and was so elated to be making a man's wage for the first time that he celebrated with a pork pie, a respite from a life until then filled with hunger. "Pleased as I was, I think my dear old mother was more overjoyed than I was. She felt then that there was to be an end to the terrible pinch of poverty from which we all suffered."[79] When the orphaned John Buckley ran away from his apprenticeship, he found work as a carpenter on a large country house, and ended up being awarded a pay bonus due to the quality of his work. "What pleasure there is in running your fingers through your first payment for work!" he exclaimed.[80]

No matter how excited they had been about their household contributions, autobiographers who had begun working as children had fond memories of the respite from work that Sundays provided. George Parkinson, who spent so much of his waking life underground, noted, "The Sunday became the veritable jewel of the week; when the cares and miseries of the workdays vanished from memory, and the joys of family life, of sunlight, and of unwonted ease made a little Paradise." Moreover, the ability to sleep later gave him "feelings of intense joy and satisfaction such as no words could express."[81] Charles Shaw, working up to fourteen hours a day making pottery ware, agreed: "Those Sundays for children! Who can tell their value? Besides the light and freedom they brought, there was the ever-fresh joy of the Sunday School. I am thrilled many times even yet as I think of those simple joys in contrast with the hardships." James Corben worked as an apprentice to his uncle, a quarryman; he was constantly underfed and overworked, and his uncle did nothing but find fault with him. Sundays were the happiest days of his week; kind words from the minister or his daughters caused him to shed tears of joy.[82] James Dunn, who entered a coal pit at around eight years of age, noted that he didn't see the sun from one week to the next until "Sunday came round and was hailed with delight by the poor collier lad, as on that morn he was privileged to see God's beautiful light."[83]

Frank Forrest used Sunday mornings to escape from Dundee into the countryside: "I breathed more freely, and the joy that I felt was sweeter than the delight of an aspiring monarch on gaining a crown. So intense were my emotions that I often said to myself, 'Surely God has made this a day of rest for the benefit of mill boys.' "[84] Richard Boswell Belcher of Banbury recalled with delight riding with his father in a gig, to spend Sundays in Chipping Norton to attend the Baptist church there.[85] Nor were sleep and fresh air the only benefits; Ellen Ross has noted that London's working-class families saved their most nutritious and satisfying meals for Sundays, even though this meant stinting their consumption during the rest of the week.[86] William Arnold went to work in a field scaring crows and minding other children, and remembered being hungry, but part of his wage included dinner on Sundays: "The dinner they gave me made the Sunday the greatest and happiest day of the week. I used to have as much as I could eat, and that never happened at home I could tell you." The house's servant also sent him home with a bag of food to eat during the week.[87]

While some autobiographers found compensations in the form of increased status within the household and Sundays off, others remembered their early work experiences as traumatic. Rose Allen's feelings of happiness and security were completely disrupted when her father died and her family was forced to break up. Her twelve-year-old brother went off to sea, and she had to enter service. Allen's employers, Quakers, forbade music, even the singing of hymns.[88] Allen's second position was in a house so chaotic that servants were often forced to go without meals.[89] Her third employers were distressed country gentry trying to keep up appearances, which required stinting on fuel, bedclothes, and food; at one point, they found a false pretext on which to dismiss a maid whom they had failed to pay for a year, and left her without a character reference.[90] George Meek, who grew up to be a bath attendant, lived with his grandparents as a child, and his best childhood memories included particularly delicious meals, Guy Fawkes Day celebrations, and walks home with his grandfather from the brickyard. Even the fact that he often had to eat dinner alone did not detract from the memory of his childhood as a happy time.[91] All of this changed when his beloved grandfather died and his mother (his only living parent) returned from the United States. Upon her return, with additional new siblings in tow, Meeks's mother was disinterested in her son, a disinterest that intensified when she took up with an abusive married butcher and cabdriver. Beginning at age twelve, Meek alternated between working at jobs he hated and turning all his money over to his mother, and running away from home.[92]

Sometimes the passage from childhood to adulthood was precipitated by events other than the beginning of worklife. William Collison, who went on to form an organized society of strikebreakers at the end of the nineteenth century, told one of the most poignant tales about an abrupt and traumatic passage from childhood to adulthood. The son of a policeman, Collison had been spending time on a lazy summer day in the street playing with a humming top, when cries of "Murder!" reverberated through the neighborhood. A crazed man, who had just killed his wife with a knife, ran down the street, stopped directly in front of the boy, and then cut his own throat. Collison's father commandeered his son to hold the bleeding man's head steady in the horse-drawn cab while they rushed to the hospital, but the man died on the way. "The humming top was the perfect expression of that perfect afternoon . . . it was good that it should hum no more," Collison noted.[93] David Kirkwood recounted a similar tale. In the midst of a childhood that "seemed eternal . . . every day was a day of joy, food and home, and games and fun with other boys," he had learned that a man had been burned to death by steam in Parkhead Forge. Kirkwood witnessed the funeral procession and heard the funeral band playing a hymn that mentioned the passing of childhood and the existence of cares, sorrows, and unknown hidden snares in the future. Although he had heard, and sung, that same hymn many times, for the first time he had a glimpse of the fact of adult responsibility and then of mortality, and was "transfixed with horror"—a horror that he viscerally reexperienced on writing about the event. Even as an adult, he regretted that moment of loss of innocence. "Children should set out in a brave new world of high endeavour and radiant happiness, for life is a glorious thing."[94]

As this chapter has shown, the vast majority of working-class autobiographers, like autobiographers in the nineteenth- and twentieth centuries from other backgrounds, recounted the happy moments from their childhoods in detail. They regaled their readers with stories of the importance of families, interpreted broadly; the inculcation of familial and regional cultures; innocent pastimes, favorite foods, and early work experiences. These commonalities show us not only the relative deprivations of working-class childhoods but also that many children adapted their happiness to straitened circumstances, keeping their expectations low and cramming as much joy into Sundays as possible. Both girls and boys were forced to become contributors to the family economy at an early age, with girls were often sent into domestic service, while boys living at home took pride in contributing their wages.

Ultimately, even for those autobiographers who remembered childhood fondly, it served as a rhetorical counterpoint to the trials of adulthood, and this was a literary tendency that autobiographers understood. As Robert Scott noted of his childhood, "The mind then free from worldly care, kept up by hope, unaw'd by fear; My juvenile mind was kept in peace; directed by some unknown grace."[95] Once he had reached adulthood, the quest for work, and the care of his children, ensured that "real happiness can never be found by man, while he's above the ground."[96] Mary Weston had married a carpenter, and "we spent many a happy Sunday in the first years of my married life, and I can well recall my delight in seeing my elder children off to church with their father, looking so neat and so healthy, that he could not be proud enough of them."[97] Unfortunately, their young twins died of scarlet fever. "I remember listening to the glorious words of the burial service in an absent, dreamy mood, and then starting into a welcome flood of tears when a robin on a neighbouring tree began to sing and exult, as if sickness and death, rifled nests and stolen nestlings, were all unknown in bird life."[98] As if the twins' deaths were not bad enough, her older daughter, Martha, died at the age of seventeen after a very long illness that Weston viewed as a possible punishment from God for disobeying the Sabbath. Weston noted that "some people say it is a mistake to call youth the happiest period of life, since we should grow wiser as we increase in years, and happier as we become wiser. It may be so, but in my case sorrow came with wisdom, and to the day of my death I shall lovingly remember and tenderly regret the happy days of my early life."[99]

THREE

Work and Flow

MODERN PSYCHOLOGISTS AND ECONOMISTS have commented on the importance of meaningful and enjoyable work to positive evaluations of life, and this seems to have been just as true—if not more true—for industrial-era working people.[1] Of course, in an era without a comprehensive social safety net, many of the physical comforts crucial to happiness, including food, clothing, and shelter, were insecure without steady employment, so that steady employment was a necessary but not a sufficient condition for happiness. Workers in increasingly routinized occupations like textile manufacturing experienced few psychological compensations for their work, other than wages.[2] But in the face of uneven industrial development, workers who succeeded in early industrial or artisanal fields, or who started their own small businesses, had to have mastery of their tools and materials and of all of the contingencies that might arise when working. They were forced to strategize solutions to problems on the fly, and follow products in process from beginning to end.

According to the psychologist Mihály Csíkszentmihályi, such a combination of challenging work and an identifiable outcome can produce a "flow state"—a period of "peak experience" in which a person is so fixated on what they are doing that time slips effortlessly past.[3] Csíkszentmihályi correlates the flow state with happiness and enjoyment, noting that stories about experiencing a flow state are common to "assembly-line workers, welders, Alpine farmers, an Egyptian hobo, a Chinese cook, and so on."⁴ This kind of happiness, the happiness of "engagement," differs from hedonism or sensory pleasure, and also from eudaimonia, or the longer-term sense of a life well lived. As this chapter will show, many nineteenth-century workers described experiencing flow states. Autobiographer Timothy Claxton recalled being deep in thought on the solution of a mechanical problem, "which I found was more easily done in the night, when the family had retired to rest, and all around was still. At such times, sleep would be banished from my eyes, there being something so fascinating in my pursuit, that the hours flew unconsciously by."⁵ Aspects of the workplace that could facilitate these experiences included creativity, autonomy, a feeling of a good "fit" between worker and task, a healthy work environment, pleasant colleagues, and a sense of adventure.

Other historians have been hesitant to draw conclusions about the correlation of work and happiness. In her analysis of the framework knitter Joseph Woolley's diary, Carolyn Steedman wrote that "we would apply twentieth-century industrial psychology to an early nineteenth-century worker were we to ask" whether workers found happiness through their work.⁶ Early in his career, the historian John Burnett noted that few working-class autobiographies discussed work itself; that work "was taken as a given, like life itself, to be endured rather than enjoyed; most were probably glad enough to have it at all, and to expect to derive satisfaction or happiness from it was an irrelevant consideration."⁷ It is true that not everyone was in a position to find enjoyable work: the drudgery of domestic service or of one's own housework, the repetitive labor of the factory or of the mine, were unlikely to make flow possible.⁸ Although she was German, Ottilie Baker probably encapsulated the experience of many English seamstresses when she noted:

> I can't say that I was always very happy. I'd hoped for something else out of life. Sometimes I was just sick of life; sitting year after year at the sewing machine, always the collars and cuffs before me, one dozen after another; there was no value to life, I was just a work machine with no hope for the future. I saw and heard nothing of all the beautiful things in the world; I was simply excluded from all that.⁹

But Burnett's generalization does not apply to all autobiographers.¹⁰ And as David Vincent pointed out, many working people in the nineteenth century who were not "literate" in the sense of being able to read and write fluently had still mastered vast corpuses of knowledge about the arts and mysteries of their trades. "The true artisan, like the true artist, never stopped learning, never repeated himself, never exhausted the possibilities of his material."[11]

Many working people living on the cusp of industrialization still retained some control over their workplace activities, and, moreover, did not hew to a conception of happiness requiring relentless acquisition of goods, saving for the future, or aspiring to upward class mobility. Thus, a wide variety of occupations could spark joy. J. H. Powell, bound as an apprentice to his engineer father, "entered on this new sphere of action with delight, resolving to devote myself, heart and soul, to my duties . . . my brain was stored with countless visions of undeveloped mechanism. I wrought early and late, and acquired skill amid a delirium of delight." He designed two model steam engines and a lathe, and continued modelmaking in his spare time as well as on the job.[12]

James Nicol, although trained as a cooper, had always dreamed of going to sea. "To me the order to weigh anchor and sail for the Nore was the sound of joy; my spirits were up at the near prospect of obtaining the pleasures I had sighed for since the first dawn of reason."[13] He recounted being "unconscious of the lapse of time" while watching French loggers pole up and down the St. Lawrence River, and "as happy as any person was to see anything" when he had the opportunity to visit China.[14] Henry Burstow, in training to become a church bell-ringer, loved the inimitable sounds of the bells so much that he was chastised for ringing the Sunday curfew for twenty minutes rather than the scheduled five.[15] Burstow took such delight in bell-ringing that he trained himself to ring various sets of changes, and walked eight miles to a neighboring town on Saturdays to play the bells for an impressed audience, and then adjourn to a local pub for a singalong. He found his "fellow campanologists" made "light and easy my advance through every phase of life, and [have] given me a very pleasant outlook upon human nature."[16] An engineer, a sailor, a bell-ringer: all of these examples represent flow as a function of work.

Socialization in the connection between work and flow began in childhood. Although John Burnett argued that generally working-class children dreaded the end of childhood innocence, many autobiographers wrote about looking forward to the day that their education ended and they could finally take on an adult role in the workplace.[17] They associated work with novelty; with the pleasures of gaining the social respect due to working-class adults; and being able to contribute to the family economy. William Henry Lax became a messenger boy at the age of eleven, and recalled having to spend an entire Christmas day trudging through the snow on errands, yet being "perfectly happy," with a sense of purpose and the ability to turn over his first half-crown to his mother.[18] Miner George Parkinson entered his first coal pit as a trapper boy at the age of six alongside his father and grandfather. When he exclaimed with fear about descending in the cage into the mine for the first time, his father "said, in the pitmen's vernacular, 'Dinnet be flaid, hinney, aw hev had o' thee' . . . at length the downward motion became slower and still slower; and suddenly there appeared an opening, a light, and my own grandfather standing at the bottom to lift me off and calling me a brave lad."[19] For Parkinson, the mine was an extension of the family circle. Left alone in the dark with only some stubs of candle, Parkinson noted, "I felt pleasure in opening and closing my door as the bigger lads drove their horses and wagons, sometimes very quickly, along the rolley-way. In a few hours I was quite at home in my work, and proud of doing it without a mistake."[20]

Although he was not a good student, Joseph Keating studied hard to pass his fifth-standard exam so that he could finish his education at the age of twelve. The day before he reached school-leaving age, he presented himself and his certificate of school completion at the pit.[21] Once he was underground at the mine, every new sensation was joyous: the distinction of working in a dangerous place, the fun of working alongside jovial men and boys, the impressiveness of the pit mules.[22] Capping off his first day at work was the opportunity to walk home through his small Welsh village with his clothes and body completely blackened by coal, the outward sign that he had reached manhood. "Through all the marvels of that wonderful day my soul was in a state of elation . . . Finishing time came as a disappointment," Keating wrote.[23] Unfortunately for Keating, the novelty of work underground eventually wore off.[24] "Formerly, my days in the mine were short and happy. Now an hour there seemed to be a month. The pit had changed into a dungeon of darkness, and my agony in it was terrible. From the moment of going down in the morning I thought only of the moment for going up."[25]

Andrew Carnegie loved school, but when his family relocated from Dunfermline to Pennsylvania when he was thirteen years old, he went to work to support the family. A bobbin boy at the local textile factory, he worked from before dawn until after dusk each day. He found the work itself unpleasant, but it was outweighed by the cheering reassurance that he was doing something to help his family. "I have made millions since, but none of those millions gave me such happiness as my first week's earnings. I was now a helper of my family, a breadwinner, and no longer a total charge upon my parents."[26] Shortly afterward, Carnegie was hired as a telegraph messenger boy, which he found to be a much more pleasant job because he had the opportunity to work outdoors, to learn all the streets, firms, and eminent men in the neighborhood, and to receive praise, compliments, and even the occasional food-based gratuity if he did his job well.[27] But what made him happiest was knowing that his contributions to the family income facilitated the purchase of an occasional piece of furniture or clothing to add to the family's scanty supply, and eventually the discharge of the original debt that had enabled the family to move to America in the first place.[28] Slightly later, when he received a raise for being so efficient at his job, he noted, "My whole world was moved to tears of joy."[29] John Gough, whose family was destitute, had similar memories of the first time he was able to bring money home to his mother; he had earned a reward for reading aloud to a man in the library. "I can, in all sincerity, say, that never . . . have I received money since then, which has afforded me such solid satisfaction; and some of my most pleasant reminiscences are circumstances connected with that boyish incident."[30]

In addition to describing flow states, working-class autobiographers correlated workplace enjoyment with freedom from direct supervision, the ability to choose or reject tasks, work-life balance, and the feeling of a "good fit" between their own skills and those required. Some opened small businesses; the failure rate of such businesses was high, but the barriers to entry tended to be low, and the conventional wisdom of the time portrayed success as a natural function of persistence.[31] John Birch Thomas, the son of a cyclically penniless grocer, took the initiative, as a teenager, to move to London. There, he answered ads for shop clerks and messenger boys, found his own lodgings, and fed himself (albeit poorly) on eight shillings a week. For Thomas, while the work itself was not inherently interesting, his progressive ability to provide for himself made him happy. While working at a bootmaker's shop he picked up side jobs opening and putting up shutters on two other businesses, and attempted to go into business in a small way as a brass-polisher. William Ablett, who had been a draper since the age of thirteen, remembered being elated when he first rented his own London shop. Left in the middle of the dimly lit and empty space, he started "running as hard as I could down from the top to the bottom out of sheer exuberance of spirits."[32] Joseph Terry, who had been a boatman for many years, became a miller's clerk, but during his first job in that field was plagued by having a boss who expected all of his workers to put in the same long hours that he did, and then upbraided him for refusing to enroll as a Special Constable during the Chartist agitation in 1848. Terry finally left that employment over the question of work on Sundays, and started his own mill. "I felt great pleasure in my business especially as I knew I was making it pay," he noted. "I felt like a gentleman visiting the markets, seeing the world, and enjoying the fresh air."[33]

A Good Fit

Given the casual nature of much low-paid work and the discontinuous occupational histories of many working-class people, not all work opportunities were going to be enjoyable, but workers had a concept of a "good fit" between the worker and the task. An anonymous stonemason, born in the 1840s, experienced long periods of unemployment, casual labor, and even a period of tramping around the United States and Canada looking for work. Nonetheless, he enjoyed the job that brought him entry into that field, as a bricklayer's helper, noting, "I never felt better in my life than when working on this job."[34] George Cooper of Stockport had many jobs during the period of his working life, which started at the age of six. He worked as a weaver, was terminated for his political and union involvement, and eventually leveraged his way into owning a shop and a pub. A trip to the United States even resulted in his serving in a Pennsylvania cavalry regiment for a period of time. But the career that he remembered most fondly was that of his old age, when he served as a model for students at an art school. "I can tell you that I love to think about those happy days and the pleasant associations connected with them. I delight in recalling to mind each face of the bright band of students who gathered around Mr. Partington and his gifted son. I felt as though I were an inseparable constituent of the organization." Cooper's wife had died of heart disease years before, so his work as a life model was essential in integrating him into a wider social network.[35]

A good fit between the worker's skills and the work to be done produced feelings of mastery, confidence, and self-esteem. Frederick Rogers, a vellum binder, was doing the prosaic work of binding account books, but "I always loved to see and to handle a well-bound book, and was never tired of hearing about the masters in my craft who had bound famous books, knew rapidly all their names, and spent many an hour in the British Museum and places of a similar kind, poring over not the insides, but the outsides of the wonderful books of medieval days."[36] The anonymous miner who wrote an essay for the *Commonwealth* worked for a while outside of the pit selling books, and then at a coppersmith's shop in Glasgow, but ultimately found he was only able to support his family by going back into the mine. "Strange as it may seem, I experienced a degree of joy on my return to the pit, which can only be accounted for thus—I was resuming a trade of which I was master, where the opprobrium of stupidity could not be so often cast in my face."[37]

While attempting to get a foothold in the entertainment industry, Harry Lauder trained as a miner, but a miner's life was not for him. In contrast with his stifling work underground, he found that touring with a company of comedians, even as the man responsible for setting up stage sets and posting bills, was thrilling. "I loved every minute of it. Compared with my old life as a miner I felt like a bird suddenly liberated from its cage. It seemed as though some good fairy had waved her wand over me and had changed all the drabness of my life, the colourlessness of my former existence, into the romance of travel, the glory of fresh air, sunlight, freedom!"[38] Finding intrinsically pleasurable work could mean less longing after "leisure" as a separate category of existence. As Henry Lax noted, "I never had a hobby. I have none now—except my work. By all that I have heard about the absolutely necessity of a hobby for health and happiness, I ought to have been of all men most miserable . . . Is it true, after all, that it is the people with hobbies who are seeking for happiness, and who die seeking it?"[39]

Chester Armstrong worked in the mines for fifty-two years, the vast majority of them as a colliery weighman. On the day of his retirement he found he experienced both elation and depression. "It was a source of acute pain to know that I was bidding a final adieu to the centre of so many associations and pleasantries that had gone far to neutralize the depressing, monotonous nature of my employment." At the same time, he found joy in the prospect of freedom, probably in large part because his entire identity had not been subsumed in the category "colliery weighman." A student of sociology, he had read extremely widely, and even taught an adult education class on the topic.[40] In retrospect, Armstrong was able to reenvision, and then write, the narrative of his life as a quest for intellectual enlightenment. "Whilst there is nothing in my life that may be strikingly eventful, I look back upon it as a great adventure, and romantic in the best sense of that world. No one endowed with a vivid sense of imagination can set out on a lifelong quest of enlightenment without meeting adventure and romance at every turn."[41]

A "good fit" could also mean satisfying a sense of vocation or calling. Despite hardships ranging from armed attack to the deaths of two of his wives to bouts of malaria and dysentery, Thomas Lewis was happy as a British missionary in what is now Angola because "at last I had come into real touch with my life's work" and "thoroughly enjoyed preaching to these responsive negroes."[42] Making Christian converts was a challenge, but when he and his fellow missionaries had finally baptized five converts, "my joy was too great for speech."[43] Similarly, Robert Gammage, as a young Chartist lecturer in his late teens, walked miles each day in all weathers from one public meeting to another, but had an appreciation for his surroundings that made the long walks like a vacation: "the whole day I felt happy."[44] The meetings themselves primed his optimism, because the discourse revealed the native intelligence of the working people, even though they had only attended the "school of necessity": "I attended every meeting with feelings of delight."[45]

Finally, a good fit between the worker and job accommodated that particular worker's notion of a balanced lifestyle. Isaac Mead of Essex preferred to be constantly occupied. He remembered his days working at the mill as one of the happiest times in his life: his work kept him busy, his employer put his confidence in Mead, and Mead was eager to please.[46] Later in life he bought his own windmill and various farms, and said of work in general, "Work done well at the right time always pays, and one of the pleasures of life is to work as if each thing is the most important thing at the time that needs doing. A busy person is very often a happy person."[47] Similarly, James Campkin had his autobiographical alter ego Frank West wonder, "How cheerful people always feel when they are busy and have their hearts in their work."[48]

Having one's heart in the work was an important part of this equation. William Andrews, a Coventry ribbon weaver, complained that he was forced to wake before 5 a.m. to reach his workplace, had no time to eat anything until 1 p.m., and didn't get home before 7 p.m. "The long hours, the incessant harass, and the impossibility of obtaining sleep owing to the fear of being too late in the mornings are beginning to affect my health," he complained to his diary. "I am gradually becoming unwell."[49] For the printer W. E. Adams, the nature of the work to be performed was crucial: "The labour problem will never really be solved till means have been found to make every man feel an affection for his work and a desire to excel in it."[50] Speaking for himself, "I, who have tried other avocations, know of no condition of life to be preferred to that of the workman who has constant and regular employment at the trade that he likes, provided he is fairly paid for the best he is capable of producing."[51] Regular work at regular hours and for regular wages stabilized Adams's home life, giving him time each night "which I could spend in my own pleasures or my own pursuits—in reading, writing, taking a stroll, or attending a class.

Life was no longer a weariness; it was a real enjoyment. I was happy and contented."[52] Hugh Miller, a young mason, expressed a similar sentiment more succinctly: "I wrought hard during the hours allotted to toil, and was content; and read, wrote or walked, during the hours that were properly my own, and was happy."[53]

Creativity

Challenging work could bring opportunities for creativity. George Jacob Holyoake began his work-life alongside his father, a whitesmith (a worker in tin and other light metals). Holyoake delighted in designing mechanical implements for his own use, and was proud of the recognition that he received, even as a young teenager. "I often swung the striking hammer for my father at the anvil, and to this day I have more pleasure and aptitude for that form of exercise than for any other." The final enjoyable aspect of his work was the aesthetic pleasure he took from it. "Good, well-made, well-contrived, well-finished machinery always gives me as much enjoyment as a good painting."[54] Allen Davenport remembered the delight he had taken as a boy in building small replica farm implements with moving parts.[55]

Barnabas Britten, who spent an afternoon building a canoe with his older brother Charlie, recalled it as one of the high points of his boyhood.[56] Similarly, inspired by a meeting with an elderly eel-catcher, rural laborer George Baldry attempted to make his own fishing boat and described the effortless passage of time associated with the flow state:

> I went home and made a start and once going was so interested in it—while building—that I worked at it all one day, then lighting two candles about seven to go on the early part of the night. Was so much engrossed in what I was doing that I forgot even my own presence, and went on working until I found the candles were growing dim and going out, and when I come to look round found it was daylight. I was surprised to think that I had been working fourteen hours, and thought no more of the passing of time than I should have done had I been asleep.[57]

As Julie-Marie Strange points out, the joy that Baldry obtained from boat-building was quickly crushed by personal tragedy: upon finding out that Baldry and his brother had taken some of their father's materials to build a boat, the elder Baldry destroyed the boat and burned the wood.[58]

John Kelso Hunter started off his worklife as a shoemaker's apprentice, although due to a bad placement he only learned how to make very inferior shoes. His real vocation was art. One of his friends, also a working-class autobiographer, recalled Hunter's way of working: "At first he would not do any painting except when the mood was on him, and then he would get up from his cobbler's bench, throw down his tools, take up his brush and palette, which, with his easel, were always at hand, and paint until he felt that the inspiration had left him, and then he would resume his cobbling again."⁵⁹ Although it took a long time for Hunter to gain art patrons, when he eventually did earn money for his art, he was overjoyed. "I was going to do everything with that five pound . . . in my stupor, I had begun to run without knowing that I was doing so . . . it was a joyous sort of delirium. I reached home in safety. The secret of success was too good to keep."⁶⁰ The poet John Clare's highest ambition had been to "let my parents see a printed copy of my poems[.] [T]hat pleasure I have witnessed and they have moreover lived to see with astonishment and joy their humble offspring noticed by thousands of friends and among them names of the greatest distinction."⁶¹

Frank Bullen had many experiences with work that didn't suit him, noting that workingmen were always better for "a love of the work for its own sake, and not at all from any hope of reward for his achievement outside of the satisfaction of his own innate desire for perfection." Through experimentation and asking questions of professionals, Bullen taught himself the art of framing pictures, and "I was now much happier . . . I was both surprised and delighted to find that I actually had some mechanical skill." He strove to improve his skills not only to please customers "but for the great delight of admiring the work of my own hands before handing it over to customers."⁶²

Adventure

Although military or naval occupations entailed less creativity, some autobiographers reveled in these roles that offered opportunities for adventure, travel, and companionship. When George Calladine joined the militia, his posting allowed him to roam relatively freely. "I was very comfortable and happy, as we were our own masters and went where we had a mind, a reasonable distance from our station." Calladine picked hops in the nearby countryside, and spent hours in the company of a girl he had met.⁶³ Later in his military career, when posted at Ceylon, he and his fellow soldiers cooked up vast cauldrons of "toddy" made of fermented coconut juice, sugar, and eggs, and "pass[ed] along the day in the greatest of pleasure, good company, and hilarity."[64]

Robert Butler, a fife-master posted to India, recounted the importance of like-minded compatriots, including one plowman he referred to only as "W. H." He recounted how they "used to spend many a happy hour together when in barracks, and even upon the march, talking over old stories, and singing the songs of our native land." The two enjoyed sharing memories of friends and family and "in this sadly pleasing retrospect, and joyful anticipation, we lost the sense of our sorrows, and journeyed onward with increased vigour."[65] Butler's other friends included his company's tent-carrying elephant, and a young woman who was a second-generation Anglo-Indian.[66] As a soldier in India in the 1840s, John Pearman spent most of his time not actually fighting: "Our enjoyment in Barracks was such as any young man Could Like. We had Books to Read. Cards to Play. Draught Boards. Chess Boards. Back Gammon and outside the Barracks. We had skittles and Cricket and once a Month we had a Bon Ton and all the Females of the Station invited to it."[67]

John Shipp, orphaned at an early age and persecuted by his first employer during his work on a farm, dreamed of nothing more than becoming a soldier, and was perfectly content to be drafted into an experimental regiment made up of teenaged boys. He delighted in his new clothing, his position as Fife-Major, and the opportunity that barracks life gave him to play practical jokes on his bunkmates.[68] After a short stint in Cape Colony, Shipp was transferred to India, where he reported being happiest. Shipp completely believed in the East India Company's mission; he described arriving in Calcutta and being "cheered by all the bystanders. Every face was wreathed in smiles, every heart beat high for glory. The country through which we passed seemed fertile and well inhabited, prosperous and contented, British justice prevailed, and the pariah in his reed-thatched hut, and the thrifty farmer with his ripening crops, were equally protected."[69] Although Shipp often recounted having seen wartime atrocities and the deaths of civilians, he maintained a positive assessment of soldiering. He had pleasant workmates in the Irish soldiers he commanded, who were unfailingly both amusing and generous; his wife was also supportive.[70] Shipp identified his happiness and his identity so much with soldiering that his court-martial for insubordination and his banishment from India distressed him as much as his young wife's death in childbirth: "I was no longer a soldier, and the thought of that bowed me to the earth."[71]

Interestingly, Shipp, whose greatest happiness in battle was carrying the flag, described battle as a flow state, a time when "an indescribable elation of spirits possesses the whole being, a frenzied disregard of what is before you, a heroism bordering on ferocity."[72] Joseph Donaldson, once shipped to the Continent during the Napoleonic wars, also described a mid-battle flow state: "I could scarcely define my feelings during the action; but so far from feeling fear . . . I felt a sensation something resembling delight; but it was of an awful kind—enthusiasm, sublimity and wonder, mixed with a sense of danger—something like what I have felt in a violent thunder storm."[73] Of course, not every soldier enjoyed his job, even considering the retrospective mental pressure to make the best of bad situations by finding good aspects in them. An anonymous private, who wrote his autobiography to raise funds so that he might find some other work than in the military, characterized soldiering as "a life of weariness, resulting from the absence of all honourable aims and useful duties."[74]

Many sailors recounted enjoying aspects of their work: fine weather, the sparkling of sunlight off the seas, interacting with fish and sea mammals. Frank Bullen, then about twelve years old, recounted serving as a sort of plaything on board due to his small stature, and his ability to sing in a high treble voice. "Surrounded by the crew I warbled the songs I knew, while not another sound disturbed the balmy evening, but the murmur of the caressing waters alongside, and the gentle rustle of a half-drawing sail overhead"; he felt as though this was one of the pleasantest recollections of his life.[75] John Rattenbury, who signed on with a privateer as a boy, felt the same way about shipboard life. "I can recall the triumph and exaltation which rushed through my veins as I saw the shores of my native country receded, and the vast ocean opening before me; I was like a bird which had escaped from the confinement of the cage, and obtained the liberty after which it panted."[76] As Joanne Begiato has pointed out, in the century from 1750 to 1850, the ordinary sailor had become a kind of cultural synecdoche for nationalistic masculinity, imbued with all the emotions from the romantic canon: bravery, daring, a commitment to duty, the ability to be moved to tears, and even joy in battle.[77]

On the other hand, some sailors thought the revelry of their fellow sailors to be a sort of whistling past the graveyard.[78] Samuel Leech, who served in the Royal Navy, thought his fellows tried to drive away misery by creating a party atmosphere on board. "A casual visitor in a man-of-war, beholding the song, the dance, the revelry of the crew, might judge them to be happy. But I know these things are often resorted to because they feel miserable, just to drive away dull care."[79] For Leech, the life of a sailor was like that of a slave; "where severe discipline prevails, though cheerfulness smiles at times, it is only the forced merriment of minds ill at ease."[80] Naval recruits not only lacked autonomy, they were also subject to harsh discipline at all times and to the very real risk of death or dismemberment. Charles McPherson, who fought at the Battle of Navarino in 1827, described scenes of mortal wounds so horrific that the ship's surgeon had banned all nonmedical personnel from a lower deck. "All the upper part of the deck was splashed with blood and brain; lumps of human flesh sticking to it; and in the eyebolts of the deck several of the same disgusting reminders of mortality met my view."[81] Among the dead lay McPherson's friend and messmate Thomas Morfiet. McPherson retrieved Morfiet's body and, crying, sewed it up in a hammock and consigned it to the water. Similarly, W. John Stradley, who grew up in a foundling hospital, chose a career as an armorer's mate in the Royal Navy, but nearly died when his ship was torn apart by storms in the Caribbean. When he finally reached shore, traumatized by his experience, he sought to work for the arsenal at Woolwich, but even while employed, constantly had to evade press gangs to avoid going aboard ship again. When the war was over, he noted, "I got clear of that miserable Situation of a Seafaring life, and was reentered in the Arsenall[.] I again rejoiced in my liberty and thought it a great happiness to be free from Parental Constraint or the Constraint of Tyrannical Officers."[82]

Social Ties

So far, we have seen that working-class autobiographers described happiness as emanating from meaningful work, autonomy, creativity, and adventure; but social ties—the company of pleasant colleagues and masters—were also a major determinant of happiness in the workplace. Elizabeth Oakley, a milkmaid, fondly remembered playing games with one of the children in the family she worked for.[83] Alexander Mitchell, who plowed and took care of cattle as a young man, signed up for successive six-month stints of servitude, as was the custom in Scotland. When he wrote his autobiography, in his seventies, he was most pleased by memories of his co-workers and employers at every place he was hired. "Everybody was so agreeable that it made me feel happy and contented," he noted of one assignment. Of another, "They were all extremely nice and kind. They were all blessed with cheerful dispositions, always ready to crack a joke or to get a laugh." Mitchell, who loved horses, felt as though it was "a treat" to work them; but he also formed lifelong friendships with his fellow servants.[84]

Henry Broadhurst, who started his worklife as a stonemason and ended up as an MP, called his days in one employer's shop the happiest of his life, due to the good relations between master and man. The balance of work and free time was kept on the honor system, so that sometimes he had free days, and other times he worked overtime without charging extra. Because his employer, Mr. Lloyd, often had repair jobs in the countryside, Broadhurst and Lloyd traveled together, "taking our lunch in roadside inns and enjoying our pipes while the pony was halted. Pleasant times were these." Broadhurst noted that "the struggle for a living wage has put an end to the friendly relations often subsisting between employer and workman."[85] Similarly, James Mullin, an Irish cartmaker who through strenuous educational efforts eventually became a physician, remembered two years spent as a contract doctor to the demanding colliers of Blaenavon. The work was trying, both mentally and physically, but it was also pleasant: "The pleasure arose from feeling the acquaintanceship between me and my employer ripen into a very warm friendship, which became a charm that lightened my toil and allured me to remain in that limbo of labour far longer than I intended."[86]

Workplace companionship could facilitate the transfer of skills from one generation to the next.[87] The carpenter Joseph Buckley loved to work alongside an elderly journeyman, a superior workman who also seemed to enjoy his work. "He found pleasure in what he was trying to think out and work out. It was a joy to work with such a man, and his object was to turn out the best work, and when the job was finished we congratulated ourselves that there was no better work in the town."[88] Duncan Campbell did a variety of manual labor jobs to put himself through the equivalent of secondary school, but remembered with special fondness building a wall in the Scottish Highlands with a co-worker decades his senior. "Donnachadh Ruadh and I were, notwithstanding the great disparity of age, the best of friends and the best possible companions. He was an old experienced hand, and I was a young willing one at the work on which we were engaged."[89] Peter Taylor, an apprentice mechanic in his teens, was paired up with an older worker named Alexander Watt, who had few friends and was struggling to support himself so that he wouldn't be a burden on his adult son. Watt taught Taylor mathematics and methods of calibrating the speeds of gearing, and helped him to get his first post-apprenticeship position. "Many a happy, happy day old Sandy and I had together. He was very lonely, and his love fell upon me. I could use great familiarity with him, without giving any offense." Moreover, unlike some of the other workers in the shop, Sandy didn't tell dirty jokes.[90] Frank Bullen was paired on a job casting ornaments in cement with "an old soldier of the Mutiny time, and garrulous in the extreme about his experiences," which made Bullen "quite happy."[91]

Nineteenth-century workdays were long, and workplaces could provide some of the only opportunities for workers to form friendships. John Leatherhead worked in a velvet-weaving workshop, surrounded by "affable and courteous" workmates who were all "ardently bent on acquiring knowledge," so that it was "a pleasure to be among them." He and his workmates combined their funds to buy books and form a mutual instruction society.[92] Because Leatherhead was weaving on a single loom, and his work was repetitive and mechanical, he used his work hours to think about the concepts he had read the night before.[93] An anonymous Scottish printer who became a pastor spent much of his autobiography describing his former friends in the church, including the other ministers in his district, as bound together by sympathy, work, and mutual affection. "The past IS to me a present; so that now there are mental memories of happy hours spent together," he mused.[94] The comedian Harry Lauder remembered with fondness his early collaborative partnership with the musician Mackenzie Murdoch, who first worked with him on his early comedic tours of Scotland. Murdoch notated the melodies that Lauder sang, and the two men also spent much of their leisure time together. "If I was sad Mac and his fiddle could always make me glad; if I was cheery and blithesome Mac and his fiddle could make me laugh for very joy." One of Lauder's more poignant regrets was that as he became more well-known, Lauder ended the partnership, leaving his friend with no one to work with.[95]

Some workplaces were playful, enabling momentary hedonistic pleasures. As a young man, George Meek worked in a bakehouse with other youths. They passed the mornings singing and telling stories, but they had also rigged a gun out of pipe so that they could shoot raw dough at passersby through a hole in one of the windows.[96] Charles Shaw's childhood workplace would have seemed happy to an outsider; the men drank and laughed and played practical jokes on each other, including hiding full greenware buckets of water on the top of doorways to drench people as they were coming in. But looking back at these events sixty years later, Shaw saw not happiness, but debasement caused by overwork and exploitation. "In all these tricks and customs there were the fun and folly, the wild momentary abandonment which always attend recklessness . . . any revelry, any corruption and any cruelty might go on if no scandal arose, or if the week's work were done."[97] James Bent, who was promoted over the course of his career from police constable to superintendent, fondly remembered playing practical jokes on the constables in his unit.[98] Frank Bullen recalled communal times aboard ship as some of the happiest of his young life. He described the antics of two sailors as "spontaneous and side-splitting, seeming superior to all external influence—a well of continual merriment bubbling up. Song, quip and practical joke followed one another incessantly, with all the thoughtless abandon of happy children, and mirthful enjoyment that might have thawed an anchorite."[99]

Other workplaces were less playful, but matched the preferences of serious workers. As David Vincent has noted, many autobiographers emphasized their own respectability by contrasting their own seriousness with the dissipation of their workmates.[100] Robert Spurr was miserable when his workmates drank and swore, because as the sole source of support for his son, he could not go to the public house. When he found a workplace full of religious co-workers, who sang hymns and did not drink, "I had more comfort than I ever had at any previous shop for some years . . . this put more joy in my heart than all the vanity and folly I ever had."[101] James Hillocks, having risen in the world from yarn-winder to schoolmaster and druggist, was happy despite hard work, because he worked alongside his young wife, had a prospering family, and "what will two who work hand to hand not do to stand upright and honourable."[102] For Hillocks, to be able to serve the children of the poor as a schoolmaster was not only a social good but also made him a representative of success for his class, "and I felt something like the same feeling; it elevated my desires and hopes, and I once more wished . . . to be enabled to make more and greater advances by way of improving myself and others, of doing my duty, and forwarding the happiness of man."[103]

Eric Horne, author of *What the Butler Winked At*, worked for fifty-seven years as a domestic servant in the houses of the great; his memoir illustrates the sources of domestic servants' unhappiness. As a young worker, he was happy as long as he was treated well and the close community of servants had little interpersonal conflict.[104] There were occasionally moments for amateur theatricals, or dances accompanied by Horne on the violin, that made the servants "just one great big happy family."[105] This was not always the case, however. As Horne pointed out, many other employees might work with disagreeable people, but at least at the end of the day they left their work behind. "In service one has to be with them, living always in the same house, night and day, Sundays and weekdays."[106]

As Horne's duties became more onerous, he found it increasingly galling that a footman's tasks were so repetitive—largely cleaning things that had been dirtied by others: "So that at the end of his day's work he can show nothing that he has done. He has made nothing, produced nothing, yet he has been constantly on the alert all day, not knowing where his next job will spring from."[107] Horne maintained his own family in a separate residence, but due to the nature of his job he was unable to live at home, even when his wife's blindness made it dangerous for her to run the household. He had enough abusive employers to hammer home to him the complete lack of power in the employment relationship, given that domestic servants could not find jobs without a "character," and this was not something that employers were compelled by law to provide. He fondly remembered being the servant to an Indian prince who had moved to Britain, who "appreciated all that I did for him, and what was more acceptable, he treated me as though I was a human being. It was a pleasure to serve him."[108] But other employers, or would-be employers, treated him with no "more consideration . . . than a piece of dirt sticking to the heel of her boot."[109]

A Comfortable Workplace

Closely related to companionable workmates and respectful employers was the nature of the work environment itself. Farm labor was extremely taxing, but autobiographers appreciated being outdoors or working with animals, or belonging to a community whose members were working on the land. The poet John Clare was sent to the fields at the age of ten to scare birds or weed grain, but "the old womens memorys never faild of tales to smooth our labour, for as every day came new Jiants, Jobgobblins, and faireys was read to pass it away."[110] George Lansbury, later a well-traveled Socialist politician, had fond memories of delivering parcels during an otherwise difficult sojourn to Australia with his family. "The job seemed to get into my blood. I always had good horses to drive and had always been very fond of them, so the work was a real pleasure to me."[111] Thomas Holcroft, who had lived an economically marginal existence for his entire childhood, was delighted to become a stable-boy as a teenager, not least of all because it meant he ate daily, but also because "I was mounted on the noblest that the earth contains, had him under my care, and was borne by him over hill and dale, far outstripping the wings of the wind."[112]

Similarly, the Scottish farm laborer William Milne enjoyed his work, particularly when he worked in sight of a ruined castle, "for every spare hour I had from my work I wandered about the old place, and in my fancy re-built and re-peopled the ancient structure. I felt great delight in pondering and speculating over the former greatness of the baronial pile."[113] Milne thought that farm service ought to be "the happiest of all human callings, an occupation in which there is the greatest variety of food for the contemplative mind, where the procession of the seasons on their never-ceasing annual round are an endless joy to the seeing eye, and the heart which adores and loves all that God has set before it in the marvelous arrangement of the beautiful world."[114] According to Milne, the distance between this ideal and reality was only created by miserly masters who failed to feed and clothe their farmworkers adequately or to encourage them to socialize other than furtively in the middle of the night. John Buckley, who began farm labor as a ten-year-old, would have agreed with the positive elements of Milne's assessment. He found haymaking and working with the even-tempered ploughman enjoyable:

> To ride a mile on a horse in the grey twilight, with a long whip and a bag on one hime, with a bacon dumpling and a chunk of bread, and on the other a small wooden bottle of small beer, was the perfection of happiness . . . if the farmer and his labourers could only have lived by it would have been a happy life, but there can be no happiness in a constant struggle for existence."[115]

John Leno, later a printer, recalled one of his first jobs, which was delivering the rural post. Although the job involved walking many miles a day, "my daily round was through pleasant fields, where birds sang, and flowers grew. I saw the squirrel leap from tree to tree, wild rabbits sporting, the partridge whirring from my feat, the mowers and reapers at their labours, and, better still, I was welcomed wherever I went." Beyond the fact that the arrival of the post was a major social event, Leno was pleased when illiterate people asked him to read their letters for them. "I had the power to create smiles and draw forth tears. I was a boy and the listeners adult personages."[116] Leno also enjoyed being sent out into the countryside at harvest time to join other young people in gleaning. Although the gleaners worked long days, at noon they took a break for "bever" time, when those with the best voices—including Leno—were invited to sing for the rest.[117] "I attribute much of the extreme happiness

I enjoyed in Dunstable, Windsor and London, to my capacity to sing a song," he noted.[118]

The poacher John "Lordy" Holcombe professed to never be happier than when he was poaching. He excused his illegal proclivities by noting that it was impossible to support a family through honest labor in the countryside when he took up poaching as a boy; and that his activities enabled many families in his town to survive.[119] Similarly, the poacher Frederick Rolfe said he loved the excitement of the job, including the frisson of "knowen that you had got Keepers and Police beat, and that went a long way towards recompence for the danger and risk run."[120] Rolfe was later hired as a gamekeeper, which enabled him to work legitimately while using his poaching skills to catch others. "Looken back I see that this was the happiest ten years I have ever knowen," he wrote.[121] Ironically, John Wilkins, who worked as a gamekeeper, expressed just as much delight about his exploits catching poachers.[122]

Even those whose farm labor jobs were extremely repetitive could glean some mental compensation from the pride they took in their work. Robert Roberts described his grandfather's pride at being able to create round hayricks, his neighbor Tom's pride in plowing the straightest furrow, and his neighbor Jack's pride in being able to mow and reap with the best of them. "Now these little matters of pride may be trifling enough, but they had their use; they gave a little zest to the dull, mechanical monotony of their work. I should think the life of a ploughman, for instance, utterly intolerable otherwise."[123] Later, Roberts felt his own sense of pride when he became a translator of political pamphlets: "I was proud of being reckoned a literary man, although only a translator, so I was very happy and contented."[124]

Depending on the individual's perspective, many different workplaces could be interesting enough to provide aesthetic compensations. Franz Bergg, a German waiter, noted the pleasure to be gained from a beautiful workplace, even by one who was there to work rather than to enjoy leisure. "There were the blinding white tablecloths, the tasteful, multiply folded napkins, the big silver bowls and shimmering metal platters, the artistic, richly segmented centerpieces, the finely polished, nobly formed drinking glasses; the pleasingly arranged bouquets. In all its richness it offered a constantly shifting feast for the eyes."[125] Mrs. Scott, a felt hat worker, enjoyed one workshop "in a lovely room, six stories up, with big windows and a splendid view of the hills," in which "we had some good times."[126] Henry Riddell, a Scottish shepherd, "delighted in" the pastures that it was his responsibility to tend, since he was required to walk through the woods, looking at vistas that inspired him to write poetry.[127] Of course the necessity of working encouraged workers to adapt their expectations, but for many, the workplace environment had its own compensations.

Women and Work

As noted in chapter 1, working women wrote autobiographies less frequently than men did, and it is harder to make generalizations from a smaller sample size, but it is possible to infer several things from the autobiographies that do exist. Working-class women had fewer vocational opportunities than men, their work had fewer mental and physical rewards, and job tenures tended to be shorter. Emma Griffin has argued that when it came to financially remunerative work, the family was not an egalitarian institution, and the weight of inequality fell most heavily on women and girls in a vicious circle of low expectations. Often pulled from school to satisfy family needs for childcare and housekeeping, girls were neither allowed to complete their educations nor, in many cases, to learn skills that would enable them to pursue careers other than in domestic service. Lacking the skills to earn a self-supporting income, women were then forced to make pragmatic marriages. Women who married men capable of supporting the family tended, with a few exceptions, to retreat from the paid labor market entirely.[128]

Eric Horne's complaint about life being a never-ending round of cleaning up after other people would no doubt have resonated with many women, including those who worked inside the home. Still, some women described finding pleasure in aspects of work. Hannah Cullwick, who worked a number of different jobs as an under-maid, professed to enjoy even the roughest, hardest manual labor. She enjoyed her work partly because it gave meaning to the subservient identity that she had crafted with her friend and later husband, Arthur Munby, who fetishized her when she was at her dirtiest. As she wrote in one of the diaries she kept at his insistence, "As I once said to Massa, 'I was *born* to *serve*, and *not* to order.' "[129] She took pride in being able to do the most physically demanding jobs—cleaning knives and boots, for example—as well as a man might do them. She worked eighteen-hour days at some jobs, took on the work of other servants in order to give them time off, and blacked fire-grates with her bare hands. She also took satisfaction in being noticed as an ideal-appearing servant—wearing the clothes of domestic service to best advantage, and having large biceps, rough, hard, hands, and a weather-beaten face. The pride that she took in her appearance was reflected in the number of times she allowed herself to be photographed either blackened with soot or on the floor, scrubbing.[130]

Women's work outside the home could provide a respite from an unpleasant home environment. Hannah Maria Mitchell had been brought up on a farm in the Derbyshire Peak District, by a mother who was a violent-tempered taskmaster and prevented Mitchell from acquiring any formal education. When Mitchell was finally sent into the nearest town to learn dressmaking from a local woman, "for the first time I realized that work could also be a pleasure."[131] A couple of years after running away from home, she was employed in a workshop where "for the first time in my life I found myself in congenial company . . . we were very happy. Miss T. was so kind and clever that under her tuition I soon became a fairly skilled worker. She was just the friend I needed then, forthright and sensible."[132]

Although Mary Loughran, who moved from Ireland to Scotland at the age of sixteen, was maliciously refused a "character" by one employer and then interrogated and disbelieved by the next about why she didn't have one, she did find some aspects of domestic work pleasant. Her distrustful employer had one son and six daughters ranging in age from five to sixteen. "I was up with the lark now and had a heart as light as a feather, for had I not seven beautiful creatures to love, and sometimes to play with."[133] Like Eric Horne, the butler, Loughran enumerated many ways in which domestic servants lacked autonomy: employers misrepresented the number of people who would regularly need to be served in the household, or limited their servants' freedom on their days off with suspicions about their behavior.[134] But Loughran exercised what autonomy she could by immediately leaving unpleasant situations. She left one posting because it was infested with rats; several because there was no Catholic church close enough for her to walk to; and another because among the lodgers were a couple of women waiting to be admitted to a lock hospital (for treatment of venereal disease). As she noted of one situation, "With the greatest difficulty I put in three days. On the evening of the third day I sent up the dinner and ran away while they were in the dining room."[135]

Mary Ann Ashford, who became a domestic servant at age thirteen due to the death of her father, endured one unpleasant situation after another, suffering from insufficient food and constant scolding. For the most part, she was too busy with the demands of life to contemplate her own happiness; in seventeen years, she had thirteen different employers.[136] But she did note of one family that "they were very pleasant people to live with; and I gave them great satisfaction and did their work with pleasure."[137] Ashford ended up as a cook in an institution for the orphaned boys of soldiers. She enjoyed working there, but, distraught about being dismissed without good cause, she contracted a practical marriage with an elderly sergeant who was the master shoemaker of the institution. He died after thirteen years, leaving her with six children, including an infant, and no other recourse than to marry another elderly soldier, this time the master tailor for the institution. When at the age of seventy-six he was forced to stop work due to an injured arm, she doggedly, and ultimately successfully, secured his back pension for him by interceding with the royal family. At the end of her narrative, she noted that her struggles through life reminded her of a poem she had read in the newspaper: "Let us, then, be up and doing, with a heart for any fate; Still achieving—still pursuing, Learn to labour and to wait."[138]

Annie Kenney's work organizing and participating in the militant suffrage movement of the Edwardian period was pleasant to her in spite of periodic imprisonment, hunger strikes, and forcible feeding, largely due to the fun and companionship she felt within the movement. Organizers strove to keep members happy by matching people with tasks that suited their temperaments. "Suffragettes were always happy, always laughing. We had a lot to laugh at!"[139] Participation in the movement took her to parts of the country she admired, exposed her to educated discussions about politics, and provided her with the companionship of "sitting in front of a rosy fire, with kind people."[140] At least as she crafted her autobiographical persona, part of Kenney's joy emanated from her optimistic temperament. "Joyous laughter is one of the best antidotes against the serious disease of depression," she mused. "There can be no melancholy where there is genuine laughter."[141] Her determination to find the silver lining in every situation (while a little frustrating to the modern reader) led her to construe even a prison sentence as a positive development, since it allowed her to relax and daydream. On the other hand, release from prison made her so "sick with joy" that she could not eat.[142] "The joy of release! It was almost worthwhile going to prison for the supreme happiness of getting out."[143]

・・・・・・

As this chapter has shown, in the nineteenth century, work—which for a full-time worker occupied the majority of waking hours—could be a crucial factor in facilitating or detracting from happiness. Unsurprisingly, neither male nor female factory workers expressed job satisfaction, but they are also underrepresented among working-class autobiographers.[144]

While industrialization writ large notoriously could transform a workplace into a stultifying environment of repetitive toil and long hours, some working people found enjoyment, and even flow: particularly those who were able to incorporate autonomy into their work projects or schedules. Contributing to the family economy, cultivating feelings of personal mastery, good relationships with co-workers and employers, and fulfillment through adventure and creativity were good predictors of happiness among autobiographers. Although working-class women had fewer options, some of those in domestic service appreciated being able to escape from abusive or entrapping home environments, or found satisfaction in some aspects of their jobs.

FOUR

....

Life Is with People

REWARDING PERSONAL RELATIONSHIPS are closely correlated with happiness in modern studies; loneliness and unhappiness are correlated.[1] The direction of causation is somewhat unclear; it is probable that people with happy demeanors are better at attracting friends and partners, and not simply that good relationships with others promote happiness. Just as modern studies show that "psychosocial wealth" is crucial to subjective well-being today, so community was arguably even more important to the nineteenth-century working-class individual, whose experiences and emotions were validated by his or her social context in ways that could make life, upon reflection, seem satisfying or not.[2] For nineteenth-century working-class men and women, connections to the communities of the family, the workplace, the town or village, and for many, the church, were crucial.[3] Social contexts bound people together through what Susan Broomhall calls "spaces for feeling," which could be shared physical spaces, shared experiences, or shared concepts.[4] In contrast to late twentieth-century British working-class autobiographies, many of which were nostalgic for specific geographic spaces, early nineteenth-century life writing reflects that this was a society on the move, so that community consisted of relationships with people and with rituals rather than (for example) with neighborhoods.[5] As this chapter will show, the vibrancy and centrality of social ties helps to explain working-class people's participation in networks of "prosocial" behavior: lending or borrowing items or resources, feeding people who were down on their luck, graciously accepting help from others who were similarly situated.

The smallest of the concentric circles of belonging was marriage. Working-class marriages existed not just to sanctify sexual relationships, and clearly not primarily to protect inheritances (a motive that continued to restrict the choice of marriage partner for the wealthy), but rather to pool emotional and economic resources needed to create and support families.[6] Each member of a marital partnership had a prescribed economic role. For a husband, that role was breadwinning, and men often assumed the prerogative of retaining a disproportionate fraction of the total family income as pocket money. Men were entitled to the largest and most protein-rich meals, and could expect to some extent to be insulated from their children's daily care. Mothers, in contrast, were generally tasked with budgeting, child care, shopping, and meal preparation. They might stint themselves in order to stretch wages to cover family expenses, take in boarders, scavenge for food and fuel, and pawn clothing items on a weekly basis, but were expected to maintain the household without their efforts impinging on their husbands' happiness.[7] Some men described their wives' pragmatic contributions to their families rather than their wives' personalities or intellects, but it is clear that these relationships—and recalling the early days of these relationships—were valued.[8]

Even as marriage was pragmatically important for survival, working-class relationships and subsequent marriages were also founded on emotional attraction. Ginger Frost's study of breach-of-promise suits indicates that although the ideal of companionate marriage percolated through the working classes incompletely and over time, attraction was important. Couples often met through rituals like "walking out" together; sexual activity after engagement but before marriage was not uncommon.[9] David Vincent, Anna Clark, and Claire Langhamer have all shown that, while shy about intimate details, many working-class autobiographers described loving and romantic marital relationships.[10] Relationships between working-class men and women had the potential for tension, since couples might fight over authority within the relationship or about anything that straitened the family finances.[11] In such a context, when autobiographers wrote at length about the quality of their relationships, they were not just making descriptive statements about their lives but also normative statements about respectability.

Many couples met in late adolescence or early adulthood. James Bowd, who married in 1849, noted that his young wife had a close call giving birth to their daughter, but survived, "and you may be sure that I was very pleased for I was as fond of my wife [as] a Cat is of New Milk I felt as if I Dare not tell her how much I Loved her because I thought she would be trespising on [where] I should be and that would be the Head of the House."[12] Dyke Wilkinson, who was in love with love as a young man, noted that the earliest days of his business career were the happiest of his whole life. "Business was so full of promise, and I so full of love for a meek-eyed frail young thing, the gentlest and truest human being I have ever known."[13] F. H. Crittall met his wife when she was seventeen and he was a young working man of twenty-one, and he professed having been instantly delighted with her "irrepressible sense of fun and kindly banter that bound people to her with silken cords . . . Oh, the rapture of those Birmingham nights when we found delicious romance in a cup of coffee and a slice of cake from our favorite coffee shop!"[14] Thomas Whittaker referred to his home as "the one green spot on earth to me; my wife the bonniest bit of all the beauties with which I began to feel that the world was filled, making my life a perpetual sunshine, and my hopes full of bloom."[15] Chester Armstrong recalled falling in love with his wife as being "wholly absorbing," throwing every other experience into insignificance. "Owing to the almost perfect harmony of our marriage union, this period of courtship is always remembered as a very happy interlude, when the world around us acquired a new colour and interest, and a new-born purpose and joy in life assumed idealistic proportions."[16]

Couples as yet unburdened by children could get by with little. James McCurrey, a temperance advocate, dedicated his autobiography to his wife of fifty years; he had married Margaret when he was nineteen years old, and spent the evenings of their early wedded days threading needles for her so that she could have no interruption in her sewing of umbrella covers. To his mind, that was true dedication after a long day at work. He noted, "My deliberate opinion is, after more than fifty years from that needle threading time, that the best treasure in a poor man's house, or a rich man's either, is love."[17] At eighteen, Robert Lowery married his cousin, who was a year older, and professed that although the two of them lived in a garret and had two young daughters within three years, those days were the happiest of their married lives. The two shared a love for self-cultivation, sometimes going without dinner so that they could pay the weekly fee for library membership.[18] Charles Manby Smith fondly remembered the early childless years of his marriage, when his wife and he lived in London and spent the evenings walking through the street markets and watching the people, or indoors playing piano duets or painting watercolors: "Ah! Those were happy days, when we were beginning to play the game of life, and, like children at school unwilling to peril the loss of a new toy, played it 'in fun' and not in earnest."[19] Henry White, living in Cirencester and working as a tea salesman, recalled similarly carefree days: "How sweet it was then, to sit with her and talk over all the events of the day, while the tea and toast were fast disappearing. Ah, this was a pleasant time indeed, for both, he sun shining all round us."[20]

Few autobiographers discussed physical intimacy. When "Jacques" moved to Aberdeen, where he didn't know anyone, he felt incredibly lonely; "But in the crowded thoroughfares; in the busy streets; in every human throng, I felt then, what I have often felt since, an oppressive solitariness, an indescribable isolation of my individual self . . . I became moody, restless, and unhappy, never, at the same time, suspecting the operation of another, and probably the veritable cause, of so much uneasiness." He realized that he was pining away for a girl whom he was raised alongside in his small town. When she came to Aberdeen for a visit, he spent three days systematically wooing her, and the two of them continued to exchange letters when she went back home. In 1822, he traveled to a place in the countryside where they had conspired to meet, and "all the language in the world which I can command would be deficient alike in appropriateness and power to describe the sensations of joy, 'pure as angels' kisses,' which we on that, and many subsequent occasions of a similar kind, so fully experienced."[21] Henry Price, a London cabinetmaker who married a girl from the country after knowing her only a few weeks, said something similar about his early married life: "Oh the Joy and Bliss of loving. A Furnish room was a Paradise to us."[22] John Clare married his wife, Patty, out of a sense of obligation, because she was pregnant; and only then after waiting until the last minute to actually hold the ceremony. Although he "fell in love by accident, married her by accident, and esteemed her by choice and sure enough had I not met her I should have at this day been a lonely solitary feeling nothing but the worlds sorrows and troubles and sharing none of its happiness."[23]

While romantic love was elevated as an aspirational ideal, it was not a necessary condition for an acceptable marriage. The autobiography of an anonymous handloom weaver published in the *Commonwealth* demonstrates this through a comparison of his first and second wives. He had fallen in love at first sight with his first wife when he was only ten years old. He pined silently after her for years until finally, when she was recuperating from an illness, he visited her and managed to tell her that he liked her. Fifteen months later they were married. "I cannot give even a faint idea of the fulness of my joy when she became irrevocably mine. I wondered how one human heart could hold so great an amount of happiness; and in the exuberance of my bliss, I never took time to think that everything here must end." Within a short time she had died of consumption. When he married again, the feeling of being in love was absent, but "though I may not experience the ecstatic joy which I felt in the society of her who is gone, I have great reason to thank God for having a second time directed time to a partner in life who is in every way worthy of my most unlimited confidence and sincerest love."[24]

Ideals of Domesticity

Working-class autobiographers often professed gratitude for the burden that their wives bore.[25] Joseph Livesey described his wife as "no lady wife, though respectably connected . . . she did all the house work as well as attending to business, and she would sit up past midnight making and mending all the children's clothes." Livesey described her happiness as "bound up with the happiness and well-doing of her family," and he appeared to derive great happiness from his children, thirteen of whom were born, and eight of whom survived to adulthood.[26] The pitman Thomas Burt married a workingman's daughter with a poor education, but felt that she "possessed every attribute of womanhood requisite to make a loving partner and a happy home." Burt's wife was relatively uninterested in his later political career as union leader and MP, but he was contented that given his wife's skills, he "could give little attention to matters domestic" and his children would be well cared-for.[27] Alexander Murison met his future wife Ellen when they both were twelve years old and attending the same rural school. An educated woman, Ellen worked as a schoolteacher for several years before her marriage, but endeared herself to Murison's working-class parents by being accomplished at housewifery as well as literate. As he noted at the end of his memoir, "I may say, with profound admiration and gratitude, that to her love and wisdom I owe the blessing of a most happy life and the inspiration of the best I have done and been."[28]

Joseph Terry, whose unpublished autobiography was clearly influenced by tropes of middle-class domesticity, wrote at surprising length about how useful his wife could make herself. "While few ever consider the constant demand on a mother with a number of young children, fewer still ever notice as they ought to be able to appreciate woman's worth, the amount of business they can get through when necessity requires it." He described in idyllic terms what it was like during the evenings when their older children were asleep, and his wife had one child on her lap and another in the cradle next to her, and nursed the children and knitted something with a book propped up in front of her. "I sat by her side reading or composing [poetry] . . . happy in her company and in my thrice happy home, while we occasionally exchanged a remark or read aloud some pithy passage interesting to both."[29]

As the autobiographer David Johnston explained, those who had experienced unhappy childhoods particularly appreciated finding partners who could make happy homes.[30] Such seems to have been the case for Joseph Gutteridge, whose stepmother banished him from the household when he was still in his teens. He described his first meeting with the girl who would become his wife as "one day of happiness [that] was like a gleam of sunshine flitting its radiant beauty across the dreary wilderness of my life."[31] On the other hand, Andrew Carnegie had grown up with very close family ties, and lost both his mother and brother to illness shortly before his marriage at the age of fifty-one. "My life has been made so happy by her that I cannot imagine myself living without her guardianship," he noted.[32] Carnegie's additional reflections on his wife are interesting; he noted that he "could not endure" the thought of living after her, but "then the thought of what will be cast upon her, a woman left alone with so much requiring attention and needing a man to decide, gives me intense pain."[33]

Male autobiographers appear to have gained significant emotional compensations from marriage. William Hutton was married to his wife for over forty years, and professed that "she had never approached me without diffusing a ray of pleasure over the mind, except where any little disagreement had happened between us." He wrote of his wife's memory with tears in his eyes.[34] "No event in a man's life is more consequential than marriage; nor is any more uncertain. Upon this die his sum of happiness depends."[35] Hutton's happy home life caused him to redouble his efforts, "for the pleasure of providing for a beloved family is inconceivable."[36] Robert Blatchford fell in love with Sarah Crossley when she was sixteen, and married her after a seven-year engagement. He described married life as "delectable," delighting in doing chores for his wife, singing and walking together; ultimately, they lived together until she died at the age of seventy. He identified the love of a like-minded woman as the highest value in human life: "For me, fame, title, power and wealth would be dust in the balance against the gold of a woman's love."[37] Ultimately, his longing for her companionship even facilitated a shift in his belief system, from materialism to spiritualism, in the hopes that she might be able to communicate with him from beyond the grave.[38]

Men who had experienced happy marriages tended to remarry. Peter Gabbitass, a carpenter and poet, married four times, having been predeceased by three wives, and opined that "the companionship of an affectionate wife would be better than sitting at ease, with no one to please."[39] Joseph Millott Severn, later a phrenologist, married twice. He said of his first wife, "we had a very happy time . . . reciprocative conjugal companionship and new interests and responsibilities having come into our lives after many years of waiting. It was glorious, exhilarating springtime, too, when nature was abounding in a wealth of new life." Unfortunately, his first wife only lived for nine months. "Hitherto there had been much in my life which called for fortitude and courage, but this period was the most disconsolate I ever experienced."[40] Severn proposed to his second wife after only two weeks of face-to-face acquaintance, and their marriage lasted thirty-eight years and resulted in two children. Second marriages were often contracted as matters of financial convenience, since men's and women's designated roles around breadwinning and care for children necessitated either a partner, or some other resource like adopting out children or reliance on extended families.[41] Within remarriages, the existence of children and of debt from prior marriages complicated happiness.[42]

To what extent were the paeans to happy marriage motivated by genre expectations? On one side of the balance, working-class men who were unhappy in domestic situations could and did leave their relationships, as Jane Humphries's research has shown, so we might expect men who remained in the domestic circle to be happier than those who left.[43] On the other side, those who did stay married to wives whose personalities clashed had the option of not discussing those aspects in materials intended for publication. Patrick Joyce's analysis of the diary of dialect writer Edwin Waugh demonstrates that in a medium intended for his eyes only, Waugh described his wife as coarse and uneducated. For a man as deeply concerned with respectability and propriety as Waugh, his wife's personality detracted from his own self-fashioning.[44]

Women and Marriage

Fewer female autobiographers detailed the emotional compensations of marriage. Although her daily life was an unending round of difficult household chores, Hannah Cullwick professed that the meaning of her life was her love for Arthur Munby, the middle-class "sweetheart" who she had met at the age of twenty-one and to whom she had made herself a slave. Cullwick preferred their unconventional relationship to marriage, since it enabled her to engage in the aspects of being a woman that suited her and avoid the others.[45] Mary Mockford, although not the author of an autobiography herself, edited the autobiography of her husband, who had begun life as an impoverished farm boy and ended it as a successful Baptist preacher. Mockford noted that although she and her husband had only been married for seven years, "I shall ever look back on the years we spent together as among the most happy of my whole life." This was the case despite the fact that at the time of their marriage he was in his seventies and often ill, requiring much hands-on care.[46]

Much more typical among female autobiographers was Deborah Smith, who found happiness in spite of being married rather than because of it. After her first husband died of complications of alcoholism, she married again, but she and her husband could not get along. "I could never make a companion of him; somehow, he always misunderstood me. I thought of all I had missed, yet by living my own life, filling it up with work, I had not been unhappy."[47] Louise Jermy had grown up in an abusive household. When she was finally courted, she had trouble reading her suitor's rather obvious signals (he had traveled 120 miles to see her, and had also talked to her father about his intentions). She described talking about her conflicted feelings with a woman friend in Birmingham, where she lived as a domestic servant, "and she suggested that my doubt and fear were bred from my memory of the past, the unhappiness of my girlhood and the way I had to make my own way in life had made me think that any real happiness was too good to last." Unfortunately, Louise's niggling suspicion that her suitor, William, was insincere turned out to be correct. After getting her hopes up, he dashed them, saying that his previous marriage had been so happy that he could not imagine getting married again. "He had struck my life's happiness from me at one blow, and all the best that was in me went with it," Jermy wrote. "My faith and trust in him and in people in general, was gone forever."[48] In the wake of her breakup with William, she suffered from anxiety and contemplated suicide, but ultimately came to peace with the situation and even laughed when she heard that he was subsequently sued by another woman for breach of promise. Eventually she did meet the man she would marry, through their common employer, and married him not because she was in love with him, but because he was a decent man who kept his word.

It can be hard to separate women's attitudes toward the institution of marriage from the larger constraints and hardships of their prescribed role. Hannah Maria Mitchell's life story well illustrates the way in which working-class women's workload and lack of opportunity could leave them feeling dissatisfied. As her grandson Geoffrey Mitchell wrote of her, "Life in many ways had toughened and hardened her and she seldom showed affection or even, all that readily, kindness to those closest to her."[49] Mitchell had run away from home after being endlessly run ragged by her perhaps mentally ill mother, who had refused to allow her to be formally educated. Later in life, after her marriage to a fellow Socialist, she found that running a household, and especially trying to eke out meals with a scanty budget when she hated cooking, made it hard to be happy. Even so, some periods of her life as a young wife were happier than others; a move to the village of Newhall meant cheaper food, and the presence of friends, and her baby thriving by being in the open air. But with no library nearby, Mitchell also lowered her ambitions: "In many ways those three years were the happiest years of my life . . . I was more content, having, as it seemed then, given up the idea of study and intellectual development."[50]

Working-class women had to bear the cost of exploitive relationships. Charwoman Betty Dodds (Martha Grimes) described working as housekeeper for a man whom she called " 'Arry" in her memoir. When the other household employee had the night off, Betty's employer plied her with drinks, made a sexual advance, then made fun of her for wanting to get married. When she could no longer hide her pregnancy, " 'Arry" fired her. For Betty/Martha, while the relationship had ended, the prospect of her impending baby brought her happiness. "I 'ad loved, and seen life with a gent. Nobody could take that mem'ry from me . . . Besides wich, wen a woman makes 'her fust baby close she feels a kind of solemn joy a'-liftin' of 'er up." The joy that the narrator felt in her children—particularly when successive partners/husbands turned out to be abusive—was real.[51]

Families and Friends

Expanding beyond the marital dyad to the nuclear family, relatively few male autobiographers detailed the delight their children brought them, even though, as Julie-Marie Strange has described, working-class fatherhood could involve emotional involvement and play, not just economic provision and discipline.[52] Thomas Preston, who married a widow with three young children, "found myself surrounded with family anxieties without the pains of waiting for them," but professed to be "sensibly alive to the sweets of domestic happiness." Unfortunately, after giving birth to another four daughters, his wife absconded to America with a lover, "and from a situation prosperous and happy I was suddenly plunged into the deepest abyss of wretchedness." Without a wife, Preston found running his household to be immensely challenging.[53]

One exception to working men's silence about their children was James Burn, who addressed his autobiography to his son Thomas in the form of a series of letters. Burn noted of Thomas's birth that "if anything was calculated to increase my happiness, this event could not fail to do it."[54] Thomas was to be the first of sixteen children born to Burn and his two wives, and these children were sources of real pleasure.[55] John Harris, the Cornish miner and poet, was an involved parent, taking his two daughters and two sons into the countryside to play while he tried to think up verses. "My children became my companions. They were never happier than with me, nor I than when with them . . . Often have I rocked my children in the cradle, and hummed my song into existence at the same time, which helped to lull the little ones to sleep."[56]

The next concentric circle was that of the birth family, and the extended family members often referred to as "friends."[57] James Campkin had his alter ego, Frank West, note that the home "was the centre of my world, the place where I could turn when all else was dark and frowning. And what was that one thing which rendered it so attractive? *Love for each other.* If one was in difficulties, we all felt for him or her; and if any little triumph was achieved we were all equally delighted."[58] Limited literacy and the cost of sending mail hampered communication among members of families separated by military service, the search for work, or emigration.[59] As a result, reunions with family members loomed large in their memoirs.[60] Donald Stewart's father was a sailor, and he remembered the childhood joy of seeing him again after long voyages. Although he and his brothers had always accumulated an arrears of punishment—the nineteenth-century equivalent of "wait till your father gets home"—Stewart wrote that "when the old man did actually arrive however, the jubilation was so great, that the material threats vanished into thin air."[61] Joseph Severn, whose unhappily married parents separated, was sometimes taken to see his mother clandestinely, since she worked as a domestic servant for another family. "Oh! The joy of seeing mother again, and what a delightful few hours we had together; then the pangs of parting," he remembered.[62] Scottish farmhand Alexander Mitchell had a surprise visit from his aunt, who had served almost as a mother to him when he was a child. "I need hardly say that there was no one I could have been more delighted to see," he wrote. Their meeting was bittersweet, however. "Before parting we sat down by the roadside and had a good cry." He never saw her again.[63]

James Mullin's mother was widowed when he was a child, and his later success in life was due to her self-sacrifice; she skimped on her own meals and worked in the fields to pay for his school fees and later university tuition. "I remember running forth to meet her and welcome her with a kiss, and I still look back on those meetings as the happiest moments of my life," Mullin remembered.[64] Later, when he boarded with a master cartmaker and came home on weekends, "the prospect of spending a whole two nights at home with my mother made me the happiest of mortals. She generally walked to meet me about a mile outside our town, and no two lovers ever met with greater raptures of delight."[65] Alf Ireson left home at the age of fifteen to pursue a girl and a career as a mason, and did not return for several years, by which time he had a fiancé, some savings, and a union card. "The first sight of my dear mother was pathetic. I burst into tears, and mother did the same. Neither of us could speak. She clasped me in her arms, and kissed her run-away Alf. After weeping together for a time, tears were dried, for the happy home feeling cheered me." Although it was just a visit, and he had to leave again after a few days, "the memories of that visit were a great comfort to me."[66] These kinds of descriptions retroactively instantiated these working-class women as members of the self-sacrificing middle-class maternal ideal.

Robert Roberts, who rose from the position of laborer to become a scholar, noted that some of his most pleasant moments were the times he returned from acting as a school headmaster or a parish curate to visit with his family. He was their pride and joy, and was constantly asked for advice on all kinds of issues; and he remembered with particular fondness climbing the nearby hills with his father after dinner and spending "some pleasant hours in a kind of pleasant reverie." As a curate, he was able to help out his parents and siblings financially: "I always felt better after a visit to the old folks; my pockets were lighter, but so were my spirits." As he wrote his autobiography, he noted that "I have had many dark days since those serene ones, and I am glad that the happiness of those early times was not clouded by anticipation of evils to come. It is not much satisfaction that I have had from my life, but it is a little satisfaction to reflect that I was some comfort to my parents."[67] The Unitarian minister Adam Rushton, who had been a miner during his early years, looked forward to an annual hiking trip with his brother. "Memorable occasions were these, every one of them. Much was said, but much more was felt which could not be expressed. Reminiscences crowded on our minds. Incidents of our pilgrimages over the Derbyshire and Cheshire hills were recalled with the greatest delight."[68]

Other autobiographers returned to family after extended or geographically extensive separations. James Bywater migrated to the United States in 1848 and did not return for a visit until 1852, at which time his parents failed to recognize him because they had assumed he was dead. Once reacquainted, "we had a joyous greeting all around."[69] Having converted to the Church of Latter-Day Saints while in the United States, Bywater was able to visit England two more times as a missionary, and made sure to reunite with his surviving family members each time. When James Burn had finally crossed the border into England and returned to the land of his mother's people, around the Tyne, he noted that "my heart was filled with unspeakable emotions of joy."[70] Printer Charles Manby Smith reunited with his family after several years working in Paris. "Everything appeared new and foreign to my delighted eyes, which somehow would be dropping moisture, though my heart was laughing with pleasure."[71]

Henry Carter had the misfortune to be imprisoned at the beginning of the Napoleonic wars and kept in captivity for two years. When Carter was ultimately reunited with his brother Frank, "At first I took him in surprise, at first I could Hardly make him sensible I was his brother, being nearly two years without hearing whether I was dead or alive. But when he came to himself as it were, we rejoiced together with exceeding great joy indeed." His reunions with two other brothers were similarly emotional.[72] Alexander Stewart was imprisoned even longer—eleven years elapsed from his capture as a thirteen-year-old to his final reunion with his family, the members of whom had trouble recognizing him (and he had a ten-year-old sister whom he had never met).[73] After spending three years in the Cameroons, Thomas Lewis finally returned to his home in Wales to visit his elderly father. He described the visit in detail, noting that he "enjoyed every moment of my stay in the old thatched cottage, and the chats with friends at night around the blazing fire in the smithy." As his friends quizzed him about his experiences, "my father was very quiet, but I am sure that he was the happiest of men. He pretended to work, so as to prolong the talks, and he listened to every word. It was delightful to watch him as he tried to disguise his pride in his missionary son."[74]

Working-class autobiographers often recounted strong bonds with adult siblings, who had served as their first friends and companions in childhood. Thomas Oliver, a Cornish miner who had moved to Australia, heard a knock at the door of his cabin and opened it to a man he didn't recognize. The man introduced himself as Oliver's brother, who had migrated to Australia sixteen years earlier. "As I gazed at him I could see his curly locks and high forehead. I said Sampson, my dear brother, and fell on his neck and kissed him until we both wept with joy."[75] Bricklayer James McCurrey had moved from Glasgow to London with his family, and his long-lost brother John "went to every new building he saw, inquiring for a young Scotchman . . . Judge of my joy when I saw my favourite brother, and heard the old familiar speech of my childhood."[76] After having been a footman for two years, Henry White returned home. "Oh! What pleasure I experienced as I saw in the old chimney corner . . . How it all seems to cling to the memory, and with what force does it come back to me, painting each thought with bright colours of the past."[77] White's autobiography explicitly states what many other autobiographies suggest: the return to a childhood home brought nostalgia.

After spending six years in the army before returning to his hometown, Allen Davenport found words insufficient to describing the emotions of his family reunion. "No language, no arrangement of words, can express the palpitating emotions of my heart, and the wild transports and trembling delirium that thrilled through every chord and fibre of my soul!"[78] The entire village turned out to greet him. Davenport noted that, but for the fact that the girl of his dreams was still in Scotland, he would at that moment have been the happiest man in the world. Jim Blake of Clonave, a painter's model in Ireland, was joyful upon coming to London for the first time to see the old friend who had first painted him in his hometown.[79] The evangelist Raymond Preston described S. F. Collier as "one of my closest and dearest friends. We loved each other as David and Jonathan did. I shall never forget our meeting in Brisbane, after many years of separation. Our joy was beyond all description."[80] "Beyond all description": not finding the words to describe the magnitude of their emotions, working-class autobiographers invoked the ineffable, the "emotional sublime."[81]

The prospect of losing a family member forever could lead to the greatest emotional wrench of all. George Parkinson described the aftermath of the explosion at the Houghton-le-Spring colliery on November 11, 1850. When he reached his own home after his own brush with death:

> My father and mother, hearing the noise, sprang out of bed; my mother ran to the door, and, seeing me running, stood speechless till I lifted my hand, and called out with a faltering voice, 'Mother! I am no worse.' . . . words for some moments were few. Suffice it to say there was a deep sense of thankfulness and a subdued feeling of joy in that house, mingled with sadness and sorrow for the fate of others.[82]

The entire community gathered at the coal pit, fearing the worst, when the surprising announcement came that due to a ventilation shift underground, many workers were still alive (in the end only twenty-six were killed). Relief made onlookers unusually emotionally effusive. "Men involuntarily grasped each other's hands in wild excitement as they thanked God for the joyful news. Mothers, wives and daughters, whose tears had been dried up in the bitterness of their sorrow, wept again in gladness and wrung each other's hands for joy."[83] As the rescued men and boys, or their recovered bodies, were brought to the pit bank, "some received their own in a silence they could not break, and others in an excitement of feeling they could not control." In a situation like this, he recounted, "strong men wept."[84]

Friends and Neighbors

The social ties of working-class autobiographers extended from their family members to a series of concentric networks of friends, occasional companions, neighbors, and acquaintances. As Carolyn Steedman has noted, the word "friends" carried ambiguity in this period; working people tended to use the term to refer to the network of family members and patrons who might be turned to in times of economic distress.[85] Particularly among working-class women, intimacy tended to be restricted to the family circle, due to fears that taking non–family members into one's confidence could only bring trouble.[86] But the idea of friendship was beginning to evolve. David Vincent has sketched out the importance of working-class friendships to intellectual advancement, since the formal education available to working people in the nineteenth century did not encourage critical thinking or the formation of new connections. For example, Vincent quotes the Chartist poet Thomas Cooper remembering the influence of his friend John Hough: "With him I discussed questions relating to mind, to religion, to history, and general literature; and these weekly conversations, as I returned to my reading and studies, gave me a new impulse to thought and inquiry, He also used to say 'You do me good. You freshen my mind weekly.' "[87]

Some working people remembered with great happiness close friendships with those outside the family, transcending the earlier definition of "friends" that encompassed mainly relatives.[88] As Barbara Caine and Mark Brodie have noted, this more expansive definition tended to be associated with working-class upward mobility, baked into institutions like the Mechanics' Institutes or the Friendly Societies.[89] One of the most intimate descriptions of friendship came in the autobiography of Frederick Herbert Spencer, who rose from a working-class home and a background as a pupil-teacher to become a certified teacher. His closest friendship, with an unnamed colleague, was forged at the Borough Road Teacher Training College, and he called the two years he spent there the happiest of his life: "We were happy together. We had much in common, intellectually and spiritually. And our interests and abilities were sufficiently diverse to induce a mutual appreciation." The two young men promised never to part, and in fact later both worked briefly in schools in Nottingham, and shared a bedroom in their lodging house. "We were sufficient for each other. No woman disturbed our friendship."[90] Robert Watchorn, a coal miner who immigrated to the United States, recounted the letters a friend from home wrote to him every week, which were "an unabatable joy and inspiration."[91]

Through all of the tenuous years in which Frank Bullen tried to make a living as a picture-frame and fancy-goods seller, his closest friend was a costermonger who had previously sold Bullen's family their fruits and vegetables. Bullen's friend Bob was invariably there to help him shift furniture or set up his shop, lend him money if necessary, and dine with him. "I know all about self-help and have been compelled to practice it all my life, but the joy of having a friend, how great and how pleasant it is!"[92] George Herbert, a Banbury shoemaker, had many "hobbyhorses" during his life, including electroplating, photography, and playing the trombone, but none of these pleased him as much as afternoons spent with his friend George Bolton and family:

> We used to have our tea set-out in the farm-yard with George's father and mother and his brother Bill, his two sisters and Mr. G. Gardner and Mr. Gunn, and I have many times thought of it, as I never met so much happiness all round as this party used to be, as everyone strove to make each other happy, and always so successful I have thought of these Sunday teas many a time and thought they were the most happy family I had ever seen."[93]

George Ratcliffe of Leeds, a candy-maker, recalled forming "a sort of Lodge" with some of his closest male friends. They met for an annual feast, with hot-pot, wine, and tobacco smoked from commemorative pipes. Over the years the table gained vacant places as the members of the informal fraternity died, but, as Ratcliffe mused, "the sweet memories of the happy times we spent together will not die out."[94]

Before the commodification of leisure through activities like the music hall, working people depended on each other for companionship and entertainment. Henry Snell, who grew up in a Nottingham village, was worked hard as a child, but had "the happiest memories" of the smith's workshop, which became a sort of information entrepôt. There, listeners learned about the latest news, prospects for crops, and got to enjoy the "brightest, warmest, and most attractive place in the village."[95] George Meek, as a young man, worked with the grandsons of an old carpenter who was full of stories, and spent many happy evenings listening: "I used to delight to hear the old gentleman's stories of old times and old people in Eastbourne: of the lady of the manor, Mrs. Gilbert, who, with a Major Willard, the magistrate of that day, ruled the town; of the time of the Chartist rising, when the farmers, shopkeepers and other well-to-do people stood or slept behind barred and bolted doors with guns loaded, expecting a raid by the peasantry."[96] Inclusion in a larger sense of community was particularly important for the marginalized. Richard Hampton, a mentally impaired laborer from Cornwall, was tormented by others due to his appearance and manner of speaking. When he finally found his calling as a lay preacher, his tormentors took pity on him, and his inclusion in the community at last filled him with joy. "My sawl was so happy! Everybody wud cum foath cimmin to shaw how kind they cud be . . . I wus happy, and full of love," Hampton's amanuensis recorded.[97]

The kinds of community activities that could bring delight to working-class people were very often free or inexpensive. Joseph Lipton wrote that his happiest moments in childhood were spent by the river, watching the ships enter Glasgow harbor, seeing the goods unloaded, and quizzing the sailors about where they had come in from. For Lipton, this activity was related to his own self-education; he purchased an inexpensive map and used it to trace the voyages of those he had met.[98] Henry Herbert, a Gloucestershire shoemaker, visited the Great Exhibition, which charged working people a penny for admission, and remembered "the wonders which I saw with joy."[99] But Herbert's greatest joy came when he and fellow temperance advocates formed a Band of Hope.[100] In contrast, one of Jack Jones's happiest memories was taking his wife and five children on a trip to the seaside, funded with his World War I military bonus; it was the only trip they had ever managed that was not to visit relatives. While Jones and his children thoroughly enjoyed the splurge, he described his wife—normally in charge of stretching the family income to cover the family consumption—as having been so uncomfortable at the thought of the expense of the day trip that she was unable to enjoy herself.[101]

Community Traditions

Family, friends, and communities were embedded in a structure of annual traditions that punctuated the daily routine. These included events like the Middleton Wakes, during which people competed to see who could bring the most rushes to cover the floor of the church; Guy Fawkes Day bonfires; and an annual pig-washing, which had the tendency to devolve into a fully clothed swim meet.[102] William Hutton remembered his eleven trips to the Nottingham races as the most delightful he ever took, "for although I knew nothing of the horses, the winners, or the company, nor was interested in the event, yet the body was at ease, the mind divested of care, everything was new, pleasant, and above all, I was accompanied by a sister who I loved."[103] John Harris and his family looked forward to their parish feast on November 11 "with great delight, making it the subject of conversation both morning and evening as we sat around the great chimney fire."[104] Robert Blatchford remembered the annual fair with particular vividness: "I delighted in the fair. It was life. And it lasted a whole week."[105] Henry Burstow, a Horsham shoemaker, remembered with pleasure festivals that united the community: the coming of age of a local squire's son, celebrated with a baron of beef and some personalized fireworks; May Day; July Fair; and the bonfires of November 5. Burstow emphasized that given the scarcity of organized amusements for the working classes, those that did occur were much more significant in people's lives.[106]

The farm laborer William Milne remembered one of the best moments of his young working life—a Harvest Home celebration offered for the plowmen and maidservants by the lord of Pearl Bank House. "The joys of that one night of unalloyed and innocent pleasure! Has remained a memorial with me as one of the nearest approaches I have ever made to a joy which I thought the nearest to those of paradise!" he wrote.[107] The men and women, dressed in their finest clothes, promenaded into the large house through a grove of trees, surrounded by late-summer beauty arm-in-arm:

> After a little we found our way up a broad stair; on reaching the head of which such a flood of light was shed from over a hundred richly-decorated wax candles. These lights, with the floral adorn-

ments of that charming place, fairly dazzled the eye, and whatever the others thought of it, I remember I thought it like a scene from the Arabian Nights Entertainments, those grand tales of Oriental splendor!"[108]

There was music, and dancing, and at the end of the evening, their patrons surprised the servant girls by passing out a series of sealed envelopes, each of which entitled the bearer to a gift of some article of dress. Similarly, a workingman from Norfolk remembered being sent to pay his master's tithe for the year, a job that earned him the most lavish dinner that he had ever experienced, complete with roast beef, plum pudding, music, dancing, and drinking to excess (and as Vic Gammon has pointed out, drinking entailed an entire culture of treating, toasting, and song).[109] The man noted that "I never went to but one tithe feast, and it was such a treat that I remember it just as if it was yesterday."[110]

Norfolk rural laborer George Baldry—whose father had destroyed his boat—rarely mentioned happiness or pleasure in his narrative. His family was so desperately poor that many of his early experiences involved working: working for a farmer in exchange for a turnip, using a ferret to try to catch rabbits, and building traps to catch eels. Unlike the autodidact members of the working class, Baldry was no scholar; school was held over his head and those of his siblings as a punishment if they failed to behave, and his left-handedness often earned him a beating from the teacher.[111] But even Baldry recounted a series of amusing anecdotes that illustrate warm memories of community activities: attending the local fair, participating in a horse race against gypsies, and serving as a lookout when his father and his father's friends went poaching.[112]

Some autobiographers remembered momentous one-off celebrations of historic events. Thomas Carter fondly recalled the bonfires and bells marking the 1802 cessation of hostilities against the French.[113] Christopher Thomson attended the parade to celebrate fifty years of George III's reign: "the procession, the banners, and military array—the bonfires, sheep-roastings, and drunken men . . . The illumination was to me the most magical."[114] The shoemaker Robert Askham, seven years old at the time of the passage of the 1832 Reform Bill, remembered the happiness and general celebration on July 6 of that year.[115] The Chartist and printer William Adams remembered delighting in the ceremony that delineated the bounds of the parish, and the illumination of all of the houses in his town for the coronation of Queen Victoria: "The effect of the burning candles, so regularly disposed, so uniformly bright, and so many thousands in number, was almost entrancing. I had never seen anything so beautiful before, and I am not sure that I have ever seen anything in the way of illuminations so really effective since." Thomas Oliver, later a Cornish miner, was greatly delighted by the coronation celebrations in Penzance: "Market Jew Street was spanned with arches rigged up with branches of trees and decorated with flowers, processions headed by bands of music were perambulating the town. The cannons were booming and there was a fine time of it."[116] In Clandown, Moses Horler and other masons paraded through the streets with their mortarboards, and then all sat down to cold roast beef and plum pudding and beer.[117]

As the nineteenth century wore on, economic development created the possibility for more commercialized forms of communal enjoyment. Many working-class autobiographers recounted being delighted by touring theatrical performances, or even taking part. Benjamin Brierley, a young velvet weaver, formed a Mutual Improvement Society with other young men from his town, and traveled to Manchester to see a theatrical performance: "the way in which the play went was a treat to be remembered for a lifetime."[118] When they returned to their village, the young men started a theatrical society.[119] Billy Purvis (Joseph Robson), born in Newcastle in 1784, was apprenticed to a carpenter but after seeing an exhibition of gymnastics, took up slack-rope walking and eventually clowning, which he enjoyed more than anything else. "I lived like a fighting cock and was happy as a king."[120] Jack Jones's love of theater began when a circus set up a tent near his family home in Wales. Already a coal miner, he took up an evening shift selling candy and oranges at the local theater. His interest in performance continued with his writing plays and appearing in performances as an adult.[121]

Finally, we know how important community ties were to working people because they mentioned their absence. William Hutton, who had apprenticed to a stocking weaver but was unable to find work in that field, started his own bookbindery in Birmingham. "Having little to do but look into the street, it seemed singular to see thousands of faces pass, and not one of them that I knew. I had entered a new world, in which I led a melancholy life; a life of silence and tears. Though a young man, and rather of a cheerful turn, it was remarked 'that I was never seen to smile.' "[122] Joseph Millott Severn, working in London as a carpenter, often walked the streets of London observing human nature but "felt what a joy it would be, and how one could hardly contain the rapture of delight, if one could only meet just one individual whom one knew."[123] For working people, life was with people.

Happiness and Prosocial Behavior

To be good is to be happy: angels
Are happier than men because they're better.
—Nicholas Rowe, *The Fair Penitent*[124]

Connections with people also include connections forged through charitable activities. Modern happiness studies scholars have noted a link between happiness and prosocial behavior, a category that includes charitable giving and volunteering. Those who have written about the correlation explain that giving one's time or money produces happiness more than once, since recalling prosocial behavior promotes happiness. Life satisfaction particularly increases when people give for altruistic rather than self-serving reasons.[125] Some scholars hypothesize that this kind of altruism is hard-wired in humans because it was evolutionarily adaptive.[126] Was there a link between subjective well-being and prosocial behavior in the nineteenth century? Working-class autobiographies indicate that prosocial behavior and happiness were linked, both for those who depended on help from others and for those who had good experiences helping others.[127]

Many working-class autobiographers relied on, and recognized in their autobiographies, the centrality of other people's generosity to their survival.[128] Benjamin Brierley described life in Lancashire before the development of matches. Those whose fires had gone out went from one house to another with a candle, in the hopes of lighting their fire from someone else's fire. "Often have I been invited to shelter under a girl's cloak, and take a bite of her butter-cake, when either could be ill spared," he commented.[129] James Dawson Burn had a difficult childhood, presided over by a drunken stepfather who often beat him and who was intermittently jailed for various infractions. Burn fondly remembered other children's parents, who treated him with respect and kindness and gave him food.[130] When Burn finally ran away from home, his foot festering with a wound he had incurred while working outside without shoes, he reached a house on the border of Scotland and England. There, an elderly woman finally dressed the wound on his foot and allowed Burn to sleep in bed with her husband. "I lay with the old man, and slept as soundly, and rose as happy, as if I had been a lord's son. What a truly happy provision in nature it is that our capacity for the enjoyments of life are to a great extent regulated by our condition. With a little kindness, a belly-full of food, and a good night's rest, my mind was as much at ease as if I had no earthly want to provide for."[131] On another occasion, Burn attempted to walk from London to Hexham in Yorkshire without either food or money; a man's gift of a half-crown filled him with hope.[132] William Cameron, who passed through a number of occupations before becoming an itinerant tinker and beggar, called Yorkshire "the most charitable county in the three kingdoms, if not in the world."[133]

John Struthers, who as a young man worked at a farm where he was ill fed and ill used, remembered the happiness that he experienced when he was sent to a nearby farm to fetch milk. The neighboring farmer had "a large and a fine family of sons and daughters, all intelligent, cheerful, and good humoured, and the daughters all too beautiful." Milk night was, "by the young folks there, devoted to mirth-making, song singing, tale telling, etc."[134] At one point in his life the weaver Joseph Gutteridge and his young wife were destitute, with neither food nor furniture and with young children to care for. When the elderly woman who minded the children learned of the family's straits, she surprised them with a bed and bedclothes, and food and fuel. "The old nurse's large-heartedness was all the more notable when it is remembered that she herself was very poor and needed help," he mused.[135] James Dunn, who worked as a city missionary in the poorest parts of London, noted that the poorest were the most willing to share their little food with those who had none.[136]

James Nye, an agricultural laborer and the father of twelve children, described being the recipient of charity on many occasions. When his entire family was "felled with scarlet fever," ladies sent the family food, and the doctor attended his family "as if I was a gentleman." The doctor forbore to collect on his debt even though Nye eventually owed him more than four pounds. At other times friends and even strangers provided cash, wine for ill family members, outfits to replace his ragged clothing, and the resources to pay for baby linen for his ninth child.[137] Because each of these windfalls followed a session of prayer, Nye considered them to be God working through individuals, rather than actions undertaken through their own free will.

Workers depended on each other. Albert Pugh, a railroad worker, noted that "it is a recognized practice among men on public works to take a pal, when on tramp looking for work, to his home or lodgings, feed and sleep him, although it nearly always means three in a bed, and send him away the next day richer in pocket."[138] Henry Broadhurst, tramping around the countryside looking for stonework jobs, was supported at times by his friends in the militia, who allowed him to share their mess; and at others by a charitable landlady at an inn, who invited him to share her meals. "The old saying, 'The best friends of the poor are the poor,' was exemplified in my experience," he noted.[139] An anonymous Derbyshire apprentice spinner had finished his apprenticeship but could find no job and no food, until he met a young man in Stockport who brought him home to his mother. "She took me in and gave me something to eat, found me a good bed, and was very kind to me. She went with me the next day seeking work . . . She was a mother to me. Whenever I go to Stockport, I always go to see her and sometimes she comes to see me."[140] The anonymous navvy chronicled in *The Autobiography of a Working Man* noted that, unlike their employers, the navvies took up collections to provide decent funerals for workers who died on the job.[141]

John Hunter Kelso, in his memoirs, recounted suffering a setback in his early artistic career. The disappointment "always made me strong in muscle by producing a sort of savage feeling at everybody and everything." But before he could follow through on his rage by attacking some pedestrians he met on the road and stealing their food, they offered to share it with him. One of them lent him a winter coat to wear during his walk, and when he reached the man's house, shared food and offered a bed for the night. "The time I was in the company of that young man and his father was little longer than I have taken to write a report of it. Yet it has left an impression on my mind that pure Christianity was practiced by them. It was so accepted on my part that it can never be obliterated while life lasts. It left sunshine where it found sadness."[142] James Dunn, whose family only survived an illness because other working people extended their charity, noted that "a remarkable trait was common among the very poorest, and that was the willing way they would share their scanty meat with those who had none."[143] Joseph Terry, who lived with his mother in a destitute community in the North of England, recalled a kind of communal living, in which the residents of the poorly equipped houses shared all kinds of items from brushes to barrels to beds, sleeping in each other's houses when their own had too many people to accommodate. Terry's mother, whose mental illness caused her to wander, was often absent from home, and the mother of the most desperate family in the poor neighborhood, Mary Walker, would come over and take care of Terry and talk to him.[144] "I have often looked in vain, in the higher walks of life, which I have since trod, for the same self-denial and voluntary sacrifice for the good of others, and the same willingness to share the blessings of life with those who are in want," he noted, suggesting that such charity was harder to find among the rich than among the poor.[145] Jane Andrew, an invalid, lived on a farm with her brother, but the two lost all their capital when their cow died. Their friends, hearing of the disaster, collected twenty-five pounds to buy another cow.[146]

Many of these stories show that the poor largely helped the poor. Modern social psychologists who study Britain have noted that people with lower incomes donate proportionately more of their incomes to charity than do wealthier people, and that, additionally, they tend to prefer charities that directly help the poor (rather than, say, the environment or the arts). They propose that some people with lower incomes have a sense of fellow feeling rooted in a commitment to their struggling class or neighborhood and that others recognize their own plight in people with similar struggles. Scholars who study prosocial behavior note that giving can make people feel a warm glow or a "helper's high."[147] Working-class autobiographers who documented their own prosocial behavior seem to have been motivated by the same constellation of motivations as modern givers.

Robert Dottie, later in life a writer of dialect humor, worked as a butcher's boy for his grandfather. Meat left unsold on Saturdays would be wheeled around on Mondays, and as Dottie was told not to bring any back to the shop, he often gave away pieces "to somebody too poor to buy, even hiding it from the view of a possible customer—so that some needy expectant might not have to turn away from the friendly barrow empty-handed and disappointed."[148] J. H. Powell described finding a gold piece among the tips collected after a hypnosis demonstration, assuming it had been paid in error, and seeing it returned to the owner. "The woman expressed many thanks . . . and went away, I doubt not, with a lighter heart than she came. And I left double recompensed in the pleasure the sight of the poor woman's happiness afforded me."[149] John Buckley, who was abused as a child, remembered being pitied by his elderly neighbor, who gave him food, bathed his injured feet, and bandaged them. "I sat on a little bench in the chimney-corner and cried with gratitude for her kindness, which is as fresh in my memory today as if it had happened yesterday. Forty years after I returned her kindness by helping her to a small annuity, which she enjoyed many years."[150]

The bookbinder Frederick Rogers paid back a debt by reading to the elderly doctor who had cured his spinal issues. "He was glad for me to read to him, and to me it was a joy unspeakable to serve my venerable friend."[151] The strolling player Joseph Philip Robson, writing as "Billy Purvis," described putting on a benefit show in Sunderland in 1835 in the immediate wake of a shipping disaster. Having raised five pounds for the widows and orphans of that disaster, he "felt happy to know that I had done my duty" even though he was subsequently chased out of town by the local magistrate. On another occasion, he attended a furniture auction, bought the goods of a widow who had had them distrained for debt, and presented them back to her. "As I puttered my way towards my lodgings I felt a satisfaction in my breast which amply repair me for the trifling sum I had expended."[152]

Those who had achieved worldly success described taking pleasure in giving back to their communities. Thomas Okey, a London basketmaker, used his spare time to learn languages and attend public lectures, and culturally enriched himself by sneaking away from work to visit the museums and look at Italian art. Over time he established himself as an expert in Italian culture and wrote several books, on the strength of which he was ultimately appointed professor of Italian at Cambridge University:

> The search for happiness? If the quality of happiness may be applied to any aspect of human life on the planet, the happiest period of my life—and by happiness I mean the satisfaction of heart and mine and peace of soul—has been when in spare time I was absorbed in teaching, lecturing, organizing or other educational or social work in East London without any thought of material or personal advancement or gain.[153]

Disturbed by the poverty he observed in Ireland at the turn of the nineteenth century and the failure of the British government to respond appropriately, the poet Robert Anderson divided his income with the local poor and organized charity fundraisers.[154] The policeman Robert Bent, moved by scenes of grinding poverty that he had witnessed among Manchester children, used his own money to start a police-run soup kitchen that eventually served over a thousand children each day with soup and bread, supplied some of them with clothing and shoes stamped with the word "police" to discourage their resale, and organized an outing for the children once a year.[155]

Some autobiographers found joy in the nexus between their prosocial behavior and fulfillment of religious expectations. As Callum Brown has noted, most British people in the nineteenth century, influenced by the ubiquity of evangelicalism, had a Christian worldview, and visiting was "essential to the personal development of the converted Christian."[156] Robert Butler's religiously motivated good deeds included accompanying various brothers-in-arms as they lay on their deathbeds (mostly dying of intestinal complaints) while serving in India. Of his friend Alexander Chevis, Butler remarked, "Whenever my duty would permit, I was consequently in the hospital, reading and conversing with him; and on the two Sabbaths that he lived after this, I remained with him nearly the whole day; but my attendance on him was richly rewarded, for I learned more from this dying saint of what is really worth learning, than I had done all my life before."[157] Butler and his wife also adopted two orphaned children from the regiment, and when he was invalided out of the service in 1814, brought them back to Scotland and saw that each child was housed with its grandparents.[158] Robert Blatchford recounted having won the undying love of the wife of the sergeant of his regiment by arranging a funeral for the woman's stillborn child.[159]

William Thomas Swan, born in 1786, first reported feeling joy in his life one evening as a teenager when returning from Chapel. His strong religious beliefs motivated him to leave home before he could support himself financially.[160] After joining the Baptist church, Swan found happiness ministering to the sick. "O the felicity to be found in this service! I believe it to be a most important part of religion, to visit the fatherless and widows, the sick and distressed. And the more self-denial, the more enjoyment in helping."[161] Raymond Preston, an uneducated factory lad who later became a Methodist preacher, roamed Cardiff looking for a girl who had run away from her parents. When he finally found her and successfully implored her to go home, he noted the "joy of restoring her to her parents," a moment that deepened the girl's own religious belief.[162]

Although she barely supported herself by making dresses, Sarah Martin spent her spare moments visiting and ministering to women in prison and women and children in workhouses.[163] She appointed herself a sort of amateur social worker, providing former inmates with clothing, work, and encouragement, and even contacting faraway parents to convince them to take back in their formerly imprisoned children. She described the work as making her feel "in the happy presence of God, as an insect basking in the sunbeams, in the light of peace, hope, and joy."[164] George Lewin, a chimney sweep who had a religious conversion in adulthood, said something similar: "I have often said that if persons who call themselves the followers of Jesus were to do a little more sick-visiting they would become better Christians. I have had some of my happiest times in the sickroom, singing, reading and praying with the lonely ones."[165]

But autobiographers could also be motivated to prosocial behavior by pity and empathy. The soldier George Calladine, posted to Ireland in the 1820s, had orders to destroy illegal liquor-manufacturing operations, but his sense of duty conflicted with feelings of pity: "I have often been afflicted with feelings of compassion for the poor wretches when their rent depended on what was at once doomed to destruction to see the pot-ale flowing in streams down the filthy yard and their poor, half-naked children striving to dam it up till we might leave the place, with the hopes of being able to save a part of it."[166] John Clare, who was the object of charity at many points during his career, noted that "objects of compassion" moved him so strongly that one of the only times he wished he were wealthier is when he had an opportunity "for the pleasure of relieving their wants." Upon giving his only fourpence to a "poor African" begging outside St. Paul's in London, Clare was so moved by the man's gratitude over such a small amount that he made sure to fill his pocket and give more the next day. Unfortunately, when he tried to track the man down the next day, he had disappeared.[167]

Others gestured toward a duty to mankind in general. An anonymous dissenting minister who wrote an autobiography opined that "the recognition of social claims is characteristic of every benevolent mind. To live for the good of others is a noble consecration. If men generally would do this, how amazingly would the sum of human happiness be increased!"[168] James Burn, who would not have survived his years as a wandering beggar were it not for the charity of others, thought that everyone should experience the joy of helping others, because empathy makes us human. "However unbounded our knowledge, the magnitude of our thoughts, or the profundity of our genius, if we have not the electricity of love in our hearts, sufficient to make us feel for the sufferings of others, the chief end of our creation is unfulfilled."[169]

Before Andrew Carnegie made his millions, he worked in the telegraph office of a railroad during the Civil War, helping parents seeking to bring home their dead soldier's remains or arrange a visit to a sick one. "I am indebted to these trifles for some of the happiest attentions and most pleasing incidents of my life. And there is this about such actions; they are disinterested, and the reward is sweet in proportion to the humbleness of the individual whom you have obliged."[170] The positive feedback encouraged him to become a philanthropist: "He is the happy man who feels there is not a human being to whom he does not wish happiness, long life, and deserved success, nor one in whose path he would cast an obstacle nor to whom he would not do a service if in his power."[171] George Edwards, who worked to provide war pensions for widows and children impacted by the Great War, found through this work "the greatest satisfaction. It was a humane work and a labour of love. It is the greatest joy of my life to know I have been able to do something for these poor widows and children."[172]

· · · · · · ·

As this chapter has shown, nineteenth-century working-class autobiographers described many ways in which marriage, children, family, friends, and community ties were central to the experience of happiness. Particularly for working-class men, marriage was emotionally rewarding as well as being pragmatically essential. Autobiographers strove to describe their closest relationships in ways that emphasized respectability, including the self-abnegation of women in service of the family.

Social ties encompassed everything from intimate relationships through extended kin networks that could bind people together even through long periods of separation for work or due to migration. Workers forged friendships around common interests (and, as shown in chapter 3, at the workplace). In a period before the widespread commodification of leisure, participation in annual fairs and festivals, and community observance of major events in the life of the nation, created lifelong memories that made their way onto paper decades later.

The centrality of social ties meant that many working people considered themselves enmeshed in wider networks of mutual assistance. Many depended for their own happiness on the charitable inclinations of others, and were not embarrassed about receiving help from others like them. And finally, many working people found helping others—even strangers—produced pleasure, through the empathy, the "recognition of social claims," the thanks of others, and the pride that they took in living up to religious doctrines.

FIVE

The Natural World

BY THE NINETEENTH CENTURY there were few untouched landscapes in Britain. The late eighteenth century had seen an explosion in timber clear-cutting, coal mining, and turnpike building, as areas of the country that had been primarily agricultural and far from markets were monetized and brought into a larger commercial system. New canal construction even cut through the Pennines, leveling some of the hills rather than trying to accommodate the landscape. As Matthew Osborn notes, some contemporaries depicted the commodification of the landscape as a progressive and positive development; as a Suffolk doctor noted in the 1790s, "The Scarcity of Timber ought never to be regretted, for it is a certain proof of National Improvement, and for Royal Navies, Countries yet barbarous are the right and proper nurseries." But the commodification of the landscape also produced visible externalities, like the enclosure and privatization of common lands formerly available for pasturing animals, and moorlands previously used for recreation.[1] At the same time that these changes were occurring, autobiographers forged their own identities dialectically with the character of the nearby countryside: its plants, animals, and geologic formations. The natural world thus served the dual function of constituting the self, and then, when accessed in memory, nostalgically revisiting the self.[2]

Autobiographers understood the magnitude of the change that was taking place. John Finney noted in his autobiography that "all is now covered with houses. Then down by the old toll-gate and where the delightful grove used to be, not a tree was to be seen."³ James Ashley remembered that in 1862 Bermondsey, "in back of the house there was a large field of mangel-wurzel and the larks honoured us with their company and song. There was for a long distance country used for market gardens but now covered by thousands of houses."⁴ William Henry Lax remembered the glories of the Borsdane Wood and the stream that ran through it: "Even now my heart leaps at the memory." In contrast, he remembered that even as a boy, the sight of the local mine and mill intruding mechanistically on the landscape filled him with pain.⁵

One of the most surprising elements to emerge from my reading of working-class autobiographies is the degree to which workers' happiness flowed from their appreciation for and interaction with the natural world. Working people in the nineteenth century, especially those with access to areas outside urban centers, expressed their own sense of environmentalism. Although for some working people the countryside was the site of physically painful outdoor labor, many autobiographers regarded the countryside as an important resource aesthetically, for recreation, solitude, novelty, and for the provision of nonmarket goods.⁶

The conflict between technological change and nature—the machine in the garden—was part of the cultural zeitgeist, reflected in the Romantic poets' paeans to the natural world.⁷ Alexander Murison, born to a working wright in the North of Scotland, remembered the natural beauty of his childhood surroundings in language that these poets would have recognized: "Out of school, it was a charming world; brown under the plough and the barrow, yellow with waving corn, green with the lush grass, white under the sheet of show, sunshine, rain, snow—singing of birds, lowing of cattle, wimplings of the burns, rushing and howling of wind—all alike enjoyable in turn." He particularly remembered in 1858 "on turning a corner of a wood we came right in face of the Great Comet, blazing magnificently in a clear sky—a most impressive spectacle."⁸

Working people who were sufficiently literate to write autobiographies understood dominant genre conventions, so to some extent, one might expect them to laud the beauty or majesty of nature, or lament the way in which the natural world was changing.⁹ But overall, working people's autobiographies tend to recount their personal, hands-on experiences with nature—a kind of bodily knowledge—rather than an appreciation for nature's aesthetic beauties in the abstract. Stefania Barca, who studies transnational working-class environmentalism, has suggested that historians should think more about the interaction of workers' bodies with the environment, and to a large extent nineteenth-century workers' testimonies about interactions with the environment lend themselves to that perspective.[10]

For workers trapped inside mines or mills or workshops all day, nature represented bodily freedom and autonomy.[11] Frederick Rogers was lucky enough to secure a four-day vacation from his job binding vellum documents in London, and decided to walk to Oxford. He described walking through meadows, being entranced by a stream, jumping into the water naked, and air-drying himself on the grass. "I had reached the pinnacle of human joy as I knew it then—as a young man knows it when Nature has a voice of friendship and a hand-grip for him; it is a joy that passes as the years pass, but while it was with me my cup of happiness was full, pressed down, and running over."[12] He and his friends from the workshop enjoyed Hyde Park, despite the presence there of people from higher social classes. "To spend an afternoon strolling idly among the flower-beds, talking and laughing, speculating about the world of which we knew little, and occasionally finishing the day with a dip in the serpentine, was a delight as great to us as any pleasure the people in the chariots knew."[13]

Rogers credited his mother for having nurtured his love of nature. When she stood at her East London front window ironing, she looked at the trees outside. "She called them her trees and talked to them, and of them, and pointed out their natural beauty to me summer after summer, and built up in my character a sense of beauty in life which remains still." As a sickly boy in childhood, Rogers "found a summer joy in lying on the grass and staring dreamily into the sky; there came to me often a sense of the limitless greatness of the world in which I lived."[14] Like Rogers's mother, young Mary Ann Hearn was distracted from her household chores by the view from her window. "Often I have stood with tears in my eyes, and my heart throbbing with love and gladness, and tried to say something to God to let Him know what I was feeling . . . I was never allowed to stay long enough to satisfy me, for the cheery voice of my mother would call me into the house to amuse my brothers and sisters, or do some work."[15]

Walks in the countryside offered beauty, a change of scenery and access to resources.[16] As the shoemaker and poet John Askham recalled, being born in a town and consigned to work in a town in a sedentary occupation from the age of ten onward made nature seem like a wonder-filled contrast to the everyday.[17] Similarly, John Urie recalled his desire "to tramp over the moors, and through the glens and straths, to the burns and locks of our native Highlands, leaving all the cares of business behind, and developing a healthy appetite and that weariness that produces sound, refreshing sleep."[18] James Mullin, an Irish cartmaker who eventually became a doctor, spent his one day off per week driving or walking through the countryside around his Cardiff home, describing these trips as "a source of infinite pleasure." During the summer, when he could take a month off, he relocated to some other part of the British Isles and spent every day strolling, staying at farmhouses or cottages instead of hotels. "I would observe every object worth observing, and stop at every bit of beautiful scenery until I had satiated myself with its charms, and then I would pass on and retaste the pleasure in the discovery of some newer attraction."[19] Hamlet Nicholson, who considered himself a "good walker" until he was into his eighties, remembered with pleasure a multiday trek with his father from Rochdale to Sunderland and back. "As we walked along the roads in the early morning, the blue smoke from the turf fires rising, and the air impregnated with its pleasant odour, the birds singing, and the sun shining brightly, everything was most delightful; and even at this late hour of my life, my mind takes pleasure in recurring to that happy time of my boyhood."[20]

The natural world could provide opportunities for families to escape the pollution and overcrowding of urban areas. John Pearman, a police inspector, had little discretionary income, since he and his wife had eight living children, but "I used to save some money every year so as to give them a days outing sometimes 2 day and go to Sandhurst and this gave me more pleasure than anything." He remembered giving his children picnics of cake and wine along the way and "it lives in my mind's eye and I can even enjoy the sight now when I think of it and picture their happy young faces."[21] The phrenologist Joseph Millott Severn's family delighted in walks in the Sussex countryside. He noted of his wife that "scarcely anything afforded her more pleasure than a walk in the country, and gathering wild flowers." The Severns used their excursions to gather herbs to make herb beer, and to bring home buckets of blackberries, wild strawberries, hazelnuts, and armfuls of primroses, daffodils, violets, and bluebells.[22] James Campkin spent hours of his childhood wandering in the woods and fields and learning the names of wildflowers. "In this retreat were spent some of the happiest years of my life. I knew no cares but such childish whims as crossed the path of every wayward child." [23]

Streams and lakes afforded opportunities to watch living creatures, hear rushing water, and expand a monotonous diet. Hugh Miller delighted in exploring the shores and woods of his native Cromarty. For Miller, long walks in the woods hearing birds sing and watching fish inspired him to write his own poetry, and produced "a happiness ample enough to compensate for many a long hour of toil, and many a privation."[24] Later, when he took an interest in collecting aquatic specimens, he and his wife would take a skiff out and fish and eat. "I do retain recollections of these evenings spent in my little skiff . . . that not merely represent enjoyments that have been, but that, in certain moods of the mind, take the form of enjoyment still."[25] Standing in a stream fishing, Thomas Todd experienced the transcendent experience of being "part of the wonderful order of things . . . The glow of perfect health tingled in my blood; the murmur of the stream dwelt as music in my ears. I was radiantly happy."[26] The anonymous journeyman baker who wrote a prize autobiographical essay worked at a flax mill at eight years of age, spending twelve hours a day indoors, but "notwithstanding the confinement, I enjoyed many happy summer evenings on the banks of the beautiful Leven. Many trouts I caught and carried home to mother. I also became an expert swimmer, an exercise which has afforded me great pleasure."[27]

As Katrina Navickas has shown, proponents of the open space movement, even those motivated by religious belief, found it difficult to stifle their class prejudices about the way working people sometimes rowdily used open spaces.[28] It is also true that Victorian reformers like Octavia Hill, and organizations like the Commons Preservation Society, celebrated activities like rambling and gardening as forms of social control, meant to inculcate virtues of thrift and self-help, provide salutary alternatives to the pub, and prevent workers from gathering in groups and discussing issues that might radicalize them. Middle-class readers of periodicals about gardening were treated to stories about window boxes bringing nature indoors even to the dirtiest of slums, drawing slum-dwellers' attention to their own surroundings through the extension of care for plants. Social reformers celebrated the way allotments kept workers busy, kept them from being a public charge for the taxpayers, and even raised the aesthetic value of their cottages if they were well cultivated.[29] But even with all of this cultural weight pressing down, preference for the outdoors was not exclusively an imposition on working people. Rather, it harmonized with what many found pleasant.[30]

Working people who lived where plots of land were available gravitated toward allotments—a tendency accelerated by the Chartist Land Company's promotion of landownership as the key to independence. John Finney, a potter, looked for a plot of land as soon as he was married, and began gardening with his friends on his allotments at night and on Sunday mornings, sometimes "with a wee drap of lotion."[31] As Margaret Willes described in her excellent *Gardens of the British Working Class*, poorer people had been gardening for centuries, growing food, herbs, and medicinal plants for their employers and for their own families. In the nineteenth century, working people living in urban or semi-urban areas tilled allotments, small back gardens, rooftop gardens, and window boxes, growing not only useful plants but also decorative flowers. For those who worked indoors or underground, work on an allotment, although physically difficult, might be a pleasant respite, and their popularity was evident in cities like Nottingham, which reportedly had five thousand gardens in the 1840s.[32] By the 1860s, urban gardening had been valorized as emblematic of energy and respectability; working-class gardeners were said to understand the benefit of sunlight and fresh air, and to have the time and inclination to avoid the pub in favor of the metaphorical greenhouse.[33]

Working people with allotments most commonly grew potatoes, wheat, legumes, and vegetables, and some also raised pigs or ducks. Some built their own gazebos or "summerhouses," shady nooks where they could take a break from work to have a drink, or even camp out on the weekends.[34] George Edwards described going out each morning early to cultivate his vegetable garden, which was planned so that there was always something to harvest. He was fond of marrows, which so proliferated that his wife made them into pies.[35] Elizabeth Layton's greatest joy after the passing of her husband, who had worked for the railway, was to work on her allotment.[36]

By the second half of the nineteenth century, there were floral competitions especially for working-class people, who might bring their plants to be judged inside broken crockery rather than beautiful baskets. The author of a book on window gardening recounted the story of an urban child who had created a window box for plants out of an old soap container, filled it with street ash, decaying leaves, and sand, decorated it with old rags, and managed to cultivate a variety of plants.[37] William Farish, later a handloom weaver, cultivated flowers in a box garden and raised birds.[38] George Ratcliffe, who rose from a working-class home to become a major candy trader and politician in Leeds, made a point of eating with flowers on his dining table and wearing a flower in his buttonhole for his entire life, since flowers gave him so much pleasure. He saved some lilies that he had dried, and garnered simple pleasure from looking at them. Late in life, when he had amassed enough wealth to buy a few acres of land, he grew bluebells and hawthorn and acacias and laburnums. "No one could be happier than my wife and I are amidst these surroundings."[39] Betty Dodds (aka Martha Grimes), a charwoman, dated her love of flowers back to a period in her childhood when she lived near Hadley Woods. Her uncle kept bees, which she sat on a milking stool watching. "Oh, I was so 'appy them dear old days. I used to sing 'cause I was so full o' rejoice. Never knowed afore I 'ad a voice, fur me and singin' was strangers at our 'ome."[40] And even Edwin Waugh, whose mental world was riven by the conflict between respectability and his own behavior, found a "kind of peace of mind" in flowers he saw on his rambles.[41]

Working-class autobiographers recounted having treasured the natural world as children because nature provided not only endless entertainment but also the possibility of foraging for free food. "The fat-of-the-land was to be obtained for the snaring; the fish of the river and becks, for the guddling or putting down of night-lines," Thomas Todd remembered of his teenage years.[42] Edward Rymer, who began working in a coal mine at an early age, remembered that as a child "every wood, dene, pond and whin-cover was known to us in our search for blackberries, mushrooms, 'cat haws,' crab-apples, nuts, and not a bird's nest in wall, hedge, or tree for miles round Houghton could escape our vigilance."[43] Joseph Terry, who grew up on his father's keelboat, remembered being taken into the countryside by his uncle and plied with wild cherries and apples.[44] John Fraser, later a career soldier, remembered with pleasure childhood weekends spent in the Norham countryside, where he "learned the names of birds and flowers, and trees, lay in the grass and leaning over bridges puzzling ourselves as to whether the shadows were caused by trout or by something less intriguing, sought birds' nests, and lay dreaming on banks, eating a dozen things—sorrel and young hawthorn leaves, peeled bramble shoots, wild strawberries, blueberries, and the nuts of hazel and beech."[45]

A childhood preference for the outdoors is logical, since working-class homes were crowded, busy workspaces and the woods and fields were freer from adult supervision. Thomas Martin Wheeler, later a Chartist leader, fondly remembered his boyhood raiding birds' nests, hunting otters, fishing for snigs and flooks (eels and flatfish), and helping salmon fishermen to haul in their nets. His fascination with nature and love for the natural world continued into adulthood, when he took up one of the allotments allocated by the Chartist Co-Operative Land Company and submitted paeans to the beauty of that community to the press.[46] J. H. Powell walked along the train tracks into the woods to gather nuts and birds' nests, "loving the pastime the more, because I knew it to be wrong."[47] William Heaton spent his leisure time hiking, in order to collect shells, eggs, nests, and insects that became the kernel of a natural history collection that he then traded with others.[48] Henry Broadhurst, son of a stonemason and later an MP, collected hedgehog quills and sold them for extra money.[49] Deborah Smith, one of fifteen children, noted that she and her siblings had no playthings to speak of, but that nonetheless, "I was a happy child, rambling in the fields, gathering the flowers, making chains with the daisies, playing by the brooks. We enjoyed ourselves with the things Nature provided."[50] Another resourceful working-class child, James Edwin Saunders constructed a model building out of "kexes," or old, dried cow-parsley that could be lashed together.[51]

Thomas Jones of Rhymney recalled being indifferent to the beauty of the countryside as a boy, but nature contained the cost-free resources that he needed to enjoy himself: "I could find whinberries and lie on my back on the green turf listening to the larks, or sit on the banks of a mountain stream weaving bullrushes into whips or into love knots, or whittling away an ash twig . . . These were Saturday afternoons and they filled the heart with happiness."[52] Thomas Cooper recalled that some of his happiest moments had been spent rambling through the forests and identifying and picking flowers.[53] Samuel Bamford fondly recounted outdoor pastimes that included digging in the dirt, wading, seeking birds and moss.[54] On another occasion, he and his father walked to their old home in Middleton. When they stopped for a rest:

> Here I luxuriated amongst the butter-cups and daisies, and the glint of a little peeping primrose or two cast a whole stream of sunny thoughts and pleasant feelings into that happy moment. The trees seemed to wave a broader and richer foliage; the air was balmy and refreshing; the sun itself was more life-fraught, than when I felt it shining against the high walls and the flagged yards of the workhouse.[55]

One of the biggest promoters of the countryside, the poet John Clare, was enraptured by everything having to do with nature from childhood on, "with the same raptures as I have done since but I knew nothing of poetry."[56] Charles Shaw, consigned to work in the potteries from the age of seven, treasured the occasional days when the man who paid his wages decided to give him an unpaid day off. He went down to the nearby Trent River and caught "Jack Sharps [sticklebacks] in the tiny stream, and gathered buttercups, daisies, and ladyflowers along its banks." Like other poor children, he also visited the Little Wood for birds' nests and blackberries. "Blackberries then meant not only a luxury, but meant also less butter and less treacle to be used in the poor homes of the people in the town." To gather the berries, the children would have to evade gamekeepers and dogs, but the happiness of success was worth the risk.[57] The shoemaker Hamlet Nicholson, who later invented the compound cricket ball, remembered the happy hours he spent playing in the fields near Rochdale, "gathering daisies, buttercups, and primroses."[58] As a boy George Herbert, who grew up to be a Banbury shoemaker, put himself in harm's way to rob birds' nests, not just for the entertainment value of the activity but because the churchwarden paid a bounty for the head of each sparrow brought to him.[59]

Nor was the enjoyment of the natural world limited to boys, although they do seem to have had more latitude to roam. Elizabeth Layton's love of nature was a leitmotif through her entire life. She grew up in Bethnal Green but was continually drawn to the country, once walking all the way from her home to Epping Forest and back while carrying her baby brother, in order to see the woods. One of her most memorable experiences was the five weeks she spent with an aunt and uncle near Cambridge, where she played with farm animals and village children. "There were some very fine trees just outside my aunt's window. The birds sang most delightfully in them, but the delight of my life was to watch the larks rise up out of a cornfield singing as if their throats would burst."[60] Later, she walked all over the countryside with her father, and then relived some of their more enjoyable journeys by tracing over them with maps.[61] Another of the few women to write an autobiography, Betty May, was born into squalor in London to a destitute mother and decrepit father. While her early life consisted of abuse and neglect, she remembered being sent to live with an aunt in Somerset and experiencing the country for the first time: "For a week or so I found it lovely. I was awakened by the crowing of cocks, to open my eyes upon fruit trees gently swaying against a blue sky . . . I dangled my sun-bonnet by its strings. I stuck poppies and daisies in my hair. I was plump and brown and healthy . . . I suppose in a way this time in the country was a happy one."[62] This brief happy interlude was followed by four unhappy marriages, drug addiction, involvement with gangs, and many hand-to-mouth moments.

For those who worked in urban settings or indoors, nature was synonymous with things that were otherwise rare: solitude and quiet. William Tayler, a London footman, lamented being stuck indoors. "The life of a gentleman's servant is something like that of a bird shut up in a cage. The bird is well housed and well fed but is deprived of liberty, and liberty is the sweetes [sic] object of all Englishmen. Therefore I would rather be like the sparrow or lark, have less housing and feeding and rather more liberty."[63] Thomas Oliver, the Cornish miner, noted that "often when taking my walks abroad with no other company than my little dog, I have been so much delighted with the beauties around me, had it not been that I was afraid to be heard, I should shout aloud for joy."[64] At least for Oliver, shouting aloud for joy at the beauty of nature was beyond the socially prescribed norm for emotional expression by a grown man; but the fact that he wanted to indicates the intensity of emotion that nature was capable of eliciting.

Although the outdoors is hardly silent, the absence of noise is a common refrain in these memoirs. James Croll, who had quit his job as a joiner due to an injured elbow, loved to walk in nature. "Almost from boyhood I had a love for retired, solitary walks in the country. On these occasions I can enjoy a congenial companion, but I would rather be alone to meditate. It is more sweet, more pleasant. The stillness of nature adds to the charm."[65] David Love, whose travels as a soldier and a ballad-seller had taken him all over the country, noted that "I would prefer a rural life to any other, for there is none better, as there is peace and contentment in that happy state; there is no hurry nor bustle, no rattling of coaches, no bawling nor noise like that in cities or towns; but only the beautiful works of nature around them."[66] Henry Broadhurst, who had grown up in the rural area around Oxford, was shocked by the noise and commotion when he moved to London to find work. "I began to long for the sunlight on the quiet fields, the green hedgerows, and the music of the woods. Even the Houses of Parliament, with the great Clock Tower, my chief delight, could not compensate for the absence of the joys of rural life."[67] The same "newly awoken craving for solitude" that propelled so many working people to become autodidacts and avid readers (see chapter 6) could also send them outside.[68]

The urban soundscape consisted not just of moving carriages and horses, shouting children and vendors, and industrial noise but also church bells, organized song, and sometimes political contention, all conspiring to produce a clamoring din.[69] It is interesting to note that one of the only working-class autobiographers to profess to enjoy walks in the city, John Kitto, was profoundly deaf: "the numberless curiosities, new inventions, and interesting objects which fill the shop windows on the one hand, and the little street incidents and endless varieties of human character and costume on the other, have at all times furnished to me a fund of amusement which no frequency of resort could extinguish or deaden."[70]

Clearly, the natural world provided an intensely pleasurable outlet for urban dwellers. But even those whose work involved being outdoors often expressed a love of nature. Henry White first noticed the natural world when he worked as a crow-scarer; he befriended a little beetle and kept it as a pet, making a house for it and feeding it bits of his lunch. Later, he began birdwatching, particularly in the spring: "It was at such times as these that the love for natural history began to force itself on me."[71] As an adult, he collected specimens of both birds and insects, and learned taxidermy.[72] William Milne, a farm laborer in Scotland, remembered being allowed to go outside with a young playmate after their introductory reading lessons. "Glory and sunshine! Daisy-chains, and rushworm caps! Cornel whips and sauchen whistles! And the rolling about on the green grass! I now believe that we were then about as happy as it is possible for sentient beings to be."[73] Alexander Mitchell spent all of his teenage years as a farm servant, transitioning in later life to a job as stableman for an aristocratic estate. Despite the fact that his work kept him outside most of the time, he waxed the most joyful about spending his leisure time outdoors. A visit to the summit of Benatchie, "in the balmy days of summer, when the bloom is on the heather, and all nature dressed in its most gorgeous robes," conferred enormous pleasure. He also loved to watch the birds preparing their nests on the lower slope. Later in life, when he worked for an aristocratic household, he had permission to fish the local stream, at one point catching a trout that weighed over sixteen pounds. Finally, in his sixties, he acquired a bicycle and began to take day trips of as long as thirty miles.[74]

When Joseph Severn, then not even twelve years old, was employed as a farmer's boy, he thought "it was glorious to work on the beautiful summer days in the sunshine at haymaking," when "all nature was exuberant with the joyous promise and fulfilment of her abundant fruitfulness; everyone was unusually sociable and happy; class distinction broke through the bonds," and people in the village joined together to take a break from their normal employment to bring in the harvest. Interestingly, alongside this warm nostalgia, Severn recounted in detail the enormous number of rodents and birds nesting in the corn who were accidentally beheaded by people wielding scythes.[75] Nature was beautiful, but it was still red in tooth and claw.

James Edwin Saunders, who took over the running of an old mill when he was only eighteen years old, loved to climb up to the top of it to survey the countryside, and to lie down in front of it in the dark to see the stars. This led to some almost orgasmic reflections about nature in his autobiography:

> In the night there is a splendid sense of being alone with nature. You come into direct contact with her in all her changing humours as you cannot in the daytime. There is no disturbing or distracting element, and you experience a closer feeling of oneness and communion. Lovers may and do enjoy each other's society in company; but the richest happiness by far is when they are alone together, heart leaping into heart, with none to see or hinder. So it is with Nature, the great Lover of us all.[76]

Saunders noted that he also greatly enjoyed battling the elements during storms at the old mill: "Often I was only just in time; and there was a strange exhilarating delight when I got back in the dry and took off my dripping coat, to hear the storm beating on the boards outside, while I was back in shelter, and all was safe."[77] Henry Snell reveled in climbing mountains, both because doing so was challenging and because of the incredible payoff of reaching the summit. "When at last, aching and breathless, you stand alone on the roof of the world, the conquest made and with nothing between your tired body and the infinite blue, you look out upon the earth and feel that life is good."[78]

Nor were these the only autobiographers to identify the natural world with superlative pleasures. The sailor and poet Robert Anderson fondly remembered his tutor taking him fishing and foraging—activities that were crucial to survival for the impoverished teacher but for a child were unmitigated entertainment.[79] For Anderson, the natural world "harmonizes the soul, producing an ecstasy of bliss, unknown to the millions who glorify in society."[80] Thomas Carter, tailor, rhapsodized about "the early flowers, the first butterfly, the renewed song of birds, the milder temperature of the atmosphere, and the increased splendor and warmth of the sun," all of which brought him "delight and joy."[81]

As these testimonies show, the outdoors provided aesthetic pleasure, exercise, improvised playthings, and free food. The natural world also provided no-cost novelty, of the kind that people with greater opportunities might find in books or museums. Finally, the natural world was important to working people because in areas where land was increasingly commodified and privatized, space was at a premium. As Katrina Navickas has pointed out, the moors provided a place for the city dwellers of the Southern Pennines to hold large-scale gatherings and protest meetings. The open space of the moors could be very dramatic, whether they were lush and green with the Pennines in the background, or bleak and barren and rocky. As she shows, even the reporting on Chartists' torchlit meetings reflected the Romantic sensibilities of the time, describing the lines of protesters as "picturesque" or "sublime."[82] By taking their protests outside, working people in large numbers became part of what was so impressive about nature.

This is not to claim that all interactions with the natural world were pleasant ones; working-class autobiographers—even those who sometimes appreciated the outdoors—occasionally adverted to its discomfort and danger. Joseph Stamper, whose life included a period of vagrancy, found the countryside "frigid and inimical. You have got to live in a town to properly appreciate the country . . . half the beauty of the country depends on its contrast with the town, and one's lack of experience of the country's cold and callous indifference to human beings."[83] Henry Snell, who began working as a crow-scarer at the age of eight, was outside for twelve hours a day, alone, in all weathers. The length of the workday meant that he had neither time nor energy for play. He noted that farm labor "involved exposure and risk, and nearly every conceivable bodily hardship, and very few of those who managed to escape from it ever returned to it of their own free will."[84]

Without warm and protective clothing, child workers suffered outdoors. George Mockford "had no stamina about me for outdoor exposure," yet was taken from school when he was ten years old to help his father. "I had to work getting turnips out of the pie, as we used to call this heap of turnips, covered over with straw and earth. I had some old leather gloves on, but the dry earth used to get into the gloves and fill my sores, and so bad did they become that the doctor was called in." To harden him further to outdoor work, his father sent him to pull turnips in the frozen fields with no gloves on, only stopping when his own workmen chastised the father about it.[85] William Milne had only one suit of clothes, so that getting drenched with rain meant shivering in wet clothes through dinner and not being able to get warm until bedtime.[86]

Elizabeth Oakley remembered being sent into the "marshes to seek for ducks and geese and I have many a time come home with my feet wet up to my knees with walking in the marsh after the fowls and then when I got to bed on a night I used to have the cramp in my legs so bad that I had to jump out of bed and rub on my legs and stand on the cold boards to get them right."[87] An anonymous "Norfolk labourer's wife" described starting to work at age eight or nine, and being so small that she was only paid threepence a day for crawling on her hands and knees to weed charlock out of the turnip fields. The prickly stalks made her hands so raw that she had to stay away from work for them to heal, but she was more upset about the lost pay than she was about the physical pain.[88] The anonymous blacksmith who wrote his life story for the *Commonwealth* spent part of his childhood working outdoors as a farm laborer, and noted that even if the day was too cold for the cattle and horses to be outdoors, it was not thought to be too cold for the servants.[89]

While some who worked outdoors came to identify the natural world with their physical pain, as this chapter has shown, working people's assessments of the natural world were overwhelmingly positive. Some authors expressed paeans to nature that were squarely in the vein of Romanticism, but the majority that did mention nature enjoyed it because of their direct hedonic experiences in nature. The natural world provided much that was lacking in working-class lives during a time of uneven industrial transition: a sense of expansiveness, fresh air, commodities available outside the market, novelty, beauty. Many may have moved to urban areas in search of higher wages and better opportunities, but there are few paeans to cities, wages, or opportunities in their recollections. What emerges, instead, is a picture of the outdoors as a source of joy; a working-class environmentalism predicated on direct experience of the body in nature rather than passive observation.

SIX

Self-Cultivation

THE NINETEENTH-CENTURY British philosopher Jeremy Bentham famously argued that there was no appreciable difference between simple and complex pleasures; the game of pushpin and the appreciation of poetry were equivalent:

> The utility of all these arts and sciences,—I speak both of those of amusement and curiosity,—the value which they possess, is exactly in proportion to the pleasure they yield. Every other species of preeminence which may be attempted to be established among them is altogether fanciful. Prejudice apart, the game of push-pin is of equal value with the arts and sciences of music and poetry. If the game of push-pin furnish more pleasure, it is more valuable than either. Everybody can play at push-pin: poetry and music are relished only by a few.[1]

Philosopher John Stuart Mill, although like Bentham a utilitarian, disagreed, claiming that the higher pleasures of art, music, poetry, literature, and philosophy would be preferred by anyone who had had a chance to experience them: "It is better to be a human being dissatisfied than a pig satisfied; better to be Socrates dissatisfied than a fool satisfied."[2] Charles Campbell, a Scottish cotton worker and sailor who wrote his memoir while confined in a Glasgow prison, was one of many working-class autobiographers who would have agreed with Mill: "A taste for knowledge and science is of such noble origin, as to confer a kind of luster on its humblest possessor. There is something in the pleasure it yields so superior to the gratification arising from commonplace topics and the tittle-tattle of life, as to rank the poorest gleaner in the harvest of literature at least a degree above the herd of bipeds."[3]

As this chapter will demonstrate, nineteenth-century working-class autobiographers described finding pleasure in education, particularly self-education. In so doing, autobiographers were not just compensating for the lack of free state-provided education, they were also indicating how well they fit into the bootstrapping spirit of the times. *The Pursuit of Knowledge under Difficulties* was more than just a contemporary book title; it was also a passion and a badge of respectability.[4] Samuel Smiles's book *Self-Help* (1859), aimed at artisans, was wildly popular, going through seventy-three printings in one hundred years. Smiles celebrated self-making, persistence, and perseverance, reminding its readers that "great men of science, literature and art—apostles of great thoughts and lords of the great heart—have belonged to no exclusive class nor rank in life . . . the poorest have sometimes taken the highest places."[5] Of course, those autobiographers who dilated on the joys of reading or music or self-directed research to the exclusion of the joys of drinking or attending fairs were, through their narratives, marking out a place for themselves on a spectrum of political and social respectability, but that doesn't mean that their narratives were contrived or untrue.[6]

The working-class autobiographers who wrote their own narratives rather than dictating them had received some education, whether formal or self-provided. In the nineteenth century, working-class children who did attend school had to cobble together an education from a patchwork of Sunday schools, dame schools (akin to modern-day daycare centers), schools arranged on the Lancastrian system in which students were taught through rote education by slightly older students, and schools at which "pupil-teachers" apprenticed with schoolmasters.[7] The quality of these educational offerings varied widely, although in general the public education provided in Scotland was better than that in England.[8] John Burnett has noted that for many working-class children, education was stultifying and brought negative emotions like fear or boredom rather than happiness. And although Jonathan Rose disagreed with Burnett's assessment, he did admit that many of the fee-paying schools for working-class children that existed before the 1870 Education Act wasted children's time and resulted in boredom, sometimes punctuated by corporal punishment.

The same cannot be said of self-guided education, which autobiographers reported was a major source of happiness.[9]

A few autobiographers recounted really enjoying formal education. The industrialist Andrew Carnegie, who grew up in a working-class household in Dunfermline, remembered school as having been "a perfect delight," and the Nonconformist Mary Smith, who later became a teacher herself, loved Sunday school and "believed it helped to bias my mind for many good impressions."[10] Adam Rushton recalled the "exquisite pleasure" of learning to write in Sunday school, "the glorious time of straight strokes, pot-hooks, and ladles . . . Then, more exhilarating still, came forth words, and sentences, and even my own name, written in large, strong strokes of my quill pen."[11] Robert Roberts, saved from a life of rural servitude by mentors who saw that he was gifted, noted that "study was always a pleasure, not an irksome task," and that the "hours of schoolwork, which many look back upon with anything but pleasure, were to me days of unalloyed delight."

But while few autobiographers praised school, almost all who discussed their intellectual lives characterized self-cultivation, and even learning for its own sake rather than instrumental learning, as positive. They used a variety of strong emotional terms to describe their feelings, to the point that David Vincent has argued that "the discovery of useful knowledge amounted to a secularized conversion experience which left no part of the readers' lives untouched."[12] What aspects of self-directed learning were so well appreciated? Jonathan Rose writes that although working-class readers—particularly those who read on their own—tended to read what we might consider "canonical works," this reading was not an imposition of middle-class values but rather empowered workers who faced stereotypes about the intellectual attainments possible for workers.[13] Kelly Mays emphasizes that male workers found reading to be emotionally emancipating.[14]

Habits of Reading

Workers read avidly, often consuming whatever various texts they could get their hands on and combining them in innovative ways.[15] Adam Rushton described making a curriculum out of magazine articles, using a notebook to jot down the most important ideas. One of the magazines prescribed a course of study for young men, and Rushton and a friend immediately embarked on studies of religion, various histories, and science.[16] Outside of a school setting, working-class readers were not hemmed in by educational rules about how to read a text; a single text could be interpreted in different ways. *Pilgrim's Progress*, for example, could be read as a heavy Christian allegory or as a thrilling adventure story about an actual protagonist named Christian.[17] And for those who did read it allegorically, it could be a template for their life stories' own narrative arcs.[18] Thomas Cooper professed in his autobiography that "the happiest hours of all I had in early years were spent alone, and with books," remembering with particular fondness rereading *Pilgrim's Progress*.[19] An anonymous dissenting minister who had been ill as a child called *Pilgrim's Progress* "like the discovery of a new world, Columbus could not have exulted more when the western shores gladdened his eye."[20] The same book also brought joy to Samuel Bamford, son of a weaver and later cotton mill manager; the weaver James Inches Hillocks; John Leatherland, a carpenter's son from Kettering; the pit-lads Thomas Burt and John Harris; the future labor leader John Wilson; the teacher James Campkin; the Dundee factory boy Frank Forrest; and the future socialist Robert Blatchford. None of the children perceived the story to be allegorical.[21] "I rambled with Christian from his home in the wilderness to the Celestial City; mused over his hair-breadth escapes, and his conflict with giant Despair. I was very much delighted with it," wrote the weaver William Heaton.[22] Even Elizabeth Oakley, a rare female autobiographer, was captivated by the book, which opened the world of reading to her "and from that time on I have loved reading, especially when I was young. O how I enjoyed sitting up after everyone else was in bed to read and study anything that I wanted to learn, or that was interesting."[23]

Of course, the first step in becoming a lifelong learner was learning to read. Those who didn't learn in dame school or Sunday school might teach themselves. The prize essayist who called himself "Jacques" had learned to read while a teenaged apprentice to a flax-dresser, and when his health ebbed and he had to go through a spell of enforced idleness, he read for pleasure. "It has now become a habit, and has proved ever since to be one of the cheapest and most pleasurable sources of my enjoyment," he wrote. Later in life, when he was struggling as a tanner's clerk, supporting a growing family and snatching his leisure time when he could, he noted that "the 'pursuit of knowledge under difficulties' I found to contain much that, even in itself, was truly pleasant and exciting; and hours, yea, even minutes were snatched from days of oppressive toil and like 'stolen waters' were experienced to be refreshing and sweet."[24] Jacob Holkinson learned to read from posters and bills stuck on walls and by loitering in front of bookshops, and in a short time reading became his main source of enjoyment. Ultimately, his interests led him to write poetry and to study botany, and "the pleasure I derived, and still continue to enjoy, in the prosecution of this subject, it would not be easy to describe." He and a friend traveled to see all the plants within an eight-mile radius of his town, and he even discovered some fossilized fish while walking in a quarry.[25]

Avid readers often started in childhood. Frank George Marling, born in 1863, remembered his father's bound volumes of the *Illustrated London News* for 1851. His father had been to the Great Exhibition. "What splendid books they were! . . . I can see the pictures now, the wonderful Crystal Palace in building, the soldiers marching round the galleries to test them, the trees over which some parts of the building were erected . . . how we feasted on these and many other pictures." Later in life, Marling's greatest joy was working with Sunday school scholars. "I always felt myself one with the children and it was a delight to talk to them and enter into their thoughts and feelings. I think it was because I had such a vivid recollection of my own thoughts and ideas as a child that I felt so much at home with the children and they with me."[26] Learning to write, and then using literacy to express one's own ideas, was an additional challenge. Thomas Whittaker, a textile worker who later became a temperance lecturer, had two books in his library when he began his studies: the Bible and the autobiography of Benjamin Franklin. He read them over and over, copying out particularly helpful portions of each and showing them to his wife. Of course, to copy them out, he had to teach himself to write, buying pens and copy-books and making the letter "O" repeatedly.[27]

As David Vincent has pointed out, much of the knowledge working people needed in the nineteenth century was *techne*, the skills learned on the job, and that these might not require or be aided by extensive literacy. But one of the key functions of literacy for working-class children was to exercise the imagination and expand the known world, and this brought joy.[28] Joseph Donaldson, born in the 1793, remembered getting his hands on a copy of Robinson Crusoe, and found his imagination set free. "An island to one's self! I thought what a happiness! I have sat and dreamed for hours together, on what I would do in such a situation."[29] Further underlining the difference between school and voluntary self-cultivation, he reported skipping school to read his favorite books outside on the top of a nearby hill. J. H. Powell, who worked in a mill, stole moments from work to read James Fenimore Cooper. "I well remember the excited state of my mind and the intense pleasure I experienced as I grew familiar with the melodramatic incidents and wonderfully graphic descriptions of scenery which characterise his style," he noted. But a move to the drying loft at work, which was enervatingly hot, took away his desire to read.[30] Mary Ann Smith could not remember a time when she could not read; her father even indulged her by buying an odd lot of tattered books, including Shakespeare's plays. "My delight, which I kept to myself, was irrepressible . . . whenever I had done what work I set about to do, my chief pleasure was to slip away unobserved into some quiet spot, where all unseen I could read."[31] John Harris also remembered being introduced to Shakespeare. As he read his first play, *Romeo and Juliet*, he invoked the emotional sublime, writing "the delight I experienced is beyond words to describe."[32] Working-class autobiographers were more likely to cite "improving" authors like Shakespeare and Bunyan over the broadside ballads and tales of murders and intrigue that were the steadiest sellers in the first two-thirds of the nineteenth century.[33]

William Dodd, the self-titled "factory cripple," described his early life as a catalogue of woe, as one might expect in a memoir intended to attack the factory system. But even Dodd could not help describing the pleasure that he got from reading. On Sundays he went for long walks in the woods, to find solitude and read borrowed books; "these were seasons of real pleasure to me."[34] Similarly, Rowland Kenney, consigned to full-time work in a cotton factory at the age of fourteen, discovered Robert Blatchford's articles in the *Clarion*, and "was raised to what seemed, in comparison with my usual morbid state, the acme of delight."[35] Hugh Miller of Cromarty, the son of a shipmaster, was lonely until he learned how to read, and then reading became one of "the most delightful" of his amusements; he particularly admired the prints in *Pilgrim's Progress*.[36]

The Informal Economy of Books

Having learned to read, whether in childhood or later, autobiographers next had the daunting task of finding reading material. Frank Bullen, who became a ships' lad at the age of twelve and then ended up in Liverpool after a shipwreck, had the good fortune to be housed in a Sailors' Home with a library. "I found a volume of Captain Cook's Travels, coiled myself up in a big armchair, and passed at once into another world. Thenceforth, during my stay, that peaceful chamber was my home. Except for a little exercise, sleep, and meals, I scarcely left it, and long ago though it is, I can vividly remember how entirely happy I was."[37] An anonymous letterpress printer averred that his life was not full of excitement, but that he took great pleasure in reading, and that reading was of great benefit for working men because it didn't involve going out and spending funds on drinking or other amusements. By dint of such thrift, the printer had managed to amass a library of over 150 volumes.[38]

In the absence of lending libraries or their own libraries, working-class readers borrowed books wherever they could, revealing a network of readers willing to help each other. Reformer Francis Place as a boy stood at book stalls reading until he was chased away, and then found a bookseller willing to rent him one book at a time. Later in life, his landlady borrowed books for him from the rooms that she cleaned.[39] George Meek borrowed books from the shoemaker in his small village.[40] John Harris borrowed books from "Captain" Jemmy Thomas, a mining entrepreneur, and from the local rector.[41] After being forced to leave school and work to support his family, Andrew Carnegie delighted in having access to books through the patronage of Colonel James Anderson, who lent out some of his four hundred books to working boys to read in their spare time. Carnegie credited Anderson with having given him the idea to endow libraries as one of his major philanthropic projects.[42]

Chester Armstrong, who had entered the mines as a young child, discovered the joy of reading around the same time he began courting his wife. A Sunday school friend "loaned me a small pocket edition of *The Aristocrat of the Breakfast Table* by Oliver Wendell Holmes. I can easily recall the exquisite pleasure I derived from this little book."[43] Armstrong felt personally indebted to the author for having expanded his horizons. After his marriage, he continued to educate himself, becoming interested in social and economic questions, helping to form a debating society for the workers of Ashington, and ultimately discarding his Methodist religious beliefs when they could no longer be reconciled with his standard of proof. Like John Stuart Mill, Armstrong branched out from political economy to poetry, particularly enjoying the works of Robert Burns, with whom he sympathized on class issues, and Walt Whitman.[44]

Robert White, who had worked as a cattle-herd and a millwright, found a patron in his father's landlord, who lent him Sir Walter Scott's poems, "with which I was delighted." White soon afterwards secured a job as a clerk, and later used his skills as an assistant in a counting house and then as the secretary to the owner's widow. When she died, she left him several thousand pounds. While he never married, he published antiquarian articles and accumulated a large library of books. "I am fortunate in possessing the very best works ancient and modern of our most distinguished authors, hence my library has been a source of the purest pleasure in health and prosperity . . . if I possess my books, I shall not be without consolation."[45]

Henry Price was indifferently educated in the workhouse, and yet became a reader and writer in adulthood. He kept accounts of his expenditures for decades, donating his account books to the British Museum (they remain in the British Library's collections today). He also kept a commonplace book, filled with his own poetry, essays, and pictures, and wrote an autobiography. As a young man, Price spent five years in the United States working as a cabinetmaker. There, he befriended Evan Griffith, a wealthy shipping agent for the Erie Canal. One day, Price was in Griffith's house and saw his library—he had never seen so many books. Griffith said he could borrow anything. "I found something to start with. It was Rollins' *Ancient History*. No novel that I have ever read, perhaps except Uncle Tom's Cabin, gave me more pleasure . . . I read in my meal time. I read after being in Bed til 12 and 1 in the morning, and filch'd bits out of my work time."[46]

The Joys of Research

Although most working-class autobiographers were unable to delve deeply into topics due to the difficulty of obtaining reading materials, some embarked on self-directed research careers.[47] The dispersed nature of Victorian science meant that observation, categorization, and cataloguing of plants, animals, rocks, insects, or fossils could be carried out without much training, and popularizers of science were beginning to conduct sustained outreach to nonacademic audiences.[48] It was even possible for a Scottish shoemaker to make a name for himself as a naturalist and to become a scientific hero, as Anne Secord has documented for the case of Thomas Edward.[49] The autobiographer John Younger became a keen observer of bird behavior as a young child, impressing his friends with his knowledge of the flight patterns of larks by predicting each lark's next move.[50] Joseph Gutteridge of Coventry, too frail to engage in rough-and-tumble activities with the other boys, collected plants and made watercolor plant illustrations and leaf rubbings.[51] Later in life, he built his own microscope, using it to study the cell structure of plants and the nature of pollen, and noted that "it would be almost impossible to describe the intense pleasure or the valuable instruction received from these examinations of the structure and function of plant life."[52] He also found joy exploring the countryside looking for fossils, and sharing his knowledge with his friends and with young people.[53] As he wrote in his memoirs, "In the ups and downs of life I could not dominate my own prospects in a financial sense, but I have been taught a lesson not soon to be forgotten, that man may in all conditions of existence make life much happier by conforming to those principles which will lead him to seek the highest good not only of himself, but also of his fellows." The study of nature was "a joy forever" because in addition to being intellectually stimulating, it was morally elevating.[54]

Samuel Taylor, a Hanley potter, attended astronomy lectures at his local Mechanics' Institute: "Anything more deeply interesting than those lectures it was impossible to hear, there was a grandeur and sublimity we had never imagined. They affected people powerfully. Instead of sleep they were wandering in the immensity of space, visiting double suns, and suns of every hue and magnitude."[55] The Cornish miner Thomas Oliver had bought a book on astronomy that caused him to wonder how scientists calculated the distance of planets from the earth. Realizing he needed to know some math to understand the question, he arranged to study with one of his town's two schoolmasters. Later, when he traveled to Australia to try mining there, he was "never happier than when collecting natural objects."[56] After his return to England he became interested in zoology and botany and became a proponent of evolutionary theory. Joseph Millott Severn, while a young teenager working in an ironstone mine, discovered that another young man in the village not only shared his fascination with phrenology but also had the "student set" of bumpy ceramic heads and their accompanying instruction books. The opportunity to cultivate a friend with the same interest was "a joy that I had not anticipated."[57]

Bathchair-man George Meek educated himself about science, "to get as near to the truth of the meaning of life as I possibly could." But he also identified as a Socialist and an agnostic, and dedicated himself to reading "some of the best productions of all ages, from ancient Greece to modern France and America."[58] John Wilson was late to self-cultivation, but in his early thirties embarked on a self-designed program of "grammar, logic, history, shorthand, and the dictionary."[59] Joseph Keating, who had finished his formal education at the age of twelve, took up reading philosophy, history, politics, and novels later in his teens. To Keating, the awakening of his mind was associated with the awakening of his physical capacities:

> I was tremendously alive at this period. Everything interested me. Every hour, every minute, was crammed with my activities in one direction or another. New mysterious emotions and passions seemed to be breaking out like little flames from all parts of my body. As soon as the morning sunlight touched my bedroom

window, I woke. I did not rise, I leapt up . . . a glorious feeling within me, as I got out of bed, made me sing. My singing was never in tune, but my impulse of joy had to express itself.[60]

Unfortunately Keating, who had mood swings, lost interest in study, decided that he hated the desk job that made time for study possible, and "when I left the office of an evening, and walked over the bridge to my lodgings . . . my thoughts were chiefly of suicide."[61]

Occasionally, working-class scholars who had to overcome difficulties to gain access to education were able to leverage their studies into social mobility based on academic merit. James Mullin, born during the Irish famine and raised in abject poverty, delighted in books as a boy. Reading "has been the charm of my existence—the sunshine that converted the gloomiest of prospects into a paradise where my imagination luxuriated amongst the richest fruits and fairest flowers of human intellect, while the squalid realities that surrounded me were lost in the divinest of all companionships."[62] Many of his early years were spent accumulating toys that he could use to barter with other children in exchange for any books they had at home; later, any two pence he could find were invested in reading material on any topic, even religion (in which he was otherwise uninterested). Mullin's incessant reading eventually enabled him to try for, and win, a scholarship to Queen's University, Galway, making him the rare working-class youth to earn a university degree and practice medicine.

Another good example of this phenomenon can be found in the career of Henry Jones. Jones's father, a shoemaker, had almost no education, although he rejoiced in the ability of his three sons to win medals for their educational achievements from their days of elementary education onward. When Henry Jones had the opportunity to gain further education by alternating days at schools with days in his shoemaking workshop, he "ran towards home from sheer gladness of heart for a full mile."[63] Study ended up being much more captivating than shoemaking, and Jones applied for scholarships, first to Bangor Training College for Teachers, and then to the University of Glasgow. In between stints at university he taught primary school in the Welsh mining and iron town of Brynamman and was "exceedingly happy," throwing himself into the task with the energy that a twenty-year-old teacher can muster. The school flourished, the community was kind to him, and he even found employment for one of his brothers as his helper.[64]

Having discovered what he loved, Jones ultimately became a university professor of philosophy. At this level, teaching gave him "greater joy than ever before," because of the great autonomy that position afforded him. "I was granted the opportunity of making the most of any powers that I had, and of carrying my students with me if I could, imparting to them as vital the truths which seemed vital to me."[65] Of course, a university professorship brought with it other, less enjoyable duties, and, in one of the most engaging and relatable passages of his narrative, Jones described finishing with his last meeting as a member of the St. Andrews Faculty Senate, "by far the most painful gatherings I ever knew."

> I rose from that great oval table around which members of the Senate sat, left the room, and quietly closed the great door. I stood for a moment on the map outside the door and at the top of the staircase. Then a wild wave of uncontrollable joy broke over me ... I danced in silence on that mat like a madman, every sinew and muscle in my body working, and I knew for the first and last time the full *savagery* of joy.[66]

The Love of Poetry

In addition to sharing the experiences of learning to read, unleashing their imaginations, and cultivating their connections to borrow books, many working-class autobiographers described in vibrant emotional detail their love of poetry. When John Clare discovered blank verse at the age of thirteen, it made his heart "twitter with joy."[67] The vellum binder Frederick Rogers noted that Shakespeare had been a part of his intellectual life since he remembered ever having one, and that "I enjoyed his verse as I enjoyed the sunshine and the trees, and no higher enjoyment can be got out of poetry than that."[68] Robert Story, who later became a poet, remembered being given a book of Watts's *Divine Songs for Children* when he was a child, carrying it everywhere, and memorizing its contents. "Its effect upon my mind was magical. It gave me the feeling of a new existence. The mountains, the clouds, and the skies took an aspect of poetry and religion."[69] John Plummer discovered a book of songs commemorating the patriot Kossuth in a Chartist bookshop in London, and was instantly transported. "Never till my dying hour shall I forget the glorious enthusiasm of that moment, when a new and heavenly existence seemed opened up before me."[70] John Fraser considered the poetry of Shelley and Keats, to which he was introduced while a soldier in India, to be "unexpected and glorious beyond dreams."[71] Joy, magic, glorious, heavenly, transported:

clearly, for these workers, poetry produced a transcendent experience.

Some working-class autobiographers found poetry so compelling that they sought out further poetic education. W. E. Adams described taking poetry classes at the Working Men's College, as "such a feast of reason and flow of soul as almost never was since Shakespeare had his bout with Ben Jonson at the Mermaid."[72] The Scottish shepherd Henry Scott Riddell befriended a professor who allowed him to attend lectures at no charge. "To share in the conversation of those possessed of high literary taste and talent, and, above all, of poetic genius, is the highest enjoyment afforded by society," Riddell wrote.[73] Jack Goring found one work of poetry so delightful that he wrote to the poet, and to his surprise was sent not only a note of encouragement but also a complete edition of his poems. "I never was and never should be a scholar and when I think of books and myself I seem to have played the butterfly rather than the bee yet somehow or other I have gathered something of the sweets of satisfaction," he noted.[74]

The invention of the Stanhope iron press lowered barriers to entry into the publishing business.[75] As Andrew Hobbs has opined based on a statistical sample, proliferating newspapers may have published as many as five million pieces of original poetry during the Victorian period, providing ample opportunity for working people to see their names, initials, or pseudonyms in print.[76] Some of these organs had a large circulation; even working-class women might have their poetical works printed in the *Northern Star* and other Chartist and radical periodicals, thus reaching a wider audience than all but the most accomplished poets.[77] For additional poetic outlets, poor poets could publish chapbooks by taking up collections among patrons.[78]

John Jones, a footman and poet, was celebrated by Robert Southey, who said that there were in his poems "such indications of a kind and happy disposition, so much observation of natural objects, such a relish of the innocent pleasures offered by nature to the eye, and ear, and heart, which are not closed against them, and so pleasing an example of the moral benefit drawn from those pleasures, when they are received by a thankful and thoughtful mind," that he was persuaded to sponsor Jones's poems.[79] In a short autobiography that he sent to Southey, Jones described his worklife as a footman, punctuated by many delightful hours he had been able to spend reading from the open bookcase at the house where he served.[80] Southey expressed surprise that the intellectual exercise of writing poetry had pleased Jones without also making Jones discontented with his station in life (one of the fears surrounding educating members of the working classes).[81]

Nor was Jones the only working-class versifier who took pleasure in the exercise. Mary Smith began to write poetry in her head, using the time while scrubbing floors or walking outdoors to practice her verses. Later in life, when she opened her own school, "poetry indeed was through all the hard periods of my life, my joy and strength, the uplifter of my soul in trouble."[82] John Taylor, the seventeenth-century waterman and poet, wrote poetry for its own sake and was proud of his talent.[83] Ann Yearsley, a milkmaid and mother of six children, wrote verses because they made her happy; and John Frederick Bryant, a tobacco pipe maker, read Virgil and Homer over and over again, and then wrote a paean to the dog that turned the family's hearth spit.[84] Mary Ann Hearn loved day school and Sunday school, and memorized long scriptural passages.[85] She called the world of poetry a "wonderful world of vivid imagination and unutterable joy" that opened to her after she encountered the poem "The Better Land" by Felicia Hemans: "I wish I could describe, even if only so far as I am able to live it again, the strange, sweet emotions which overcame me as I read those lines."[86] These emotions impelled her to pick up a pen and try her own hand at poetry. Like other working-class autobiographers whose first poetic attempts were shared anonymously, Hearn had "a moment of keen joy, not unmixed with pride," to hear them praised.[87]

An anonymous poem could be taken on its own terms, divorced from the status of its author. Allen Davenport, a sometime shoemaker and radical Spencean politician, wrote a poem and anonymously stuck it to a tree in his small village. When he later heard his verse being sung by various people, he compared his happiness to "the joy of Columbus when he first beheld the new world; of Archimedes when he exclaimed Eureka, or that of Franklin when he pierced the thunder cloud, and drew down the fire of heaven!"[88] Davenport described his first published poem as one might describe a newborn baby: "the poor little bantling—my first born, clad in a robe of typographical splendour."[89] William Heaton, who spent his hour of daily leisure from weaving writing poetry, had similar feelings when one of his first poems appeared in the *Leeds Intelligencer*. "Judge then of my delight, the first time I was so gratified. I read it, rubbed my eyes and read it again, as if afraid there might be some delusion in it."[90] The Cornish tin and copper miner John Harris became an ardent composer of poetic verses. "The love of song grew with my physical growth, and was dearer to me than the smile of friendship," he professed. He used every available implement and surface for writing on: sharp rocks and pieces of slate; blackberry juice and cast-off tea wrappers.[91] When he finally managed to get his first poetic production—a dirge on the death of some miners killed on the job—into print, "these verses were given to a poor blind man; and I remember with what intense joy I listened in the crowd as he sang them up and down the market at Camborne."[92]

The poems produced by working-class poets, with few exceptions, were snugged inside a straitjacket of mostly conservative expectations about form and rhyme. Most Chartist poets produced calls to action, summoning up the specters of wan factory children, wage slaves, and mammon-worshipping capitalists; although Thomas Cooper's *Purgatory of Suicides*, a Dantean journey through the afterlives of historical suicides, represented the zenith of what a self-educated man could do within certain literary restrictions. Other working-class poets produced paeans to the countryside, or likened unspoiled nature to heaven.[93]

Fewer working-class autobiographers branched out into writing fiction, although Frank Bullen is one who did. A failed tradesman by the time he took up writing for profit, Bullen found that getting a story published gave him "a sudden gleam of joy, a bit of pleasure so keen that it made me forget for the time all my troubles."[94] Having spent his teen years aboard ships, his background coincided with a national interest in adventure stories. "There was a glow of strange delight in my heart, to find that when I took my pen in hand and sat down to write, all that early life on many seas stood out bold and clear upon the background of my mind, and I lived its incidents over and over again." Writing was so delightful that Bullen didn't even mind that he never knew how much he would be paid for his writing, or when.[95]

Happiness and Music

Just as working people often found exposure to poetry transformative, so exposure to professionally played music could be eye-opening and spark a desire to participate.[96] In between jobs as a domestic servant, Rose Allen once attended a concert, which "seemed almost more than weak mortality could sustain . . . for years this concert gave me intense pleasure."[97] Alexander Somerville, who had grown up a farm laborer, went to a vocal concert as a young man and said of one female singer that "the electric effect was as great upon me as if heaven had opened, and a singing angel had descended . . . the memory of that delightful entertainment served me to think upon, and refresh my spirit with, as I toiled in the saw pit at the long saw, for weeks after."[98]

Of course, singing in public was ubiquitous and popular, requiring nothing more than a reasonable voice and the ability to carry a tune. Henry Burstow, a shoemaker and bell-ringer, found singing to be his "chief mental delight," accompanying him on every stage of life from infancy forward. For Burstow, singing involved a process of committing 420 sets of lyrics and melodies to memory, sometimes after only a single hearing. Burstow's most personally significant moment came on his mother's deathbed, when he was able to sit, her hand in his, and sing her favorite song to her.[99] William Heaton bought comic songs, "altered them to please myself," and then memorized them, so that he could sing at public houses.[100] James Nye as a young man was drawn into bad company because he was a "of a cheerful disposition and a pretty good songster," learned to play music and formed a band, supporting himself this way for three years. Later in life Nye crafted musical instruments and wrote hymns.[101]

Fifes and flutes were also relatively inexpensive. Serjeant Butler was fascinated by music from childhood on. He remembered a weaver in his town who was a famous whistler, "and he used to gratify my musical desire by whistling a tune to me, until I had got it nearly correct, and then gave me another." In his teens, he used part of his scanty earnings to buy himself a fife, "and this cheering companion beguiled many a hungry hour, for I was remarkably fond of music." He was able to leverage his knowledge of music into a position as an army fifer: "I found pleasure in nothing but music and musicians."[102] William Clift of Bramley, who began life as a farm laborer and later became a tenant farmer, taught himself to play the church organ by transposing notes from the flute, which he already knew how to play, to the organ. "The first time I was able to play with both hands at once, that is treble and bass, I was so delighted with the advancement that I hardly knew how to leave the organ to go home."[103]

As was the case with books, patrons sometimes gave working people instruments or access to instruments. Thomas Davies thought he had lost everything in his life: he lost his sight, his daughter died only three days after birth, his wife passed away, and his friend Martha also died. But some young women in his town of Haverfordwest presented him with a piano, and "I took so much delight that I soon came to play on it." The women then brought him a harmonium, and he worked constantly to improve his skills.[104] John Shinn, whose family often went short of food, was trapped in his childhood house due to insufficient outerwear, and regretted never having had a formal education. Despite this, he loved to draw and paint, so whenever he could earn a halfpenny he spent it on paints and paper, "which afforded me very great pleasure, and occupied my time and mind." Later, Shinn obtained permission to practice on a piano, and taught himself to play, using a cheap piano book. Although he continued to work as a cabinetmaker, his growing musical skill led to his obtaining church accompanist positions, and to an appreciation of organ music by the great organists of nineteenth-century London. Ultimately, by dint of some unpaid labor, lots of walking, and much musical practice, he was able to turn to music full time.[105]

While the correlation between self-cultivation and professions of happiness is very strong, it is important to note that these autobiographies were written against a backdrop of great social pressure to conform to norms of respectability. Upwardly mobile working men professed to find the most joy in activities related to learning. William Lovett, who had pulled himself up from ropemaker to cabinetmaker to small shopkeeper through enormous persistence, spent his young married life reading and tutoring his wife in the rudiments of social and political understanding.[106] He later reflected that the leisure activities of the working classes—particularly the "drunken revelry of the pot-house"—contributed powerfully to their oppression.[107] Like John Stuart Mill, Lovett favored rational pursuits that had the potential for deeper, more meaningful happiness and personal uplift: "If they were encouraged to admire the beauties of nature, to cultivate a taste for the arts and sciences, to seek for rational instruction and amusement, it would soon be found that their vicious habits would yield to more rational pursuits; man would . . . be better qualified to enjoy happiness in any future state of existence."[108] Mary Ann Hearn seconded Lovett's opinion, noting that when working people could finally gain access to the "higher pleasures and pursuits which have been for so long a time been the exclusive privileges of the favoured few," they would appreciate them more "because they understand and value them."[109]

Those workers who were unable to focus on cultivating themselves sometimes took pride and joy in promoting their children's educational fortunes. James Ashley, a London hat-shaper, worked so hard that Sundays were his only respite. But the happy moments noted in his autobiography were all identified with his children's educational successes. The entire family sacrificed so that the eldest son, Will, could go to a competitive school and from there to Oxford. Although Will earned a first-class honors degree and was passed over several times for positions "on account of class," he eventually became a history professor at the new university in Birmingham.[110] George Smith, a Romany traveler, extended his stays in various cities so that his children could attend school, "and it is with pleasure I feel in having done so, it will assuredly be to their interest and welfare."[111]

Narratives of self-cultivation were also much more prevalent among male autobiographers. As Kelly Mays has noted, working-class women's ability to cultivate themselves intellectually depended on time, money, solitude, social approval of women's education, expectations about women's fulfillment, and others in the house willing to share the chores normally associated with women. Women's education, especially in the nineteenth century, was not viewed as helping to advance the fortunes of the working class.[112] Toward the end of the nineteenth century, however, as compulsory education brought more girls into the classroom, working-class women began to identify happiness with self-cultivation. Mrs. Scott, a felt-hat worker who later became a justice of the peace, recalled reading J. M. Barrie's books: "one laughs and cries, and feels with Grizel that one can sit and rock and hold oneself tight with sheer delight."[113] Although their reading was largely done on rare vacations or "in time stolen from . . . sleeping hours," fellow Women's Cooperative Guildswomen wrote to the central office of their organization with lists of books that they had read and requests for other book suggestions. "To read a book is one of the luxuries that I am looking forward to with a great longing," Mrs. Russell from Liverpool wrote wistfully.[114]

· · · · · ·

As this chapter has shown, working-class autobiographers not only benefited from literacy in being able to tell their life stories, they also found fulfillment in other aspects of the life of the mind. Whether they learned to read in school or despite school, they read avidly and often unsystematically, leaning on a network of patrons and friends to gain access to more reading materials. Some became self-directed researchers, often delving into the natural world around them, collecting, or making conclusions based on keen observation of birds or plants. Some acquired musical instruments and learned to play, a factor that could open additional opportunities for income as well as being personally satisfying. And many wrote in formats aside from autobiography, including and especially poetry, and felt the joy of seeing their works in print.

Of course, genre conventions influenced the degree to which autobiographers focused on their intellectual pursuits, but the degree to which both men and women emphasized the joy of learning over other kinds of recreational activities suggests that autobiographers would have sided with Mill over Bentham. Unlike pushpin, which might provide a moment of fleeting happiness, self-cultivation produced a scaffolding for new knowledge, the building of skills, and continual enjoyment, and enabled individuals to enjoy retelling the stories of their own intellectual development.

SEVEN

The Way of Duty

THE MODERN POSITIVE PSYCHOLOGY MOVEMENT HAS developed more decidedly in the direction of the maximizing of pleasures than in the direction of *eudaimonia*, a good life as defined by the satisfaction of some objective set of life goals.[1] But many working-class autobiographers chose not to write at any length about transitory pleasures. The "good life" that each presented to the world reflected a collection of values and virtues expressed in the doing. For writers in the nineteenth century, a life well lived was likely to have an external definition, based on duty, social recognition, or the usefulness of that life to mankind.[2] To some extent, the autobiographers who dedicated their lives to causes were engaging in prosocial behavior, which, as seen in chapter 4, had its own rewards; but often they encountered long stretches of hardship as they struggled toward their definition of "the good."

Many working-class autobiographers wrote from the perspective of old age, and had the tools to assess whether their lives had been well lived in retrospect. Those who embraced a eudaimoniac definition of happiness as duty fulfilled mainly had dedicated their lives to social, political, or religious change. By the early twentieth century, writing about one's life in trade unionism, social reform, temperance, or religious practice had become a trope, in turn influencing the trajectory of these narratives.[3] Many of the men born in the 1850s and 1860s began their work in politics when the Labour Party emerged as an organization. Some worked as aldermen; others became members of Parliament. Some worked as editors, and others in the temperance movement or in home missionary work.[4]

Many working-class autobiographers were nominally Christian but not particularly formally observant, or, as Nan Hackett has written, they used religious institutions for instrumental purposes like free meals or education.[5] In *Destiny Obscure*, John Burnett argued that for most working-class autobiographers in his sample, religious observance brought neither despair nor joy, and was more associated with fear and anxiety than with other emotions.[6] But many autobiographers defined the good life as the fulfillment of religious duties, participating in the expansive economy of Protestant evangelicalism described by Callum Brown in *The Death of Christian Britain*.[7] Moreover, even awe at the natural world, the joy of self-improvement, or self-sacrifice in the name of scientific progress could be written about in ways that echoed the conversion narrative.[8]

The Conversion Narrative

Autobiographers seeking to proselytize wrote their memoirs in a form that will be familiar to any student of nineteenth-century evangelicalism. They described their pre-conversion ignorant sinfulness: having taken great pleasure in drinking, gambling, swearing, or other vices (or, in the case of Caroline Hopwood, showy dress).[9] Then, some exposure to religion left them uneasy and in a state of fear and contemplation of sin; and then finally, the religious doubts were overcome with a feeling of joy or at least contentment. Their autobiographies show that, particularly for male writers, the religious autobiographical narrative could provide an acceptable space for emotional catharsis.

Conversion narratives often included documentation of mood swings, from the deepest despair to the highest elation. The anonymous handloom weaver who contributed his life story to the *Commonwealth* imagined that he had committed some unpardonable sin, and literally had visions of the devil coming to his bedside before he was assured of grace.[10] The Methodist tanner Jonathan Martin thought that God was communicating with him through his dreams; his behavior was considered so extreme that he was institutionalized.[11] An anonymous Scottish boy, living in Glasgow in the 1820s, tried to make himself sad, convinced that without conviction of sin and painful experiences, religious conversion would never come. "I thought I must weep over sin and have a sadly crushed spirit. To evoke within me these feelings, I read the awful parts of the Bible, alarming books, and would set apart hours to think over my sins and their consequences. Notwithstanding all efforts I never could experience the anguish I thought necessary."[12]

Conversion narratives required both conviction of sin and the experience of having that sin forgiven. Margaret Davidson, a poor but religious Irish woman who had lost her sight to smallpox as an infant, had moments when she longed for death, perceiving no benefit to living since it kept her away from God. The family's minister "exhorted my parents to read diverting books to me, and to send for a physician to inspect into my disorder, but my heart swelled with seraphic joy."[13] Despite her parents' objections, Davidson eventually left home to join a community of Methodists, and for seven years her mood oscillated between fear and delight. "I cannot recollect one week wherein I was not sensible of two very different feelings in my soul . . . I was like one under the scorching influence of the material sun, for three or four days at once—then my soul was refreshed with streams from heaven."[14]

James Nye, an agricultural laborer and Calvinist, believed that because only the elect would attain salvation, every moral failure or sin testified to his own unfitness. Nye loved music—"there is something in music and singing which touches so clean on my natural part that I cannot help being carried away with the sound instead of the substance," he noted. But while he felt happiness when he played for his friends, as soon as he went away again "my conscience would begin to flog me most severely, and then I would promise to go no more. But these promises were soon broke and at it I went again in spite of all my convictions."[15] At the moments in his life when he felt the most spiritually self-assured, Nye was ecstatically happy; after one sermon, "the tears of joy run . . . freely," and soon afterward, as he walked around outside while reading the New Testament, "I walked and read and wept for joy."[16] More often, his self-assurance was undermined by his difficulties with feeding his twelve children, two of whom were invalids for a time; and with repeated legal troubles that threatened the family with eviction. During his periods of darkness and doubt Nye could not bear to go to church; his longest absence lasted three years. "I think that nature never taught this lesson; no nature never can rejoice in tribulation. It is a very easy thing to thank and bless and praise a giving God, but there must be something more than nature to thank and bless and praise a taking God," he mused.[17] Nye was a man at war against himself.

Coming from a very similar Sussex background and eventually sharing exposure to some of the same religious influences, George Mockford described at one point being so short of food that he contemplated kill-ing himself. He was rescued by a helpful Samaritan who gave him work and dinner. A heart problem made it hard for Mockford to hold a job, but he reported feeling ambiguous calls to the ministry. Ultimately, assurance that his soul was saved brought him the greatest happiness. As he describes in his memoir: "The first day I walked out of the house by the river-side, O, the blessed peace I was favoured with! . . . everything in nature looked new; all spoke of the goodness and praise of God . . . I cannot in words describe the blessed state I was in . . . a measure of his happiness lasted several months."[18] Ultimately, all of Mockford's material cares disappeared once he became pastor of a Baptist church.

The Coventry weaver Joseph Gutteridge hit one of his life's lowest points as religious questions filled him with despair. "My mind was so much exercised with these doubts and fears respecting the great mystery of a life hereafter, that I often longed that I might drink of the water of Lethe to *drown in oblivion* the memory of the past and the present." Gutteridge's religiously inspired depression wreaked havoc on his household and on his wife's health. Ultimately, after her untimely death, he became interested in spiritualism, unwilling to contemplate a universe in which she didn't continue to exist in some form. "What is it that upholds the upright man in his day of desolation but the cheering hope of a happy and glorious life hereafter?" he asked his readers.[19]

Eli Ashdown, a miller, experienced whipsawing emotions because he perceived that God was punishing him for his unredeemable sins. Sometimes he had to stop reading the Bible because the prospect of damnation so terrified him. On December 3, 1863, as he walked to the mill, he noted that "all creation seemed happy compared with me; for my breast ached with sorrow; I said in a loud voice, 'I am a lost man! I am a lost man' and the eternal decrees of God seemed to seal my doom." Inside the mill, he opened a window, and "a sense of love and mercy flowed into my soul, and increased until I was lost in wonder, love, and praise. Tears filled my eyes, and my sins and terrors were gone."[20] Ashdown, like many of his co-religionists, felt an entire spectrum of strong emotions: ecstasy, terror, depression, and tears. This emotional cycling continued as Ashdown suffered family illnesses, the death of his eldest son in adulthood, and unexpected obstacles that impelled him to give up the milling business. "Satan wrought on my natural affections, till at times I was almost beside myself in distress and sorrow, feeling my poor children would soon be motherless," he wrote of one episode.[21]

Henry Carter, a Cornish smuggler, was so weighed down by thoughts of his own sinfulness and unworthiness for salvation that he was in a permanent funk: "I had hardly the least hope left of Christ, Heaven, or happyness."[22] Bereaved of his beloved wife, he found himself obsessing about whether she had "gone happy" (that is, had died with assurance of her own salvation). His mood fluctuated with his level of certainty about salvation rather than with his material circumstances, which ranged from captaining his own privateering vessel, to hoeing Indian corn alongside Black farm laborers in Long Island, to being imprisoned during the Napoleonic wars.[23] Convinced that God would be more favorable to him if he practiced self-denial, he habitually under-ate—a fact that had his fellow prisoners begging him to eat—and even, at one point, wrapped a cloth around his body, under his clothes, a sort of "tightening of the belt" intended to make him eat less. His weight dwindled from 200 to 135 lbs.[24] Although he was rarely happy in captivity, Carter described spending so much time in prayer that he was barely cognizant of having a will of his own: "my will was loste in the will of God."[25]

The sailor Joshua Marsden's autobiographical letters to his children testify poignantly to the impact of religious beliefs on the experience of many emotions. As a child, Marsden was terrorized by religious fears, including the fear of "apparitions and spirits."[26] His unsettled mind, troubled with the fear of death, prevented him from having a happy childhood, "for while his companions seemed full of mirth and gladness, he was often pensive, and his heart was torn with inward anguish."[27] Marsden may have been mirroring his mother's depression and anxiety: "Many an hour has your father (then only eleven years old) lain weeping, waking, trembling and agitated beyond measure; not, indeed, on account of his own sins, but through sympathy with the gloomy despairing state of his mother's mind."[28] Eventually Marsden's mother experienced her own conversion experience, becoming a prayerful presence in his life. In response, he rebelled, taking pleasure in dancing, singing, playing cards, and performing practical jokes.[29] He ran away to sea, where he experienced several accidents that wrecked or nearly wrecked his ship. During the last incident he promised God that if he were saved he would serve him always, jumped ship in Wales, and walked two hundred miles to his home. As it was 1795, and Marsden, as an able seaman, was likely to be pressed into the Royal Navy, he began spending time with the Methodists, and became a missionary to British North America at the age of twenty-two. Ultimately, he founded the first Methodist church in Bermuda.[30] As he assessed his life, Marsden concluded that the purpose of life was to be happy—"Happiness is the end and aim of our being"—but that only religion brought true happiness, because only the pleasures of piety were uncorrupted by guilt and regret.[31] "The poorest, possessing this treasure, is rich in eternity's joys," he noted.[32]

Religious autobiographers also chronicled their feelings of shame. William Smith, a poor boy trained as a shoemaker, documented the activities of his pre-conversion youth: participating in and facilitating cockfights, badger-baiting and bear-baiting, working in a public house, hiking, camping, and swimming. Later, when he converted to Methodism and became a part-time preacher, his previous worldly pleasures embarrassed him. "I think I have said enough about my black and sinful way of life that I now write I feel ashamed of it and I say to myself, what pleasure had I seen in those things whereof I am now ashamed. I would give all I have if I could blot out from my memory that part of my life."[33] John Donkin McNaughton, a tailor born in the North Riding of Yorkshire in 1774, had reveled in hedonism for the first thirty-five years of his life, until his landlords introduced him to Methodism. At first he felt shame about his own sinful life; and one of his fellow congregants "told me I should not say anything of the kind, because it would occasion people to conclude that religion makes its professors unhappy."[34]

For religious autobiographers, rejecting hedonism could promote feelings of self-satisfaction. The anonymous printer who wrote *Scenes from My Life* was contemptuous of other working-class people, whom he thought failed to prepare for the future: "If one was to take his stand at the corner of the street, and asking the question, 'What object are you living for?' of each passerby, with power to obtain a truthful answer; what would be the answer of the majority? 'To enjoy myself.' "[35] As a boy, he had been placed as an apprentice with a family of indolent Spitalfields weavers, and remembered himself with "no higher enjoyment than to tattoo his arms, empty a pint of beer at a draught, squirt tobacco juice as far as Bob Mears could and repeat all Dibdin's sea songs."[36] When he grew up, the printer found himself with a sick wife, two children, and a marginal existence. A Methodist class teacher asked him if he was happy, and he responded, "I am poor, and in debt, out of temper with myself and all the world, and over head and ears in every bad habit, not fit to live, and afraid to die."[37] Ultimately, his despair drove him to a religious conversion, which if it did not bring him happiness, at least brought him a "calm confidence."[38]

A religious context could legitimate emotional expressions that might be inappropriate elsewhere. John Wilson, a miner, attended a Primitive

Methodist class meeting shortly after swearing off drinking and gambling. When asked how he was getting along spiritually, he burst into tears of joy:

> It was to me a happy cry. I must let the cynic and sneerer explain it, but he must not do it on the ground that I could be easily made to cry. That statement would be falsified by my life. I had seen too many of life's stern battles to cry, except it was at the sight of other people's distress. In this class meeting there was no distress. All was joy, and not the least joyous was myself, even while the tears were chasing each other down my cheeks.[39]

Wilson here acknowledged to imagined "cynics" and "sneerers" that it was surprising for men to shed tears, but at the same time attempted to push back against perceived rules of working-class male emotional display. Another autobiographer, Robert Roberts, observed rather than participated in the religious enthusiasm that spread through his Welsh valley when he was a boy. He described the emotional wrench produced when a young preacher told the story of "the woman who was a sinner." "Tears streamed down aged cheeks—strong men sobbed with emotion; the hum of voices grew louder, and when he concluded the audience was melted into a strange sort of tearful joy . . . though there were few tearless eyes, there were as few lips that did not wear a contented smile."[40]

A fifer and drum-major who spent seven years posted in India, Robert Butler complained often in his journal that his fellow soldiers drank and swore and consorted with Indian women. He was overjoyed when he managed to locate either religious books or sympathetic company. Finding a copy of Doddridge's *Rise and Progress of Religion in the Soul*, he described being "so overjoyed that I hardly knew that my weak limbs had a body to support . . . I read it over again, until I had almost the whole substance . . . by heart."[41] When he was invalided out of the army and returned to the British Isles, his feelings upon attending a church service for the first time were extreme. "I found it too much for my feelings, for I thought that my heart would have burst with alternate joy and sorrow."[42] Butler's religious feelings invoked the ineffable: "I trust, my dear reader, you will excuse me, when I tell you that I am unable to describe my emotions at this time."[43] Religious ceremonies could provoke an emotional catharsis that was acceptable in few other situations.

Autobiographies written with the purpose of religious witness asserted that real ecstasy could only be found in religious contexts. Birmingham native Henry Holloway, having been ejected from his home by an abusive stepfather, recounted drunken sprees, dancing, boxing, and card playing, interspersed with jail sentences for forgeries that had been intended to raise funds. "On then I went in my mad career, not caring for anything. I picked up new associates—bad men like myself. Having lost sight of going to work again, nothing appeared to remain for me to do but to be a man of the world."[44] Holloway's jailhouse religious conversion resulted in such a state of ecstasy that the prison warden upbraided him for loudly singing hymns at night.[45] Even after his transportation to Gibraltar, Holloway delighted in singing with the prison choir; upon his release, he became a wandering preacher, bringing crowds around by ringing a "gospel bell."[46]

The tailor Thomas Carter described many moments of transcendent bliss, all of which were spurred by thoughts of the afterlife, whether they occurred to him while walking in a graveyard or sitting in church and watching beams of light come down on the congregation through the windows.[47] John Vine Hall spent his young adulthood in bouts of drunkenness that almost led to him losing his life several times as he nearly fell into coal pits. He described a repeated process of becoming blackout drunk, sobering up, regretting the episode, and then hating himself, but the tears he shed over this were God's tears. "The tears ran down my cheeks, I knew not why. The more I tried to suppress them, the more they would flow. Finding it useless to go on with business, I went upstairs; but there I got worse, and I began to think, surely this is the voice of mercy once more calling me to repentance."[48] Over seven years, Hall attempted and failed to stop drinking, and was wracked with liver pain that caused him to contemplate suicide.[49] Only prayer could lift him from grief into paroxysms of joy. "My pain was gone, and my gratitude seemed as if it would drive me into a delirium of joy. Now this may be considered to arise merely from a strong irritation of the nervous system. Well, let all this be called by whatever name it may by others, I would humbly attribute it to the forgiving mercy of God."[50] With the help of a doctor who (surprisingly) had concluded that addiction had a biological basis, Hall weaned himself from any use of alcohol, and eventually became as committed an evangelist as he had been a drinker. In 1821, he wrote a religious tract that would be translated into thirty languages and see the printing of three million copies, and made it his life's work to pass out tracts and bend the ear of everyone he met, "in steam-boats, coaches, railways, omnibuses, and anywhere when opportunity has occurred." "No tongue can tell, no mind can conceive of the ecstasy of my soul when exercised in promoting the glory of God," Hall wrote.[51]

Similarly, the actor, clown, and "man monkey" Harvey Teasdale, although he had enjoyed intermittent success on the stage, rejected his former vice-filled life after having a religious conversion while imprisoned on an attempted murder charge. Once released from prison, Teasdale joined a revival band, and destroyed his former worldly stage props and costumes in front of an audience.[52] Afterward, Teasdale obtained a barrow and became a roving peddler, barely earning enough to support himself, but "I was happier, far happier then, even with poverty and persecution—for I had both—than ever I had been in the possession of wealth and sin."[53]

Some autobiographers fused into a single memoir the idea that life was not primarily meant to revolve around happiness and that only religion promoted happiness. Charles Humphreys, a milk-boy who had some sketchy friends and who drank heavily, found through religion the first unadulterated joy he had ever known. He prayed several times a day for salvation, and "I had just been praying, when a light came over my soul and happiness in my heart, which overwhelmed me, and I shouted for joy . . . I could explain nothing more than I had a heavenly feeling, and so full of joy that I jumped and praised God."[54] Humphreys believed in a "Second Blessing," a second religious conversion that completely purged one of sin. "I had had many and many bright and happy days when there was not a cloud to hide my Saviour from mine eyes, and this experience of what God could do by His grace, led me to believe that what he could help me to do for one day, He could help me to do for weeks and months."[55] When two of his children died suddenly of an illness, the idea that this was God's will, and that God should be praised for allowing two of his other children to survive, conditioned his reaction to what otherwise would have been a tragedy.[56]

At the same time Humphreys, who later became a bookseller and a Salvation Army preacher, considered righteousness rather than happiness to be the goal of human existence. God was not a strictly loving entity, but hated hypocrites and sinners, and Humphreys took it upon himself personally to punish those sins. He proudly described beating his own children when he thought it was necessary, getting into several fistfights with hecklers who interrupted his outdoor meetings, being upbraided by other religious figures for calling his auditors pigs and swine, and calling for the damnation of the Sultan, moneylenders, and barristers who tried to defend obviously guilty clients.[57] "Nearly every ass believes that God loves us all alike. He couldn't be such a fool, He loves you according to what you are worth, what you do and how you do it. In no case bulk, but quality."[58]

As Humphreys's reaction to his children's deaths suggests, religious conversion sometimes promoted happiness by validating fatalism. Sarah Martin did not find happiness in religion until she decided that salvation came only through grace, and thus all her laboring after her own salvation was useless.[59] William Bowcock, a Lincolnshire drillman, warned others to submit entirely to God's will. "There is always something to interrupt our joy and disturb our tranquility. Certainly it is right that it should be so; for if we had everything that the heart could wish, we should be for making this our home, forget our dependency on the Lord, and rob him of his rights."[60] James Dunn, who had to sacrifice dreams of education to enter a coal mine as a young boy, described undergoing a complete mental transformation through religious conversion. For Dunn, belief meant turning over all worldly cares to God. As he lay ill on what his family thought was his deathbed, Dunn said, "I have given up all to Christ, if I live, I live to Him, if I die, I go to Him . . . tell the men at the factory that I have no fear, but am perfectly happy."[61] Circumstances that would have driven Dunn crazy before his conversion were now just a chance for God to surprise him with some exercise of Divine will.[62] Thomas Lewis, a Baptist minister in Wales, despite his "apparent brusqueness," was described as having lived "a well-spent life, rich in labour, service, and abiding fruit."[63] Although he described few moments of happiness—all associated with sermons—he took the notion of duty extremely seriously. The recurrent thought that he was not saving souls left him disconsolate, while the deaths of two of his daughters failed to traumatize him because they were completely compatible with his worldview.[64]

Taking fatalism to its most extreme point led to a sort of Panglossian contentment. The cooper William Hart interpreted Divine Providence as having ordered all things for his good. He interpreted an attack of smallpox as a benevolence, since when he could find no one to lodge him during his illness, he was sent to the pest house to recover at no charge.[65] He even attributed to godly intervention his lack of attraction to his female tenant while her husband was away at sea for eighteen months. "I think that when the Lord leads us into temptation (if I may be allowed the expression) he grants his special race an almighty power to prevent us from being overcome," he mused.[66] Later in life, he credited to Divine Providence his attraction to his first cousin (whom he later married), and the West India Dock Company's decision to raise him to a salary of 105 pounds per year.[67] Toward the end of his life, Hart remembered most the trials that his family had faced, one after another: losing his job and being left with a small pension; failure in business; having to split up his family. His most difficult conundrum was an unemployable son, who fell into "loose and bad habits which brought him and his parents into such troubles and sorrows as tis heartbreaking to reflect on." Nonetheless, Hart was convinced that his son was meant to teach him a moral lesson, even if he could never figure out what that might be.[68]

So far we have seen that religious autobiographers, variously, downplayed worldly happiness, claimed that religious belief was the only thing capable of making humans really happy, or interpreted the world around them as God's plan for their own good within a system that they might not fully understand. Religious belief was also a salve for economic disappointment, since riches were more dangerous to living a good life than was poverty. Edward Anderson wrote, "I envy not the proud, the rich, the great; to riches happiness is not confin'd. For they can never ease a troubled mind: When the world smiles on us the most of all, We are in danger of the greatest fall; The poor it seems are in the safest place, But rich and poor may all be rich in grace."[69] The sea captain Henry Taylor would have agreed: "Gratification of any kind palls the appetite, and a continued sameness of indulgence creates disgust. A chequered life is the best and safest; it makes men thankful for prosperity when they are favoured with it."[70] Isaac Mead, born in Essex in 1859, complained that too much education of the wrong kind had set common people above their place and inflicted them with the disease of envy. "The poor man, too, has his share of troubles, but by making provision for sickness and by thrift, not having too high ambitions, spending only what he can afford, he too can be contented and happy."[71] Similarly, William Henry Lax asserted that happiness had little to do with economic welfare. "You can have abject misery in a palace; I have seen rapturous joy in a slum tenement. Only by bringing one's life into harmony with God's will can one attain that real happiness which is independent of environment or circumstance."[72] William Huntington, a manual laborer, turned to religion after a hernia disabled him from work and his first child died of unknown causes. "My lameness, poverty, distress of mind, suffering of my wife, loss of my child, sense of God's wrath, were the most complicated distresses I had ever felt."[73] With God's help, Huntington could bear hunger, the poverty that condemned him to continue his work as a coal-heaver even while preaching, and the illnesses of his many children.

A few autobiographers did notice that the religious emphasis on the soul-burnishing effects of poverty could conveniently rationalize poverty. The Cornish miner Thomas Oliver served as a preacher for a long time, until he began to develop heterodox views about the soul (none existed), free will (an illusion), and social injustice (perpetuated by greed). After being excommunicated, he noted: "We may pride ourselves on our civilization and quite right too, but I think if ministers of the gospel would preach sermons that are calculated to make happier lives and happier homes instead of prating for half an hour on some mystical subject that can do nothing but mystify their audience, they would do far more to attract people to church."[74] Such criticisms were rare, however.

Finally, religious belief could promote happiness by providing a sociable community of fellow believers or an aesthetically pleasant environment. Rowland Kenney found himself isolated from his fellow Lancashire factory lads by his love of reading and of the English language. Although he was an agnostic, the beauty of the Anglican Church service captivated him.[75] Mary Ann Hearn, born in 1834, wrote religious tracts and lectured under the pseudonym Marianne Farningham. She spent her childhood doing housework, but also daydreaming: "It was a beautiful world of fancy in which I lived, and I saw lovely sights, and did heroic deeds; and my everyday life was beautiful too, for it was filled with love, the joy of doing, and much running about in the open air."[76] Because her father was religious, she was surrounded by the chapel community, with Sundays spent in services and socializing with other parishioners in the vestry. "The joyousness of these Sundays was wonderful. The chapel was the centre of intense love and loyalty."[77]

Although Farningham never married, she formed a household with a school headmistress. "We both loved the fields and the meadows, and took walks to the pretty villages which lie so near to the town, and our home-life was peaceful and joyous."[78] Supposedly because she did not think her appearance would attract a suitor, Farningham filled her life with religious work. She taught Sunday School classes; enjoyed nurturing her students; traveled around the country giving lectures on Christian womanhood; supported herself as a writer; and served as editor of the *Sunday School Times* for over two decades. "In a very real sense my work has been my life," she noted.[79] While autobiographies written by women born before 1870 are rare, collections of women's oral histories from a slightly later date confirm the importance of church- or chapelgoing as a source of sociability, aesthetic pleasure, and even romance for respectable young working-class women.[80]

David Kirkwood, whose major interests were economic and political, associated the "gladdest days of my life" with the Sabbath morning children's meeting at the local church, led by the charismatic "Mister Buchanan," a man so warm and friendly that Kirkwood summoned up

Buchanan's mental picture every time someone mentioned Christ.[81] Henry Snell called his association with the Unitarian chapel and school "the happiest experience of my young life" (until he was banished from the school for being a bad influence on the other young people, which transformed the experience into his greatest grief).[82] William Henry Lax, who grew up to be a Methodist minister in London's Poplar section, remembered his early religious life as "jolly," enabling him to enjoy himself to the full.[83] Of his Sundays, spent entirely in either church or Sunday school, he argued that "when I compare those Sundays with the Sundays of today, spent in open disregard of divine sanctions and in frantic seeking after pleasure, without finding it; in futile pretense of happiness, I declare that for thrill and for satisfaction those old days far surpassed the present."[84]

Social and Political Reform

Even as religiously motivated autobiographies had clearly delineated generic features, some of those same features were carried over by working-class autobiographers who embraced nonreligious righteous causes. Many of these causes—including temperance—were energized by Protestant evangelicalism, and some working men came to organizing with religious experiences in their backgrounds.[85] Joseph Livesey catalyzed the temperance movement in Britain from its very beginnings in Preston in the 1830s. He edited a newspaper, *The Moral Reformer*, and crossed the countryside giving temperance lectures. He so firmly embraced abstinence from alcohol that even when he was ill and writhing with pain, and his doctor prescribed medicinal wine, he refused to take it, on the grounds that if it did make him feel better, then this would be a good advertisement for alcohol.[86] He spent much of his time in slums, but "though pained at what I witnessed, I always felt pleased that I had sought out the wretched and miserable, especially the great sufferers through drink, and had secured the opportunity of giving them good advice and encouragement amid their poverty." Livesey enjoyed his work among the poor; "I feel happier at any time at the fireside of a poor man's cottage, chatting with his family, than in the drawing room of my richest friend," he professed.[87] But most of all, he liked the feeling of being useful: "My notions of life are very simple, for man, I believe, is the happiest when removed from either poverty or riches, has tolerable health, and is pursuing day by day a useful object."[88]

One of Livesey's protégés, Thomas Whittaker, saw his life as literally a series of battles for teetotalism. Commitment to total abstinence from alcohol was so controversial that it earned him physical beatings from drinkers. Even so, he called temperance work "a joy to us, and our success was our reward." He had occasional moments of extreme happiness: "At times my delight was so great that I shouted, and literally ran and jumped."[89] But for the most part, he saw the good life as the fulfillment of duty. "Entertainment is not life, it may do as paper and string to wrap up life, but it is not life," he opined. "The greatest luxury in the world is the luxury of doing good." Occasionally, Whittaker met people who told him what an impact his temperance lecturing had made on their lives: "these things are constantly happening to me, and they are the sunlight in my evening sky."[90] A third temperance reformer, James McCurrey, had no regrets about investing his energy even though drinking continued to flourish in Britain: "We, a mere handful of humble men, attacked the most popular delusion, the most seductive vice, the established national sin . . . our only weapons were truth and energy."[91]

While the connection between evangelicalism and temperance is obvious because drink was thought to cause sin, many completely nonreligious causes were animated by the same energy to improve mankind. Will Thorne, an overworked brickmaker who ultimately led one of Britain's largest trade unions, described his life story as a continuous struggle to save others from the horrendous working conditions he had experienced as a child and young man. He recalled early workdays that involved hours of lifting bricks, bookended by long walks to and from his employment. After working as a navvy and a gas worker, Thorne rose to lead the Gasworkers' and General Labourer's Union. "My new duties as secretary of the union brought longer hours, and an even greater strain on my mental and physical resources, than the hard labour of the gasworks. But I was working for more than wages. I was working for the lives of men, women and children. The work was as a religion, a holy mission. I gloried in it."[92] He closed his memoir with a promise to continue the work until he died, and noted, "I can never forget the horror of my childhood days and the misery and suffering I have seen, and if I can leave the world a better place than I have found it I shall die content."[93]

John Hodge, a Scottish steelworker who later became a trade union official and then an MP and cabinet member, also portrayed his own life as less important than the virtues of honesty and fair play that he sought to propagate. Hodge described himself as a peacemaking voice of reason, who always emphasized that employer and employee could act in harmony if they had properly cultivated trust. When Hodge felt he deserved a pay raise, he simply enumerated the ways he had saved his employer money or had increased productivity, and expected that these explanations would constitute an unassailable argument. When a company experienced prosperous times, Hodge expected that company to reward its employees, and when the economy declined, that the company would make protecting jobs a top priority. Later, during the First World War, Hodge managed a pension fund for disabled veterans, to which he applied the same expectations: that justice to the disabled was part of the contract made with soldiers.[94] One of Hodge's only references to happiness occurred on the last page of his memoir, as he assessed his life's contribution: "I carry away with me many pleasant memories and happy thoughts of many friendships of long standing that nothing can shake. I have had a long innings. If that innings has given joy and pleasure to many and injury to none, then I am happy and content in the results of my life's work."[95]

While creating the persona of a self-sacrificing tribune of the people might be seen as self-aggrandizement, the autobiographers who created such personas had vision of the "good life" that went beyond personal well-being. The Spencean radical and shoemaker Thomas Preston found himself convinced by the arguments of Corresponding Societies to advocate for reform:

> Ardent, young and cheerful, I found I possessed a heart, that before never knew its office; I found that I had confined that sympathy and affection to private circles, which was due to the whole nation. Nor were my wishes confined to England; I thought, and (I have ever since cherished the principle,) that the great universal mass of society ever claims the impartial attention of the political philanthropist. He who truly loves liberty loves her everywhere.[96]

As if to burnish his own reputation, Preston recounted the many times he relieved other poor families out of his own scanty savings. "Without ostentation, I declare, that I have, on numberless occasions, parted with my last shilling to the poor and needy," he noted. Preston was jailed for his political beliefs, accused of treason, tried and found not guilty, and reiterated to readers of his autobiography that he would continue to direct his efforts to "that parliamentary purity (which reform only can effect)."[97]

The notion of duty to humanity was so pervasive that it could structure narratives of nonbelievers. The printer James Watson, a proponent of freethought and Owenite socialism, in 1834 was jailed for a third time in connection with the sale of unstamped newspapers. He wrote to his wife, Ellen, noting that his only goal in life was to make "you happy and endeavouring as far as possible to make the world, or rather its inhabitants, more comfortable."⁹⁸ Watson's professed disinterestedness in his own happiness continued, as he became a prominent Chartist, and then a supporter of the Mazzinian revolutionary movement of the late 1840s. The "severe and self-denying" nature of his life earned him a written encomium from his friend William James Linton: "The evening of his life was worthy of the morning. Happy in his home with a wife who loved and honoured him; loved and honoured too by many friends . . . he had the well-deserved reward of all his conscientious work, his self-denial and devotedness for the good of others."⁹⁹

Nor was Watson the only Chartist autobiographer who sought to fulfill duties toward his fellow men. John James Bezer described an early life of almost unremitting misery, broken only by exposure to literacy (*Pilgrim's Progress*) and a short stint of happy work in a Camberwell garden. In Bezer's telling, as a child he suffered from the ills of society. His father, a barber with a drinking problem, had been psychologically damaged by mistreatment while in naval service, and his mother could not afford to support the family. Bezer himself only had one useful eye, having lost the other through a bout with smallpox. Without money, Bezer could not be properly apprenticed, and so only learned slop shoemaking work. When he lost his job, he took to begging in the streets, and found that even the Mendicity Society had rules verging on the Kafkaesque, preventing him from taking bread and cheese home to his starving wife and child. For Bezer, the decision to become a Chartist was the most momentous act of agency taken in a life of prior helplessness.¹⁰⁰

Similarly, the printer and later reporter W. E. Adams, who spent his early career as a Chartist and then a Republican, was convinced that there was more to happiness than "beer and skittles. Higher aspirations entered our heads, suffused our thoughts, coloured our dreams. 'Happiness,' we had been told, 'is a poor word: find a better.' "¹⁰¹ For Adams, as a young man, "better" meant living in a barebones printers' cooperative, then tramping around the country in one uncomfortable situation after another, even suffering fleas if it meant being able to distribute Republican tracts. Despite their poverty, Adams and his fellow Republicans also donated funds to advance revolutions in Europe.¹⁰² Robert Lowery dedicated his young manhood to the Chartist movement and later became a temperance lecturer, believing that both causes would increase the general happiness by alerting people to simple changes that would better their lives. "History informs us that our forefathers were free and happy . . . we work harder than they did . . . if so, how is it that so many of our countrymen are starving, sinking into an early grave from over-labour and want?"¹⁰³

William Lovett, who hardly ever mentioned being happy or pleased after having reached adulthood, threw himself into social and political reform efforts, including Chartism. Lovett thought men could achieve happiness only when they had the right to make their own political decisions. For Lovett, "virtual representation"—the notion that each MP represented the entire kingdom rather than a particular constituency—was unlikely to result in good policy. Given that people often had difficulty identifying their own best interests, representatives operating at one remove were even less likely to promote the best interests of all.[104] When direct petitioning of the government to extend the right to vote failed, Lovett optimistically turned to advocating education, since in his opinion an intelligent and well-informed populace (something that workers had the potential to become) simply could not be denied the right to speak freely and to make their own decisions. His vision of a future with an educated populace, encapsulated in an address by the London Working Men's Association, was almost utopian:

> Imagine the honest, sober and reflecting portion of every town and village in the kingdom linked together as a band of brothers, honestly resolved to investigate all subjects connected with their interests, and to prepare their minds to combat with the errors and enemies of society—setting an example of propriety to their neighbours, and enjoying even in poverty a happy home. And in proportion as home is made pleasant, by a cheerful and intelligent partner, by dutiful children, and by means of comfort, which their knowledge has enabled them to snatch from the ale-house, so are the bitters of life sweetened with happiness.[105]

For Lovett and members of the Working Men's Association, education would produce universal happiness by emphasizing the brotherhood of mankind.[106]

John Bedford Leno, also a printer and Chartist, showcased his political participation and commitment to working-class causes. "In my long term of life, I have had but one strong desire and that has been justice and freedom to all mankind," he noted. "For what thought can be more consoling than that you have avoided doing injury to others, striven your best to uplift them and striven to adhere to personal principles?"[107] Emmanuel Lovekin, of Donnington Wood, Salop, a low-level Chartist organizer, declared, "I even thought myself Somebody. I felt very earnest in the work I had to do, which was not very small, meeting almost every night," and at one point attending a meeting of twenty thousand people.[108] Chartist autobiographies and autobiographies of religious missionaries illustrate a common set of values, in which individual happiness was de-prioritized in favor of larger uplift.

Chartist autobiographers set the pattern for subsequent generations of working-class activists. Born decades after William Lovett, the syndicalist activist Tom Mann represented himself as having had a similarly single-minded commitment to reform. Although he was married and had several children, Mann never mentioned his family in his autobiography, as he traveled around the globe, ejected from one country after another for his radical lecturing.[109] In some places, the only reception he received was hostile, but he described such instances of cultivating "virgin soil" as a pleasant challenge. For Mann, to work toward the true freedom of the working man was almost a religious goal. "To engage in this work is to be occupied in the noblest work the earth affords," he wrote, and "I look for the coming of associations of equals, working co-operatively to produce with the highest efficiency, and simultaneously to care for the physical and mental wellbeing of all."[110]

The Socialist politician George Lansbury professed his dedication to the proposition that "human life and human happiness were much more valuable than all the property in the world." He supported civil disobedience by women's suffrage advocates, and served two short prison terms for these and similar beliefs.[111] Lansbury began and ended his autobiography with a paean to the friendship of those he had worked alongside. He cherished the memory of their optimism and fight. "In doing this we are confident that we have gained more of true satisfaction, more of the real joy of life through participation in the struggles on behalf of impersonal causes than would have been possible under any other conditions." Lansbury stated that while neither he nor his wife ever became financially independent, they felt "privileged to be soldiers in the army of the workers, engaged in the task of overcoming ignorance and establishing the Kingdom of Love."[112] Lansbury anticipated a Socialist millennium, not just in Great Britain, but also in the Soviet Union, a place he greatly admired.

The Socialist Frank Kitz described a life similarly dedicated to high moral seriousness. In his memoir Kitz placed himself within a much larger picture: the development of the Socialist, Anarchist, and Communist movements, not only in Britain but also in Germany and the United States. He wrote his narrative to advance this great movement and to provide a long-term perspective for those young people new to the cause. He viewed his life as emblematic of the lives of an entire class at the time:

I decorated the walls of my lonely room with pictures of the French Revolution, which I purchased out of my scanty earnings. Brought up in the neighborhood of the West End, with the evidences of wealth and luxury confronting me—wealth unearned, comfort undeserved—and with my own undeserved hardships, I needed no lectures upon surplus value or dissertations upon economics to cause me to challenge the justice of a system which confers wealth upon the parasites of society and clouds the lives of thousands.[113]

Kitz's particular happiness paled before the importance of the Socialist movement's success.

Commitment to the uplift of humankind could create cognitive dissonance because of the hardship that the life of duty could pose to autobiographers' families. Jack Jones, a successful public speaker and local secretary for the Miners' Federation in Wales, realized when his wife became ill that he had neglected his family while pursuing political causes. This realization brought him to tears.[114] John McAdam also struggled with the conflict between doing right by his family and doing good. After twenty years spent in Canada and the United States, McAdam returned to his native Glasgow in 1847 and, for the rest of his life, worked for the cause of Continental revolutionary movements. Materially and morally, he supported Kossuth, Mazzini, and Garibaldi, even traveling to Naples to visit British troops who were there working for Italian unification. In his autobiography, McAdam said almost nothing about his own family, except in a concluding paragraph:

> In this quiet corner provided by my exceptionally industrious and well-doing family, I sometimes ask myself, what has often been asked of me, whether I have done right in devoting so much of my time and means towards these great national questions. As regards my own family I admit frankly that I ought to have studied their interests *first* rather than the interests of strangers, but I had for many years been interested in them before I had any family, and I could not desert those brave men while struggling for national existence ... After all I took great pleasure in it. [115]

Other autobiographers kept their comments about family to a minimum. The farmworker-unionizer Joseph Arch produced an autobiography with little discussion of childhood or of family pleasures. Although he complimented his partner as "a good, clean wife and a good mother," he also complained that "she was no companion to me in my aspirations."[116] Arch sought not to maximize his own happiness, but rather to maximize the independence and autonomy of his fellow laborers. Ironically, even though it was probably not his professed goal, he also achieved public recognition for himself.[117] He presented his life as a telos. To hear him tell it, he had learned the importance of independence from his mother, who refused to be dictated to by the parson's wife; built his own material independence, one ill-paid farm labor job at a time; and then built the Agricultural Labourers' Union, almost single-handed, so that "the lower classes of society [might] rise and become thrifty, and provident, and happy, with plenty to eat and plenty to do, with good wages fairly earned, and then every other class of society will be raised, will be strong and happy in proportion."[118] Another agricultural union organizer, George Edwards, was hardly at home from one week to the next, putting over six thousand miles on his bicycle in a single year. Nonetheless, this accorded with his idea of the good life. "In spite of the hard work and the long weary miles I cycled on lonely roads, often late at night, still it was a pleasant year's work, as I felt I was building up an organization that would accomplish some great thing for this long-neglected class."[119]

On the other side of the political spectrum, but on the same issue, William Collison was a soldier in the battle against Trade Unionism and Socialism. Collison was born into poverty in Stepney and worked as an omnibus driver and dockworker. But run-ins with his trade-union colleagues over minor matters, and his exclusion from dockwork because he was no longer a member of a trade union, made trade unionists his enemies for life. Financially supported by employers, Collison founded the National Free Labour Association, funneling strikebreakers to the sites of bitter industrial disputes before the First World War.[120] Except briefly during childhood, Collison never described his own happiness; he was often angry. He nearly killed a striking worker, and was prosecuted on numerous occasions, either for defending women of the upper classes from what he described as vile language by workmen, or ejecting trespassers from the NFLA offices.[121] In the last chapter of his autobiography, entitled "The Apologia," Collison portrays the battle between trade unionists and strikebreakers as part of the eternal cycling of the human condition, a battle between good and evil that goes back as far as recorded history. "There is eternity in me, William Collison, the strike breaker and the enemy of Trade Unionism. As they rise up from their ashes, so shall I arise from mine, and so shall we renew our world old antagonism. We fought each other thousands of years ago, and it may be that we are destined to fight thousands of years hence."[122] Like Nietzsche, Collison celebrated the *Übermensch*, except his ideal man was the skilled workman, free to strike whatever bargain he could with his employer. "The unfit and the inefficient will always organize and combine," Collison sneered.[123]

Self-Sufficiency

Karen Chase Levenson has argued that Victorian middle-class society broadly embraced utilitarian versions of happiness as the individual pursuit of pleasure and avoidance of pain, but that this conception of happiness, although dominant in literature, was not exhaustive.[124] As in literature, so in life: many of the most interesting conceptions of happiness were not utilitarian. As we have seen, one way to configure the "good life" in Victorian Britain was to help mankind. Another was to fulfill social expectations even at great personal cost. Being financially self-sufficient was a cornerstone of Victorian masculinity. Many Victorian autobiographers from the midcentury on, in the mold of Samuel Smiles, considered their lives to have been successful if they had been able to raise themselves from working class to middle class or higher by dint of their own exertions. So William Ablett used his knack for selling clothing—he was such an accomplished salesman that he was able to convince patrons to buy goods above the retail price—into his own clothing shop and ultimately a shop in the fashionable West End.[125] George Mitchell began life as an immiserated farm laborer, but insisted on learning stonemasonry although no one would take him on as a regular apprentice, and was eventually able to leverage his hard work into large construction contracts.[126]

An anonymous weaver whose short memoir was published in the *Kendal Mercury* in 1841 described a life of great abstemiousness, hard work, and self-improvement through saving and through mechanics' institutes. Although he made no reference to happiness in the sense of joyousness, he equated well-being with economic self-sufficiency: "You must cease paying attention to those men who tell you that happiness is to come from others, and not from yourselves; depend upon it, you have more power over your own happiness than any other person or persons."[127] John Passmore Edwards's autobiography embodied high moral seriousness; "Do the best for the most" is the epigram that appears on the work's title page. Born into a poor Cornish family, Passmore Edwards leveraged ill-paying work as a reporter into the purchase of a series of magazines. When these failed, he made paying back his creditors the pole star of his existence. He served on committees promoting peace and free trade and temperance; he gave lectures for mechanics' institutes on the importance of dedicating one's life to good causes.[128] After finally achieving financial success, Passmore Edwards decided to repay society, not out of philanthropy but out of duty, which he considered to be prior to, and superior to, philanthropy. He donated buildings for twenty-four public libraries, and a number of mechanics' institutes, hospitals, asylums, convalescent homes, and even drinking fountains, all with the guiding philosophy that national strength depended on developing the abilities of the British people.[129] "I entertain an idea that every sunbeam that kisses the earth enriches the earth, and that every disinterested act performed by one person for the benefit of another person enriches the performer or receiver, or both, and survives both."[130]

Finally, some who saw fulfillment of duty as the central value to be maximized in life embraced neither politics nor religion. The tailor Thomas Carter, born in 1792, explicitly traded his own enjoyment for a good life based on the fulfillment of duties. As a young child, he was frequently ill, and found children's games exhausting. His parents put him to work knitting and doing other household chores. While he found these responsibilities unpleasant, he credited them with keeping him on the path to respectability.[131] Carter remembered avoiding other children at school and staring out the window, "almost losing myself in vague yet delightful anticipations of the happiness which I then hoped to realize even in this life. This, however, has proved to be a waking dream; yet it was a dream so delightful, that I could wish to have it repeated, almost at the certain expense of a similar disappointment."[132] At first, Carter thought that if he could just acquire a certain material standard of living, he might acquire happiness. Later, he bitterly chastised himself for ever having entertained such naïve thoughts.[133] As an adult, Carter made few friends, since he disapproved of what he considered to be the dissipated habits of people of his class, but he assessed his life positively because he carried out his duties toward his family despite his debilitating chronic asthma and the loss of several of his children.[134] Defending his choice of virtue over pleasure, Carter wrote,

> I would not exchange the pleasure which is derivable from the seemingly unpromising sources that are within my reach for any amount of the childish, trifling, and irrational mirth which too frequently is dignified by the name of pleasure. I am bold to affirm that it is not only possible, but also comparatively easy, to draw certain, that the review of any given portion of time spent in the discharge of these

important and imperative duties will afford a vastly larger amount of mental satisfaction than can, under any circumstances, be drawn from the recollection of merely trifling and perhaps vitiating pleasures. To have contributed in any degree towards either the present or the future well-being of relatives or friends, or to have lent a helping hand to the great work of social improvement, whether physical or moral, must ever call up far more pleasurable reflections than any that can follow upon a course of mere amusement.[135]

While he professed commitment to the well-being of relatives and friends, Carter condemned Chartism, socialism, republicanism, and large public gatherings.[136] Even if Carter's focus on fulfilling duties was mostly psychological adaptation to a nonoptimal situation, it enabled him to sort through his life and give value to his sacrifices.

Even those who committed themselves to a notion of duty that they were never able to achieve could consider their lives well lived. Peter Gabbitass, the former carpenter turned "Clifton Poet," dragged a large barrow with his own printed verses to and from the marketplace, where he stood outside in all weathers. He thought he provided a public service, and lamented that the public did not understand the importance of materially providing for the poet, "especially when he is battling with the evils of the age, and trying to uplift mankind into a purer, nobler, and a better life."[137] Similarly embracing the idea of eudaimonia, the shoemaker and poet Robert Askham adjusted his expectations: "I shall never, perhaps, get all my wishes fulfilled with regard to devoting myself to literature, but whoever got all he wanted? I am blessed beyond thousands of my class. I have general good health, obedient children, a kind wife, a willing heart to work as long as I am able, and hitherto I have kept out of debt." Askham's biographer characterized him as "hopeful."[138]

· · · · · ·

As this chapter has shown, many working-class autobiographers gravitated toward a version of the good life that prioritized duty—to family, to God, to their oppressed fellow men, to social uplift—over positive emotional states. Autobiographers who underwent religious conversion set up expectations for the genre. The greatest variety of emotional expression appeared in religious memoirs, since the shift from conviction of sin to assurance of salvation was supposed to be accompanied by emotional whipsawing, from tears to ecstasies. Even within religious memoirs, however, authors expressed a range of views about religion and happiness, from the ecstasy of salvation to the lower-key enjoyment of religious community to the contentment that accompanied fatalism.

The autobiographies in this chapter show that working people had a more complex definition of the good life than a focus on happiness as hedonism would account for. Commitment to the success of Chartism or Teetotalism or a trade union organizing campaign could sometimes bring the personal contentment that accompanied dedication to a virtuous cause, but these activities were often associated with drudgery, disappointment, the inability to spend much time with family, or even imprisonment, depending on the cause and the era. Even the role of breadwinner or family provider could structure a vision of the good life that transcended personal happiness. Autobiographers comforted themselves by viewing their social or political work as a step toward a man-made millennium; if they were not around to see it, they could at least take comfort in having brought it closer.

EIGHT

Absent Happiness

AS SARAH AHMED HAS POINTED OUT, the conditions of happiness may not be available to everyone. We can learn something about the nature of happiness in the nineteenth century by noticing where reference to happiness is missing. If autobiographers writing about their own happiness helped by pointing out the objects of happiness, authors who were not happy raised public consciousness about the structures that made happiness unattainable.[1] Some autobiographies contained no reference to happiness—not because their authors were following the way of religious or social duty, but rather because their lives were so immiserated due to poverty or physical pain that they lacked the ingredients for human flourishing. These autobiographies constitute their own, jeremiad-like genre, intended to explain the bitterness of their lives or to settle long-standing scores; happiness appears by its absence, as deprivation. As this chapter will show, some autobiographies failed to reference happiness due to pain, illness, or disability. Other authors lacked the basic necessities of life, including food, safety, health, and human dignity. Still other authors seem to have assumed their emotional lives were of no interest to readers, lacked the language to talk about their emotions, or didn't have the time or inclination to reflect on how they felt about a world in which they lacked much agency.

The fact that some lives were largely unhappy produced discomfort. The soldier and later police inspector John Pearman grappled with this discomfort in his own memoir: "My firm belief is that man was sent into the world to be happy and joyful as all animated nature are." Happiness could be the lot of any man who didn't think too deeply about acquiring happiness: "I must say I done very well in the Police Force. But as I said before it is not a happy life. But what I am thinking of how much of happiness is the lot of the poor. The more he thinks the less is his happiness my idea is the less a poor man is taught the more happiness he will enjoy as he is more content with his hard life."[2] Some types of media—stories about Victorian street children, for example—acted as spaces for middle-class readers to exercise their feelings of pity. But the fact that autobiographies lacking happiness may have evoked pity in some readers should not detract from the fact that these were real working people's lived experiences, and that they pointed to social and political shortcomings in an otherwise prosperous country.[3]

Pain, Illness, and Disability

Autobiographers with illnesses or disabilities operated in an environment in which unhappiness and physical pain had already been firmly linked. Nineteenth-century literature emphasized the connection between pain and unhappiness, portraying people with pain, illness, or disabilities as objects of either pity or menace. As Avi Ohry writes, "Disabled or deformed children are depicted as innocent victims, while their older counterparts are most often viewed as corrupt victimizers whose physical deformities are outward manifestations of their inner depravity."[4] Tiny Tim from Dickens's *Christmas Carol*, with his apparently life-shortening unspecified orthopedic ailment, and Bessy Higgins of Elizabeth Gaskell's *North and South*, dying of tuberculosis contracted in a workplace full of cotton fluff, are heart-rending examples of the former, while Mr. Smallweed of Dickens's *Bleak House*, unable to walk and constantly nagging "Shake me up, Judy!" represents the latter. Nor did working-class people fit into the stereotype of genteel, middle-class invalidism embodied by Willkie Collins and Harriet Martineau.[5]

Physical pain, illness, or disability could be a barrier to happiness but also a reason to write an autobiography, either to appeal to the public for economic help or as a kind of narrative therapy. Elizabeth Storie recounted a significant turn in her fortunes at the age of four, when health and happiness were replaced by "a life of suffering and misery without redress." An incompetent physician had dosed her with so much mercury and hydrochloric acid that her mouth disintegrated, her cheek skin fused to her gums, and her clenched jaw blocked food from entering, so that she had to be fed through a straw. Her narrative, published with the aid of charitable subscriptions, detailed her relentless pursuit of the doctor in court, the legal system's denial of her claim at all levels, and even the local minister's refusal to grant her communion. By her own description, she ended up "depressed by permanent bodily suffering—deprived of the power of speech—disfigured and disabled in appearance by medical experimental abuse—subjected to the contumely of the thoughtless, wanton, inconsiderate and unfeeling, and still, with any strength I had, compelled to struggle for my bread."[6] The publication of her story was part of that struggle.

John Munday, born in 1821, lived a life of abjection after the premature death of his mother. The closest he got to recounting happiness was a memory of working as a cow-keeper in early life, one of the only times he had plenty to eat and drink. As was the strategy among some working-class families at the time, Munday slept on the streets while his brothers lived in the workhouse.[7] Too poor to be apprenticed, he eventually picked up enough knowledge of plastering to work in construction, but this trade subjected him to one injury after another: a split-open forehead, a permanent back injury that left him in lifelong pain, and a lost eye.[8]

Josiah Bassett spent his early years in and out of workhouses, and was never formally apprenticed because he seemed incapable of learning. He briefly mentioned falling in with "wicked boys" at the ropework where he was employed turning a wheel, but the "fairs, races, plays, and other places of amusement" did not bring him any lasting happiness.[9] Bassett existed hand-to-mouth; he traveled from the northern tip of Scotland to Cornwall and Wales, relying on shelter and charity for every meal. On the occasions when he had the material good fortune to be locked up in a house of correction where food was supplied, he had nothing more interesting to pass the time than to count off the seconds of each minute on his hands.[10] Ultimately, according to the minister who heavily edited his autobiography, Bassett's greatest joy came from joining the Church.[11] But even after a religious "conversion" in jail, Bassett felt confused that this experience had brought him neither mental comfort nor physical comfort; he was often the butt of mean-spirited pranks and the victim of theft.

Thomas Jackson entered the militia at the age of seventeen and was assigned to the Coldstream Guards. He and his regiment enjoyed themselves immensely until they were sent to Holland to fight in the wars against Napoleon. At the 1814 Battle of Bergen-op-Zoom, Jackson sustained a grave leg injury, was taken prisoner, and kept in wretched conditions while his leg festered. When he finally was discovered and returned to the British side of the conflict through a prisoner exchange, an old surgeon amputated his suppurating leg with a dull saw. The bone fragments embedded in his leg caused inflammation every time he tried to walk, an ordeal that dragged on more than a year. As much as he resented his luck, he, like Elizabeth Storie, resented people's stares even more, and he brooded because passersby failed to thank him for his military service.[12]

After his injury Jackson and his wife had two children, but her death at the age of thirty-four yoked Jackson with all the responsibility for supporting his children. Like many workers who had sustained injuries, he was able to do light work, keeping the books for a coal-seller for a while, then turned to teaching school (a job that he hated) and then finally working as a plater. Remarriage alleviated some of the pressure, but in 1832, he and his second wife nearly died in a cholera epidemic. By the time he reached his fifties, Jackson was obsessed by health anxiety, and began to understand the relationship between his mental state and the way that he narrated his life to himself. "The cowardly nervous mind, incubus-like, is constantly brooding over dismal things, and ruminating on fearful, visionary bodings, such as poverty, misery, and death, with a thousand other illusive thoughts, calculated to still depress the brooding spirit."[13]

As Jackson's example illustrates, the availability of prosthetic limbs, the expectation that employers would find light work for people injured on the job, and the variety of tasks available at the workplace before the assembly line helped to mitigate injured workers' economic situations by providing opportunities. Still, the lack of structured social provision for people whose illness or disability left them unable to work put the risk and responsibility on the impacted people and on their families, with some assistance from Poor Law unions or friendly society and sick club payouts.[14] For those who were unable to work, the home might provide an adequate level of care for a person with a disability who needed help with the activities of daily life, but income remained a problem.[15] In their study of miners who were injured in the workplace, David Turner and Daniel Blackie note that serious injuries could inflict emotional harm by inverting the gender dynamics of the family—forcing male breadwinners to depend on wives and children—which could lead to domestic violence. On the other hand, surviving a disabling accident could be read as a miraculous deliverance by God and an opportunity to display "Christian cheerfulness." Thus, the onus was on the individual to adjust to their challenges.[16]

Autobiographers appear to have felt pressure to temper their expectations about happiness. Jane Andrew, an invalid dependent on her brother for her entire life, mentioned no moments of happiness, but found compensation in the idea that happiness was not really the purpose of life. "As to all my trials and afflictions, which have been neither few nor small, they have all been sent for my soul's good," she argued.[17] A disabled seller of nutmeg-graters whom Henry Mayhew interviewed endorsed this position, noting, "I've always been led to think He's afflicted me as He has for some wise purpose or another that I can't see. I think as mine is so hard a life in this world, I shall be better off in the next."[18]

Disabled working people might also console themselves with the thought that their suffering could heighten their anticipation of continuous contentment in the afterlife. The velvet weaver John Leatherland was injured in an omnibus accident, confined to bed with a hugely swollen side and in excruciating pain. When he had recovered he noticed that just being able to walk outside filled him with exquisite pleasure. "The thrill of pleasurable sensation experienced seemed to compensate for the suffering endured, suggesting the thought that perhaps the natural evils to which all are more or less doomed in this world, are mean only to enhance the appreciation and intensity of the bliss in that angelic state when 'sorrow and sighing shall forever flee away!' "[19]

The right social support could buffer the experience of disability. A best-case scenario is illustrated by the life of John Kitto, who lost his hearing at the age of twelve. While working with his father to slate a house roof, the boy fell thirty-five feet from a ladder and ended up with a deafening head injury. Unlike congenital or acquired blindness, acquired deafness was not necessarily thought to preclude many types of employment.[20] While he was also put out to work long hours at an unspecified manual labor job, Kitto was lucky enough to have access to books.[21] Ultimately he learned enough to support himself through his writing, including a two-part book called *The Lost Senses*. The first section, largely autobiographical, explored his experience of deafness. Although he had lost all the beauty of hearing nature, he "developed a sense of the beautiful in nature and art, and a love for it—a passionate love—which has been to me a source of my most deep and pleasurable emotions."[22] He loved looking at physical landscapes and enjoyed travel, in some ways having fewer issues with communication than people who struggled with a language barrier. Kitto even enjoyed parties, usually enlisting a friend to sit with him in a corner and translate the flow of the conversation to him using finger-spelling. His one notable regret was his inability ever to hear his young children's voices, and his major fear that he would not hear danger, such as a fire, or traffic approaching him from behind; but he was embedded within a community of family and friends who ensured that he didn't have to struggle by himself. Kitto's happiness demonstrates adaptation to circumstances, but also a more favorable set of circumstances than some other working-class deponents with disabilities.

Poverty

Poverty was another major obstacle to happiness. Some working people lived lives of such economic marginality that happiness seemed to pale beside the goals of a full belly or a little bodily comfort.[23] Unlike the "waif stories" so popular among reformist late-nineteenth-century writers and readers, the autobiographies of the poor did not necessarily have a satisfying narrative arc culminating in religious and physical salvation.[24] Isaac Anderson, who worked as a farm laborer in Essex, remembered being hungry enough to pilfer eggs, to eat water and flour, and feeling "so fatigued and hungered I could have eaten my fingers if it had been possible. I could scarcely walk home at the end of a day's work."[25] George Atkins Brine, "King of the Beggars," begged enough to eat, but his existence was monotonous. The names of the men and women who accompanied him on the road changed, and his days were punctuated with stints in jail or in the workhouse. Every time Brine's life settled into stability or he earned a little money, he spent it all on alcohol, repeatedly regaining sobriety only to realize that he was again destitute. He did not give the reader a sense that this cycle was in any way enjoyable.[26]

J. H. Crawford's *Autobiography of a Tramp* documented a similar experience, exacerbated by the fact that the poorest Britons were looked upon as barely human. Its protagonist, young Dick, had never lived in a house in his life. His parents miserably subsisted by selling baskets made out of reeds and eating vermin they were able to catch in the countryside, or else whatever they could steal. Dick and his family lived completely outside the boundaries of respectable society, earning the angry glares of pub-owners, policemen, and even churchgoers. To add insult to injury, Dick's father alternated between deserting the family and physically abusing Dick's mother, who ultimately died as the result of the father's abuse.[27] Another desperately poor autobiographer, William Marcroft, was a second-generation unfortunate. When his mother Sally was pregnant, his father's family refused to allow the couple to marry, so she gave birth to William in a poorhouse. A second baby, with the same father, died immediately after birth. Sally Marcroft supported herself and her son as best she could by sewing, but ended up marrying a man who earned very little himself, in order to escape sexual pressuring by the father of her first two children. This marriage resulted in a large number of births and infant deaths, and then in Sally Marcroft's institutionalization for mental illness. Her son, by this time a teenager, was forced to support himself and his younger siblings, and lived what he described as a completely joyless existence.[28]

While some autobiographers suffered from both poverty and the deprivation of dignity, others were unhappy because their lives, as they lived them, clashed with their own hopes for themselves, or with the overweening expectations of a larger "improving" Victorian culture. One Preston weaver, jailed for stealing wool, had led a dissipated life, lying to women about his desire to marry them so that he could get money from them. He described giving his young children whiskey to drink, in order to stay at the bar longer. Ultimately, his wife also became a drinker: "Both parents drunk in bed, with their clothes on—in the middle of the day-time; one throwing up on one side, and the other on the other side; and this in the presence of three children! The oldest lad would have said 'Mam! Art thou drunk? Art thou drunk like my dad?'"[29] Betty May, the artists' model, dancer, and general bohemian-about-town, did not find her life rewarding. "The feeling about my life is in many ways one of great dissatisfaction. In spite of my adventures I do not really think that in many things I have got the best out of it, and yet when I look back on it I find it equally difficult to imagine myself having behaved in any way differently when I remember the various problems with which I have been faced."[30]

Life circumstances could collide with an inner lack of resilience. William Gifford, born in the 1750s, was raised by his mother, with occasional visits from a drunken, cold-tempered father who frittered away the family money. Gifford was orphaned at the age of thirteen; unlike his baby brother, who was put into the almshouse, Gifford was considered old enough to fend for himself, with his godfather placing him in one employment situation after another. He wanted to become a schoolteacher, but his godfather apprenticed him to a shoemaker instead, and when Gifford spent his time reading instead of making shoes, his master confiscated Gifford's books and writings, including a satire of a Methodist meeting that the shoemaker did not find very funny.[31] The frustration of all of Gifford's hopes plunged him into despair. "It was a period of gloom and savage unsociability; by degrees I sank into a kind of corporeal torpor; or, if roused into activity by the spirit of youth, wasted the exertion in splenetic and vexatious tricks, which alienated the few acquaintances which compassion had yet left me."[32] Ultimately, a mentor who could tell that

Gifford had native intelligence took up a subscription to purchase the rest of his time from his apprenticeship, giving him writing supplies and the opportunity to support himself by writing verse. With the mentor's encouragement, he found a position at Oxford and began translating Latin, but the untimely death of his mentor plunged him into another deep depression. "I seemed to be engaged in a hopeless struggle without move or end; and [t]his idea, which was perpetually recurring to me, brought such bitter anguish with it, that I shut up the work with feelings bordering on distraction."[33] One bright spot was that Gifford was able to channel this bitterness into a job as a satirist and editor of the *Quarterly Review*, where he became famous for his facility in lampooning poets and authors.

While the absence of happiness in some life writing is evidence of struggles with poverty, disability, or unresolved desires, other working-class autobiographers summarized the events of their lives without reflecting much or at all on their emotions. Did they lack the language to describe how they felt about past events, or did they not think such details were interesting or relevant to their imagined audiences?[34] Nathaniel Dale, a gamekeeper on several aristocrats' estates, wrote an autobiography that richly detailed his worklife and relevant close scrapes that he and others got into, but which contained no self-reflection. His autobiography gives the reader a good sense of his personality; he was quick to anger and to fight, very confident in his own abilities, and devoted to the aristocrats whom he served. He was not poor; his perquisites included a house, fuel, and permission to sell as many rabbits as he could catch. He and his first wife had a total of nine children, all of whom he was able to establish in trades. Dale never stepped back to reflect on his feelings about his life or accomplishments.[35]

An anonymous thief narrated his criminal career to the chaplain at the Clerkenwell prison. Born in 1853, the man's first memory was of being beaten by his father with a leather strap and then tied to a bed for stealing fruit; the rest of the narrative is a catalogue of thefts interspersed with brief stretches of time in prison. Although the author, according to his own narrative, had plenty of money for entertainment, which he spent mainly at the theater, music hall, and on drink, he never mentioned happiness or pleasure. Aside from a brief cohabitation with a Whitechapel prostitute who left him while he was serving time in prison, he did not report having any friends or family connections. And at one point he double-crossed the man who was fencing stolen goods for him, explaining that his motto was "Do anybody, but mind they don't do you." The brief thought that he "had threw away the only chance I had of doing better" made him miserable, but it was a misery quickly chased away with alcohol.[36] A different felon, author of the anonymous "Autobiography of a Convict," described two moments of happiness in his life: during his apprenticeship as a tailor, when he was slowly sliding into sinfulness and idleness without any conscience to be bothered, and then after his imprisonment for burglary. "Now, in the consciousness of being actuated by just and virtuous motives, I feel a new and comparatively happy man." He explained that he had been exiled, but was looking forward to starting a new life in the land of his exile, "hoping to acquire, by diligence and industry, contentment and repose."[37]

Working-class autobiographers might write in the style of the picaresque, describing their hair's-breadth escapes from complete destitution, or the speculations they were able to make with their last sixpence. These autobiographies strove to be entertaining but tended to express little emotion. A good example is the narrative of David Prince Miller, a traveling showman, who performed magic, acted as a barker for a circus sideshow, and ultimately became the manager of the Adelphi Theater in Glasgow for a period during the 1840s. Although he was sometimes moderately successful, and married and had several children, he never mentioned anything making him happy, or revealed his emotional state, but throughout his narrative expressed a calm confidence that he would always be able to get by, no matter how many times he was bankrupted.[38] William Cameron, or "Hawkie," spent most of his adult life as a perambulating beggar; his successful begging was punctuated by episodes of drunkenness and of brief cohabitation with various women, but he seemed devoid of self-reflection until he was finally interned in a hospital in Glasgow. Cameron's lack of public reflection on "the good life" did not mean he had no thoughts on the matter. In a letter to the man who would ultimately edit his autobiography, he described himself as "quite happey in my sitewation, although not altogether content. I must be thankful for the appearing respite I have got, and considering I never was willing to do mutch."[39]

Finally, one of the most important external factors explaining the presence or absence of thoughts on happiness was the slow and uneven development of rules for autobiography as a genre. Even within the brief period from 1750 to about 1930, one can detect change over time. Working-class autobiographies written in the nineteenth century, whose authors were born in the eighteenth, tend to be short on emotional insight. Some authors did not even describe their lives as continuous narratives. For example, Anthony Errington's memoirs are more of a string of briefly recounted remarkable events than "a life." His tale includes numerous episodes of near-deaths or actual deaths of miners working underground; three examples of times that he used a prayer to coax recalcitrant butter into being; and a time that he and some other men found large spiders in the coal pit and made money during the fair exhibiting them.[40]

In contrast, many of the autobiographers of working-class origins who benefited from post-1870 compulsory education, and who wrote their memoirs in the Freudian twentieth century, were trying to explain their own upward mobility. They understood that to their readers, the inward journey—the *Bildungsroman*, the story of becoming—was just as important to document as the outward journey. Rowland Kenney, whose life had encompassed manual labor, writing, editing, political activism in the service of the Socialist party and then public service, first in postwar Poland and then at the Foreign Office, recounted three major emotional turning points. The first had occurred when he was unjustly punished at school at the age of nine. Kenney attributed all of the resentment that he possessed in later life to being made to stand on a stool in the corner and withstand being hit with a cane.[41] As an adult, Kenney experienced a second epiphany, when an activist in the Socialist movement who was also a Christian Scientist encouraged him to adjust his attitude by repeating to himself "All is good!" The affirmations resulted in what Kenney described as almost a mystical experience:

> Ten minutes ago the sunshine had seemed thin and weak; now it was rich with power and promise . . . I realized then that what I usually saw were mere masks which hid these people from me, but the masks had now become transparent and through them shone an inner light of essential good and right-being. The whole world had sloughed off a scaly skin of pettiness, greed, hate, evil, and unscrupulous self-seeking, and shown itself as the beautiful being it really was.[42]

Kenney's third turning point came after the 1919 airplane crash that permanently injured him; he was plagued with nervousness and nightmares that today might be characterized as post-traumatic stress.[43] Kenney used these emotional turning points to explain how he became a follower of Gurdjieff and Ouspensky.

Will Thorne also spoke the language of psychology when looking back over his life, as he tried to identify the moment that he took on the mantles of working-class identity and union leadership. The navvies (manual laborers on construction projects) with whom he worked represented the ideal of rebellious self-defense. "Living and working with them, and then leaving navvying to become unemployed for some time, did not give rise at the time to any definite thoughts in my mind. That came later. But it was at the time I was with these big free-hearted men that my subconscious mind was at work."[44] J. E. Patterson, born in 1866 and having published his autobiography in 1911, was also familiar with the idea of psychological development. After his mother died when he was seven years old, he was sent to live with his grandmother. The next few years were full of his own brutality as he worked out his rage: against a goose that he beat to death with a hammer, against a young playmate whom he purposely exposed to a billy-goat attack, against a nanny who was hired to watch him, against the windows of an empty cottage, all of which he broke with rocks, and against an aunt, with whom he engaged in a knock-down, drag-out fistfight that left her bloodied. At one point a small firecracker that he attached to the housekeeper's skirt set her on fire.[45] The only time he experienced joy as a child was when he ran away from home. Had he been born seventy-five years earlier, he might have commented on his own sinfulness or perhaps not reflected on his motivation at all. Instead Patterson suggested that a lack of parental nurturing was partly to blame: "perhaps the one great fault was a lack of consistent tenderness . . . closer watchfulness and less stern commanding might have led to a better understanding of the rebellious enigma."[46] As these examples demonstrate, the genre of working-class autobiography shifted over time to become more explicitly focused on writers' inner states.

While absence of evidence is not necessarily evidence of absence, this chapter suggests that there were several reasons why documentation of happiness might be omitted from an autobiography. Some working-class authors lacked elements essential to happy lives, like autonomy, physical safety, or freedom from pain. Others felt burdened by the lack of social respect, as they faced homelessness or floundered economically in a society in which material success and personal morality were assumed to correlate. And before the advent of the *Bildungsroman*, there was less pressure on authors to reveal inner thoughts and emotions. Autobiographies like these tended to lack the catharsis of resolution, identifying some of the major flaws in nineteenth-century British society but proposing no solutions.[47]

NINE

Sadness, Fear, and Anger

DESCRIPTIONS OF NEGATIVE EMOTIONS like sadness, fear, and anger are less often detailed in nineteenth-century working-class autobiographies than are happiness, joy, and contentment. There are various contributory explanations for this. Autobiographers may have assumed that audiences would be less interested in their failures than in their successes, or have been loath to revisit some of the more challenging times in their lives.[1] Social pressure probably played a role: as Joanne Begiato has noted, respectable Victorian men were expected to project emotional self-control.[2] Furthermore, sadness and depression can sap the desire to engage in life writing, or any kind of writing for that matter. John Ward O'Neill, a weaver who kept a diary in the 1860s, noted that he had stopped writing in it for nearly two years "because I was sad and weary. One half of the time I was out of work and the other I had to work as hard as ever I wrought in my life, and can hardly keep myself living."[3] Nonetheless, it is worth examining displays and descriptions of sadness, fear, and anger, because these descriptions provide some balance in the assessment of working-class lives, and even hint at inner turmoil caused by conflicts between individual experience and social expectations.

Sadness

In *Weeping Britannia*, Thomas Dixon chronicled Britons' attitudes about shedding tears, from the medieval period to the present. He posited that Britons' stoicism stemmed from their self-identification against the emotional Other. He identified three turning points in the history of emotional display around sadness: the Protestant Reformation, because weeping was associated with Catholicism; the French Revolution, because too much emotional display was associated with French radicalism; and empire-building, because emotional display was associated with colonized peoples.[4] Dixon drew his examples of emotional display rules from such varied sources as religious biographies, plays, poetry, and art, but his examples were more often normative than descriptive.

In contrast, as Julie-Marie Strange's work has shown, working-class autobiographies can provide thick description of the experiences of sadness and grief. Two of the working-class autobiographers in my sample clearly had lives structured by trauma. Born into a family of Scottish fishmongers, Christian Watt had a reasonably happy childhood and young womanhood. But she lost one family member after another, including five of her seven siblings, who died over a short period when she was in her teens. The tragedies destroyed her parents, and "my two remaining brothers were abroad, so I had to carry the whole burden of a sad and broken world. I did not think I would ever smile again."[5] After some indecision about her life course she married, but the happiness of married life was interrupted when her son Peter died at the age of thirteen while working aboard a herring boat. Next, her eleven-year-old son Joseph, who was working as a mason's assistant during the school vacation, died of tetanus after a workplace accident. Her two remaining brothers and her husband died over a three-year period, leaving her with eight remaining children, all under the age of eighteen, and no provider.[6]

As a woman, and a person who spent so much time in the care of mental health professionals, Watt was much more open about her emotions than almost all other working-class autobiographers. She had undertaken the writing as a form of therapy, encouraged to journal by her doctors. "For a long time I suffered the terrible pain of the loss of my husband and family," Watt wrote. "It was an appalling grief. I now had to be father and mother with so little and no prospects of any betterment, for though you worked your fingers to the bone you could not save a penny for the results were so poor."[7] According to Watt, the stress of repeated loss and struggle culminated in several stays in asylums for the mentally ill, and the burden of housework, cooking, and the care of a toddler fell upon her ten-year-old daughter, Isabella.

While Watt found her stays in the asylum to be peaceful and therapeutic, they signaled the end of her family's prosperity. The stigma of mental illness was such that when she was released, former workmates refused to work alongside her, and parents of possible suitors for her children refused to allow the marriages. Watt reported that as a last-ditch effort she attempted to migrate to the United States, only to be rejected by the consulate due to her mental health history. Broken, she attempted to burn down her house, and was committed to the asylum for the rest of her life, although like many autobiographers who grew to be very old, she eventually found peace with herself. "At the closing of my days I have encountered so much kindness, I am blest every time I breathe. My life has been hard but I would not say it has been a sad waste, for my purpose has been to shed light in a dark place, and I have kept the faith, for which we are told we will be rewarded with a crown of life."[8]

As Allan Beveridge and Fiona Watson point out, Watt's documentation of her emotional life contrasts greatly with the medical records kept by the asylum that housed her.[9] She was described as "manic," suffering from religious delusions, and incoherent on various occasions. Beveridge and Watson speculate that Watt was kept in the asylum not because she found it restful, but rather because she was considered too dangerous to live in outside world. For the purposes of this study, however, it is sufficient to say that Christian Watt was the expert on what it felt like to be Christian Watt, and that she generally felt depressed.[10] The experiences of other working-class women with depression were also refracted through the perceptions of others. Tommy Buller Mitchell described his wife Eliza's alarming postpartum depression: "Her strength was failing and her spirits began to get very low at times, so much so that Tommy had to think serious about it. One day, I had been out to work and returned home in the evening; she was sitting by the fire and she looked up at me and said 'I am so glad you are come, I was just going to throw the baby under the grate.' "[11] Mitchell took the baby from Eliza and made sure that she got enough rest, but she experienced anxiety and depression intermittently for the rest of her life.

A second emotionally introspective working-class autobiographer, Robert Roberts, grew up in a small village in Wales, where he was regarded as a genius since having learned to read at the age of three. With luck and patronage he gathered together the rudiments of education. He learned first at home, by wide reading, then at a local grammar school, then at a Methodist training college at Bala, and finally at St. Bees Theological College, a school to train prospective Church of England ministers who were not wealthy enough to enter Oxford or Cambridge. Roberts described being plagued throughout his life by self-doubt, catastrophic thinking, and bouts of illness and fatigue. During one stint of school teaching, he noted, "I crawled into the school in the mornings, fought against my illness with the desperate energy of one who knew that if he failed, he had nothing to look for but a few evil days of poverty and an early close to his hapless life with all his work undone."[12]

As a curate Roberts worked diligently and enjoyed some of his postings where he thought he was doing some good, but his sensitivity to criticism could lead to a downward spiral. Getting wind of some negative gossip about him from his fellow curates caused him to ruminate on the idea that "I am a humbug, there is no question about it. My whole life is a long humbug . . . I took to learning because it comes natural to my taste like cream to a cat . . . it should have been my duty to think first of proving some credit to those who had shown so much love and kindness to me but I did not do so."[13]

In an astounding passage, Roberts related walking for miles, filled with self-hatred and self-accusation, opening one closet door after another in his mind: "What do we find here? Pride. Ah, dry, haggard, skeleton. How many a time hast thou made a fool of me?" He stopped walking when he reached a chapel with a pile of building materials, including some flawed tiles that had been cast aside. "I am a tile with a flaw in it. There's something wrong in the baking. The flaw has not yet been found out, but it will someday and I shall be cast aside like that, a useless bit of ugly pottery."[14] Roberts eventually lost his curacy after a widely reported bout of drinking, which turned him inward even more. He ran away to Australia, and supported himself by tutoring, but eventually returned to Wales, destitute. He died at the age of fifty of a laudanum overdose. Roberts's description of his own unhappiness stands out in contrast to the other nineteenth-century autobiographies, so much so that John Burnett and H. G. Williams, who wrote the introduction to the modern reprint of his memoir, conclude that it had not been meant for publication. "One of the things that makes Roberts's life story so untypically Victorian," they note, "is the failure of self-help to produce a happy, honoured and contented being who triumphed against the odds."[15]

Christian Watt and Robert Roberts are atypical, as most of the sadness expressed in working-class memoirs was situational, emanating from the deaths of loved ones. Writing in 1980, David Vincent argued that many working-class people could not afford to grieve for their deceased loved ones, since the conditions of everyday life were often precarious due to poverty, and work needed to go on.[16] And there are examples of what Vincent described. When George Sanger's firstborn son died suddenly in a convulsive fit, he and his wife had no savings to hold a funeral, and were forced to swallow their grief and pretend to be merry in order to pack in the crowds to their traveling show. "There in the bitter grey weather, our hearts as heavy as lead, we had to mount jests and smile to win the people to our show so that our loved one might be laid decently to rest . . . the mummer must smile though his heart be breaking."[17] The lack of a decent funeral grated against community expectations of respect for the dead, and deprived mourners of the support that other members of the community were able to express by just showing up.

But even when the practicalities of life demanded that mourners persevere, autobiographers continued to struggle with grief and loss; extended meditations on the deaths of family members in memoirs written decades later served as ongoing memorialization.[18] Samuel Fielden, later hanged for participation in the Chicago Haymarket Riot of 1886, lost his mother when he was a young child. He described rushing home from the textile factory where he worked, and his father sat down in a chair with Samuel on his knee and tried to tell him what had happened, but no words would come. Samuel ran upstairs and saw his mother gasping for her last breaths. "Words cannot describe my feelings. It seemed as though the bright summer day grew black, and my life seemed to be going out as that of the form before me was going. But I will not dwell upon this painful scene." Fielden confessed to his readers that he had never been able to banish the image of his mother's deathbed from his mind. "I do not think that there has ever been a day that I have not had it before me since the occurrence," he noted.[19] John Wilson also lost his mother, at the age of four. "And now, at seventy-one, with an interval of sixty-six or seven years, I can see the poorly furnished room and the bed in the corner upon which I was lifted. And now as I write this the tears start to my eyes, and I can feel the close pressure to her heart, and the motherly affection on her lip as she kissed me."[20] Although this was a painful memory, it was also dear to him, and he hoped he would be able to keep that mental picture as long as he lived. Mary Ann Ashford recalled the day that her father unexpectedly died. She was scolded for having left her father's bedside in the hospital and had "a violent fit of crying, which, no doubt, did me a great deal of good."[21]

But the death of a parent paled before the death of a child. No matter how common it was in an age of infectious disease and before public health measures—around 150 infants per 1,000 live births before 1900, with statistics as grim as 509 per 1,000 in some areas—the death of a child was heart-wrenching.[22] Thomas Dixon described the emotional ordeal faced by the middle-class Tait family, who lost five children under the age of ten to scarlet fever within a single year. The Taits' struggle to reconcile religious hope of an afterlife with the ugly reality of seeing children die in agony was shared by those of working-class origins, despite the common assumption that the feelings of working-class people were somehow less refined than those of their social superiors.[23] Julie-Marie Strange has argued that working-class parental relationships were wrongly classed as low in attachment; while middle-class social reformers criticized practices like the Catholic wake or the storage of bodies for burial within small working-class homes, hands-on practices like washing and preparing the corpse for burial at home expressed emotional closeness.[24] Moreover, the way that working-class autobiographers described their own grief pushed back against the stereotype that fatalism helped to blunt their feelings.[25]

Comedian Harry Lauder became his family's breadwinner at the age of twelve when his father died. Lauder worked his way up from the mines to become a famous entertainer, and to have a long and happy marriage to a woman he met as a teenager. But the most life-changing event was the loss of their only son, John, who was killed in the First World War. Upon receiving the news of his son's death, Lauder plunged deeply into depression. But his wife emphasized that their sacrifice was one shared in houses all over Great Britain, and that if he failed to fulfill his performance contract, hundreds of people would lose money and work. He described being barely able to go through with the first performance after his son's death, choking on the words of his songs, buoyed only by the sympathy that he perceived coming from the audience; and ultimately fainting into the arms of his manager after getting offstage. "You may ask why I chose to recall all these details about a night so sad, so full of grief, so charged with personal drama," he wrote. "I do so because I think it is only right and proper if I am to tell the story of my life in these memoirs."[26] Lauder's son's death became a turning point in his life, after which no moment of happiness was completely free from the thought of what he had lost. He entertained troops at the front, and traveled to the United States to enlist American support for the conflict. As he addressed crowds there, "the great surging, cheering, high-spirited concourse at Wall Street did me more good than anything else for months. I was so affected that I had to go home to my hotel and lie down for an hour or two."[27] When he received the news that he had been granted a knighthood, he was overjoyed, but at the same time flashed back to the loss of his son. "I would willingly, aye, with great joy, have bartered the lot for one smile from John, one shake of his hand, to hear him say 'Dad, old man!' once more."[28]

"Jacques," the Scottish autobiographer whose prize essay was printed in the *Commonwealth*, was a young married man when he and his wife lost their child in infancy. "Sanguine and hopeful, it were difficult to tell the anguish we both felt under this bereavement. The first loss, and the greatest cross, we had yet experienced, our young hearts smarted feelingly under the dire dispensation, and for many years thereafter we could not advert to the circumstance without enduring much of the poignancy of our early grief."[29] The loss of their son foreshadowed the loss of his wife in childbirth in 1844, immediately after she delivered their tenth child. This was a grief that recurred to him again and again: "memory—busy memory—frequently calls from its depth the more prominent features in every scene, and presents them so vividly and distinctly, that even now I dare scarcely trust myself to peruse the brief sketch that I have thus somewhat hurriedly and imperfectly drawn."[30] "Stirrup," the shoemaking author of another prize essay, lost his daughter when she was only two and a half years old. "I cannot, if I would, tell of the event. The writing of these lines, simple as they are, opens the crystalline fount of my tears and they fall like large beads upon the paper before me. Being the first death in our family, we felt the more keenly." He enclosed a poem rather than describing the death itself, but noted that "the recollection of her dying scene is as fresh and vivid to me now as if I was but gazing on it." All of the attempted consolations by religious figures were futile since the event "was like taking my heart from my body."[31]

J. H. Powell used almost the same words to describe his feelings when he lost his daughter Marion at the age of seventeen months. "To some hard natures the death of a dear child may seem like a matter to be thankful for," he mused, "but to me it seemed like the parting of life from love—the decay of hope—the separation of the soul from the body."[32] James D. Wright, who earned his living climbing and repairing steeples and chimneys in England and abroad, recalled that he and his family lived happily in Edinburgh until a smallpox epidemic struck the town, sickening one family member after another. The only one to die was his sixteen-year-old daughter, Jessie. "This blow was surely felt by me, for she was my favourite child . . . We got clear of this distress, but I could not help looking at Jessie's empty chair."[33] Somehow, the very terseness of this sentence aptly communicates grief. Devastatingly, Wright also lost three adult sons—also employed as steeplejacks—to workplace accidents. He heard about the last death by chance, from a friend, just as he was boarding a train. "I was left alone in a state of mind that I cannot describe to my readers," he wrote.[34] The emotional aloneness that nineteenth-century Britons experienced surrounding deaths in the family may have been exacerbated by the decline of customs like dirge-singing that had formerly enabled mourners to be uplifted by the participation of other members of the community.[35]

To an extent, the loss of a child or children in infancy or young childhood was expected; the loss of an adult child in whom years of care and nurturing had been invested was a severe blow. Servant and linen weaver Elizabeth Campbell's autobiography was abbreviated after she described her childhood, but she dedicated a full paragraph to the death of her adult son, who was killed by a "hair-teazing machine" (a machine to process horsehair for bedding) at a House of Industry (a workhouse). "Oh! I cannot tell what a bitter and sore trial it was for me to go identify the mangled remains of my son Willie. This was the greatest of many sorrows in my life, and I have mourned sore, and still mourn, his untimely end." She wrote a poem about the experience, wondering whether he had died in assurance of salvation.[36] The Coventry weaver Joseph Gutteridge had a similar reaction to the death of his adult son, who died of complications of alcoholism. The son had probably died without salvation, Gutteridge reasoned, since Gutteridge had raised his children in a thoroughly materialist frame of mind. When someone came to the house to tell him that his son was dying, Gutteridge fainted, striking his head so that he was neither able to visit his son's deathbed nor go to his funeral. His wife went instead, but Gutteridge noted that "these were hours of mental torture. Only those who have had this sad experience can tell the agony of mind that comes to one who feels that though he did not, he might have taught his children a higher principle than non-responsibility."[37]

High child mortality rates also meant that many working-class autobiographers had lost siblings. Adam Rushton considered his brother to be his closest friend. Summoned unexpectedly to his brother's deathbed, "Only with choking sobs could I utter parting words." At his brother's grave, "I felt as if transfixed, and with only the wish to be laid beside him there, and that my spirit should pass away with his into the heavenly realm . . . at times, for several days, my heart almost ceased to beat, and my life seemed ebbing away."[38] J. E. Patterson lost his mother who died in childbirth, and then his younger sister Mary, to illness, when she was only a baby. Although he was kept away from Mary's funeral due to his age, he eventually did visit her grave, standing there and sobbing. "The loneliness was so oppressive and impressive that I knelt by the little mound and sobbed in utter abandonment." The deaths of all of his caring female relatives had forced him to become independent before he was ready: "I tearfully left the scene, to remember it again and again in the future . . . when I should see by the mind's eye that toddling little fair-skinned sister . . . and realize how imperfect and unfinished are the heart and brain of him into whose life, especially in the impressionable years, there comes no formative touch of the divinity of womankind." As a slightly older child, he lost his only adult friend, an ostler, who was kicked by a horse. Again, he cried in secret. "Since then I have come to the conclusion that too many griefs can make the heart grow tough; too many joys must leave it half-complete."[39]

The loss of a partner after many years of marriage also left autobiographers emotionally adrift; as Julie-Marie Strange notes, the results could include economic devastation, loneliness, and the loss of a social role.[40] When his wife became ill, John Thompson of Sunderland quit his editorial job. After two years she died of cancer: "the loss of so true and noble a partner in life's struggles was a deep blow . . . this made a sad impression on the lonely husband as all his children were then married and comfortably settled in life." Although Thompson sometimes wrote in the third person, here he was dissociated from the man who suffered, becoming "the lonely husband."[41] James McCurrey, a construction worker and temperance lecturer, lost all six of his children over time, including his favorite son, who died when he was just eleven years old. But the most difficult loss was his wife. "The loss of one who had traveled the journey of life in sorrow and in joy, with me for nearly 47 years, was a grief I cannot describe and will not dwell on."[42] Francis Place, whose wife died suddenly of metastatic breast cancer, felt the same way. "On the day of her funeral I suffered more than I had ever before done and more than I believed I could suffer on any occasion." Place found himself utterly unable to attend the funeral. "I had lost, and forever, my friend my long cherished companion in all my various changes of life, she who had my entire confidence, she who gave me hers, and had loved me most sincerely during Thirty Seven Years."[43] He noted that even after her death, whenever he heard a noise in the house, he looked up, expecting to see her. As Vicky Holmes points out, women facing the death of partners tended to find themselves financially and socially worse off than did men. These problems are compounded by their silence in the historical record.[44]

David Barr arranged his autobiography in a unique way, isolating all his most emotionally challenging moments in a separate chapter entitled

"Shadows." "Although my life, now running out to the end, has been on the whole bright, joyous, and successful, it would not accord with universal experience were I able to claim that there had been no bitterness in my cup, no cloudy days, no dark and dreary nights," he explained. Barr had been predeceased by a twenty-year-old brother (who died in a workplace accident), his mother, his father, his eldest daughter, his youngest daughter, another brother, and finally a promising son, but "before closing the chapter I am constrained to acknowledge with profound gratitude the many compensations that I am able to set against the pathetic incidents on which I have only lightly touched." As he noted in the next chapter, these deaths, however hard they were to bear, were part of life, and did not impinge on his fairly modest concept of what it meant to be happy. "I have every happiness and comfort in my home, with enough and to spare of this world's goods, affectionate children united in the closest bonds and all walking in the fear of God. What more could I desire or possess to complete my happiness?"[45]

While sadness was most often associated with grief, some autobiographers grappled with sadness arising from other causes, including homesickness. Lucy Luck, a straw-plaiter, described the sadness she felt when she and her husband moved from the Thring area to London for him to work. The couple had recently buried an infant daughter. "I shall never forget my first two or three months in London. I think I cried most of the time, for my husband was on night work, and I amongst strangers and thinking of the poor child I had so recently buried. I would have given anything to have gone back to the country."[46] Alf Ireson ran away from home to join his girlfriend who was in service in Cambridge. Although he had been quite excited at the prospect of freedom and adulthood, his lodging was dirty and he "realized that I had separated myself from kind parents and a good home. I sat down and wept. The thought of the anguish of my dear broken-hearted mother gave me great distress."[47]

Economic setbacks could precipitate a sense of sadness and shame, particularly in men unable to support their families in a context that blamed poverty on individual moral failings. But writing about that shame was unusual, except when it was instrumental in causing a life change (alcoholism to temperance, for example, or unbelief to religion). Born in Kent in 1817, the son of an injured soldier, John Bartholomew Gough immigrated to the United States at the age of twelve. His mother had handed him over to a neighboring family, in the hope that by emigrating with them he would achieve a better life. Soon after, Gough's mother and sister also migrated to the United States, but the mother's untimely death left both teenagers to shift for themselves. Gough became a bookbinder, but he also had talents for comedic singing and theatricals, and without parental supervision, spent his spare time performing for free drinks at various pubs.[48] As a result, Gough soon became addicted to alcohol—an intense, insatiable physical craving that ruined his life. He lost multiple jobs, two infants, his wife who died in childbirth, his public reputation, his self-respect, his health, and, through various bouts of delirium tremens, his grasp on reality. His decline filled him with such overwhelming shame that he could barely stand to be alive:

> With the exception of the days of my childhood, my whole life had been one perpetual struggle against poverty and misery in its worst forms. Thrown at a tender age upon the world, I was soon taught its hard lessons. Death had robbed me of my best earthly protector, and Providence cast my lot in a land thousands of miles from the place of my birth ... In the very depths of my desolation, wife and children had been torn from my side. In the midst of thousands I was lonely, and, abandoning hope, the only refuge which seemed open for me was the grave.

Gough contemplated suicide on several occasions, but always went back to angrily drinking, feeling that the world had cheated him. Ultimately, he was only able to stop drinking due to the social support of the Washingtonian Temperance Society. His fellow society members even forgave him when he fell off the wagon while working as a temperance lecturer.[49] Robert Flockhart spent much of his young adulthood as a soldier assigned to India, before experiencing a religious conversion and becoming a preacher. As he looked back at his army years, the emotion he expressed most strongly was shame about his drunkenness, swearing, and sexual behavior. "I feel greatly ashamed when I remember that I myself am the very man that was guilty of the three heinous sins just mentioned, and that I went to such a length as to cast off all shame. I was worse than a beast."[50]

A few autobiographers linked their sadness directly to poverty. John Shinn, born in 1837, noted that from 1840 to 1850 his family was often short of food, and "this caused a sad depression in our childish minds, which never thoroughly passed off in after years, but caused a feeling [of] depression and sadness for our entire lives."[51] J. H. Powell had used his savings to start a magazine. When it failed, he became depressed. "I was for a time mentally paralysed, and scarcely had strength to stretch forth my hand to save myself." Later in life, he even contemplated suicide.[52] Israel Roberts of Pudsey quit his job in the mill with the intention of spending his entire savings starting his own business, but at first he struggled. "So downhearted was I at times that I used to fear anyone asking me what sort of a market there had been and when I reached home I would go right upstairs and change my clothes and then I would kneel down and have a good cry and an earnest prayer for Divine help."[53] Robert Watchorn described how uncomfortable both he and his mother were when he headed off to the coal mine for the first time at the age of eleven. "When I finally left, her sobbing was not only audible and deep, but terribly upsetting, no less so to herself than to me. It is one of those incidents in one's life that are unforgettable."[54] The discomfort was exacerbated by his experience underground, as weird stillness, the dripping of water from the roof, and the creaking of timbers alternated with banging noises and rolling trucks. "The effect upon a child can only be imagined. A creeping sort of feeling takes possession of him. He contemplates running away, but where is he to go?"[55]

Stress and depression produced physical symptoms. Bathchair-man George Meek described the despair of being a gig worker during a period of high unemployment, "If you would know the horror of black despair go out with a bathchair day after day, with chair-owner or landlord worrying you for rent, food needed at home, and get nothing. Stare till your eyes ache; pray with aching heart to a God whom you ultimately curse for His deafness. And this not for a few weeks, but year after year."[56] The suffragette Hannah Maria Mitchell described several years of activism in the movement to gain votes for women, including short periods of jail time and some rough treatment at the hands of crowds whom the police didn't bother to restrain. One day, while giving a speech, she started to see black areas in her field of vision; this was followed by what she described as a nervous breakdown, and then a year of "fits of depression when I was often tempted to end my life."[57] Only long walks in the countryside and her mother's temporary presence in the household enabled her to recover.

John Struthers, who had overcome difficult odds to become a shoemaker rather than entering into the muslin trade like his father, experienced depression when he thought about the religious sacrifices he had made in order to secure his material position. "Sometimes, indeed, his distress was very great, and it was all the greater that he was well aware it was beyond the power of man to help him. There was not indeed any one with whom he could communicate on the subject, or even to whom he could confide the secret," Struthers wrote of himself, suggesting that despair was a socially inappropriate emotion.[58] Although he continued to ruminate, he comforted himself by writing poetry and spending time with his wife, "whose invincible fortitude, imperishable hope, equanimeous temper, richly instructive or delightfully amusing conversation, and her never-failing, delightful sympathies, made her to him an overflowing fountain of perpetual sweetness."[59]

Robert Spurr's first wife died a few weeks after the birth of their child, less than a year after his marriage to her. He had to place his baby with his mother and sister to raise while he went to look for work, and had a hard time supporting himself. He was then struck with typhus, which so weakened him that he was unable to work for a year. His clothes became so worn that he was forced to sell his furniture to clothe himself. Writing about these difficult times resurrected painful feelings. "My heart was fit to break—and while I am writing, I feel the smart of it." Later, when he did manage to find work, he felt so isolated and overburdened that he contemplated suicide. While feelings of failure elicited these emotions of guilt and insufficiency, other sad events—including the deaths of four of his eight children—were just the lot of the working man in the world, and received less comment.[60]

No matter what caused the sadness, working men experienced pressure to conform to emotional expectations by suppressing its expression. So Serjeant Butler described the atmosphere onboard his ship to India, as it departed from England in 1807. "There seems much to make one unhappy and melancholy, when taking probably the last view of the land that gave him birth; but notwithstanding, all seemed now festivity and joy. Some of those who seemed so full of joy, I have good reason to believe, might, with justice, be called Solomon's merry men—in their laughter their hearts were sad."[61] Joseph Donaldson had disgraced his family once when, at the age of thirteen, he ran away to sea. After that voyage he came home, but discovered that he no longer fit in, and decided to enlist without telling his parents. When he accidentally met with his mother in the marketplace, "I could scarcely define my feelings. Shame, grief, a sort of sullen despair, a sense that I had cut myself off from the world—that I had done my worst, and a determination to push it to the utmost, were mingled together in my mind." His mother wept, and asked him to come home to say goodbye to his father, who struggled to contain his own emotions. "My father cut some meat on his plate; but instantly pushed it from him. He rose from his seat, and walked about the floor with a rapid pace. He opened his waistcoat. He seemed suffering. I could no longer endure to see the convulsive agony with which his whole frame was agitated."[62]

Donaldson's mother's weeping was bearable; his father's weeping, having crossed a line, was unendurable.

Men writing from a distance about their early lives described having wept in private. The fact that they wrote about these episodes at all suggests that emotional display norms changed over the course of the nineteenth century and into the twentieth.[63] Frank Forrest, who lived away from home during the week to work in a mill, came back on the weekend to find that his mother and brother had both been taken to the infirmary due to a fever epidemic. "When I came to a silent place, I wept aloud," he wrote. "Solitude nourishes melancholy, and I have frequently, when brooding over misfortunes or bereavements, felt, when alone in some solitary spot, a disposition to give vent to my feelings in a flood of tears."[64] Eli Ashdown, the miller-turned–Baptist minister whose emotional life was full of torment, described at many moments in his diary weeping with his doubts, but always in private. At one point after a disappointing prayer service, "When I reached home after service I felt almost overwhelmed . . . I wished in myself I had never been born, and pitied my wife, children, and friends too; for my life seemed one of inconsistencies. I walked to the bottom of our lane, then leaned back against the corner of the wall and wept till I had no more power to weep."[65]

Crying in private was a learned behavior impelled by experience, as crying in public was considered womanly. While serving in India, Robert Flockhart was assigned to care for a fatally wounded man. The patient coughed up some blood, pronounced "Oh Lord, I'm gone," and died, and Flockhart burst into tears. "My assistant told my companions in the company that I had cried at his death, and they laughed me to scorn," he remembered.[66] Martin Douglas described an emotional conflict of masculinity in his autobiography. A celebrated keelman, he was often asked to row out to help ships in trouble in his local harbor. But he also had financial issues that led to his bankruptcy, and resented other keelmen whom he claimed were unjustly taking his coal-shipping opportunities. He noted in his memoir:

> I once had the honour of dining with the gallant Marquis of Londonderry . . . he proposed my health in a most handsome manner . . . I never rose to reply and thank his lordship and gentlemen for drinking it, for in the meantime he was giving my rights away, sharing my Coals among the other fitters. I could not rise without shedding tears, as my heart was full and it would have looked unmanly of me, to be seen with tears in my eyes, in fact I could not speak.[67]

Douglas did not want to appear unmanly by crying in front of a visible audience, but he was willing to admit his inner turmoil to an unseen audience of putative readers. Thomas Davies reported a similar attitude toward weeping, when he found himself going blind at the age of twenty-seven. "I used to go to the farthest end of the garden to weep, and to pray to my Master in heaven, and I always tried to hide my sorrow and grieving from my wife."[68] Even James Dunn, who was only a boy when his mother died, went into the garden and cried, or saved his tears for nighttime when he was only perceived by his younger brother. Years later, when he was struggling with the notion of religious conversion and feeling bad about his sinfulness, he closed himself in the bedroom to cry.[69]

At some point in childhood, boys were expected to stop expressing sadness with tears. Adam Rushton recalled being emotionally overwhelmed by his first day as a worker in a silk mill at the age of eight. He noted that "the close, impure air seemed to be stifling me. The clangour of machinery deafened me. I could hardly speak a word to anyone." His fingers trembled too much to do his new job, but, probably because he was so young, his emotional outburst elicited pity rather than contempt. "On being remonstrated with, I burst into tears. I was kindly taken away to sit on a stool in the corner until my emotion was overcome."[70] Thomas Todd, also eight years of age, was sent by his employer to fetch a horse at a public house eighteen miles away. He soon found he had no concept of how far that was, and ended up hungry and thirsty and exhausted on a treacherous uphill path in the darkness. "The tears came gushing out of my eyes. I sometimes think they were the hottest tears ever shed. I buried my face on my arm, and cried until I couldn't cry anymore." When he finally reached the public house he could not stop sobbing; and given some whiskey and water, he fell asleep until the next day. "Little did I think as a child, that the recollections of that experience would be more vivid to me and more easily recalled in all its significance after the passage of over seventy years."[71] Neither autobiographer was teased for his display of emotions because an eight-year-old boy was still a child, but after childhood, tears about things other than the death of family members were evidence of fragility rather than of refined emotional sensibilities.

Fear

Shame, despair, sadness, and grief were more common topics for working-class autobiographers than was fear. Working-class autobiographies rarely conveyed fears about economic survival; many working people shared a baseline of anxiety about material success. In Barbara Rosenwein's words, "Only culture can tell us what a threat is, how we should handle and express our fear, and whether fear or some other emotion should dominate our social lives—or dominate at certain times but not at others."[72] Fear can be buffered by fatalism—the belief that when it's your time to go, it's your time to go—or by belief in a benevolent and providing God, or the belief that it is more appropriate for women than for men to express anxiety. Glimmers of all of these aspects come through in the autobiographies. Francis Place described several times in his life when his fortunes were utterly destroyed, either by the actions of others or by bad business decisions. While he remained optimistic about the future, his wife was made permanently anxious by the repeated plunges into poverty. "The miseries of poverty had made such an impression upon her, her hopes which had been raised pretty high and had been blasted . . . had made her apprehensive that she should never long together be free from misfortunes, she always expected some catastrophe."[73] Whether or not Place himself felt anxiety about the future, in his autobiography he attributed those feelings to his wife.

Working-class writers often deployed fear in their autobiographies as a sort of comic relief. Men shared anecdotes about fear in childhood, when irrational fears were to be expected.[74] The potter Charles Shaw remembered being horrified to see a man lift off the top of his head and drop it back down again; having never seen or heard of a wig, he "hardly knew whether to regard him as a man or a demon."[75] William Henry Lax remembered being gripped with fear before he started school at the age of five, due to all of the cruel rumors older children spread about the horrors of school.[76] His other fears included pigs' carcasses that had been hung up after butchering, and a disabled man with a prosthetic leg. Lax also recounted a moment of horror, upon seeing the coffin of a man who had been killed in a mine explosion: "It was some days after the explosion when the body was found; flesh and clothing charred by the fire; stark horror in his face; his hands extended as if to ward off the dreadful flames—in that attitude of terror, death had closed relentlessly upon him. Without a word, sick from fright, we ran home."[77]

Joseph Severn, whose parents separated when he was young, was sent to live with an abusive and contentious uncle who kept him from running away from home by telling him that "there were bloody bones in the well that would get me if I attempted to go home. Thus the feeling of fear was early implanted in my mind, and during my childhood I never dared to go past this well unless accompanied by someone."[78] Henry Snell told a similar story, of having been terrorized by stories that ghosts lived along the path of his two-mile walk to work. "The children of today are born into a saner and more enlightened world, and they will never experience the agony that ignorance inflicted upon the childish minds of their grandparents nearly seventy years ago. I knew every yard of those quiet and beautiful lanes, and I have never forgiven the superstition which made me fear them."[79] Duncan Campbell described belief in ghosts as general among the people of the Scottish Highlands, but noted that his personal fear of walking through churchyards in the dark stemmed from stories of Burke and Hare and having seen a suicide buried in unconsecrated ground.[80]

Autobiographers characterized fear as a characteristic not only of children but also of women and uneducated rustic people. As David Vincent has argued in the context of improving literacy throughout the nineteenth century, folkloric beliefs about supernatural beings were beginning to give way to more scientific understandings of the world's operations.[81] Thomas Bewick was himself terrified by "phantoms and supernatural things," and noted that "these wrought powerfully upon the fears of the great bulk of the people at that time, and with many, these fears are not rooted out even at this day."[82] Horace Harman, who traveled through the Buckinghamshire countryside, shared dialect tales that working people told each other about seeing ghosts.[83] John Sykes, who grew up in a Yorkshire village, recounted his neighbors' beliefs in "witches and wizards, hobgoblins and ghosts, with all their train of terror." While these folk tales didn't scare him, Sykes's neighbors terrified his childhood self on Bonfire Night. Several men dressed up as Guy Fawkes, "ferocious though motionless figures, wearing masks, black hats, black coats. They looked like dead men. Their hideous faces, with too much red about them, gleamed and glowed like a butcher's shop lit by naphtha flares." But he was much more seriously terrorized by seeing his father in a coffin as a very young boy: "I did not want to look at my father dead, and still remember the chill and terror of that ghastly experience."[84]

Anthony Errington, a barely literate mine-waggoner born in 1778, was thrown by some "friends" into a freshly dug grave. He found himself trapped between two coffins, sobbing. "I cannot describe what a smell I felt," he wrote, synesthetically—and at a historical moment when it was believed that bad smells or "miasmas" caused disease, this smell could be the harbinger of death. When he finally managed to climb out of the grave, his mother "weshed me from the Crown to feet. And I got on fresh Close, thease being burnt with fire for fear of the plage." The experience, and the fear of being buried alive, haunted Errington's sleep "for a long time after, and for severell years after I thought I felt the smell of the Dead Corps."[85]

In an era before widespread outdoor lighting, darkness exacerbated fears about ghosts and the walking dead. At age nine, William Arnold set off to work in the dark on winter mornings, and came home in the evenings "after it was dark, pitch dark, and raining, and blowing, and showing sometimes . . . Many a time my heart seemed to stand still with fright."[86] Joseph Wardle, who worked in a limeworks before becoming a Methodist minister, recalled traveling from one stop on his preaching circuit to the next, through a lonely road. "I had not gone far before I heard a noise behind me. Was it footpads, or ghosts? I was afraid to look back for fear I should see a ghost. It came nearer slowly, shuffling along." He was inclined to run but did not, instead pulling out his umbrella as the scary noise got closer. To his surprise, however, it was a newspaper being blown along by the wind. Wardle's narration of the tale, which doesn't give away the harmlessness of the specter until the end, invites the reader to share his scare but then laughs it off as nothing serious. It was a fear, but a silly fear.[87]

Mary Loughran, born in a small Irish village, worked in (as legend had it) a haunted mansion near Montrose. One night, she heard a bumping and thumping overhead and decided it was the house ghost haunting the library. "I dared not move, but kept my eyes fastened on the ceiling. I suppose I was waiting for him to appear. The noise still continued. I think it lasted about an hour." She lay awake the rest of the night, and descended blearily to breakfast the next morning to tell the tale, only to find that there was a rational explanation; a bat had flown in the window and the maid needed to move all the furniture in order to shoo it out. "I was so relieved at the ending of my ghost story that they all teased me with my credulity," she noted.[88]

The fears of rustic people or children about disembodied noises and imagined ghosts loomed less ominously than the real existential terror of the religious adherent contemplating the state of the soul.[89] John Stradley, born in 1757, was pressed into service on naval ships several times and also worked for the naval armorer. While on shore leave, he found himself falling into sinfulness and patronizing brothels. When he thought about the afterlife, Stradley felt paralyzing physical panic and feared he was being punished by God: "I was often afraid to shut my eyes, for fear of fires and ghostly figures that was painted in my emagination [sic], the terrors of a guilty conscience, Sinner be sure your sins will find you out was stamped on my very heart."[90] Jane Andrew, watching her mother suffer during the mother's last illness, experienced "great anxiety, both of soul and circumstances." She worried that she herself had transgressed God's law, and reading a Bible that warned sinners of judgment "brought such terror into my soul that I was afraid to sleep, for fear I should awake in hell." Her anxiety propelled her religious conversion, which in turn caused complete detachment and the belief God would take care of everything.[91]

David Love, a collier-turned-ballad-writer, had a similar experience at the age of ten, "by an awful dream of the last judgment, which put me in such fear that I was in a fever. I have often thought thereon with terror."[92] Religious fears also plagued Henry Hughes after a company of actors came to his town in Wales. "As they made their acts and tricks, I thought they were under the influence of the devil and that it was by his power that they could do those things." He enjoyed watching the show but "after I got home and went to bed, a certain feeling of terror and fear struck me so I could not sleep and for two weeks this fear and terror possessed me so I could hardly fall asleep and when I did, I would be awakened yelling with fear." Hughes kept his emotional struggles from his friends "for fear again they would laugh at me," again indicating the acceptable limits of emotional performance.[93] James Nye, a Calvinist who believed in predestination, "was so fearful and timid that I was afraid to go to sleep at certain times, less I should wake up in hell. And when I went to sleep I was scared with the most awful dreams that I awoke in such a fright that I really thought that I was dying."[94]

Detailing such fears was essential in conversion narratives, because only God could remove fear and sadness. Jonathan Saville described the fear he felt when first called as a local preacher. "As I was going I said to myself, 'What art thou going to do? They will never receive thy blundering preaching' . . . when I got into the pulpit and looked round, I felt faint. It was the first time that ever I felt my right thigh weaker than the other. It trembled as if I had an ague. My tongue for a long time clave to the roof of my mouth."[95] Saville could reveal his fear because God had overcome it for him, giving him the talent to convert people, including the woman who had been one of his childhood abusers. Ultimately, he explained, "I standing by the bedside in ecstacy [sic], and with a face full of joy and gratitude."[96]

Few autobiographers admitted to feeling fear for their bodily integrity, but some sailors, perhaps because the risk to life and limb from seagoing was well known, described harrowing experiences. Frank Bullen, whose *Log of a Sea-Waif* chronicled four of his early teen years, described his most extreme moment of physical terror in detail. Then aboard an

American-flagged ship, the Western Belle, he was ordered to climb to the very top of the royal pole, an extension of the topmast. He managed to climb to the top but, paralyzed with fear and trembling, found himself unable to sheave the sail line. "As I write, the cold sweat bursts from every pore, for I feel again the terrible agony of that moment," he remembered. Despite fearing that the mate would kill him for not doing his job, he climbed back down. "The whole episode may seem trivial; but I frankly declare that, having in my experience, faced death many times, I have never felt such terror as I felt then."[97]

Another sailor, J. E. Patterson, once saw a waterspout appear in front of his ship. "The thunder of its impact on the water became deafening. Surely landsmen never saw a scene like that in its awful simplicity, sublimity and threatening tragedy." The waterspout set off a mad panic, with everyone on the deck rushing astern. They could do nothing but watch the waterspout, which by now had sunk two other ships, bearing down on them. "Every instant was an age—an age of expectancy and horror." Luckily for Patterson and the rest of the crew, the waterspout lifted up at the last minute, giving his ship time to clear the vortex. The unexpected escape left everyone in a stupor.[98] Another experienced sailor, John Wilson, was personally sanguine but described the terror felt by others on a transatlantic voyage, noting that the companionways were fastened down to keep "fear-stricken passengers out of the way of the sailors." As the sea pitched the vessel up and down, "when the stern rose out of the water the great screw [the ship's propeller] would miss, and there would be a loud burring and a terrible shaking of the whole of the great fabric. This would set in a dreadful dread of danger ... indicated oft by the attitude, and oft in lamentations."[99] Having survived six hours lashed to the ship's wheel during a storm on a previous voyage, Wilson tried to keep the others calm, but it was futile.

In contrast with the physiological experience of happiness, which autobiographers rarely described, the physiological experiences of fear were central to the accounts of these brushes with death. The miller James Edward Saunders recalled trying to stop his mill from turning furiously during a severe storm. As he tried to with all his might to stop the mill gearing, he heard one of the mill timbers break. "I had no thought of death that I can remember, and certainly no fear of it, but I was startled and enthralled. Permeating and thrilling every fibre of my being was the consciousness of something new; something unfelt and unknown ever before."[100] George Sanger had similarly visceral fear when his father inadvertently picked up some "resurrectionists" (grave robbers) while driving their cart one evening. All the boy knew was that he had caught a glimpse of a corpse being carried in a bag. Eventually the grave robbers fell asleep and Sanger's father was able to alert the police and have them arrested, but the episode traumatized him. "I was for a time very sick and ill, and months later would start from my sleep, shrieking that I saw a dead woman's face near mine." Many years later, he admitted that the memory was still "horribly vivid."[101] The Scottish apprentice John Kelso Hunter, later an artist, recalled the advent of the first steam train to Scotland. As people crowded around it, the engineer opened the steam safety-valve, producing an explosive noise. "All sorts of murder shouts rose from the group. I was petrified, and held a death grip for a time, quite uncertain whether the people were killed, or I were still alive. It had on me a lasting effect."[102] These descriptions illustrate powerful, instinctive, somatic reactions, rather than the cognitive judgments often implicated in evaluating happiness.

Anger

Of sadness, fear, and anger, the last was described the most rarely. While the solid and muscular working-class body became a normative model for all men in imperial Britain, mores around fighting were beginning to change.[103] Although working-class communities had long sought to deter some episodes of domestic violence by witnessing, speaking up, and shielding battered women, respectable working men were increasingly expected to police their own behavior. Cases involving men's violence against their wives, while a staple of the police courts in London before 1850, became rarer, as middle-class beliefs about the repugnance of hitting respectable women found purchase in working-class communities.[104] As this transformation was uneven across place, time, and class, alternative ways of settling scores, such as lawsuits, were emerging as alternatives to feuding and ritualized violence.[105]

Descriptions of physical violence are most common among the earliest-born autobiographers in the sample. Writing in his diary just a few years past the turn of the nineteenth century, Joseph Woolley described his drinking companions as often engaged in physical fights, emphasizing that drink caused people to make choices they would never have made sober. When Woolley was a young man, he found physical fighting and its results to be an amusing part of life and an integral part of male conviviality, but when he got older, or if the fighting extended to domestic violence, he did not approve.[106] Thomas Bewick, born in 1753, was articled to an engraver at the age of fourteen, and recounted being followed and insulted by three "blackguard" apprentices "till I could bear it no longer, when, turning upon one of the sauciest of them, I presently levelled him, and was about serving the second in the same way, when they all three fell upon me and showed no mercy," blackening Bewick's eyes and scratching his face. "This was an abominable sight to the family, which no excuse could palliate," he recounted, of coming home to his master. As punishment for his participation in the fight, he was forced to go to church twice a day on Sundays and to read the Bible daily.[107]

While men were increasingly expected to eschew non-state-sanctioned violence, fighting remained an acceptable way for boys to work out their differences. Thomas Todd described blackening the eyes of a boy named Puggy who demanded one of the two wood pigeon's eggs he had robbed from a nest. When his mother saw Thomas's own black eyes, she only wanted to know who his opponents had been, and was glad he had given as good as he got.[108] Formulaic fighting continued in schoolyards into the twentieth century.[109] But George Edwards had to leave his post as a farm laborer at age nineteen because he and his workmate got into a fistfight with their employer, who accused them of stopping their plowing at the end of the field. "With an oath I denied this and called him a liar. He thereupon struck me with his clenched fist and knocked me down. As I got up I struck him on the side of the head with my whipstalk and knocked him down."[110]

Members of a few hypermasculine trades continued to be notorious for fighting. James Dunn, born in 1835, remembered that colliers settled their disagreements with fistfights that crowds would gather to watch.[111] At midcentury, Robert Watchorn, a coal miner and later leader of the American United Mine Workers, got into a scuffle with his boss. After being shouted and sworn at, Watchorn "blessed the rough and ready life I had been compelled to live as a Derbyshire schoolboy and pit lad." Unfortunately, the two men clashed so hard that Watchorn left the other man unconscious, and had to flee the coal mining village, learning only much later that the boss had survived their fistfight. Despite being wealthy and politically well connected by the time he wrote his narrative, he chose to recount the story, suggesting that he did not see it as embarrassing.[112]

Angry men were encouraged to subsume their anger in activities like boxing. One of the angriest working-class autobiographers in the sample, Daniel Mendoza, was led to a boxing career by his impulsive personality. Born into a humble Jewish family in London, Mendoza responded to racist insults by physically fighting.[113] As one song celebrated an opponent of Mendoza's: "So very polite, so genteel, such a soft complaisant modest face, What a damnable shame to be spoil'd by a curst little Jew from Duke's place!"[114] After his impetuousness led to the loss of one job after another, Mendoza decided to open a school of pugilism to support himself. He turned out to be a wonderful self-publicist, producing treatises on boxing that, by outlining a scientific and defensive approach, helped shift boxing from an emotional outburst to an actual sport. Similarly, Jem Mace was a teenager on the tramp, supporting himself by playing the violin, when a man came up and idly smashed his instrument, ruining his livelihood. "Never in my life did I fight so gladly, or with feelings of more bitter animosity. He had smashed my fiddle, my one possession that I cared for more than aught else, and I meant smashing him."[115] Like Mendoza, Mace became a champion boxer, channeling his inner rage into a more respectable arena.

These examples aside, autobiographers fulfilled the increasingly widespread social expectation that violence should be regretted. Some of this regret was driven by the nature of the genres in which they wrote; for example, imprisoned autobiographers were supposed to regret their crimes. James M'Kaen, about to be executed for the murder of Lanark postal carrier James Buchanan in 1797, wrote his life story at the behest of his jailers, and so, seemingly, to be an object lesson for others. He described himself as habitually enraged, noting, "I have, all my life, being a man subject to violent gusts of passion, so much so, that I could not command my temper at times, when I received but slight provocation." M'Kaen harbored a grudge against Buchanan due to some financial transactions that had taken place three years before the murder; and when the two of them began to argue, and Buchanan kicked him in the shin, M'Kaen responded by slitting the man's throat with his strait-razor. After that one violent impulse, however, he "was racked all night with the most tormenting anxiety of mind; for I declare the idea of death is nothing to me in comparison of the astonishing horror of conscience I felt at this time."[116] He managed to escape to Ireland, but was quickly taken into custody, brought back to Glasgow for interrogation, and had a mental breakdown under questioning. "When gazing on my hand that did the deed, I burst out into an involuntary flood of tears, and started up from my bed; and was fully resolved to burn my hand off my body, and set fire to my bed and bedclothes, to suffocate myself."[117] M'Kaen's narrative ended formulaically, with a confession of sin and begging for forgiveness.

But other autobiographers clearly reflected changing mores around male violence as they struggled after the fact with the "discipline" meted out by their own fathers, or by describing their own attempts at emotional control. As Julie-Marie Strange has described, they tried to rationalize that past corporal discipline within twentieth-century norms, by contrasting their own behavior with that of their fathers.[118] Francis Place described his father as angry and violent, beating his boys (but not the girls) for the smallest offense and getting into a physical fight with the housemaid who tried to protect them. Although at one point his father broke a stick across his head, causing him to lose consciousness, Place claimed to believe that his father was well intentioned. "He wished and intended that his children should be honest, sober, industrious, and in every sense of the word respectable . . . the modes he adopted for producing these desirable ends were such as he expected would produce them." Nor was Place's father alone in this since, as Place noted, soldiers during this era were routinely flogged. When Place grew to adulthood, however, he felt shame about his own anger toward his wife.[119]

Horribly burned in a childhood accident that forever impaired his vision, Edward Rymer described one moment of sheer joy in his autobiography—when he finally, in middle age, acquired a pair of glasses with very strong lenses.[120] For the most part, however, Rymer was angry. Constantly hard-pressed to make a living as a miner due to his vision impairment and rheumatism, and yet completely unwilling to give up his commitment to the idea of unionizing miners, he lost one job after another. At one point "pain and anxiety completely crushed me, and I fell under the blow . . . many saw me fall, but few put forth a hand to help me. Such is life, and such is the world's gratitude."[121] At another point, his anger was so disabling that his wife asked him to move out. "For a short time, my temper was uncontrollable, and I feared that my better nature would give way to violence."[122] In contrast with many autobiographers who found the process of looking back over their lives allowed them to relive pleasant memories, for Rymer the process was mentally destabilizing:

> And oh! When I think of this and the awful suffering of my wife and children at those times in this so called free, Christian and happy England my mind reels, my aged limbs totter under me, my eyes become sightless, and blood rushes like a seething torrent through my head. It is then that I feel the want of friends and cheerful advisers, to guide my steps from the path of temptation, for when I think of the little graves I have left behind me in various parts of England my soul is smitten and I long to fly from the haunts of men.

Leaving home and deserting his family for fear of harming them; surrounding himself with cheerful friends; throwing himself back into his nonstop, if not altogether successful, attempts to unionize miners—these were the methods that Rymer publicly admitted to using to grapple with his anger and depression.[123]

While male autobiographers experienced pressure to control their aggression or to channel it into socially acceptable forms like games and warfare, women were assumed to have less control over their negative emotions. Christian Watt attacked a farm overseer who flicked his riding crop at her: "I flew at him, attacking him like a ferocious wounded animal. I kicked his shins and with a resounding smack sent the fire flying in his face, first one side and then the other. He fled in fear." Sure that she was about to be fired from her position, she was instead called to an interview with the Master of Lovat, who was apparently attracted to her for her willingness to stand up for herself.[124] One of the crisis points in Louise Jermy's autobiography came when, after years of grimly accepting her stepmother's physical and mental abuse, Jermy snapped because her stepmother had confiscated some personal possessions. Not only would she get her Bible and other possessions back from her stepmother, she blamed her stepmother for her health condition (which seemed to be a traumatic brain injury brought on by the abuse) and swore, "I should neer forget that I would be revenged if I waited years for it, and that she would never forget it." Jermy refused to apologize for her outburst, nurturing a murderous hatred in her heart for a week.[125] Finally, as Emma Griffin has suggested, corporal punishment of children by mothers was "part and parcel of a nineteenth-century upbringing," and perhaps was an outlet for women's dissatisfaction with the narrowness and disappointments of their worlds.[126]

・・・・・・

As previous chapters have shown, happy people might cry public tears of joy as families were reunited after long absences; they might sing in unison in pubs or run and jump for joy in nature, or feel a quiet glow of pride in anonymous authorship, or experience a second round of contentment by thinking about happy moments. Working-class autobiographers' revelations about more negative emotions suggest that grief, fear, and anger had more stringent emotional display rules. The few women writing autobiographies in the nineteenth century could be less constrained in describing their emotional lives, since they were not hamstrung by rigid expectations about the bravery and composure of the respectable nineteenth-century

European white man. But this did not mean that men never felt sad or afraid or angry. Faced with the deaths of children or wives, they wept, but often in private. After banishing childhood fears about ghosts and corpses, they were encouraged to downplay their fears, although life-threatening situations could cause bodily reactions that overwhelmed them with terror. As boys, they might get angry and fight each other, but as men they were encouraged to expiate their aggression in more socially acceptable ways.

Some aspects of the emotional world of British working-class people have been reconstructed from their memoirs over the course of the thematic chapters. Some of that world is instantly recognizable to people in the twenty-first century: the joys of family and community, the emotionally restorative power of nature, the importance of having engaging work and pleasant co-workers. Some of that world may be more estranged from our personal experience: the joy of acquiring "knowledge under difficulties," perhaps, or (one would hope) the pride of a young child bringing home a first paycheck. To what extent does the emotional world of British working-class people born before 1870 support some of the generalizations current in the contemporary field of happiness studies? The next chapter sets up that conversation between the past and the present.

TEN

The Past and the Present Converse

WHAT IS "HAPPINESS"?[1] One of the major problems inherent in putting the present into dialogue with the past hinges on the multiplicity of definitions of happiness in the literature. For modern psychologists and philosophers who study this question, what is meant by happiness or "the good life" or "well-being" is extremely important, since they base their findings largely on questionnaires and surveys whose language can bias the outcome of their studies. For many people, the word "happiness" connotes emotions and mood, so when asked if they are happy, they tend to consult their mood at that moment.[2] In contrast, when people are asked how satisfied they are with the way their lives have gone, they tend to engage in a cognitive process rather than an emotional stock-taking. They assess their own achievements against some ideal state of affairs, their own goals, or the achievements of other people.[3] Some students of happiness have fused happiness and life-satisfaction into a larger category of "subjective well-being."[4]

Scholars Amartya Sen and Martha Nussbaum have proposed another way of measuring well-being, which relies on measures external to the subject. They suggest contrasting the resources people have with those needed for optimal human function, or, as it is often termed, "flourishing."[5] This method of investigating well-being can be useful for comparing happiness across disparate populations, since some people—especially the economically and socially marginalized—may adapt to the shortcomings in their environments: "To overlook the intensity of their disadvantage merely because of their ability to build a little joy in their lives is hardly a good way of achieving an understanding of the demands of social justice."[6] Unlike Sen, who proposes that there is no single list of human capabilities necessary for flourishing, Nussbaum offers ten specific qualities, including bodily health and integrity, interaction with the environment, play, the ability to reason, and the ability to affiliate with others in relationships.[7] Sen and Nussbaum's cautions about adaptation to environmental shortcomings provide a useful corrective to the idea that emotions alone tell us everything we need to know about happiness in the past; just because people may have been able to sometimes be happy does not indicate that their worlds were optimal or even acceptable.

A fourth way to identify well-being, *eudaimonia*, originated with the ancient Greeks. Like Sen and Nussbaum, Aristotle thought that a life well lived could be best assessed from the outside, but in contrast with them, he thought that no man could be counted happy until his life was over.[8] *Eudaimonia* connotes a life lived well, in ways that reach beyond the subjective experience of momentary happiness to incorporate not only pleasure and luck but also the right virtues displayed at the right time. In Aristotle's worldview, reflecting upon one's pursuit of excellence or some larger life goal might produce subjective feelings of happiness, but these are not necessary for eudaimonia to be present.[9] Eudaimonists emphasize that lives lived well must contain not only happiness but other characteristics, including autonomy and "meaning."[10]

Within England and later Britain, the word "happiness" and its cognates underwent a transformation between the sixteenth and nineteenth centuries. Happiness as a concept drifted away from "hap" or worldly fortune and toward multiple meanings connoting felicity, pleasure, the good for a man, or the good of mankind.[11] By the nineteenth century, the debate over whether public policies could facilitate happiness was in full swing, although social engineers differed about whether the best course of action for emotional uplift was the preservation of family structures, or security of income, or the provision of access to education.[12] Social-welfare promoters warned working people against ambition or jealousy that might undermine happiness, but at the same time sought to establish access to food, clothing, and shelter, without which happiness was a doubtful proposition.[13] Some Chartists and land reformers latched on to stereotypical notions of happiness (snug cottage, happy family, warm fire grate, robust harvest) to advance their demands. But Sarah Lloyd and Joanna Innes noted that even as discussions became ubiquitous about the government's role in promoting happiness, individuals considered happiness to be a feeling.[14]

In this book, I opted for a pluralistic understanding of happiness, spreading the definitional net as wide as possible so as not to foreclose the possibility that working-class Britons in the nineteenth century had differing definitions of what constituted "the good life." I read holistically, to see what these working-class deponents, all long dead, had to say to me about their emotional lives. To what extent was personal "happiness," rather than the well-being of the community, a common or even an acceptable expectation?[15] Did working people distinguish between or equate happiness and economic well-being, or did they identify other factors as promoting happiness? How were expressions of emotion displayed or muffled, encouraged or suppressed? Did working people in Britain share norms around emotion that might constitute an "emotional community"?[16] I found working-class autobiographers who made no mention of happiness at all, but who still thought that they lived good and valuable, or eudaimoniac, lives. Endorsing the notion that physiological needs must be met before happiness can be achieved, some of the poorest autobiographers dwelt more on the hardships of their lives than on any happy moments.

Putting the modern literature on happiness into dialogue with the past is helpful for several reasons. First, such a conversation can show diverging cultural values over time. For example, Jordan McKenzie points out that in Western modernity, many of us believe that people can make their own happiness, and indeed that they have that responsibility. But there is a difference between the fleeting experience of happiness, and the more lasting experience of contentment. Contentment, McKenzie argues, relies on a larger social context that gives life meaning and that social context has eroded over time.[17] Chapters 2–7 of this book do tend to support McKenzie's theory of the importance of social context, since so many of the aspects of the good life for nineteenth-century working people hinged on relationships with other people: co-workers, co-religionists, family members.

A second reason for the conversation is to test the transhistorical applicability of modern hypotheses about the preconditions for happiness. In modern studies, some conditions are strongly correlated with happiness, including being employed and having autonomy at work.[18] Close relationships promote happiness; researchers have reported that people who are married are happier.[19] A study of self-reported well-being across 142 nations noted a close correlation between well-being and social capital, defined as having dependable and trustworthy people to fall back on, belonging to associations, and volunteering; although the study also noted that there was some variance in how these features were valued culturally, and that the strongest correlations were in middle- and upper-income countries.[20] Those people who report being religious tend to report higher happiness levels; psychologists link these reports to the social networks, friends, and communities available within religious organizations, and the availability of comfort and explanation in times of stress or existential terror.[21] All of these concepts can be tested longitudinally with the addition of historical evidence.

British working people's emotional lives can also tell modern scholars something about the relationship between happiness and autonomy. According to Carol Graham, in the twenty-first-century world, people with few hopes of achieving long-term plans are more likely to define happiness as daily pleasure, particularly when they are surrounded by others who are similarly situated. Those with the ability to form and achieve longer-term goals are more likely to relate happiness to the achievement of those goals. It is possible to move from the short-term to the long-term category, and sometimes governments can facilitate this, through distributive programs, education, health provision, and other means. But moving from one category to the other—from enjoying little daily pleasures to being made aware that one might create long-term plans and goals but have significant hindrances in the way of achieving them—can decrease individuals' own happiness. If Graham is correct, we might see people living in a time of social or political transition experiencing less happiness, as they have suddenly become more aware of the arbitrary obstacles in the way of their goals.[22]

In my research, I found that nineteenth-century working-class autobiographers expressed remarkably little resentment about structural inequality, and great gratitude for the opportunities they managed to cobble together. Modern studies show that reported happiness may be positively influenced by behavioral training methods that encourage people to be aware of and thankful for what they have.[23] People are also more likely to be happy, even in a case of hard times, when they feel as though they have had some input into decision-making processes; particularly in early Victorian Britain, so much of the onus for personal success was placed on the individual that few autobiographers assigned anyone else blame for their predicaments.[24] The remainder of this chapter will use specific historical examples to reflect on some of the current hypotheses in the field of happiness studies.

Happiness and Cheerful Mood

In the modern happiness studies literature, happiness is often measured with reference to cheerful moods. Sonja Lyubomirsky, Laura King, and Ed Diener conducted a massive meta-analysis showing that in the industrialized West, people with habitually cheerful moods have better lives: more social interaction, more job success, better coping strategies, and even better health, and that the moods seem to precede the outcomes rather than the other way around. They end their article by wondering whether this has been the case across all times and places.[25] Positive emotions are thought to provide this array of beneficial outcomes by building creativity and resilience.[26] Daniel Haybron agrees, arguing that a person's positive emotional state, or psychological flourishing, is a better barometer of whether they are "happy" than a sum total of their pleasant experiences, or a cognitive assessment of their lives as a whole.[27] The philosopher Mark Walker has even called for research into pharmacologically increasing the happiness set-point for individuals who have not been diagnosed with depression.[28]

The evidence about cheerful moods from the working-class autobiographies is more mixed. Joanna Innes found that writers described outward expressions of happiness as a social norm more commonly in the second half of the nineteenth century than the first.[29] Some working-class autobiographers did endorse the connection between cheerful moods and happiness, but viewed cheerful moods as a matter of inborn temperament. John Britton, who wrote his autobiography during the 1840s (while in his seventies) characterized himself as "sanguine, cheerful, hopeful, and confident," and saw it as the reason for his long life.[30] Thomas Lipton noted that he had often been called "the world's greatest optimist . . . there's something buoyant and healthy in being an optimist. It is because of my optimism that I have gone through life smiling. That I am always in good mood and fine fettle."[31] Andrew Carnegie also reflected upon his own optimistic personality, "my ability to shed trouble and to laugh through life, making 'all my ducks swans,' as friends say I do." He noted that "a sunny disposition is worth more than fortune. Young people should know that it can be cultivated; that the mind like the body can be moved from the shade into the sunshine."[32] John Plummer, the son of a London corsetmaker, described himself as having a "natural buoyancy of spirits" that helped him deal with a miserable childhood. After a fever robbed him of his hearing, he was tormented mercilessly by the neighborhood children.[33]

But the role of moods—or what moods even were—was ambiguous. Before the emergence of materialistic theories of mind, passions and affections were thought to originate in the soul, as thoughts prior to any actions or bodily reactions. This interpretation was particularly prevalent among theologians.[34] If moods were thoughts, fluctuating moods might signal mental instability. An even temperament was an essential component of respectability, particularly for men. Women were thought to be more emotional, but even then, it was important to be steady.[35]

Cheerful moods could be ungrounded in reality. The emotional grandiosity that made Joseph Keating's happiness so fleeting comes through in his musings about his career as a novelist: "I believed that the novels which were in me and not yet written would be great, immortal books, that I would be regarded as a master, and my name spoken throughout the world. I saw myself famous for all eternity. Yet, not once did I see myself rich . . . I thought about making literature . . . with my career clearly fixed, I was happy in the present, and immortal in the future."[36] Although he wrote his memoir in prison after having murdered his wife, Charles Campbell "felt my mind endowed with a natural buoyancy that gave a sanguine tinge to my hopes, under the very worst of circumstance, and made me look with an air of indifference on all the little crosses and downfalls that marked my humble lot."[37] Even in prison, Campbell judged that he had been dealt with fairly.[38] Similarly, John Babbacombe Lee, nicknamed "the man they could not hang" after the hangman's trapdoor failed three times during the attempt to execute him, remembered being happy and sanguine throughout his trial. He smiled as he left the courtroom after sentencing, theorizing that nothing bad would befall the innocent man he considered himself to be.[39] In another instance, a young tradesman's clerk came down with an illness that had been sweeping through his hometown of Churchwick in 1834. As he lay in bed, delirious, with his family members crying around him and despairing for his recovery, he felt "indescribably happy . . . I had no pain, no anxiety, no wish—except it was that I should continue in that state of mental felicity forever." He remained in that state for about three hours.[40]

Moods, unlike character traits, could also be subject to sudden shifts. Writers of autobiographies centering on religious conversion documented mood swings so often that they seemed to be integral to the genre. The Methodist minister Joseph Barker remembered his mother oscillating between ecstasy and depression; she interpreted the former state as a sign of God's good grace and the latter as a sign of God's displeasure. His father had similar mood swings: "they both lived this up and down, this shuttlecock sort of a life for a great many years."[41] Barker's parents' lives were complicated by their belief in, but inability to achieve, Methodist "second blessing," a state of sinlessness that would result in the acquisition of a permanently ecstatic mood.[42]

Thomas Lidgett's autobiography describes similar mood swings, or what he called "fits of despondency," related to religious belief and doubt. Lidgett contemplated suicide on several occasions and once was committed to an asylum for fifteen months, but these dark moments were dispelled by an epiphany: "I remembered everything was not mine, but I said it is my Fathers; I will trust him . . . He has pardoned all my transgressions this morning and I am so happy I cannot stand still."[43] Johanna Brooks upset her entire family by insisting that she had been called upon to preach. Although her religious beliefs filled her with ecstatic joy, her husband beat her with a stick for disobeying him, and his parents insisted that she was insane and should be under a doctor's care. Ultimately, all of her family members were converted; but their immediate reaction to her religious ecstasy—suspicion that Brooks was insane—is telling.[44]

Bad moods were just as untrustworthy as happy moods. John Savage, a miller, described his own mood swings as "hypochondria." "The periods of depression and elevation lengthen'd progressively with me from one Month to three and from that to six, and used for years together to return as regularly as an intermitting fever." At his lowest point, he experienced "a deep melancholy and ardent wishes for dissolution, with very great temptations to attempt my own release"[45] Later in his narrative he noted that "the unhappy Person that is strongly affected with Hypochrondria beholds a black side to everything that he views and can't see a bright one to anything."[46] Thomas Wilkinson Wallis noted that at one point in his early worklife he found himself subject to free-floating bad moods. He dismissed these as having no rational basis, but still thought them significant enough to recount the event in his autobiography: "I suffered much from depression of spirits—nervousness, I suppose. I did not know any cause for it. I had as many comforts of life as I ever expected to have, still, life seemed a burden, and there appeared nothing in life worth living for. But this feeling was happily transitory."[47]

Cheerfulness, or the outward manifestation of happy moods, could be a false front toward oneself or others. Charles Manby Smith, a printer who had moved to Paris during a period of economic depression, found while there, among the workmen, "a factitious kind of gaiety and frivolity not at all natural to my temperament stole over me by degrees, and was the result doubtless of associations which engendered habits both of thinking and acting altogether contrary to my true disposition."[48] Ellen Johnston, who had been traumatized by her stepfather as a young teenager, felt the same: "When mixing with a merry company no one could be more cheerful, for I had learned to conceal my own cares and sorrows, knowing well that 'the mirth maker hath no sympathy with the grief weeper.' "[49] Harvey Teasdale, a strolling performer who spent much of his time impersonating a monkey, had been cuckolded by his wife but tried to cheer himself up by pretending to be happy. "How little does the motley, mirth-seeking audience of the theatre know of the bitterness of spirit that is hidden under the grinning mask and grotesque antics of the miserable clown who excites their thoughtless laughter," he mused.[50] Clearly, while cheerful moods are central to modern-day happiness studies, working-class autobiographers had a more nuanced assessment of moods.

While some autobiographers discussed moods, many emphasized the importance to happiness of resilience and low expectations. The anonymous Dissenting minister who wrote *Struggles for Life* recounted an entire series of life lessons which to him constituted happiness. He averred that no man could know ahead of time what was best for him, and so it was better not to try to anticipate the intentions of Divine Providence. A person's attitudes toward the things that happened in life determined his happiness rather than the things themselves. "Happiness must dwell within, or be an entire stranger."[51] He had learned to be contented with the bare minimum necessary for life. Work was not only a duty, but it also tended to make people happy. Finally, if unsurprisingly in a clergyman, he claimed that Christianity was good for everyone, not simply because it gave people attitudinal happiness or hope but also as an instrumental value, which "greatly improves the physical and domestic condition of those who believe in it."[52]

James Hopkinson, a nineteenth-century furniture maker and salesman, mentioned his own happiness more frequently than most other writers. His first memories of happiness were in childhood, when a woman preacher came to the Primitive Methodist chapel, and, later, when he heard a choir sing Luther's hymn at St. Paul's church in Nottingham.[53] Religion continued to be a source of happiness and joy into Hopkinson's old age.[54] Like many other working-class children, he was delighted by nature and made happy by reading outdoors.[55] As he grew older, he took great pleasure in his work, both creating furniture and showing it to people. For Hopkinson, novelty and keeping busy were important; he enjoyed teaching himself about astronomy from Herschel's lectures, and spent time fishing, playing cricket, and amusing himself with a lathe.[56] "In fact I always have had some hobby or other. I think that man is the most miserable who has no mind or inclination to amuse himself or another by an innocent relaxation or amusement. The mind of man is a very wonderful contrivance, if it has not something to employ its powers upon it becomes weak and inactive. Work, not idleness, leads to enjoyment."[57] Moreover, from Hopkinson's perspective, novelty and activity produced happy memories, which he could then enjoy at his leisure.[58]

Hopkinson's resilience gave him a good base from which to deal with disappointment. A relationship he hoped would end in marriage was blocked by disapproval of family members on both sides. When his mother refused to give him her blessing, Hopkinson broke off his relationship with his intended. He was at first "like a fish out of water," but then threw himself into work as a way of avoiding thinking about the situation. "It was ten times better than going about moaning & groaning, and looking as if I could not say boo to a Goose. Then again I am not constituted to be very unhappy for very long altogether." Hopkinson acknowledged that part of his inability to stay sad for long was constitutional: "I have always within me such a fund of enjoyment when I am well that it rises spontaneously and I cannot help it." But another source of his good humor was attitudinal: "I am a firm believer in an ever-ruling providence and that if we commit our ways to the Lord he will direct our steps."[59] Ultimately, once Hopkinson's mother died—six years later—he was free to marry, and ended up with "a good and suitable companion one with whom I could take sweet council and whose love and affection was only equall'd by her ability as a business woman."[60] Hopkinson doesn't seem to be overestimating his own resilience here; the editor of his memoir, his great-grandson, wrote, "My mother used to speak of her grandfather as 'such a jolly man.' "[61]

A father and a son wrote autobiographies that showed how contrasting temperaments and mental framing could make the difference between a happy and an unhappy life. William Thomas Swan, born in 1786, left home after a disagreement about religiosity with his parents and became a brickmaker. While in his autobiography he reflected occasionally on material scarcity, physical pain, or on the extent to which his religious belief did not match up to all that God expected from him, he generally did not want things that he did not have. "Why should I talk of brighter days when thousands would be glad to be as I am, and again how many times have I been told that mine is an enviable situation."[62] In his autobiography, William Thomas's son, William Swan (born in 1813), described his father as "one of the most happy and cheerful men in the world."[63]

In contrast, the younger William Swan was a boiling kettle of discontentment, in a way that estranged him from family and friends. His material condition was not that much different from his father's, although he was trained as a confectioner rather than entering the brickmaking trade. While his first child was born two years before he and his wife could afford to marry, they did marry, and eventually had six children who grew to adulthood, along with the several who died in infancy. But Swan's ailments (including asthma, boils, scrofula, and leg pain) made him despondent, he worried that he was not destined for salvation, and he argued with his bosses about why other people were given work but not him. One of his sons, Phillip, had risen in station from poverty to a salary of 500 pounds a year, and William Swan constantly and fruitlessly nagged him to send money.[64] Swan noted that "I had the pleasure of living to see all three sons and all three daughters married, but I also bore the contempt of being absent their weddings, my presence not being desireable. I could not help thinking, 'If I be a father where is my honour?' "[65]

Some autobiographers developed compensatory philosophies to help them adapt to their circumstances or to anticipate future disappointment. The talented wood sculptor Thomas Wilkinson Wallis believed that every experience of pleasure in a person's life would be counterbalanced, at some point, by an equivalent amount of pain. "The characteristics of our nature are not adapted to continued or lasting happiness. The very ingredients that constitute our happiness contain also the seeds of our misery."[66] Wallis had concluded this based on his own experiences as a sculptor, as eye disease rendered him unable to sculpt even though he was at the height of his artistic powers. David Johnston described the events of the first year of his married life as a catalog of the experiences that composed happiness: "To be lifted from a miserable life of servile drudgery into a snug, sweet home at the age of twenty-six years, in robust health; to be in communion with the woman you dearly love, and with whom you have been acquainted for eight years; to be blessed with a promising son; to have your credit well-established; to possess the confidence of your fellow-creatures, and all your prospects brightening, must be felt to be appreciated." Unfortunately, Johnston noted, "such felicity seldom falls to the lot of man. Indeed, I have been led to look upon happy coincidences as the harbinger of evil." To the superstitious Johnson, his awareness of his own happiness presaged his young wife's illness and death. If happiness did occur, it might not only be fleeting but the sign of looming disaster.[67] Maidservant Hannah Cullwick thought having low expectations could allay disappointment. "The greatest pleasure wears away and quickly too and I've so long learnt that to save disappointment one mustn't expect pleasures," she noted.[68] Working-class autobiographers, then, had complex definitions of happiness that did not necessarily revolve around cheerful moods.

Economics and Happiness

Economists have historically not been concerned with "happiness" per se but rather with "utility"—the positive feedback that individuals receive from the goods and services that they are able to secure with a given level of income.[69] If utility depends on income, then rising wages, under the right distributional conditions, should create better conditions for people. But Richard Easterlin questioned this correlation in the 1970s, arguing that a focus on gaining ever more income distracts people from the fact that they will adapt to greater levels of income, and then have increased expectations that require ever *greater* levels of income. In contrast, cultural goods like music and art, and social goods like health and family, provide more utility than does the acquisition of consumer products.[70] Contemporary students of happiness have explored this "Easterlin paradox": that although within any given society wealthier people report being happier than poorer people, economic growth appears not to impact the level of happiness in a society over the long term.[71] Easterlin concluded that what was most important was relative deprivation, or one's status compared with the rest of the society.

Work done on this issue since the 1970s has suggested that the correlation between income and happiness is more robust than the Easterlin paradox suggests. Income and subjective well-being do correlate, at incomes up to about the 75th percentile.[72] Moreover, people in countries with higher levels of income in an absolute sense tend to enjoy better public goods that they also may not notice but which add to happiness, like cleaner environments and better infrastructure.[73] Nonetheless, people do tend to adapt to positive changes in income, and to overestimate the degree of happiness that they will achieve with such changes in income, and to underestimate the degree of happiness conferred by such "intrinsic" enjoyments as family and hobbies.[74] Interestingly, researchers have also found that this correlation between happiness and income is expressed more strongly among male research subjects. They theorize that poor women may look for their life satisfaction measures within the home and family relationships.[75]

Contemporary scholars of happiness have noticed that people tend to resent visible divergences in status—a great gap between the rich and the poor, the powerful and the powerless, the well-educated and the deprived—particularly when there is no good explanatory factor for such differences. When poverty can be attributed to moral failure or laziness, or alternately, to God's will or natural differences of quality at birth, or when high-status people are less visible, there is less resentment.[76] A few autobiographers did express such resentment. As the papermaker William Hutton noted, "There is nothing more common than for a man to be discontented with his state. Something is always wanting, and that want, though a trifle, becomes a balance, in his own esteem, against the many things he enjoys, though any one of them is equal to the thing wanted."[77] Deborah Smith, when she was a young married woman, illustrated this discontentment through her envy of her friends' possessions. "When I went into my friends' homes, and saw the mahogany drawers with the large looking-glass on top, and their dresser with the beautiful globes on, I often felt dissatisfied and unhappy. I dreamt how some day I would have a happy home with everything my heart could desire."[78]

But working people with few expectations of upward mobility—those whom John Burnett described as having "patient resignation"—professed to feel more contentment than those who were striving but found their road to prosperity blocked.[79] In that vein, the Norfolk rural laborer George Baldry noted, "What the ear hath not heard nor the eye seen, the heart does not grieve for."[80] Henry Quick of Zennor, a Cornish working-class poet who seems to have suffered from a disability, was content without wealth but troubled by community rumors that he had a large stockpile of cash hidden away. This rumor poisoned his relationships, including that with his wife, who had been "jealous" of the imaginary fortune for the eight years of their marriage. Quick wrote: "Poverty is a grievous trouble, but harsh reflection makes it double. When poverty in doors doth hie, out window love doth swiftly fly. Content and peace is all I crave; Nor noise or strife I wish to have . . . Though poor and mean may be my lot, let sweet content dwell in my cot; Disdain no humble life to live, with gratitude ask and receive."[81]

John Plummer, a corsetmaker's son turned poet, incorporated the same sentiments into a poem in his *Songs on Labour:*

> The World grows old and Men grow cold
> To each while seeking Treasure;
> And what with Want, and Care and Toil
> We scarce have time for Pleasure;
> But never Mind, that is a loss

> Not much to be lamented;
> Life rolls on gaily if we will
> But smile and be contented.
> If we are Poor and world be Rich
> It will not be by pining;
> No! Steady Hearts and hopeful Minds
> Are Life's bright silver lining.
> There's ne'er a man that dared to *hope*
> Hath of his choice repented;
> The happiest Souls on Earth are those
> Who Smile and are Contented.[82]

In his study of English folk songs, Vic Gammon noticed a similar social psychology expressed in drinking songs; company and conviviality were important, but wealth was overrated.[83] Few autobiographers professed resenting being blocked from otherwise obtainable goals by their class position—what David Vincent refers to as "blighting consciousness." Many more expressed a sense of fatalism and patient resignation about their conditions.[84] The attempt to achieve happiness by focusing on gratitude rather than frustration was all well and good as long as a person was not destitute (the bar for destitution was set surprisingly low).[85]

A modern meta-study of happiness indicates that in developing countries, poorer people are made happier than are wealthier people by small increases in their resources. Social scientists use "need theory" to explain this phenomenon, concluding that people who are unable to meet their most basic physiological needs are the ones who benefit the most from each additional increment of income, so that additional income, fulfilling those basic needs, makes them much happier.[86] As chapter 8 has shown, people in the most desperate economic situations were less likely to reflect on happiness than were those with their basic needs met. Without the means to keep hunger at bay, other aspects of fulfillment had to be postponed. An anonymous Glasgow weaver, suffering through a work shortage in 1826, wove all day long and was still unable to earn enough to support his family. His twelve-year-old son continued at the loom after his father had gone to sleep, in order to maximize use of their capital. In between paydays the family foraged for hawthorn berries, and the father noted that "a scantiness of food for a length of time causes such an uneasiness, that there is not anything that can compensate for the want of it . . . hunger is always gnawing at us, and disturbs our peace."[87] Similarly, George Mitchell, the "skeleton at the plough," described an early life of long hours of rural labor and hunger so acute that he would drink buttermilk out of the pig's trough and root around in there for curds that the pig had missed, or gather snails and grubs and roast them to eat them. To save their self-respect his parents would pretend that he was being punished and send him to bed without dinner, "when, in reality, they had no food for me."[88]

Joseph Stamper, who spent several years wandering the country as a casually employed transient, was too concerned with his next meal and whether he had enough money to sleep in a doss-house (a flophouse) on any given evening to be happy. But more than that, Stamper resented the way in which his ragged and dirty appearance caused others to deny him dignity. As a young man, he longed for the company of women, but knew none would be interested in a man with neither a home nor a job. When he went back to his hometown, people that he knew looked right at him—almost through him—without recognizing that they knew him. The alienation from other human beings caused him to break down in tears at his mother's grave, and he reported that the experience also permanently hindered his ability to make friends. Without a certain economic minimum, human dignity was impossible.[89]

The lack of money was often compounded by the absence of physical safety. John Buckley's mother died when he was two years old, and until the age of ten he lived with an aunt and uncle who treated him with incredible cruelty. He was physically abused, starved, made to do all of the household chores, and even tied to a bedpost. At one point, as punishment, he was told that he had drunk poison (he hadn't) and then measured for a casket by the local carpenter.[90] Mary Saxby recounted a childhood of abuse, including having been robbed, threatened with a knife, and chained to a bed by her own father, who fed her only crusts of bread. Unsurprisingly, Saxby ran away from home three times by age eleven.[91] Her life, after she ran away with a group of gypsies, was never pleasant; she lived with a man who went on to marry another woman, was arrested and kept in a prison for petty offenders for six weeks for having been arrested in the company of a prostitute, and became pregnant by John Saxby, who subsequently deserted her to join the army.[92] Ultimately, after siring two more children, he agreed to marry her, but he was abusive. Saxby suffered the loss of a surviving twin and all of her worldly goods in a fire. Ultimately, she interpreted her hardships and disappointments as the result of not being "a child of God."[93]

Robert Blincoe, whose disfigured body became a synecdoche for the impact of factory toil on children, described his early life as a failed search for human dignity. At the age of four he was dumped at St. Pancras workhouse, having no memory of his family and an abiding sadness that no one came to claim him. The workhouse was so miserable that Blincoe hoped to be chosen as a chimney-sweep's boy. As Blincoe's interlocutor and scribe wrote, "Estranged from the common ties of nature, it is less to be wondered at, that propelled by a violent inclination to a rambling life, and loathing the restraining imposed by his then condition, he should indulge so preposterous a notion, as to prefer the wretched state of a sweeping-boy." Although Blincoe was not chosen to be a chimney sweep, he was "intoxicated with joy" to hear that the majority of workhouse children were going to be shipped north as factory apprentices.[94]

Edward Finlay, a chain-making Liverpool street beggar nicknamed "Penny-a-yard," was rendered obsolete by a mechanical chain-making apparatus, which made better chain faster than he was able to do by hand. Destitute, he collected subscriptions from local businessmen in order to put together a saleable autobiography that was only a tale of woe. Finlay had lost a hand and sustained deforming facial burns in childhood, the combination of which harmed his prospects for employment. He and his wife had to support seven surviving children; two had already died of malnutrition. One day when he went out to beg, and was lucky enough to get a shilling, he returned only to find that his heavily pregnant wife had suffered a stroke that paralyzed one side of her body. When Finlay was arrested for street begging, his wife was forced to shift for herself, sheltering for three weeks in a public outhouse, during which period her newborn infant died. All Finlay asked was that readers empathize with him enough to buy the chains and mats that he made.[95]

J. H. Powell remembered of his neglect-filled childhood, "for years we all suffered—suffered from want of food, want of clothes, want of happiness."[96] Henry Snell reverted to the emotional sublime—noting that his feelings could not properly be described—when he thought back to an extended period of unemployment that he had suffered: "I find it difficult to record in detail the many difficulties and privations of this period in my life, for to recall them even in my own memory is very like the pain associated with the reopening of a recently healed wound. I can only assure the reader of this book that behind these general phrases there is a grim background of physical impoverishment and emotional suffering that I do not care to describe." He described unemployment as a "mental hell," stifling him in his desire to be a constructive member of society, and nurturing in him a sense of grievance against the world. "The memory of those days still bites into my soul like a hot iron."[97] Stories like those of

Blincoe, Finlay, Buckley, Powell, and Snell demonstrate that a certain economic minimum was needed to ensure that people could be free of hunger, live autonomously, have relationships with others without being shunned as social outcasts, have any leisure time, or be able to avoid certain kinds of arduous labor.[98]

Adaptation

Many of the working-class autobiographers adapted to their circumstances because they had very modest expectations. A tramp who went by the name of Dick Arch, interviewed in prison, described a life history that, while it never included a stable home or a job, had its enjoyable moments. Arch was raised by an adult beggar who had informally adopted him when he was three years old. Later in life, he fell in love with a "van girl" named Jenny, whose job it was to shake a tambourine and encourage people to see a sideshow. That relationship, he confided, was "the beautifullest, happiest time that ever a poor chap could know." Although he and his girlfriend Jenny were homeless, they were comfortable living outside while it was warm, and fed themselves by working as street musicians. Unfortunately, by the time winter rolled around Jenny was heavily pregnant and their housing situation was insecure. One night when they were unable to pay for any indoor shelters, she died of exposure. Arch's interviewer intended the autobiography to serve as social commentary, noting that in some way the system was failing such men. But Arch's indomitable refusal to obey social norms, and desire to live autonomously if poorly, comes through very strongly in the dictated autobiography.[99]

Frederick Rogers remembered reading works like *All Sorts and Conditions of Men* that described the grinding poverty of East London, where he grew up. "I had lived there all my life, and had got solid happiness out of the conditions . . . they were not terrible to me. Poverty there was, and I had shared it; but I knew—even though a thin wall stood between them and the workhouse—there was often happiness and upright, honorable lives among the poor."[100] Rogers particularly admired his mother, an uneducated farmworker who had moved to London, for being able to create a "clean, happy, righteous home" on twenty-five shillings a week. Frank Forrest, who began to work in a Dundee mill as a boy after his father was transported to Australia, resented living in an overcrowded and dirty city and hated his work, and particularly the people he worked with. But he noted that "happiness surely depends more on the state of the mind and heart, than on the factious trappings of worldly circumstances; for, even amidst our misfortunes, wretchedness, and poverty, rays of felicity sometimes penetrated and relieved our minds from the painful monotony of unceasing misery." He particularly felt his mother's love, and her appreciation for the contribution he was able to make to keeping them both fed and clothed.[101]

Some working people took pride in their very poverty, arguing that their lack of money enabled them to cultivate superior, nonmaterialistic values. Joseph Mayett of Quainton worked on a farm before enlisting in the army. As soon as he had saved a little money, he noticed himself changing his spending habits, becoming miserly not only to his friends but also to himself. Ultimately, he shook off this negative personality change by spending all of his money. "Here I lost my Spirit of Covetousness and I am sure I lost the worst torment I ever had in my life for in all my Straits in poverty I was never so miserable as I was in the love of money," he noted.[102] Thomas Oliver comforted himself with the same thoughts. "My readers will see that my life has not been all sunshine as far as wealth is concerned; but I can assure them that it has been a very happy one. I know if I had the mind I could have accumulated more wealth, but more wealth would not have produced more happiness." For Oliver, who was made happiest when studying nature, an attachment to wealth have made him a slave.[103]

The "cheap jack" William Green, who hawked goods at fairs, scoffed at "certain people who really believe in themselves, and are constantly cuddling the idea that money makes happiness."[104] Similarly, Tom Barclay, who later became a Socialist, writer, and secularist, grew up in a household that he described as having no comforts whatsoever: "What a monotonous childhood! No toys, no picture-books, no pets, no going 'ta-ta.' No carpet on the uneven brick floor, no mat, no wallpaper, what poverty!" Having reached the age of eight in slum conditions, Barclay went to work, variously in rope-walks, shoemaking, and textiles, his long days punctuated by punishment meted out either by his various employers or by his often-drunk father. Barclay was bored and disappointed, but unconvinced that those born with more advantages were any less likely to be bored or disappointed with life.[105]

As this section has shown, the experiences of working-class autobiographers bear out the notion that some minimal level of income is necessary for comfort, safety, and dignity, without which happiness is very difficult to achieve. On the other hand, in contrast with people in modern developed nations, few nineteenth-century autobiographers rode the hedonic treadmill. The autobiographers often adapted to the conditions that made upward mobility impossible, through stoicism, fatalism, nostalgia for the moments of joy in their lives, and a kind of repeated cognitive reassurance that the lives of the wealthy were not more likely to be generally happy than those of the poor.

Happiness and the U-Shaped Curve

Some modern scholars of happiness (including philosophers, psychologists, and economists) have posited the existence of a U-shaped happiness curve: people who are surveyed profess to be happiest in youth and in old age, with the financial and familial cares of middle-age producing a low point in relative happiness.[106] Controversies about whether the curve is shaped like a sine wave rather than a U, or whether it is fair to calculate the shape of the curve without controlling for factors like income and health, muddy the initial impression somewhat, but it does seem clear that, particularly when "life-satisfaction" is measured (a cognitive assessment of happiness) rather than "happiness" (an assessment of one's current mood), subjective well-being dips in adulthood and then rises later in life, perhaps dipping again for the oldest old. Social scientists have posited various hypotheses about the happiness curve, including that older people might feel happier due to less work-related stress and fewer social expectations, or that older people might be better at emotional regulation and thus have adapted to the circumstances of their lives.[107]

Scholars in this area note that longitudinal studies are scarce; this is where autobiographies can add to the conversation.[108] Many working-class autobiographers described experiencing a U-shaped subjective well-being curve. The Coventry weaver Joseph Gutteridge wrote: "In taking a retrospect of life I am struck at its various phases. Sometimes its complexion has been bright and beautiful, as in my younger days while roaming the fields and lanes in search of plants and wild flowers. The aspect of Nature transformed the world into a veritable paradise, made happier by the loving care and protection of earthly parents."[109] Like other autobiographers, he described childhood, the period pre-dating financial responsibility, as particularly magical. He continued:

> After this period came shadows—privations and trouble—but viewed from the standpoint of old age these were as nothing in their effects upon manhood compared with the blighting influence of the dark shadows of Materialism which enveloped the mind for about eighteen years of the best part of life. This materialistic philosophy

of non-responsibility almost brought me to a state of unreason, so dark and gloomy was the prospect.

Not only did Gutteridge and his young family face near-destitution at several intervals while his children were young, but his firm conviction that there could be no afterlife also depressed him, putting strain on his wife that he thought sent her to an early grave. After her death, he turned to "the study of various physical sciences and the investigation of spiritual phenomena . . . the pleasure experienced in these pursuits led to the resolve not to live for self alone, but to place at the service of those who were struggling for 'more light' whatever knowledge I had gained. The power to help others confers a pleasure beyond all expression." In his old age, then, Gutteridge's focus shifted from hedonic pleasures, happiness as experienced in a particular moment, to whole-life satisfaction. Being able to retrospectively structure his life as a heroic narrative, triumphing over adversity and turning his purpose to help others, gave him great contentment, and he looked forward to the afterlife that he was now convinced existed.[110]

As chapter 2 showed, many working-class autobiographers fondly remembered childhood with great detail. Young adulthood and middle age, when families were growing, and children needed to be supported, were often more difficult phases of life. In the words of the artist John Kelso Hunter, who at one point had nine children living, "The morning and evening of life seem nearest each other. The middle department is more bustle and confusion."[111] Authors described old age with fondness as their responsibilities receded. Of course there is narrative pressure to end any story—even a life story—with a happy ending, but autobiographers also provided explanations for their positive assessments of old age. One of these was being able to relive pleasant memories; as George Sanger noted, "In old age—perhaps as one of its compensations—the memory is able to picture with unusual brightness the scenes of one's very early days."[112]

Elderly writers experienced happiness observing their descendants or other young people. A Scottish printer who had become a pastor and spent most of his work in Christian outreach was comforted by reading literature that lauded old age as one of the happiest times. He appreciated the ability to visit a nearby happy family, and to have time to write articles and tracts.[113] Joseph Philip Robson, who tragically lost five of his six children between infancy and young adulthood to disease and workplace accidents, found joy in the family of his only living child. "He is married, and has three fine little girls; so that the halo of happiness still encircles our humble hearth. The flowers of childhood are ever sweet. They bring back the memories of the loved and lost."[114]

James Mullin, whose life took him from abjection to eventual comfort as a doctor, looked back at his life from age seventy-one with satisfaction as one well lived, and supposed that the difficulty of his early days made his satisfactions as an adult even sweeter. He enjoyed the process of writing his memoir, and "in listening to Nature's sweetest music—the prattle of my grandchildren—I am transported back to the happy days of childhood, which I can imagine but have never experienced." Even though he was writing during the period of the Great War, the war of "Right against Might, of Light against Darkness," gave him optimism for the future. Like other writers who looked back from the perspective of old age, he professed to find pleasure in being free from temptations. "The pleasures of youth and manhood are the pleasures of the senses, and their intoxication is often followed by unpleasant reaction. The pleasures of old age are the pleasures of the intellect and affections, pleasures that soothe and sweeten and beget no regrets."[115]

Other writers looked forward to spending time in leisure after lives spent in manual labor. Although the Socialist journalist Robert Blatchford had lost his wife ten years before writing his autobiography, he professed at the age of eighty to "enjoy literature and the cricket news and music and poetry and detective stories and gardening and the beauty of clouds and trees. Mentally and spiritually I am as young as I was at forty—and younger, happier, more cheerful, more serene."[116] Blatchford explained this phenomenon as the loss of anxiety about the future; he no longer had to worry about supporting his family financially, or providing his wife with a home, and his desires and ambitions had contracted with age.[117]

Having found the perfect job, Anthony Grundy titled the section of his memoir in which he began to work on the railroad, "Happy at Last." While he had a successful fifty-year career, however, he felt just as happy to be retiring: "Some people think it is a serious mistake to retire after leading an active life, but I hardly think this will apply in my case, as I am never so happy as when I have a spade in my hand getting the best out of good old Mother Earth; or a pitchfork during haymaking time; or better still, a sporting gun over my shoulder and accompanied by a well-trained spaniel."[118] William Henry Lax, who was in his late sixties when he wrote his autobiography, emphasized that while the body had no choice but to grow old, cheerfulness could keep the mind young. "Make up your mind to maintain a buoyant outlook on life. When the sun shines, let it shine on you ... Hang on to your sense of humour with both hands." Maintaining the "thrill and zest of life" could keep a man young: "his sense of wonder at the beauty of a sunset, or the glory of heroism and self-sacrifice, or the intricate markings on a butterfly's wings."[119]

The Pleasures of Memory

For many older writers, having time for the act of remembering constituted a pleasure in itself, allowing the sort of wool-gathering impossible in the press of midlife business. John Younger apologized to his readers for dwelling on his childhood, but noted that "I am feeling a certain pleasure in thus recalling the memory of those scenes which so interested at the time, and which to me can never again return."[120] Alf Ireson noted that as he wrote:

> Personal recollections, incidents of one's ancestors which were impressed on the infant mind. All return with a precious freshness. It has been a time of joy to me to write these lines. The mind has been taken back to the happy days of boyhood, and I have lived once more through the years of parental love. In fact, my dear mother has seemed very near. Her voice and smile! And at times it has seemed I felt her touch. She loved her Alf.[121]

John Wilson, who had been happily married for forty-six years, noted of writing about his deceased wife that "as I write these words, with the memory of that happy marriage day—better for me than I ever imagined—still living in my heart in its most minute detail, I am buoyed up and cheered."[122]

Although Alexander Mitchell, who served decades as the stableman to an aristocratic family, never married or had a family of his own, he found assessing his own life an enjoyable exercise. "It has been a great pleasure to me to have all these early and late reflections brought vividly to mind, and I am thankful that I have been spared to note down these particulars of what has been, on the whole, a happy life." Mitchell attributed his happiness to his good health, which in turn was due to the hard work he had done as a farm laborer.[123] Frederick Rogers, who was active in the bookbinders' union and in the national campaign for old-age pensions, noted that

> in these pages there is no quarrel with life, there is an appraisement of it as it presents itself to me after nearly threescore years and ten

of its experiences.... With all of its ups and downs, life has been to me a wonderful panorama, a rich banquet... one of its many paradoxes is that happiness is not found by those who set out to search for it, but is often found by those who do the work nearest to hand, because they feel it wants doing, and try to do it as well as they know how.[124]

At the end of his narrative, Rogers circled back around to the notion of the pleasure of old age. "It is well to have lived, to have helped one's fellows, to have enjoyed the sunshine of the good old earth, and that larger sunshine of the intellect and the soul."[125] As Emma Griffin has noted, many autobiographers writing in the late Victorian period or the early decades of the twentieth century pointed to positive social change that had occurred during their lifetimes; by ending their autobiographies on a happy note, they were reflecting the positivism of the age. Walter Freer noted that "mere youngsters" of sixty or sixty-five teased him about his optimism; but for him, at the age of eighty-three, his long life span had itself produced much pleasure. He had been able to see many of the improvements of the late nineteenth century: the phonograph, the internal combustion engine, electricity—and even those of the twentieth, including aviation. Societal improvement and the extension of the franchise had given him great optimism in the ability of man to progress—optimism that even the Great War didn't seem to have quashed.[126]

This is not to claim that every autobiographer found remembering to be pleasant; all, however, seem to have considered a summing-up of their lives to be important. James Houston, a comedian, packed his memoir with amusing anecdotes to entertain his friends, but noted at one point that looking over an old concert program gave him a "feeling of extreme sorrow," since ten of his friends listed on the program had since passed on.[127] James Dunn noted that "in recalling memories of the past seventy years, from the coal mine until now, I have had mingled feelings of pleasure and pain, of joy and sorrow, of thankfulness and regret."[128] John Fraser, who had kept his expectations fairly modest, considered himself blessed throughout his life: he had a successful career in India, a wife and six children, only one of whom died; and a post-retirement career of thirty-seven years as a Yeoman Warder in the Tower of London. "I have enjoyed myself while writing this book, as old men like myself do enjoy themselves in reliving past sorrows and gladnesses, tragedies and comedies... I have had a good time for most of my life."[129] Writing memoirs helped authors to give their lives some ultimate meaning, a narrative through-line where there may have seemed to be none before.[130]

As this chapter has demonstrated, nineteenth-century working-class autobiographies support some modern scholars' conclusions about the nature of well-being: for example, that childhood and old age may be experienced as more pleasant than midlife, due to the combination of relaxed expectations and narrative rethinking. Other scholarly assertions, including the notion that hedonic treadmill effects interfere with happiness, seem to be linked with a time and place. Autobiographers found ways cognitively to adapt to their situations, using fatalism or ideas about the balance of good and bad experiences to offset dissonance. While many modern scholars of happiness focus on mood and mood inventories, many nineteenth-century working-class autobiographers distrusted moods, viewing happiness as an underlying character trait or a reaction to external circumstances. For British working people, a level of income that did not provide safety or dignity or respite from hunger was inconsistent with the achievement of happiness, but few autobiographers expressed class-related grievances or openly compared themselves with others who were more prosperous. I would argue that these sorts of changes in the way that people experience and explain emotions to themselves are indicative of larger changes in the structure of values over time.

Conclusion

WHAT IS THE SIGNIFICANCE of this deep dive into the happiness of the British working class? Ever since Friedrich Engels wrote his *The Condition of the Working Class in England,* based on his firsthand observations in the 1840s, questions have circulated about the impact of industrialization on workers.[1] For decades, economic historians participated in the "standard of living" debate, attempting to intuit from data whether the short-run impact of urbanization and mechanization was positive or negative.[2] It is true that studying longitudinal wage series, working hours, the heights of birth cohorts over time, and differential life expectancies provides important guidance in this direction. But some aspects of life are not reducible to modeling, particularly without an understanding of the priorities, values, hopes, fears, and sources of enjoyment of those undergoing change, and their capacity for adaptation to circumstances. This study joins an expanding literature that adds qualitative evidence about those experiences by going to the source: the words of those who lived then.

As the foregoing chapters have shown, despite posing some epistemic challenges for the researcher, working-class autobiographies provide a rich window into the emotional lives of Britons born between 1750 and 1870. They link assessments of happiness and "the good life" with common themes and experiences. Autobiographers recounted the happy moments from their childhoods in detail. They remembered their nuclear and extended families, the oral transmission of the stories of their parents and neighbors, their outdoor play, and their favorite foods. Together, their autobiographies illustrate that working-class childhoods sometimes did include much more work than children should ever have to undertake, but that children adapted to their long workweeks, punctuated by the joy of Sundays. The existing evidence, heavily weighted toward male autobiographers, suggests that girls had fewer opportunities to take pride in their earned income, since they were sent away for domestic service.

Work could be a crucial factor in facilitating or detracting from happiness. While factory workers were underrepresented among working-class autobiographers, and factory toil was notoriously unrewarding, enjoyment and even "flow" were possible in some workplaces.[3] Workers discussed the pride that they took in their economic contributions. They celebrated moments in which they were able to use their creativity to solve problems. They understood the importance of a good fit between a worker and a workplace, and happy workers enjoyed good relationships with fellow workers and some employers. As with childhood experiences, the picture of women's experiences at work is harder to decipher, although it seems that even domestic service had the potential to offer moments of satisfaction.

One through-line in many of the foregoing chapters has been the importance of community and social ties to the happiness of British working people in the nineteenth century. Increasingly, working-class men and women formed marriages for companionship as well as economic survival. Children depended on parents and other relatives, and many counted their interactions with elders among their happiest childhood memories. Families relied on their individual members to contribute economically, and close family ties persisted even through physical separations, as shown by the ubiquity of references to emotional reunions. But community was also essential in other ways. Older workers and younger workers paired up on the job, facilitating the transmission of skills. Autodidacts learned with the help of those who lent books, joined in group study with curious individuals, or read the poetry that working-class novice poets produced. Many poor people extended assistance to others that they could ill afford, as part of a larger economy of prosocial activity that helped to substitute for the lack of distributive justice. A sense of duty to others impelled many autobiographers to participate in movements—temperance, missionary activity, Chartism, trade unionism—that promised to uplift people.

Another through-line in this study is the degree to which many of the aspects of happiness for nineteenth-century workers were low-cost or free (the opportunity cost of leisure excepted). For those living in crowded and uncomfortable homes, "outside" was an additional and essential living area. Those with access to the natural world could obtain ad hoc children's playthings, supplementary food, solitude, and beauty. Even working people without that immediate access might till allotments or window boxes to bring the natural world closer. In the realm of entertainment, individuals could learn to read through a number of inexpensive methods, including dame schools and Sunday schools, and sharing books and other materials made self-education accessible. Religious ceremonies, which many found uplifting, were accessible at no cost to anyone with clean and sufficient clothing. The persistence of community and of noncommercial forms of leisure into the industrial period may have helped to buffer some of the impacts of long hours, low wages, and urban pollution.

But even as community, nature, and self-cultivation offered accessible pleasures, some working-class autobiographers gravitated toward a version of the good life that prioritized duty over positive emotional states. The conversion narrative, part of the expansive menu of evangelical ideas available to nineteenth-century Britons, could provide even to the nonreligious a narrative frame for examining their own lives. They described their lives' arcs by focusing on religion, or political transformation, or social uplift. As they converted to teetotalism, or Chartism, or trade unionism, or Socialism, or anti-unionism, workers brought closer whatever worldly millennium they envisioned, even at the cost of transitory pleasures for themselves and their families.

This study has also hinted at a conclusion endorsed by Emma Griffin for a slightly later time period: that working-class women, particularly in cities and towns, had less access to the sources of happiness than did working-class men. Particularly after marriage, women had little leisure time. Most of their responsibilities were carried out indoors, often surrounded by children who required supervision, so such leisure activities as reading, or finding solitude in nature, were largely foreclosed. The round of housework was never-ending, the load made heavier by the physical challenges of childbearing, nursing, and childcare. Women had less access to adult friends. It is no wonder, under the circumstances, that church and chapel, sources of community and novelty as well as reassurance, attracted female congregants.

Nineteenth-century working-class autobiographies endorse some themes in the modern field of happiness studies and call the transhistoricity of others into question. Nineteenth-century autobiographers were skeptical about cheerful moods, but endorsed the ideas of cheerful dispositions, and particularly emphasized the importance of resilience. Perhaps as part of the cultivation of that resilience, most adapted to their social stations, professing to find contentment with little, as long as they possessed safety, dignity, and enough to survive. While autobiographers portrayed themselves as largely free of the "hedonic treadmill" effects that characterize many in the twenty-first century, they do share with contemporary people a tendency to describe contentment in old age and nostalgia for childhood.

Finally, autobiographers went into more detail about the sources of their happiness than about their unhappiness. Part of this is a result of self-selection and the desire of life-writers to give their lives meaning in retrospect. Even so, examination of sadness, fear, and anger in the autobiographies suggests that there is much more to be learned about emotional experience and expression among British working people, and particularly about the way in which such emotional displays as tears, irrational fright, and aggression helped to define working-class gender expectations in the nineteenth century.

NOTES

Introduction

1. William Hutton, *The Life of William Hutton, FASS* (London: Baldwin, 1817), 247. Modern scholars comment on the existence of a U-shaped happiness curve over the course of a lifetime, suggesting that childhood and old age are the periods of greatest happiness. Hutton's narrative coheres with this interpretation. See chapter 10 for more details.

2. John Britton, *The Beauties of Wiltshire* (London: J. Noves, 1825), xlvii.

3. Kristen Lindquist, Karen S. Quigley, Erika H. Siegel, and Lisa Feldman Barrett, "The Hundred-Year Emotion War: Are Emotions Natural Kinds or Psychological Constructions? Comment on Lench, Flores, and Bench," *Psychological Bulletin* 139, no. 1 (2013): 255–63; Kristin Lindquist, Suzanne Oosterwijk, Maria Gendron, and Lisa Feldman Barrett, "Do People Essentialize Emotions? Individual Differences in Emotion Essentialism and Emotional Experience," *Emotion* 13, no. 4 (2013): 629–44; Nicole Eustace, Eugenia Lean, Julie Livingston, Jan Plamper, William Reddy, and Barbara Rosenwein, "AHR Conversations: The Historical Study of Emotions," *American Historical Review* 115, no. 5 (December 2012): 1487–530, at 1506.

4. Fred Feldman explores the various theories and their proponents in *What Is This Thing Called Happiness?* (Oxford: Oxford University Press, 2010), passim.

5. On happiness and other emotions as "cluster concepts," see Alan H. Goldman, "Happiness Is an Emotion," *Journal of Ethics* 27 (2017): 1–16. On the qualities that render happiness an emotional state, see Mauro Rossi, "Happiness, Pleasure, and Emotions," *Philosophical Psychology* 31, no. 6 (2018): 898–919.

6. The chronological cut-off point provides a manageable sample of life-writers who were forced to adapt to the economic changes of the nineteenth century.

7. Darrin McMahon, "Finding Joy in the History of the Emotions," in *Doing*

Emotions History, ed. Susan J. Matt and Peter Stearns, 103–19 (Urbana-Champaign: University of Illinois Press, 2013).

8. See, for example, Darrin McMahon, *Happiness: A History* (New York: Atlantic Monthly Press, 2006); Nicholas P. White, *A Brief History of Happiness* (Oxford: Blackwell, 2006); Adam Potkay, *The Story of Joy: From the Bible to Late Romanticism* (Cambridge: Cambridge University Press, 2007).

9. Thomas C. Buchanan, "Class Sentiments: Putting the Emotion Back in Working-Class History," *Journal of Social History* 48, no. 1 (2014): 72–87.

10. Jan Plamper explores the history of the tension between biological theories of emotion and social constructivist theories in *The History of Emotions: An Introduction* (New York: Oxford University Press, 2015), 76–146.

11. A good summary of the historiography can be found in Susan J. Matt and Peter Stearns, *Doing Emotions History* (Urbana-Champaign: University of Illinois Press, 2013), 17–38. For the crucial early works on the history of the emotions, see Carol and Peter Stearns, "Emotionology: Clarifying the History of Emotions and Emotional Standards," *American Historical Review* 90 (1985): 813–36; and *Anger: The Struggle for Emotional Control in America's History* (Chicago: University of Chicago Press, 1987); and Peter Stearns, *Jealousy: The Evolution of an Emotion in American History* (New York: NYU Press, 1989); *American Cool: Constructing a 20th-Century Emotional Style* (New York: NYU Press, 1994); *Battleground of Desire: The Struggle for Self-Control in Modern America* (New York: NYU Press, 1999); and *American Fear: The Causes and Consequences of High Anxiety* (New York: Routledge, 2006).

12. Christina Kotchemidova, "From Good Cheer to 'Drive-by Smiling': A Social History of Cheerfulness," *Journal of Social History* 39, no. 1 (2005): 5–37; for a great modern example of emotionology, see the export of American smiling practice to Russian McDonalds employees in Alix Spiegel, "Changing Social Norms Can Save Your Life," *Invisibilia* Podcast, National Public Radio, available at https://www.npr.org/2016/06/17/482443233/listen-to-the-episode.

13. William Reddy, *The Navigation of Feeling: A Framework for the History of the Emotions* (Cambridge: Cambridge University Press, 2001).

14. Barbara Rosenwein, "Worrying about Emotions in History," *American Historical Review* 107, no. 3 (June 2002): 821–45; Barbara Rosenwein, *Emotional Communities in the Early Middle Ages* (Ithaca, NY: Cornell University Press, 2006). On the clashing of historical schools, see Rob Boddice, *The History of Emotions* (Manchester: Manchester University Press, 2018), 208–10.

15. Thomas Dixon, "The Psychology of the Emotions in Britain and America in the Nineteenth Century: The Role of Religious and Antireligious Commitments," *Osiris* 16 (2001): 288–320.

16. On the evolving history of concepts of happiness or the relevance of happiness as a category, see Robert Darnton, "The Pursuit of Happiness," *Wilson Quarterly* 19, no. 4 (1995): 42–53.

17. Iris Mauss, Maya Tamir, Craig Anderson, and Nicole Savino, "Can Seeking Happiness Make People Unhappy? Paradoxical Effects of Valuing Happiness," *Emotion* 11, no. 4 (2011): 807–15; James E. Crimmins, "Jeremy Bentham," in *The Stanford Encyclopedia of Philosophy* (summer 2020 edition), ed. Edward N. Zalta, available at https://plato.stanford.edu/archives/sum2020/entries/bentham, last accessed October 11, 2020.

18. Roy Porter, "Happy Hedonists," *British Medical Journal* 321, no. 7276 (December 23–30, 2000): 1572–75.
19. Thomas Hardy Society, "Negotiating the Emotional Habitus of the Middle Classes in *The Mayor of Casterbridge*," *Thomas Hardy Journal* 28 (2011): 44–67.
20. Caroline Austin-Bolt, "Sarah Ellis's *The Women of England*: Domestic Happiness and Gender Performance," *Nineteenth-Century Contexts* 37, no. 3 (2015): 183–95; Pamela Horn, *Ladies of the Manor: Wives and Daughters in Countryhouse Society, 1830–1918* (Phoenix Mills: Alan Sutton, 1991), 111–36.
21. Sarah Ahmed, *The Promise of Happiness* (Durham, NC: Duke University Press, 2010), 4.
22. Sonja Lyubomirsky, Laura King, and Ed Diener, "The Benefits of Frequent Positive Affect: Does Happiness Lead to Success?" *Psychological Bulletin* 131, no. 6 (2005): 803–55.
23. Mihály Csíkszentmihályi, "If We Are So Rich, Why Aren't We Happy?" *American Psychologist* 54, no. 10 (1999): 821–27; Barbara H. Rosenwein and Riccardo Cristiani, *What Is the History of Emotions?* (Cambridge: Polity Press, 2018), 105–7.
24. Mihaly Csíkszentmihályi, "If We Are So Rich"; Richard A. Easterlin, Laura Angelescu McVey, Malgorzata Switek, Onnicha Sawangfa, and Jacqueline Smith Zweig, "The Happiness–Income Paradox Revisited," *Proceedings of the National Academy of Sciences* 107, no. 52 (December 28, 2010): 22463–68.
25. Valerie E. Chancellor, ed., *Master and Artisan in Victorian England: The Diary of William Andrews and the Autobiography of Joseph Gutteridge* (New York: Augustus Kelley, 1969), 77.
26. Arthur A. Stone and Christopher Mackie, eds., *Subjective Well-Being: Measuring Happiness, Suffering, and Other Dimensions of Experience* (Washington, DC: National Academies Press, 2013), 78, 94.
27. Reddy, *Navigation of Feeling*, 105–6.
28. Ahmed, *Promise of Happiness*, 24.

Chapter 1: Interrogating Autobiographies

1. On the variety of working-class literary output, see Florence Boos, "Introduction: The Literature of the Victorian Working Classes," *Philological Quarterly* 92, no. 2 (Spring 2013): 130–45.
2. Emma Griffin, *Bread Winner: An Intimate History of the Victorian Economy* (New Haven, CT: Yale University Press, 2020), *Liberty's Dawn: A People's History of the Industrial Revolution* (New Haven, CT: Yale University Press, 2014), and "Diets, Hunger and Living Standards during the British Industrial Revolution," *Past & Present* 239, no. 1 (May 2018) 71–111; Julie-Marie Strange, *Fatherhood and the British Working Class, 1865–1914* (Cambridge: Cambridge University Press, 2015); Regenia Gagnier, *Subjectivities: A History of Self-Representation in Britain, 1832–1920* (New York: Oxford University Press, 1991); Patrick Joyce, *Democratic Subjects: The Self and the Social in Nineteenth-Century England* (Cambridge: Cambridge University Press, 1994); David Vincent, *Bread, Knowledge and Freedom: A Study of Nineteenth-Century Working-Class Autobiography* (London: Europa, 1981), and *Literacy and Popular Culture, England 1750–1914* (Cambridge: Cambridge University Press, 2011); Jane Humphries, *Childhood and Child Labour in the British Industrial Revolution* (Cambridge: Cambridge University Press, 2010);

Nan Hackett, *XIX-Century British Working-Class Autobiographies: An Annotated Bibliography* (London: AMS Studies in Social History No. 5, 1985), and "A Different Form of 'Self': Narrative Style in British Nineteenth-Century Working-Class Autobiography," *Biography* 12, no. 3 (Summer 1989): 208–26; John Burnett, *Annals of Labour: Autobiographies of British Working-Class People, 1820–1920* (Bloomington: Indiana University Press, 1974), *Destiny Obscure: Autobiographies of Childhood, Education and Family from the 1820s to the 1920s* (London: Allen Lane, 1982), and *Useful Toil: Autobiographies of Working People from the 1820s to the 1920s* (London: Allen Lane, 1974).

3. Helen Rogers and Emily Cuming, "Revealing Fragments: Close and Distant Reading of Working-Class Autobiography," *Family and Community History* 21, no. 3 (October 2018): 180–201. The database and projects based on the database are available at http://www.writinglives.org.

4. George Huntington, *The Autobiography of John Brown, Cordwainer* (London: A. R. Mowbray, 1867). Helpfully, the copy of the *Autobiography* that has been digitized by Google contains an inscription on the inside of the book explaining that Brown is "an ideal Yorkshireman, founded on reality."

5. Edith Sophia Hooper, "George Huntington," *Dictionary of National Biography, 1912 Supplement*, available at https://en.wikisource.org/wiki/Huntington,_George_(DNB12), last accessed October 12, 2018.

6. Henry Morton Stanley, *The Autobiography of Henry Morton Stanley* (New York: Houghton Mifflin, 1909), 82.

7. Stanley, *Autobiography of Henry Morton Stanley*, 94.

8. Stanley, *Autobiography of Henry Morton Stanley*, 122.

9. Tim Jeal, *Stanley: The Impossible Life of Africa's Greatest Explorer* (New York: Faber and Faber, 2007), 34–41.

10. Stanley, *Autobiography of Sir Henry Morton Stanley*, 237–38.

11. Ginger Frost, *Illegitimacy in English Law and Society, 1860–1930* (Manchester: Manchester University Press, 2016), 198.

12. Florence S. Boos, "Collaboration and the Victorian Oral Narrative: The *Autobiography of a Charwoman*," *Forum for Modern Language Studies* 52, no. 2 (April 2016): 218–31.

13. Francis A. West, *Memoirs of Jonathan Saville of Halifax* (London: Hamilton, Adams, 1843), 16.

14. James R. Simmons, ed., *Factory Lives: Four Nineteenth-Century Working-Class Autobiographies* (Peterborough: Broadview Press, 2007), 36; Liam Harte, *The Literature of the Irish in Britain: Autobiography and Memoir, 1725–2001* (Basingstoke: Palgrave Macmillan, 2009), xxvi; Humphries, *Childhood and Child Labour*, 17–20.

15. On diaristic writing, see Anne-Marie Millim, *The Victorian Diary: Authorship and Emotional Labour* (Burlington, VT: Routledge, 2013).

16. Robert Blatchford, *My Eighty Years* (London: Cassell, 1931), 62.

17. Blatchford, *My Eighty Years*, 180.

18. Laurence Thompson, *Robert Blatchford: Portrait of an Englishman* (London: Victor Gollancz, 1951), 33, 35, 66, 141.

19. Albert Michael Neil Lyons, *Robert Blatchford: The Sketch of a Personality* (London: Clarion Press, 1910), 183.

20. Blatchford quoted in Thompson, *Robert Blatchford*, 44.

21. Thompson, *Robert Blatchford*, 68.
22. Vic Gammon considers this question with reference to popular songs in *Desire, Drink and Death in English Folk and Vernacular Song, 1600–1900* (Burlington, VT: Ashgate Press, 2008), 45.
23. Richard Coe, *When the Grass Was Taller: Autobiography and the Experience of Childhood* (New Haven, CT: Yale University Press, 1984), 41, 76.
24. James Edwin Saunders, *The Reflections and Rhymes of an Old Miller* (London: Hodder and Staughton, 1938), 9.
25. George Parkinson, *True Stories of Durham Pit-Life* (London: Charles H. Kelly, 1912), ix.
26. Robert Dottie, *The Rambles and Recollections of "R' Dick"* (Manchester: Albert Sutton, 1898), x.
27. David Barr, *Climbing the Ladder: The Struggles and Successes of a Village Lad* (London: Robert Culley, 1910), 9.
28. Gagnier, *Subjectivities*, 39.
29. Vincent, *Bread, Knowledge and Freedom*, 14.
30. A Soldier [Joseph Donaldson], *Recollections of an Eventful Life, Chiefly Passed in the Army* (Glasgow: W. R. McPhun, 1825), viii.
31. John Harris, *My Autobiography* (London: Hamilton, Adams, 1882), 2.
32. Carolyn Steedman, *The Radical Soldier's Tale: John Pearman, 1819–1908* (New York: Routledge, 1988), 69.
33. Cassandra Falke, *Literature by the Working Class: English Autobiographies, 1820–1848* (Amherst, MA: Cambria Press, 2013), 65–101.
34. S. Parsons, *Poetical Trifles: Being a Collection of Songs and Fugitive Pieces, with a Sketch of the Life of the Author* (York: R. Johnson, 1822), v.
35. "Penny-a-yard: or the Autobiography of a Liverpool Beggar," *Liverpool Mercury*, August 4, 1854. Edward Finlay as "Penny-a-yard" is also mentioned in Stephen Terry, *Glasgow Almanac: An A–Z of the City and Its People* (Glasgow: Neil Wilson, 2005), 92–93, and can be found in the 1871 Scotland Census, locked up in the North Glasgow Gaol. See 1871 Scotland Census, Parish: *Glasgow Inner High*; ED: *North Prison of Glasgow*; Page: 23; Line: 10; Roll: CSSCT1871_127, accessed via Ancestry.com.
36. Simmons, *Factory Lives*, 47, 91.
37. On Mary Prince's and Elizabeth Storie's narratives, see Florence Boos, "Under Physical Siege: Early Victorian Autobiographies of Working-Class Women," *Philological Quarterly* 92, no. 2 (2013): 251–68.
38. [Elizabeth O'Neill], *Extraordinary Confessions of a Female Pickpocket* (Preston: J. Drummond, 1850), 10.
39. John Sturrock, *The Language of Autobiography: Studies in the First Person Singular* (Cambridge: Cambridge University Press, 1993), 12; Avrom Fleishman, *Figures of Autobiography: The Language of Self-Writing in Victorian and Modern England* (Berkeley: University of California Press, 1983), 471–79.
40. Falke, *Literature by the Working Class*, 135.
41. Sturrock, *Language of Autobiography*, 49.
42. David Vincent, "Working-Class Autobiography in the Nineteenth Century," in *A History of English Autobiography*, ed. Adam Smyth (Cambridge: Cambridge University Press, 2016), 165–178; Vincent, *Bread, Knowledge and Freedom*, 17–20.
43. Jane Rendall, "A Short Account of My Unprofitable Life: Autobiographies

of Working-Class Women in Britain, c. 1775–1845," in *Women's Lives / Women's Times: New Essays on Autobiography*, ed. Trev Lynn Broughton and Linda Anderson (Albany: State University of New York Press, 1997), 31–50.

44. Richard Salmon, "'The Unaccredited Hero': *Alton Locke*, Thomas Carlyle, and the Formation of the Working-Class Intellectual," in *The Working-Class Intellectual in Eighteenth- and Nineteenth-Century Britain*, ed. Aruna Krishnamurthy (Farnham: Ashgate, 2009), 167–94, at 185.

45. Falke, *Literature by the Working Class*, 160; Steedman, *Radical Soldier's Tale*, 41.

46. "Lord" George Sanger, *Seventy Years a Showman* (New York: E. P. Dutton, 1926), 3.

47. On twentieth-century working-class autobiographies, see Chris Waters, "Autobiography, Nostalgia, and the Changing Practices of Working-Class Selfhood," in *Singular Continuities: Tradition, Nostalgia, and Identity in Modern British Culture*, ed. George Behlmer and Fred Levenson (Stanford: Stanford University Press, 2000), 178–195.

48. Gagnier, *Subjectivities*, 48.

49. James Dunn, *From Coal-Mine Upwards, or Seventy Years of an Eventful Life* (London: W. Green, 1910), ix.

50. Maureen Hamish [Mary Loughran], *Adventures of an Irish Girl at Home and Abroad* (Dublin: J. K. Mitchell, 1906), 189.

51. Jacques, "Glimpses of a Chequered Life," *Commonwealth* (Glasgow), November 15, 1856, 3.

52. Dov Shmotkin, "Happiness in the Face of Adversity: Reformulating the Dynamic and Modular Bases of Subjective Well-Being," *Review of General Psychology* 9, no. 4 (2005): 291–325.

53. John Wilson, *Memories of a Labour Leader* (London: T. Fisher Unwin, 1910), 18.

54. Griffin, *Bread Winner*, 15.

55. Deborah Smith, *My Revelation* (London: Houghton, 1933), 54.

56. Smith, *My Revelation*, 75.

57. Smith, *My Revelation*, 58.

58. Ellen Johnston, "Autobiography of Ellen Johnston, the 'Factory Girl,'" in Simmons, ed., *Factory Lives*, 309.

59. Johnston, "Autobiography of Ellen Johnston," 310.

60. Louise Jermy, *Memories of a Working Woman* (Norwich: Goose and Son, 1934), 18.

61. Jermy, *Memories of a Working Woman*, 29, 34, 40.

62. Jermy, *Memories of a Working Woman*, 67, 77, 79. See also Jane McDermid, "The Making of a 'Domestic' Life: Memories of a Working Woman," *Labour History Review* 73, no. 3 (December 2008): 253–68.

63. Ann Candler, *Poetical Attempts by Ann Candler, a Suffolk Cottager, with a Short Narrative of Her Life* (Ipswich: John Raw, 1803), 4–13.

64. Marianne Farningham [Mary Ann Hearn], *A Working Woman's Life* (London: James Clarke, 1907), 232.

65. Farningham, *Working Woman's Life*, 218.

66. Saba Safdar, David Matsumoto, Katherine T. Kwantes, Wolfgang Friedlmeier, Seung Hee Yoo, Hisako Kakai, and Eri Shigemasu, "Variations of Emotional Dis-

play Rules within and across Cultures: A Comparison Between Canada, USA, and Japan," *Canadian Journal of Behavioral Science* 41, no. 1 (2009): 1–10.

67. Katie Barclay, "Performing Emotion and Reading the Male Body in the Irish Court, c. 1800–1845," *Journal of Social History* 51, no. 2 (Winter 2017): 293–312.

68. David Kirkwood, *My Life of Revolt* (London: George Harrap, 1935), 2.

69. Andrew Carnegie, *Autobiography of Andrew Carnegie* (Boston: Houghton Mifflin, 1920), 62–63.

70. "Autobiography of a Blacksmith, Written by Himself," *Commonwealth* (Glasgow), January 17, 1857, 3.

71. Wilson, *Memories of a Labour Leader*, 313.

72. David Vincent, "Love and Death and the Nineteenth-Century Working Class," *Social History* 5, no. 2 (1980): 223–47, at 228.

73. Parkinson, *True Stories of Durham Pit-Life*, 50.

74. Fritz Strack, Norbert Schwarz, and Elisabeth Gcshnedinger, "Happiness and Reminiscing: The Role of Time Perspective, Affect, and Mode of Thinking," *Journal of Personality and Social Psychology* 49, no. 6 (1985): 1460–69.

75. Russell Cropazano and Thomas Wright, "Is a 'Happy' Worker Really a 'Productive' Worker? A Review and Further Refinement of the Happy-Productive Worker Thesis," *Consulting Psychology Journal: Practice and Research* 53, no. 3 (2001): 182–99.

76. Patricia Meyer Spacks, "Stages of Self: Notes on Autobiography and the Life Cycle," *Boston University Journal* 25, no. 2 (1977): 7–17.

77. Henry Snell, *Men, Movements and Myself* (London: J. M. Dent and Sons, 1936), 264.

78. Jane Humphries concludes that, at least among male autobiographers, children who grew up in small families are overrepresented and children of agricultural workers are underrepresented, but that these qualities do not impair the use of the autobiographies for qualitative evidence. See *Childhood and Child Labour*, 80.

79. Brian Harrison and Patricia Hollis, eds., *Robert Lowery, Radical and Chartist* (London: Europa, 1979), 115; Gagnier, *Subjectivities*, 51; R. D. Anderson, "Education and the State in Nineteenth-Century Scotland," *Economic History Review* 36, no. 4 (1983): 518–34, at 524.

80. Pamela Horn, *The Rural World: Social Changes in the English Countryside, 1780–1850* (New York: St. Martin's Press, 1980), 134–38.

81. Ryan T. Howell and Colleen Howell, "The Relationship of Economic Status to Subjective Well-Being in Developing Countries: A Meta-Analysis," *Psychological Bulletin* 134, no. 4 (2008): 536–60, at 536.

82. Brook Bastian, Peter Kuppens, Kim De Roover, and Ed Diener, "Is Valuing Positive Emotion Associated with Life Satisfaction?" *Emotion* 14, no. 4 (2014): 639–45.

83. Alfred Kelly, *The German Worker: Working-Class Autobiographies from the Age of Industrialization* (Berkeley: University of California Press, 1987), 4.

84. Hackett, *XIX-Century British Working-Class Autobiographies*, 10; Hackett, "A Different Form of 'Self'."

85. Burnett, *Destiny Obscure*; Burnett, *Useful Toil*.

86. See, for example, "Notes on the Life of Joseph Ricketts, Written by Himself," *Wiltshire Archaeological and Natural History Magazine* 60 (1965): 120–26.

87. Vincent, "Love and Death and the Nineteenth-Century Working Class."

88. Strange, *Fatherhood*, passim; see also *Death, Grief, and Poverty in Britain, 1870–1914* (Cambridge: Cambridge University Press, 2009); and "'She Cried a Very Little': Death, Grief and Mourning in Working-Class Culture, c. 1880–1914," *Social History* 27, no. 2 (May 2002): 143–61.

89. Emma Griffin, "The Emotions of Motherhood: Love, Culture and Poverty in Victorian Britain," *American Historical Review* 123, no. 1 (February 2018): 60–80.

90. Heather A. Williams, *Help Me to Find My People: The African American Search for Family Lost in Slavery* (Chapel Hill: University of North Carolina Press, 2012).

91. Carolyn Steedman, *An Everyday Life of the English Working Class: Work, Self and Sociability in the Early Nineteenth Century* (Cambridge: Cambridge University Press, 2013), 27.

Chapter 2: The Simple Pleasures of Childhood

1. Anna Davin, "The Jigsaw Strategy: Sources in the History of Childhood in Nineteenth-Century London," *History of Education Review* 15, no. 2 (1986): 2–17.

2. On childhood generally, see Hugh Cunningham, *The Invention of Childhood* (London: BBC Books, 2006); Joanne Begiato, "Selfhood and 'Nostalgia': Sensory and Material Memories of the Childhood Home in Late Georgian Britain," *Journal for Eighteenth-Century Studies* 42, no. 2 (2019): 229–46, at 231.

3. Cf. Strange, *Fatherhood and the British Working Class*, 92–110.

4. John Younger, *Autobiography of John Younger*, ed. William Brockie (Kelso: J. & J. H. Rutherfurd, 1881), 2.

5. Anna Davin, *Growing Up Poor: Home, School and Street in London, 1870–1914* (London: Rivers Oram Press, 1996), 18.

6. Thomas Holcroft, *Memoirs of the Late Thomas Holcroft* (London: Longman, Hurst, Rees, Orme and Brown, 1816), 2.

7. Holcroft, *Memoirs of the Late Thomas Holcroft*, 24.

8. Christopher Thomson, *Autobiography of an Artisan* (Nottingham: J. Shaw, 1847), 28. On parents singing, see Begiato, "Selfhood and 'Nostalgia,'" 234.

9. Charles Shaw, *When I Was a Child: Growing Up in the Potteries in the 1840s* (n.p.: Dormouse Press, 2013 [1903]), 12.

10. Thomas Lipton, *Leaves from the Lipton Logs* (London: Hutchinson, 1930), 49–50. Illegitimate children often had more troubled childhoods due to lack of parental attachment or to constant circulation among parents, institutions, foster parents, and extended kin. See Frost, *Illegitimacy in English Law*, 222. On aristocratic children, see Horn, *Ladies of the Manor*, 28.

11. Thomas Cooper, *Life of Thomas Cooper* (London: Hodder and Staughton, 1872), 4–5.

12. Parkinson, *True Stories of Durham Pit-Life*, 2.

13. John Harris, *My Autobiography* (London: Hamilton, Adams, 1882), 11. Furze is a plant often used for kindling.

14. Elizabeth Oakley, "Autobiography of Elizabeth Oakley," *Norfolk Record Society* 56 (1991): 113–50, at 119, 129, 137.

15. Davin, *Growing Up Poor*, 26. Historians disagree about the nature of the existing evidence. Cf. Griffin, *Bread Winner*, 235, 243.

16. Burnett, *Destiny Obscure*, 53.

17. Jane Humphries, "Care and Cruelty in the Workhouse: Children's Experi-

ences of Residential Poor Relief in Eighteenth- and Nineteenth-Century England," in *Childhood and Child Labour in Industrial England: Diversity and Agency, 1750–1914*, ed. Katrina Honeyman and Nigel Goose (Farnham: Routledge, 2013), 115–34; Alannah Tomkins, "Poor Law Institutions through Working-Class Eyes: Autobiography, Emotion, and Family Context, 1834–1914," *Journal of British Studies* 60 (April 2021): 285–309.

18. Tomkins, "Poor Law Institutions," 291.
19. Henry Price, "Memoir of Henry Price: The Diary of a Working Man Long Resident in Islington," GB 1032 S/HEP, Islington Local History Library, 9, 16.
20. West, *Memoirs of Jonathan Saville*, 8–9.
21. George Lloyd, "The Autobiography of Georgie Brawd," Burnett Archive of Working-Class Autobiographies, Brunel University (hereafter "Burnett Archive"), 16.
22. Joshua Marsden, *Sketches in the Early Life of a Sailor* (Hull: William Ross, n.d.,), 1.
23. Haggard, Lilias Rider, ed., *I Walked by Night: Being the Life and History of the King of the Norfolk Poachers* (New York: E. P. Dutton, 1936), 6.
24. Hamish [Mary Loughran], *Adventures of an Irish Girl*, 16.
25. Joseph Philip Robson, *The Autobiography of Joseph Philip Robson* (Newcastle upon Tyne: John Clarke, 1849), 16.
26. Sir Harry Lauder, *Roamin' in the Gloamin'* (London: J. Lippicott, 1928), 25.
27. William Hammond, *Recollections of William Hammond, a Glasgow Handloom Weaver* (Glasgow: Citizen Press, 1904), 8–9.
28. Duncan Campbell, *Reminiscences and Reflections of an Octogenarian Highlander* (Northern Counties Newspaper and Printing, 1910), 78. "Gray Egyptians," Campbell explains, was an epithet applied to moderately religious old people by "hysterical revival spouters."
29. Henry Jones, *Old Memories* (New York: George H. Doran, 1922[?]), 25–28.
30. Jones, *Old Memories*, 37.
31. Mary Ann Smith, *The Autobiography of Mary Smith, Schoolmistress and Nonconformist* (London: Bemrose and Sons, 1892), 15.
32. Davin, *Growing Up Poor*, 64.
33. Thomas Burt, *Pitman and Privy Councillor: An Autobiography* (London: T. Fisher Unwin, 1924), 25.
34. Burt, *Pitman and Privy Councillor*, 26.
35. Kirkwood, *My Life of Revolt*, 13.
36. Alexander Murison, *Memoirs of 88 Years (1847–1934): Being the Autobiography of Alexander Falconer Murison* (Aberdeen: University of Aberdeen Press, 1935), 33.
37. Alfred Ireson, "Reminiscences," in Burnett, *Destiny Obscure*, 84, 86.
38. Edward Anderson, *The Sailor: A Poem* (Leeds: G. Wilson, n.d.), 8.
39. Joseph Millott Severn, *The Life and Experiences of a Phrenologist* (Brighton: Severn, 1929), 15.
40. Joseph Terry, "Recollections of My Life," quoted in Burnett, *Destiny Obscure*, 67.
41. Horn, *Ladies of the Manor*, 34, 39, 107.
42. Elizabeth Campbell, *Songs of My Pilgrimage* (Edinburgh: Andrew Eliot, 1875), xvi.
43. Frederick H. Spencer, *An Inspector's Testament* (London: English Universities Press, 1937), 30.

44. Samuel Bamford, *The Autobiography of Samuel Bamford*, vol. 1 (New York: Augustus Kelley, 1967), 42.
45. Saunders, *Reflections and Rhymes of an Old Miller*, 38.
46. Thomas Jones, *Rhymney Memories* (Llandysul: Gomerian Press, 1970), 53–54.
47. Janet Bathgate, *Aunt Janet's Legacy to Her Nieces: Recollections of Humble Life in Yarrow at the Beginning of the Century* (Selkirk: G. Lewis and Son, 1894), 37, 50, 61.
48. Jacob Holkinson, "The Life of Jacob Holkinson, Tailor and Poet, Written by Himself," *Commonwealth* (Glasgow), January 24, 1857, 3.
49. Harris, *My Autobiography*, 8.
50. Chancellor, ed., *Master and Artisan in Victorian England*, 88.
51. Samuel Gompers, *Seventy Years of Life and Labor* (New York: E. P. Dutton, 1957), 49–50.
52. Burnett, *Destiny Obscure*, 59.
53. Humphries, *Childhood and Child Labour*, 98.
54. Griffin, "Diets, Hunger and Living Standards." In her most recent book, Griffin argues that by the second half of the nineteenth century, hunger issues had more to do with individual household breadwinner failure rather than actual food shortages. See Griffin, *Bread Winner*, 202.
55. Edmund and Ruth Frow, eds., *The Dark Satanic Mills: Child Apprentices in Derbyshire Spinning Factories* (Manchester: Working Class Library, 1980), 16.
56. Horace Harman, *Sketches of the Bucks Countryside* (London: Blandford Press, 1934), 22.
57. Alexander Somerville, *The Autobiography of a Working Man* (London: Charles Gilpin, 1848), 51.
58. Ben Brierley, *Home Memories and Recollections of a Life* (Manchester: Abel Heywood, 1886), 16.
59. William Henry Lax, *Lax His Book: The Autobiography of Lax of Poplar* (London: Epworth Press, 1937), 58.
60. John Clare, "Autobiographical Fragments," in *John Clare's Autobiographical Writings*, ed. Eric Robinson (Oxford: Oxford University Press, 1983), 29.
61. Clare, "Autobiographical Fragments," 31.
62. Clare, "Autobiographical Fragments," 40.
63. Henry White, *The Record of My Life* (Cheltenham: printed by the author, 1889), 14, 34.
64. Younger, *Autobiography of John Younger*, 54.
65. William Stevens, *Memoir of Thomas Martin Wheeler* (London: J. B. Leno, 1862), 8.
66. Smith, *Autobiography of Mary Smith*, 55.
67. Harrison and Hollis, eds., *Robert Lowery, Radical and Chartist*, 43.
68. Humphries, *Childhood and Child Labour*, 42–48.
69. Jane Humphries, "Childhood and Child Labour in the British Industrial Revolution," *Economic History Review* 66, no. 2 (May 2013): 395–418.
70. Griffin, *Bread Winner*, 70.
71. Lipton, *Leaves from the Lipton Logs*, 54.
72. Lipton, *Leaves from the Lipton Logs*, 60.
73. Humphries, *Childhood and Child Labour*, 240.

74. Vincent, *Bread, Knowledge and Freedom*, 82–83; Ellen Ross, *Love and Toil: Motherhood in Outcast London, 1870–1914* (New York: Oxford University Press, 1993), 160; Cunningham, *The Invention of Childhood*, 174.
75. Sanger, *Seventy Years a Showman*, 22, 24.
76. Severn, *Life and Experiences of a Phrenologist*, 29.
77. George Edwards, *From Crow-Scaring to Westminster: An Autobiography* (London: Labour, 1922), 23.
78. Peter Featherstone, *Reminiscences of a Long Life* (London: Charles H. Kelly, 1905), 12.
79. William Arnold, *Recollections of William Arnold* (Northampton: Privately printed, 1915), 37.
80. John Buckmaster, ed., *A Village Politician: The Life of John A. Buckley* (London: T. Fisher Unwin, 1897), 108.
81. Parkinson, *Stories of Durham Pit-Life*, 7, 151.
82. Shaw, *When I Was a Child*, 56. See also R. J. Saville, ed., *A Langton Quarryman's Apprentice: James Corben's Autobiography* (Langton Maltravers Local History Society, 1996), 8, 12.
83. Dunn, *From Coal-Mine Upwards*, 12.
84. Frank Forrest, *Chapters in the Life of a Dundee Factory Boy: An Autobiography* (Dundee: James Myles, 1850), 33–34.
85. A. W. Exell and N. M. Marshall, eds., *Autobiography of Richard Boswell Belcher of Banbury and Blockley* (Blockley: Blockley Antiquarian Society, 1976), 3.
86. Ross, *Love and Toil*, 38–39. Cf. Griffin, *Bread Winner*, 214.
87. Arnold, *Recollections of William Arnold*, 13–14. See also Humphries, "Childhood and Child Labour in the British Industrial Revolution," 396.
88. Rose Allen, *The Autobiography of Rose Allen, Edited by a Lady* (London: Longman, Brown, Green and Longman, 1847), 33.
89. Allen, *Autobiography of Rose Allen*, 73.
90. Allen, *Autobiography of Rose Allen*, 104, 116.
91. George Meek, *George Meek, Bath-Chair Man, by Himself* (New York: E. P. Dutton, 1910), 14.
92. Meek, *George Meek*, 46.
93. William Collison, *The Apostle of Free Labour: The Life Story of William Collison, Founder and General Secretary of the National Free Labour Association* (London: Hurst and Blackett, 1913), 6.
94. Kirkwood, *My Life of Revolt*, 47–8.
95. Robert Scott, *The Life of Robert Scott, Journeyman Wright* (Dundee: T. Colville and Son, 1801), 34.
96. Scott, *Life of Robert Scott*, 47.
97. Mary Weston, *The Story of Our Sunday Trip to Hastings, as Related by One of the Party* (London: Working Men's Lord's Day Rest Association, 1890), 18.
98. Weston, *Sunday Trip to Hastings*, 40.
99. Weston, *Sunday Trip to Hastings*, 10.

Chapter 3: Work and Flow

1. Nancy Tandler, Annette Krauss, and René T. Proyer, "Authentic Happiness at Work: Self- and Peer-Rated Orientations to Happiness, Work Satisfaction, and Stress Coping," *Frontiers in Psychology* 11 (2020): 1–16; Blake A. Allan, Casson-

dra Batz-Barbarich, Haley M. Sterling, and Louis Tay, "Outcomes of Meaningful Work: A Meta-Analysis," *Journal of Management Studies* 56, no. 3 (2019): 500–528, at 505.

2. Karl Marx, "Estranged Labour," *Economic and Social Manuscripts of 1844*, available at https://www.marxists.org/archive/marx/works/1844/manuscripts/labour.htm, last accessed January 21, 2021. In addition, as Robert Gray notes, the discourse of mechanized labor in the early nineteenth century focused on the ills of the factory system, allowing little opportunity for workers to discuss whatever happiness they may have experienced on the job. See Gray, *The Factory Question and Industrial England, 1830–1860* (Cambridge: Cambridge University Press, 1996), part 1.

3. Mihály Csíkszentmihályi, *Flow: The Psychology of Optimal Experience* (New York: Harper and Row, 1990). 19.

4. Csíkszentmihályi, "If We Are So Rich"; Mihály Csíkszentmihályi, "Happiness, Flow, and Economic Equality," *American Psychologist* 55, no. 10 (2000): 1163–64.

5. Timothy Claxton, *Hints to Mechanics on Self-Education and Mutual Instruction* (London: Taylor and Walton, 1839), 15.

6. Steedman, *Everyday Life of the English Working Class*, 195.

7. Burnett, *Annals of Labour*, 15.

8. Steven Reiss, "Human Individuality, Happiness, and Flow," *American Psychologist* 55, no. 10 (2000): 1161–62. See also Kelly, *The German Worker*, 72.

9. Quoted in Kelly, *The German Worker*, 73.

10. See, for example, Griffin, *Bread Winner*, 74.

11. Vincent, *Literacy and Popular Culture*, 56, 107, 113.

12. J. H. Powell, *Life Incidents and Poetic Pictures* (London: Trubner, 1865), 9.

13. James Nicol, *The Life and Adventures of James Nicol, Mariner*, ed. John Howell (Edinburgh: W. Blackwell, 1822), 8.

14. Nicol, *Life and Adventures of James Nicol*, 16, 96.

15. Henry Burstow, *Reminiscences of Horsham: Being Recollections of Henry Burstow* (Horsham: Free Church Book Society, 1911), 95.

16. Burstow, *Reminiscences of Horsham*, 99, 106.

17. Burnett, *Destiny Obscure*, 65.

18. Lax, *Lax His Book*, 87–88.

19. Parkinson, *Stories of Durham Pit-Life*, 19.

20. Parkinson, *Stories of Durham Pit-Life*, 20.

21. Joseph Keating, *My Struggle for Life* (Dublin: University College Press, 2005), 38.

22. Keating, *My Struggle for Life*, 44.

23. Keating, *My Struggle for Life*, 52.

24. Keating, *My Struggle for Life*, 72.

25. Keating, *My Struggle for Life*, 86.

26. Carnegie, *Autobiography*, 34.

27. Carnegie, *Autobiography*, 43.

28. Carnegie, *Autobiography*, 55.

29. Carnegie, *Autobiography*, 57.

30. John B. Gough, *An Autobiography of John B. Gough* (Boston: printed by the author, 1845), 8–9.

31. Samuel Smiles's *Self-Help* (London: John Murray, 1860), intended to appeal to an audience of just such ambitious workmen, is mostly a catalogue of individuals who succeeded through persistence.
32. William Ablett, *Reminiscences of an Old Draper* (London: Searle and Rivington, 1876), 199.
33. Joseph Terry, "Recollections of My Life," Burnett Archive, 70.
34. A Working Man, *Reminiscences of a Stonemason* (London: John Murray, 1908), 77.
35. Anne Swift, ed., *The Story of George Cooper, Stockport's Last Town Crier, 1824–1895* (Stockport: Anne Swift, 1975), n.p.
36. Frederick Rogers, *Labour, Life and Literature*, ed. David Rubenstein (Brighton: Harvester Press, 1973), 40–41.
37. "Autobiography of a Miner," 4.
38. Lauder, *Roamin' in the Gloamin'*, 86.
39. Lax, *Lax His Book*, 128.
40. Chester Armstrong, *Pilgrimage from Nenthead: An Autobiography* (London: Methuen, 1938), 259–60.
41. Armstrong, *Pilgrimage from Nenthead*, 301.
42. Thomas Lewis, *These Seventy Years* (London: Carey Press, 1930), 48, 51.
43. Lewis, *These Seventy Years*, 121.
44. Robert Gammage, *Reminiscences of a Chartist*, ed. W. H. Maehl (Manchester: Manchester Free Press, 1983), 30, 34.
45. Gammage, *Reminiscences of a Chartist*, 39.
46. Isaac Mead, *The Life Story of an Essex Lad, Written by Himself* (Chelmsford: A. Driver and Sons, 1923), 44.
47. Mead, *Life Story of an Essex Lad*, 107.
48. James Campkin, *Struggles of a Village Lad* (London: Tweedie, 1858), 17.
49. Chancellor, ed., *Master and Artisan in Victorian England*, 57.
50. William Edwin Adams, *Memoirs of a Social Atom* (London: Hutchinson and Son, 1903), 553.
51. Adams, *Memoirs of a Social Atom*, 333.
52. Adams, *Memoirs of a Social Atom*, 388.
53. Hugh Miller, *My Schools and Schoolmasters; or, the Story of My Education* (Edinburgh: Johnstone and Hunter, 1854), 165.
54. George Jacob Holyoake, *Sixty Years of an Agitator's Life*, vol. 1 (London: T. Fisher Unwin, 1893), 25.
55. Malcolm Chase, ed., *The Life and Literary Pursuits of Allen Davenport* (Aldershot: Scolar Press, 1994), 4.
56. Crispin [Barnabas Britten, pseud.], *Woodyard to Palace* (Bradford: Broadacre Books, 1958), 109.
57. George Baldry, *The Rabbit Skin Cap: A Tale of a Norfolk Countryman's Youth* (London: Collins, 1939), 186.
58. Strange, *Fatherhood and the British Working Class*, 186.
59. John Urie, *Reminiscences of Eighty Years* (Paisley: Alexander Gardner, 1908), 140.
60. John Kelso Hunter, *The Retrospect of an Artist's Life* (Greenock: Orr, Pollock, 1868), 197.
61. John Clare, "Sketches in the Life of John Clare," in *John Clare's Autobi-

ographical Writings, ed. Eric Johnson (Oxford: Oxford University Press, 1983), 4.

62. Frank Bullen, *Confessions of a Tradesman* (London: Hodder and Stoughton, 1908), 86–87, 119.

63. Major Farrar, ed. *The Diary of Colour-Sergeant George Calladine, 19th Foot, 1793–1837* (London: E. Fisher, 1922), 6.

64. Farrar, ed., *The Diary of Colour-Sergeant George Calladine*, 47.

65. Serjeant Robert Butler, *Narrative of the Life and Travels of Sergeant B———, Written by Himself* (Edinburgh: David Brown, 1823), 157.

66. Butler, *Narrative of the Life and Travels of Sergeant B———*, 166, 190.

67. Steedman, *Radical Soldier's Tale*, 148.

68. John Shipp, *The Path of Glory: Being the Memoirs of the Extraordinary Military Career of John Shipp, Written by Himself* (London: Chatto and Windus, 1969 [1834]), 15.

69. Shipp, *Path of Glory*, 43.

70. Shipp, *Path of Glory*, 219.

71. Shipp, *Path of Glory*, 227; Shipp was court-martialed over an unpaid debt.

72. Shipp, *Path of Glory*, 62, 111.

73. Donaldson, *Recollections of an Eventful Life*, 149, 161.

74. *The Autobiography of a Private Soldier, Showing the Danger of Rashly Enlisting* (Sunderland: John Richmond, 1834), 3.

75. Frank Bullen, *The Log of a Sea-Waif* (London: Smith, Elder, 1899), 56.

76. *Memoirs of a Smuggler, Compiled from His Diary and Journal* (Sidmouth: J. Harvey, 1837), 5.

77. Joanne Begiato, "Tears and the Manly Sailor in England, c. 1760–1860," *Journal for Maritime Research* 17, no. 2 (2015): 117–33.

78. And, in the assessment of Marcus Rediker, shipboard life was extremely regimented and oppressive. See Rediker, *Between the Devil and the Deep Blue Sea: Merchant Seamen, Pirates and the Anglo-American Maritime World, 1700–1750* (Cambridge: Cambridge University Press, 1989).

79. Henry Baynham, *From the Lower Deck: The Royal Navy, 1780–1840* (Barre, MA: Barre, 1970), 95, 163–64.

80. Samuel Leech, *Thirty Years from Home; or a Voice from the Main Deck* (London: H. G. Collins, 1851), 42.

81. Baynham, *From the Lower Deck*, 163.

82. Richard Barnett, "The View from Below Deck: The British Navy, 1777–1781," *American Neptune* 38, no. 2 (1978): 92–100.

83. Oakley, "Autobiography of Elizabeth Oakley," 135.

84. Alexander Mitchell, *The Recollections of a Lifetime* (Edinburgh: n.p., 1911) 32, 34, 37, 39, 43, 46, 58.

85. Henry Broadhurst, quoted in Burnett, *Annals of Labour*, 316.

86. James Mullin, *The Story of a Toiler's Life* (Dublin: University College Press, 2000), 155.

87. Griffin, *Bread Winner*, 268.

88. Buckmaster, ed., *Village Politician*, 133.

89. Campbell, *Reminiscences and Reflections*, 219.

90. Peter Taylor, *Autobiography of Peter Taylor* (Paisley: Alexander Gardner, 1903), 49.

91. Bullen, *Confessions of a Tradesman*, 37.

92. J. A. Leatherland, *Essays and Poems, with a Brief Autobiographical Memoir* (London: W. Tweedie, 1862), 10.
93. Leatherland, *Essays and Poems*, 12.
94. *Autobiography of a Scotch Lad: Being Reminiscences of Threescore Years and Ten* (Glasgow: David Bryce and Son, 1887), 84.
95. Lauder, *Roamin' in the Gloamin'*, 118.
96. Meek, *George Meek*, 71.
97. Shaw, *When I Was a Child*, 70.
98. James Bent, *Criminal Life: Remembrances of Forty-Two Years as a Police Officer* (London: n.p., 1891), 160, 168.
99. Bullen, *Log of a Sea-Waif*, 28.
100. Vincent, *Bread, Knowledge, and Freedom*, 185.
101. "The Autobiography of Robert Spurr," *Baptist Quarterly* 26 (April 1976): 282–88.
102. James Hillocks, *Life Story: A Prize Autobiography* (London: Houlston and Wright, 1860), 79.
103. Hillocks, *Life Story*, 81.
104. Eric Horne, *What the Butler Winked At* (New York: Thomas Seltzer, 1924), 35, 49.
105. Horne, *What the Butler Winked At*, 91.
106. Horne, *What the Butler Winked At*, 267.
107. Horne, *What the Butler Winked At*, 70.
108. Horne, *What the Butler Winked At*, 247.
109. Horne, *What the Butler Winked At*, 260.
110. Clare, "Sketches in the Life of John Clare," 3.
111. George Lansbury, *My Life* (London: Constable, 1928), 59.
112. Holcroft, *Memoirs of the Late Thomas Holcroft*, 111.
113. William Milne, *Reminiscences of an Old Boy: Being Autobiographical Sketches of Scottish Rural Life from 1832 to 1856* (Forfar: John McDonald, 1901), 256.
114. Milne, *Reminiscences of an Old Boy*, 285.
115. Buckmaster, ed., *Village Politician*, 16, 23, 25.
116. John Bedford Leno, *The Aftermath; with Autobiography of the Author* (London: Reeves and Turner, 1892), 8.
117. Leno, *The Aftermath*, 10.
118. Leno, *The Aftermath*, 90.
119. Caractacus [pseudo.], *Autobiography of a Poacher* (n.p.: John Macqueen, 1901), 10–11.
120. Frederick Rolfe, *I Walked by Night: Being the Life and History of the King of Norfolk Poachers* (London: Ivor Nicholson and Watson, 1935), 69.
121. Rolfe, *I Walked by Night*, 124.
122. John Wilkins, *The Autobiography of an English Gamekeeper* (New York: Macmillan, 1892), 90.
123. Robert Roberts, *A Wandering Scholar: The Life and Opinions of Robert Roberts* (Cardiff: University of Wales Press, 1991), 48.
124. Roberts, *A Wandering Scholar*, 216.
125. Kelly, *The German Worker*, 80.
126. Mrs. Scott, JP, "A Felt Hat Worker," in *Life as We Have Known It*, ed. Margaret Llewellyn Davies (London: W. W. Norton, 1975), 87.

127. Henry Scott Riddell, *Poetical Works of Henry Scott Riddell*, ed. James Bryson (Glasgow: Maurice Ogle, 1871), xvii.
128. Griffin, *Bread Winner*, 6, 36, 164.
129. Liz Stanley, ed., *The Diaries of Hannah Cullwick, Victorian Maidservant* (New Brunswick, NJ: Rutgers University Press, 1984), 85.
130. Stanley, ed., *The Diaries of Hannah Cullwick*, 59, 66, 90.
131. Hanna Maria Mitchell, *The Hard Way Up: The Autobiography of Hannah Mitchell, Suffragette and Rebel* (London: Faber and Faber, 1968), 57, 71.
132. Mitchell, *The Hard Way Up*, 71.
133. Hamish [Mary Loughran], *Adventures of an Irish Girl*, 28.
134. Hamish [Mary Loughran], *Adventures of an Irish Girl*, 153, 173.
135. Hamish [Mary Loughran], *Adventures of an Irish Girl*, 105, 120.
136. Florence Boos, *Memoirs of Working-Class Women: The Hard Way Up* (London: Palgrave, 2017), 171.
137. Mary Ann Ashford, *Life of a Licensed Victualler's Daughter* (London: Saunders and Otley, 1844), 45.
138. Ashford, *Life of a Licensed Victualler's Daughter*, 91.
139. Annie Kenney, *Memories of a Militant* (London: Butler and Tanner, 1924), 68, 155, 162.
140. Kenney, *Memories of a Militant*, 115.
141. Kenney, *Memories of a Militant*, 12.
142. Kenney, *Memories of a Militant*, 98, 229.
143. Kenney, *Memories of a Militant*, 96.
144. On the plight of factory workers, see Cunningham, *Invention of Childhood*, 156–58.

Chapter 4: Life Is with People
1. I have titled this chapter in tribute to Mark Zborowski's history of a similarly sociable world, *Life Is with People: The Culture of the Shtetl* (New York: Schocken Books, 1952). On happiness and relationships, see Vian Vittorio Caprara and Patrizia Steca, "Affective and Social Self-Regularity Efficacy Beliefs as Determinants of Positive Thinking and Happiness," *European Psychologist* 10, no. 4 (2005): 275–86; Iris B. Mauss, Nicole S. Savino, Max Weisbuch, Craig Anderson, Maya Tamir, and Mark Laudenslager, "The Pursuit of Happiness Can Be Lonely," *Emotion* 12, no. 5 (2012): 908–12; Csíkszentmihály, "If We Are So Rich," 823; Rocio Calvo, Yuhui Zheng, Santosh Kumar, Analia Olgati, and Lisa Berkman, "Well-Being and Social Capital on Planet Earth: Cross-National Evidence from 142 Countries," *PLOS One* 7, no. 8 (2012): 1–10.
2. On the social nature of emotional experience, see Jordan McKenzie, "Happiness vs. Contentment? A Case for a Sociology of the Good Life," *Journal of the Theory of Social Behavior* 46, no. 3 (2015): 252–67, at 259. On "psychosocial wealth," see Arthur A. Stone and Christopher Mackie, eds., *Subjective Well-Being: Measuring Happiness, Suffering, and Other Dimensions of Experience* (Washington, DC: National Academies Press, 2013), 34.
3. Burnett, *Annals of Labour*, 17. On working-class sociability, see Davin, *Growing Up Poor*, 56.
4. Susan Broomhall, "Introduction," in *Spaces for Feeling: Emotions and Sociabilties in Britain, 1650–1850*, ed. Susan Broomhall (London: Routledge, 2015), 1–11.

5. On the flourishing of working-class autobiographies in the 1970s and 1980s, see Christopher Waters, "Autobiography, Nostalgia and Working-Class Selfhood," in *Singular Continuities*, ed. George Behlmer and Fred Leventhal (Stanford: Stanford University Press, 2000), 178–95. On relationships through letters, see Katie Barclay, "Marginal Households and Their Emotions: The 'Kept Mistress in Enlightenment Edinburgh," in *Spaces for Feeling: Emotions and Sociabilities in Britain, 1650–1850*, ed. Susan Broomhall, 95–111 (London: Taylor and Francis, 2015).

6. Vicky Holmes, *In Bed with the Victorians: The Life-Cycle of Working-Class Marriage* (London: Palgrave Macmillan, 2017), 16. On aristocratic courtship and marriage, see Horn, *Ladies of the Manor*, 67–70.

7. Ross, *Love and Toil*, 69–86.

8. Frank Bullen, noting that the details of his domestic life were "quite private," wrote very little about his family; *Confessions of a Tradesman*, 129.

9. Ginger S. Frost, *Promises Broken: Courtship, Class, and Gender in Victorian England* (Charlottesville: University Press of Virginia, 1995), 63, 65, 67, 99, 111, 137.

10. Vincent, *Bread, Knowledge and Freedom*, 47; Anna Clark, *The Struggle for the Breeches: Gender and the Making of the British Working Class* (Berkeley: University of California Press, 1995), 64–67; Claire Langhamer, *The English in Love: The Intimate Story of an Emotional Revolution* (Oxford: Oxford University Press, 2013), 12.

11. Clark, *Struggle for the Breeches*, 74; Holmes, *In Bed with the Victorians*, 57.

12. James Bowd, "The Life of a Farm Worker," *Countryman* 51, no. 2 (1965): 293–300, at 297.

13. Dyke Wilkinson, *A Wasted Life* (London: Grant Richards, 1902), 27.

14. F. H. Crittall, *Fifty Years of Work and Play* (London: Constable, 1934), 44–45.

15. Thomas Whittaker, *Life's Battles in Temperance Armour* (London: Hodder and Stoughton, 1884), 145.

16. Armstrong, *Pilgrimage from Nenthead*, 75.

17. James McCurrey, *Life of James McCurrey* (London: S. W. Partridge and Son, 1876), 16.

18. Harrison, ed., *Robert Lowery*, 62.

19. Charles Manby Smith, *The Working Man's Way in the World* (London: W. and F. G. Cash, 1857), 259.

20. White, *Record of My Life*, 123.

21. Jacques, "Glimpses," November 1, 1856, 3; November 8, 1856, 3.

22. Price, "Memoir of Henry Price," 58.

23. Clare, "Autobiographical Fragments," 74.

24. "The Life of a Handloom Weaver, Written by Himself," *Commonwealth* (Glasgow), April 25, 1857, 1.

25. Hackett, "A Different Form of 'Self,'" 223.

26. Joseph Livesey, *Autobiography of Joseph Livesey* (National Temperance League Depot, 1885), 16–17.

27. Burt, *Pitman and Privy Councillor*, 139.

28. Murison, *Memoirs of 88 Years*, 207.

29. Terry, "Recollections of My Life," Burnett Archive, 78.

30. David Johnston, *Autobiographical Reminiscences of David Johnston, An Octogenarian Scotchman* (Chicago: n.p., 1885), 97.

31. Chancellor, ed., *Master and Artisan in Victorian England*, 109.
32. Carnegie, *Autobiography*, 217.
33. Carnegie, *Autobiography*, 220.
34. Hutton, *The Life of William Hutton*, 95. On emotional authenticity and length of marriage, see Langhamer, *English in Love*, 32.
35. Hutton, *Life of William Hutton*, 96.
36. Hutton, *Life of William Hutton*, 99.
37. Blatchford, *My Eighty Years*, 261.
38. Blatchford, *My Eighty Years*, 266.
39. Peter Gabbitass, *Heart Melodies: For Storm and Sunshine* (Bristol: n.p., 1885), xliv.
40. Severn, *Life and Experiences of a Phrenologist*, 142, 155.
41. Humphries, *Childhood and Child Labour*, 72.
42. Rendall, "A Short Account of My Unprofitable Life," 41.
43. Humphries, *Childhood and Child Labour*, 66–67.
44. Joyce, *Democratic Subjects*, 52.
45. Stanley, ed., *Diaries of Hannah Cullwick*, 170.
46. George Mockford, *Wilderness Journeyings and Gracious Deliverances: The Autobiography of George Mockford* (Oxford: J. C. Pembrey, 1901), 65.
47. Smith, *My Revelation*, 86.
48. Jermy, *Memories of a Working Woman*, 118, 124–25.
49. Mitchell, *The Hard Way Up*, 29.
50. Mitchell, *The Hard Way Up*, 112.
51. Annie Wakeman, *Autobiography of a Charwoman* (London: John Macqueen, 1900), 50.
52. Strange, *Fatherhood and the British Working Class*, passim.
53. Thomas Preston, *Life and Opinions of Thomas Preston, Patriot and Shoemaker* (London: A. Seale, 1817), 16, 18.
54. Burn, *Autobiography of a Beggar Boy*, 116.
55. Burn, *Autobiography of a Beggar Boy*, 199.
56. Harris, *My Autobiography*, 66–67.
57. In contrast, see K. D. M. Snell, "Belonging and Community: Understandings of 'Home' and 'Friends' among the English Poor, 1750–1850," *Economic History Review* 65, no. 1 (2012): 1–25.
58. Campkin, *Struggles of a Village Lad*, 16.
59. Vincent, *Literacy and Popular Culture*, 35.
60. Humphries, "Care and Cruelty in the Workhouse," 130.
61. Donald Stewart, *The Life of an Agitator* (Hull: Elson, 1921), 1. See also David Dickson, *Memorials of a Faithful Servant, William Innes* (Edinburgh: Lorimer and Gillies, 1876), 9.
62. Severn, *Life Story and Experiences of a Phrenologist*, 8.
63. Mitchell, *Recollections of a Lifetime*, 32.
64. Mullin, *Toiler's Life*, 3.
65. Mullin, *Toiler's Life*, 86.
66. Alf Ireson, "Reminiscences," Burnett Archive, 65–66.
67. Roberts, *Wandering Scholar*, 286, 344.
68. Adam Rushton, *My Life as a Farmer's Boy, Factory Lad, Teacher and Preacher* (Manchester: S. Clarke, 1909), 290.

69. James Bywater, *The Trio's Pilgrimage: Autobiography of James Bywater* (n.p.: Bywater Family Foundation, 1947), 37.
70. Burn, *Autobiography of a Beggar Boy*, 55. Robert Watchorn used similar wording in Herbert Faulkner West, *The Autobiography of Robert Watchorn* (Oklahoma: Robert Watchorn Charities, 1958), 58.
71. Smith, *Working Man's Way in the World*, 134.
72. Harry Carter, *The Autobiography of a Cornish Smuggler, 1749–1809* (Truro: Joseph Pollard, 1894), 102–3.
73. Alexander Stewart, *The Life of Alexander Stewart, Prisoner of Napoleon and Preacher of the Gospel* (London: George Allen and Unwin, 1948), 108.
74. Lewis, *These Seventy Years*, 99.
75. Thomas Oliver, *Autobiography of a Cornish Miner* (Cambourne: Cambourne Printing and Stationery, 1914), 39.
76. James McCurrey, *Life of James McCurrey*, 22. Unfortunately, John got lost at this reunion meeting and disappeared, never to be seen again.
77. White, *Record of My Life*, 69.
78. Chase, ed., *Life and Literary Pursuits of Allen Davenport*, 12.
79. Harte, *Literature of the Irish in Britain*, 62.
80. William Kingscote Greenland, ed., *Raymond Preston, British and Australian Evangelist: Life Story and Personal Reminiscences* (London: Epworth Press, 1930), 66–67.
81. This same sentiment—of being too overwhelmed to describe feelings but attempting to anyway—was common in this period in newspaper accounts of horrific workplace accidents. See Jamie Bronstein, *Caught in the Machinery: Workplace Accidents and Injured Workers in Nineteenth-Century Britain* (Stanford: Stanford University Press, 2008), 71.
82. Parkinson, *Stories of Durham Pit-Life*, 52.
83. Parkinson, *Stories of Durham Pit-Life*, 55.
84. Parkinson, *Stories of Durham Pit-Life*, 56–57.
85. Steedman, *An Everyday Life*, 75.
86. Mark Brodie and Barbara Caine, "Class, Sex and Friendship: The Long Nineteenth Century," in *Friendship: A History*, ed. Barbara Caine (New York: Routledge, 2014), 223–77, at 250.
87. Thomas Cooper, quoted in Vincent, *Bread, Knowledge, and Freedom*, 127.
88. In contrast, see Snell, "Belonging and Community," 14.
89. Brodie and Caine, "Class, Sex and Friendship," 244, 249.
90. Spencer, *An Inspector's Testament*, 150, 161.
91. West, *Autobiography of Robert Watchorn*, 42.
92. Bullen, *Confessions of a Tradesman*, 105, 107.
93. George Herbert, *Shoemaker's Window: Recollections of Banbury before the Railway Age* (Chichester: Phillmore, 1971), 33.
94. George Ratcliffe, *Sixty Years of It: Being the Story of My Life and Public Career* (London: A. Brown and Sons, n.d), 115.
95. Snell, *Men, Movements, and Myself*, 18.
96. Meek, *George Meek*, 66.
97. Richard Hampton, *Foolish Dick: An Autobiography of Richard Hampton, the Cornish Pilgrim Preacher* (London: A. Trengove, 1873), 43.
98. Lipton, *Leaves from the Lipton Logs*, 46.

99. Henry Herbert, *Autobiography of Henry Herbert, a Gloucestershire Shoemaker and Native of Fairford* (Gloucester: printed by the author, 1876), 105.

100. Herbert, *Autobiography of Henry Herbert*, 127, 133

101. Jack Jones, *Unfinished Journey* (New York: Oxford University Press, 1937), 183.

102. Bamford, *Autobiography of Samuel Bamford*, vol. 1, 159. See also Brierley, *Home Memories*, 4, 46.

103. Hutton, *Life of William Hutton*, 141.

104. Harris, *My Autobiography*, 18.

105. Blatchford, *My Eighty Years*, 44.

106. Burstow, *Reminiscences of Horsham*, 69.

107. Milne, *Reminiscences of an Old Boy*, 208.

108. Milne, *Reminiscences of an Old Boy*, 209.

109. Gammon, *Desire, Drink and Death in English Folk and Vernacular Song*, 168.

110. "Autobiography of a Suffolk Farm Laborer," in *East Anglian Reminiscences*, ed. E. A. Goodwyn and J. C. Baxter (Ipswich: Boydell Press, 1976), 45.

111. Baldry, *Rabbit-Skin Cap*, 59.

112. Baldry, *Rabbit-Skin Cap*, 129, 161.

113. Carter, *Memoir of a Working Man*, 43.

114. Thomson, *Autobiography of an Artisan*, 46.

115. John Askham, *Sketches in Prose and Verse* (Northampton: S. S. Campion, 1893), 193.

116. Adams, *Memoirs of a Social Atom*, 131; Oliver, *Autobiography of a Cornish Miner*, 10.

117. Mabel Frances Coombs, *The Early Recollections of Moses Horler* (Radstock: n.p., 1900), 13.

118. Brierley, *Home Memories*, 39.

119. Brierley, *Home Memories*, 43.

120. Joseph Philip Robson, *The Life and Adventures of the Far-Famed Billy Purvis* (Newcastle upon Tyne: John Clarke, 1849), 28.

121. Jones, *Unfinished Journey*, 50, 56, 78, 86, 211.

122. Hutton, *Life of William Hutton*, 84.

123. Severn, *Life Story and Experiences of a Phrenologist*, 94.

124. Quoted in Joshua Marsden, *Sketches from the Early Life of a Sailor*, 47.

125. Dylan Wiwad and Lara B. Aknin, "Motives Matter: The Emotional Consequences of Recalled Self- and Other-Focused Prosocial Acts," *Motivation and Emotion* 41 (2017): 730–40, at 730.

126. Lara B. Aknin, Tanya Broesch, J. Kiley Hamlin, and Julia W. Van de Vondevoort, "Prosocial Behavior Leads to Happiness in a Small-Scale Rural Society," *Journal of Experimental Psychology* 144, no. 4 (2015): 788–95.

127. Of course, working people were not the only ones gladdened by participation in prosocial activities; for aristocratic women, it justified their existence. See Horn, *Ladies of the Manor*, 124.

128. Davin, *Growing Up Poor*, 39–43.

129. Brierley, *Home Memories*, 20.

130. Burn, *Autobiography of a Beggar Boy*, 28.

131. Burn, *Autobiography of a Beggar Boy*, 54.

132. Burn, *Autobiography of a Beggar Boy*, 97.

133. William Cameron, *Hawkie: The Autobiography of a Gangrel*, edited with a preface by John Strathesk (Glasgow: David Robertson, 1888), 20, 42, 47, 74.

134. John Struthers, *The Poetical Works of John Struthers* (London: A. Fullerton, 1850), xxx.

135. Chancellor, ed., *Master and Artisan in Victorian England*, 124.

136. Dunn, *From Coal-Mine Upwards*, 99.

137. James Nye, *A Small Account of My Travels through the Wilderness*, ed. Vic Gammon (Brighton: Queens Park Books, 1981), 12, 20, 26, 27, 33, 35.

138. Albert Pugh, "I Helped to Build Railroads," *Pilot Papers* 1, no. 4 (1946): 75–98, at 89.

139. Henry Broadhurst, *Henry Broadhurst, M.P., The Story of His Life from a Stonemason's Bench to the Treasury Bench* (London: Hazell, Watson and Viney, 1901), 24.

140. Frow and Frow, eds., *Dark Satanic Mills*, 20.

141. Eleanor Eden, ed., *The Autobiography of a Working Man* (London: Richard Bentley, 1862), 52, 85.

142. Hunter, *Retrospect of an Artist's Life*, 160–62.

143. Dunn, *From Coal-Mine Upwards*, 99.

144. Joseph Terry, "Recollections of My Life," Burnett Archive, 11–12.

145. Joseph Terry, "Recollections of My Life," in Burnett, *Destiny Obscure*, 71.

146. Jane Andrew, *Recorded Mercies: Being the Autobiography of Jane Andrew, Living at St. Ives, Liskeard, Cornwall* (London: E. Wilmshurst, 1890), 36.

147. The extensive literature on this is summarized in Roger Bennett, "Why Urban Poor Donate: A Study of Low-Income Charitable Giving in London," *Nonprofit and Voluntary Sector Quarterly* 41, no. 5 (2012): 870–91.

148. Dottie, *Rambles and Recollections*, xiv.

149. Powell, *Life Lessons*, 105.

150. Buckmaster, ed., *Village Politician*, 12.

151. Rogers, *Labour, Life and Literature*, 21.

152. Robson, *Life and Adventures of Billy Purvis*, 162, 200.

153. Thomas Okey, *A Basketful of Memories: An Autobiographical Sketch* (London: J. M. Dent and Sons, 1930), 152.

154. Thomas Sanderson, ed., *The Poetical Works of Robert Anderson, Author of 'Cumberland Ballads,' etc., To Which Is Prefixed the Life of the Author, Written by Himself* (Carlisle: B. Scott, 1820), xxxi.

155. Bent, *Criminal Life*, 256.

156. Callum Brown, *The Death of Christian Britain* (London: Routledge, 2001), 49.

157. Butler, *Narrative of Serjeant B———*, 132–33, 199.

158. Butler, *Narrative of Serjeant B———*, 182, 236, 284.

159. Blatchford, *My Eighty Years*, 129.

160. William Swan, *The Journals of Two Poor Dissenters, 1786–1880* (Oxford: Aiden and Mowbray, 1970), 3.

161. Swan, *Journals of Two Poor Dissenters*, 13.

162. Greenland, ed., *Raymond Preston, British and Australian Evangelist*, 43.

163. Sarah Martin, *A Brief Sketch of the Life of the Late Sarah Martin of Great Yarmouth* (Yarmouth: n.p., 1844), 15; Rendall, "A Short Account of My Unprofitable Life," 38.

164. Martin, *Life of Sarah Martin*, 25. For similar testimony, see Barr, *Climbing the Ladder*, 75–76.

165. Rev. J. Arthur Turner., ed., *The Life of a Chimney Boy, Written by Himself* (London: Charles H. Kelly, 1901), 51. Lewin was identified through his birthplace and date (1832, London) and death-place and date (1896, Hitchin), using ancestry.com.

166. Farrar, ed., *Diary of Colour-Sergeant George Calladine*, 122.

167. Clare, "Autobiographical Fragments," 140–41.

168. *Struggles for Life: Or the Autobiography of a Dissenting Minister* (London: W and FG Cash, 1854), 7.

169. Burn, *Autobiography of a Beggar Boy*, 142.

170. Carnegie, *Autobiography*, 86.

171. Carnegie, *Autobiography*, 294.

172. Edwards, *Crow-Scaring to Westminster*, 193.

Chapter 5: The Natural World

1. Matthew Osborn, "The Weirdest of All Undertakings: The Land and the Early Industrial Revolution in Oldham, England," *Environmental History* 8 (April 2003): 246–69.

2. Begiato, "Selfhood and 'Nostalgia,'" 236; Vincent, *Bread, Knowledge and Freedom*, 89.

3. John Finney, *Sixty Years' Reminiscences of an Etruscan* (Stoke upon Trent: J. P. Fenn, 1902), 39.

4. Ashley, "Autobiography," Burnett Archive, 16.

5. Lax, *Lax, His Book*, 40.

6. In a footnote to a 1994 article, Michael Sigsworth and Michael Worboys noted that it is difficult to read working-class attitudes toward environmental and public health issues from the historical record; workers were often objectified by public health reformers. A footnote to the article indicated that they planned to mine working-class autobiographies to develop a better sense of working-class environmentalism, but that project seems never to have materialized. Michael Sigsworth and Michael Worboys, "The Public's View of Public Health in Mid-Victorian Britain," *Urban History* 21, no. 2 (1994): 237–50.

7. Vincent, *Bread, Knowledge, and Freedom*, 188.

8. Murison, *Memoirs of 88 Years*, 33.

9. Anna Pavord, *Landskipping: Painters, Ploughmen and Places* (London: Bloomsbury, 2016), 20; Joyce, *Democratic Subjects*, 33–34.

10. Stefania Barca, "Laboring the Earth: Transnational Reflections on the Environmental History of Work," *Environmental History* 19 (January 2014): 3–27.

11. Kelly, *The German Worker*, 33.

12. Rogers, *Labour, Life and Literature*, 56.

13. Rogers, *Labour, Life and Literature*, 126.

14. Rogers, *Labour, Life and Literature*, 306, 310.

15. Farningham, *A Working Woman's Life*, 22.

16. Strange, *Fatherhood and the British Working Class*, 140.

17. Askham, *Sketches in Prose and Verse*, vii–viii. See also Frank Kitz, *Recollections and Reflections* (London: Carl Slienger, 1976), 4.

18. Urie, *Reminiscences of 80 Years*, 151.

19. Mullin, *Toiler's Life*, 167–68.

20. Hamlet Nicholson, *An Autobiographical and Full Historical Account of the Persecution of Hamlet Nicholson* (Manchester: Barber and Farnsworth, 1892), 8.

21. Steedman, *Radical Soldier's Tale*, 218–19.
22. Severn, *Life Story and Experiences of a Phrenologist*, 296–97. See also Terry, "My Recollections," Burnett Archive, 77.
23. James Campkin, *The Struggles of a Village Lad* (London: William Tweedie, 1858), 2.
24. Miller, *My Schools and Schoolmasters*, 124, 188. See also Joseph Constantine, *Fifty Years of the Water Cure* (London: John Heywood, 1892), 2; Terry, "Recollections of My Life," Burnett Archive, 1.
25. Miller, *My Schools and Schoolmasters*, 509.
26. Thomas Todd, *My Life as I Have Lived It* (Leeds: Thomas Todd, 1935), 66.
27. "The Life of a Journeyman Baker," *Commonwealth* (Glasgow), December 13, 1856. 3.
28. Katrina Navickas, "'God's Earth Will Be Sacred': Religion, Theology and the Open Space Movement in Victorian England," *Rural History* 22, no. 1 (2011): 31–58.
29. Robin Veder, "The Gardener's Exercise: Rational Recreation in Early Nineteenth-Century Britain," *Proteus* 25, no. 2 (2008): 53–59.
30. S. Martin Gaskell, "Gardens for the Working Class: Victorian Practical Pleasures," *Victorian Studies* 23, no. 4 (1980): 479–501.
31. Finney, *Sixty Years' Reminiscences*, 26.
32. Margaret Willes, *The Gardens of the British Working Class* (New Haven, CT: Yale University Press, 2014), 6, 102, 106, 152.
33. Elizabeth Coggin Womack, "Window Gardening and the Regulation of the Home in Victorian Periodicals," *Victorian Periodicals Review* 51, no. 2 (Summer 2018): 269–88.
34. Willes, *Gardens of the British Working Class*, 123, 133, 149.
35. Edwards, *Crow-Scaring to Westminster*, 157.
36. Mrs. Layton, "Memories of Seventy Years," in *Life as We Have Known It*, ed. Margaret Llewellyn Davies (New York: W. W. Norton, 1975), 55; See also Oliver, *Autobiography of a Cornish Miner*, 84. On allotments and the working-class diet, see Griffin, *Bread Winner*, 206.
37. Willes, *Gardens of the British Working Class*, 155.
38. William Farish, *The Autobiography of William Farish: The Struggle of a Handloom Weaver* (London: Caliban Books, 1996), 15.
39. Ratcliffe, *Sixty Years of It*, 47, 171, 309, 325.
40. Wakeman, *Autobiography of a Charwoman*, 10, 12–13.
41. Joyce, *Democratic Subjects*, 54.
42. Todd, *My Life as I Have Lived It*, 26. Guddling is a Scottish dialect word for catching fish using one's hands.
43. Edward Rymer, *The Martyrdom of the Mine* (Middlesbrough: Jordison, 1898), 5, facsimile reprint in Robert G. Neville, ed., *History Workshop Journal* 1 (Spring 1976) and 2 (Autumn 1976). See also Severn, *Life Story and Experiences*, 7.
44. Terry, "Recollections of My Life," Burnett Archive, 4.
45. John Fraser, *Sixty Years in Uniform* (London: Stanley Paul, 1939), 28.
46. Stevens, *Memoir of Thomas Martin Wheeler*, 6, 41.
47. Powell, *Life Incidents and Poetic Pictures*, 3.
48. William Heaton, *The Old Soldier, The Wandering Lover, and Other Poems* (London: Simpkin, Marshall, 1857), xix.
49. Broadhurst, *Henry Broadhurst, M.P.*, 2.

50. Smith, *My Revelation*, 18.
51. Saunders, *Reflections and Rhymes of an Old Miller*, 14.
52. Jones, *Rhymney Memories*, 155.
53. Cooper, *Life of Thomas Cooper*, 18–19.
54. Samuel Bamford, *Early Days*, vol. 1 (London: Simkin and Marshall, 1849), 53, 86.
55. Bamford, *Early Days*, vol. 1, 76.
56. Clare, "Autobiographical Fragments," 32.
57. Shaw, *When I Was a Child*, 33–4.
58. Nicholson, *Autobiographical and Full Historical Account*, 134.
59. Herbert, *Shoemaker's Window*, 47. Sparrows were considered nonnative, grain-eating pests.
60. Layton, "Memories of Seventy Years," 18.
61. Layton, "Memories of Seventy Years," 30.
62. Betty May, *Tiger-Woman* (London: Duckworth, 1929), 29–30.
63. William Tayler, quoted in Burnett, ed., *Annals of Labour*, 185.
64. Oliver, *Autobiography of a Cornish Miner*, 69.
65. James Croll, *Autobiographical Sketch of James Croll, with a Memoir of His Life and Work* (London: Stanford, 1896), 18.
66. David Love, *The Life, Adventures and Experiences of David Love, Written by Himself* (Nottingham: Sutton and Sons, 1823), 149.
67. Broadhurst, *Henry Broadhurst, M.P.*, 13.
68. Kelly J. Mays, "Domestic Spaces, Readerly Acts: Reading, Gender and Class in Working-Class Autobiography," *Nineteenth-Century Contexts* 30, no. 4 (2008): 343–68, at 348.
69. David Kennerly, "Strikes and Singing Classes: Chartist Culture, 'Rational Recreation' and the Politics of Music after 1842," *English Historical Review* 576 (October 2020): 1165–94.
70. John Kitto, *The Lost Senses* (London: Charles Knight, 1845), 152.
71. White, *Record of My Life*, 38, 43.
72. White, *Record of My Life*, 142.
73. William Milne, *Reminiscences of an Old Boy: Being Autobiographic Sketches of Scottish Rural Life from 1832 to 1856* (Forfar: John McDonald, 1901), 24.
74. Mitchell, *Recollections of a Lifetime*, 25–26, 66, 89.
75. Severn, *Life and Experiences of a Phrenologist*, 25.
76. Saunders, *Reflections and Rhymes*, 67.
77. Saunders, *Reflections and Rhymes*, 68.
78. Snell, *Men, Movements, and Myself*, 164.
79. Sanderson, ed., *Poetical Works of Robert Anderson*, xv.
80. Sanderson, ed., *Poetical Works of Robert Anderson*, xxxiv.
81. Thomas Carter, *Memoirs of a Working Man* (London: Charles Knight, 1845), 31.
82. Katrina Navickas, "Moors, Fields, and Popular Protest in South Lancashire and the West Riding of Yorkshire, 1800–1848," *Northern History* 46, no. 1 (March 2009): 93–111.
83. Joseph Stamper, *Less Than the Dust: The Autobiography of a Tramp* (London: Hutchinson, n.d.), 78.

84. Snell, *Men, Movements, and Myself*, 8, 12. As noted above, however, Snell became an avid mountain hiker.
85. George Mockford, "Wilderness Journeys and Gracious Deliverances," Burnett Archive, 4.
86. Milne, *Reminiscences of an Old Boy*, 119. See also William Johnston, *The Life and Times of William Johnston* (Peterhead: William Taylor, 1859), 11.
87. Oakley, "Autobiography," 136.
88. "A Norfolk Labourer's Wife," in *East Anglian Reminiscences*, ed. E. A. Goodwyn and J. C. Baxter (Ipswich: Boydell Press, 1976), 27.
89. "Autobiography of a Blacksmith, Written by Himself," *Commonwealth* (Glasgow), January 17, 1857, 3.

Chapter 6: Self-Cultivation

1. Jeremy Bentham, *Rationale of Reward* (London: C. and W. Reynell, 1830), 206.
2. John Stuart Mill, *Utilitarianism* (London: Longmans Green, 1879), 14.
3. Charles Campbell, *Memoirs of Charles Campbell, at Present Prisoner in the Jail of Glasgow* (Glasgow: James Duncan, 1828), 4.
4. Vincent, *Bread, Knowledge, and Freedom*, 144.
5. Smiles, *Self-Help*, 21.
6. Strange, *Fatherhood and the British Working Class*, 143.
7. Cunningham, *Invention of Childhood*, 169–73.
8. Boos, *Memoirs of Working-Class Women*, chap. 2; Jonathan Rose, *The Intellectual Life of the British Working Classes* (New Haven, CT: Yale University Press, 2001), 59.
9. Burnett, *Destiny Obscure*, 148, 196; Rose, *Intellectual Life*, 151–56, 170; Smith, *Autobiography of Mary Smith*, 13.
10. Carnegie, *Autobiography of Andrew Carnegie*, 14.
11. Rushton, *My Life as a Farmer's Boy*, 23–24.
12. Eranda Jayawickreme, Marie J. C. Forgeard, and Martin E. P. Seligman, "The Engine of Well-Being," *Review of General Psychology* 16, no. 4 (2012): 327–42; Vincent, *Literacy and Popular Culture*, 196; Vincent, *Bread, Knowledge, and Freedom*, 136.
13. Rose, *Intellectual Life*, 19.
14. Kelly J. Mays, "Domestic Spaces, Readerly Acts: Reading, Gender and Class in Working-Class Autobiography," *Nineteenth-Century Contexts* 30. no. 4 (2008): 343–68, at 345.
15. Vincent, *Bread, Knowledge, and Freedom*, 117–20; Cunningham, *Invention of Childhood*, 122.
16. Rushton, *My Life as a Farmer's Boy*, 76, 100.
17. Rose, *Intellectual Life*, 95–105, 371; Joyce, *Democratic Subjects*, 33.
18. Brown, *Death of Christian Britain*, 70.
19. Cooper, *Life of Thomas Cooper*, 22. To some extent such a confession is predictable; Cooper became an itinerant Baptist preacher later in life, and many Chartists were proud autodidacts.
20. [Leask], *Struggles for Life*, 46.
21. On the popularity of *Pilgrim's Progress* among working-class autobiographers, see also Burnett, *Destiny Obscure*, 38. Bamford, *Autobiography of Samuel*

Bamford, vol. 1, 40; Hillocks, *Life Story*, 30; Leatherland, *Essays and Poems*, Harris, *My Autobiography*, 24; Blatchford, *My Eighty Years*, 41; Wilson, *Memories of a Labour Leader*, 54; Burt, *Pitman and Privy Councillor*, 115; Smith, *Autobiography of Mary Smith*, 62; Forrest, *Chapters in the Life of a Dundee Factory Boy*, 56; Campkin, *Struggles of a Village Lad*, 21.

22. Heaton, *The Old Soldier*, xvii.
23. Oakley, "Autobiography of Elizabeth Oakley," 124.
24. Jacques, "Glimpses," November 1, 1856, 3.
25. Holkinson, "Life of Jacob Holkinson, Tailor and Poet," January 24 and 31, 1857, 3.
26. Frank George Marling, "Reminiscences," Burnett Archive, unpaginated.
27. Whittaker, *Life's Battles in Temperance Armour*, 61–62.
28. Vincent, *Literacy and Popular Culture*, 59.
29. Donaldson, *Recollections of an Eventful Life*, 3.
30. Powell, *Life Lessons*, 6.
31. Smith, *Autobiography of Mary Smith*, 40. On Shakespeare as a nineteenth-century working-class favorite, see Rose, *Intellectual Life*, 124.
32. Harris, *My Autobiography*, 62.
33. Vincent, *Literacy and Popular Culture*, 207; cf. Rob Breton, "Genre in the Chartist Periodical," in *The Working-Class Intellectual in Eighteenth- and Nineteenth-Century Britain*, ed. Aruna Krishnamurthy (Burlington: Ashgate Press, 2009): 109–28, at 113.
34. Dodd, *Narrative*, 289.
35. Rowland Kenney, *Westering: An Autobiography* (London: J.M. Dent, 1939), 26.
36. Miller, *My Schools and Schoolmasters*, 27, 28.
37. Bullen, *Log of a Sea-Waif*, 158.
38. "The Life of a Letterpress Printer, Written by Himself," *Commonwealth* (Glasgow), February 7, 1857, 3.
39. Mary Thale, ed., *The Autobiography of Francis Place* (Cambridge: The University Press, 1972), 47, 109; Cunningham, *Invention of Childhood*, 122.
40. Meek, *George Meek*, 32.
41. Harris, *My Autobiography*, 46.
42. Carnegie, *Autobiography*, 48.
43. Armstrong, *Pilgrimage from Nenthead*, 77.
44. Armstrong, *Pilgrimage from Nenthead*, 142.
45. Robert White, *Autobiographical Notes* (Newcastle: Privately printed, 1966), 5, 22.
46. Price, "Memoir of Henry Price," 29.
47. Vincent, *Bread, Knowledge, and Freedom*, 172–73. Kelly found the same to be true for German autobiographers. See Kelly, *The German Worker*, 34.
48. Anne Secord, "Botany on a Plate: Pleasure and the Power of Pictures in Promoting Early Nineteenth-Century Scientific Knowledge," *Isis* 93, no. 1 (March 2002): 28–57.
49. Anne Secord, "'Be What You Would Seem to Be': Samuel Smiles, Thomas Edward, and the Making of a Working-Class Scientific Hero," *Science in Context* 16, no. 1/2 (2003): 147–73.
50. Younger, *Autobiography of John Younger*, 22–23.
51. Chancellor, ed., *Master and Artisan in Victorian England*, 95.

52. Chancellor, ed., *Master and Artisan in Victorian England*, 139.
53. Chancellor, ed., *Master and Artisan in Victorian England*, 151.
54. Chancellor, ed., *Master and Artisan in Victorian England*, 130, 228, 232. Samuel Smiles agreed that "Natural History is one of the most delightful of hobbies." Secord, "'Be What You Would Seem to Be,'" 158.
55. Samuel Taylor, *Records of an Active Life, with Incident of Travel and Numerous Anecdotes* (London: Simpkin, Marshall, 1886), 6.
56. Oliver, *Autobiography of a Cornish Miner*, 29.
57. Severn, *Life Story and Experiences of a Phrenologist*, 46.
58. Meek, *George Meek*, 236. A bathchair-man pushes what it essentially an adult-sized pram, conveying people who are unable to walk very far.
59. Wilson, *Memoirs of a Labour Leader*, 208.
60. Keating, *My Struggle for Life*, 113. See also Rose, *Intellectual Life*, 241.
61. Keating, *My Struggle for Life*, 145.
62. Mullin, *Toiler's Life*, 17.
63. Jones, *Old Memories*, 77.
64. Jones, *Old Memories*, 103.
65. Jones, *Old Memories*, 214.
66. Jones, *Old Memories*, 216.
67. Clare, "Sketches in the Life of John Clare," 9.
68. Rogers, *Labour, Life and Literature*, 157.
69. Robert Story, *The Poetical Works of Robert Story* (Newcastle upon Tyne: Thomas and James Figg, 1856), vi.
70. Plummer, *Songs of Labour*, xxi.
71. Fraser, *Sixty Years in Uniform*, 88.
72. Adams, *Memoirs of a Social Atom*, 381.
73. Riddell, *Poetical Works of Henry Scott Riddell*, xviii.
74. Jack Goring, "Autobiography of Jack Goring," Burnett Archive, 114, 117.
75. Vincent, *Literacy and Popular Culture*, 201.
76. Andrew Hobbs, "Five Million Poems, or the Local Press as Poetry Publisher, 1800–1900," *Victorian Periodicals Review* 45, no. 4 (Winter 2012): 488–92.
77. Meagan Birchmore Timney, "Working-Class Women's Writing in the Nineteenth-Century Radical Periodical Press: Chartist Threads," *Philological Quarterly* 92, no. 2 (2013): 177–97; Kirstie Blair, "'A Very Poetical Town': Newspaper Poetry and the Working-Class Poet in Victorian Dundee," *Victorian Poetry* 50, no. 1 (2014): 89–109.
78. Parsons, *Poetical Trifles*.
79. Robert Southey, *The Lives and Works of the Uneducated Poets* (London: Humphrey Milford, 1925), 11.
80. Southey, *Lives and Works of the Uneducated Poets*, 172.
81. Southey, *Lives and Works of the Uneducated Poets*, 12.
82. Smith, *Autobiography of Mary Smith*, 142, 156, 242.
83. Southey, *Lives and Works of the Uneducated Poets*, 35.
84. Southey, *Lives and Works of the Uneducated Poets*, 138. Adam Rushton also remembered being delighted by the *Iliad*; see Rushton, *My Life*, 49. Nineteenth-century Britons bred small dogs, called "turnspit dogs," to turn cooking rotisseries by running in circles.
85. Farningham, *Working Woman's Life*, 28.
86. Farningham, *Working Woman's Life*, 21.

87. Farningham, *Working Woman's Life*, 62.
88. Chase, ed., *Life and Literary Pursuits of Allen Davenport*, 5.
89. Chase, ed., *Life and Literary Pursuits of Allen Davenport*, 17.
90. Heaton, *The Old Soldier*, xxi.
91. Harris, *My Autobiography*, 29, 48,
92. Harris, *My Autobiography*, 58.
93. Brian Maidment, *The Poorhouse Fugitives: Self-Taught Poets and Poetry in Victorian Britain* (Manchester: Carcanet Press, 1987), 127, 137, 140.
94. Bullen, *Confessions of a Tradesman*, 198.
95. Bullen, *Confessions of a Tradesman*, 204, 264.
96. Brown, *Death of Christian Britain*, 55.
97. Allen, *Autobiography of Rose Allen*, 81.
98. Somerville, *Autobiography of a Working Man*, 109.
99. Burstow, *Reminiscences of Horsham*, 109.
100. Heaton, *The Old Soldier*, xviii.
101. Nye, *Small Account of My Travels*, 13.
102. Serjeant Butler, *Narrative of Serjeant B———*, 11, 25
103. William Clift, *Reminiscences of William Clift of Bramley* (Basingstoke: Bird Brothers, 1908), 76.
104. Davies, *Short Sketches from the Life of Thomas Davies*, 7.
105. John Shinn, "A Sketch of My Life and Times," Burnett Archive, 10, 20.
106. Lovett, *Life and Struggles of William Lovett*, 32.
107. Lovett, *Life and Struggles of William Lovett*, 78.
108. Lovett, *Life and Struggles of William Lovett*, 47.
109. Farningham, *A Working Woman's Life*, 203.
110. Ashley, "Autobiography," Burnett Archive, 29–30.
111. Smith, *Incidents in a Gipsy's Life*, 11.
112. Mays, "Domestic Spaces," 353.
113. Mrs. Scott, "A Felt Hat Worker," in Davies, ed., *Life as We Have Known It*, 92.
114. "Extracts from Guildswomen's Letters," in Davies, ed., *Life as We Have Known It*, 129.

Chapter 7: The Way of Duty

1. Alan S. Waterman, "The Relevance of Aristotle's Conception of Eudaimonia for the Psychological Study of Happiness," *Theory and Philosophy of Psychology* 10, no. 1 (1990): 39–44, at 43.
2. For a modern notion of eudaimonia as "ego complexity," see Laura A. King and Joshua A. Hicks, "Whatever Happened to 'What Might Have Been?': Regrets, Happiness and Maturity," *American Psychologist* 62, no. 7 (2007): 625–36.
3. Brown, *Death of Christian Britain*, 125.
4. Henry Manton, "Alderman Manton's Reminiscences." *Birmingham Weekly Mercury*, November 15, 22, and 29, December 6, 13, 20, and 27, 1902; and January 10, 17, 24, and 21, and February 7, 14, and 21, 1903, all p. 1.
5. Hackett, "A Different Form of 'Self,'" 220.
6. Burnett, *Destiny Obscure*, 40.
7. Thomas Dixon, *Weeping Britannia: Portrait of a Nation in Tears* (Oxford: Oxford University Press, 2015), 77; Brown, *Death of Christian Britain*, 49, 115.
8. The notion that Samuel Smiles's *Self-Help* is a sort of "lives of the saints"

martyred to science and engineering seems particularly apt. See Brown, *Death of Christian Britain*, 103.

9. D. Catherine Hopwood, *An Account of the Life and Religious Experience of D. Caroline Hopwood* (Leeds: E. Baines, 1801).

10. "Life of a Handloom Weaver," April 25, 1857, 1.

11. Jonathan Martin, *The Life of Jonathan Martin, of Darlington, Tanner* (Darlington: Thomas Thompson, 1825), 39.

12. *Autobiography of a Scotch Lad: Being Reminiscences of Threescore Years and Ten* (Glasgow: David Bryce and Son, 1887), 19.

13. Edward Smyth, *The Extraordinary Life and Christian Experience of Margaret Davidson (as Dictated by Herself)* (Dublin: The Editor, 1802), 20.

14. Smyth, *Extraordinary Life*, 77.

15. Nye, *Small Account of My Travels*, 14–15. On music as an intellectual outlet for the British working class, see Rose, *Intellectual Life of the British Working Classes*, 196.

16. Nye, *Small Account of My Travels*, 18, 20.

17. Nye, *Small Account of My Travels*, 35.

18. Mockford, *Wilderness Journeyings and Gracious Deliverances*, 29.

19. Chancellor, ed., *Master and Artisan in Victorian England*, 135, 159.

20. Eli Ashdown, *Gleanings by a Watchman on a Dark Corner of Zion's Walls . . . Being the Autobiography of Eli Ashdown* (London: Farncombe and Son, 1904), 40.

21. Ashdown, *Gleanings by a Watchman*, 68, 148.

22. Harry Carter, *Autobiography of a Cornish Smuggler, 1749–1809* (Truro: Joseph Pollard, 1894), 32.

23. Carter, *Autobiography of a Cornish Smuggler*, 41, 47, 79.

24. Carter, *Autobiography of a Cornish Smuggler*, 65, 66, 88, 96.

25. Carter, *Autobiography of a Cornish Smuggler*, 101.

26. Joshua Marsden, *Sketches of the Early Life of a Sailor* (Hull: William Ross, n.d.), 7.

27. Marsden, *Sketches of the Early Life of a Sailor*, 11.

28. Marsden, *Sketches of the Early Life of a Sailor*, 17.

29. Marsden, *Sketches of the Early Life of a Sailor*, 41–2.

30. G. S. French, "Marsden, Joshua," in *Dictionary of Canadian Biography*, vol. 7, University of Toronto/Université Laval, 2003, http://www.biographi.ca/en/bio/marsden_joshua_7E.html, accessed September 11, 2016.

31. Marsden, *Sketches of the Early Life of a Sailor*, 46, 50.

32. Marsden, *Sketches of the Early Life of a Sailor*, 3.

33. B. A. Trinder, ed., "The Memoir of William Smith," *Transactions of the Shropshire Archaeological Society* 58, no. 2 (1965): 178–85, at 182.

34. John Donkin McNaughton, *The Life and Happy Experience of John Donkin McNaughton* (Stokesley: W. Pratt, 1810), 6.

35. "A Working Man," *Scenes from My Life, by a Working Man* (London: Seeleys, 1858), 40.

36. "A Working Man," *Scenes from My Life*, 42.

37. "A Working Man," *Scenes from My Life*, 82.

38. "A Working Man," *Scenes from My Life*, 84.

39. Wilson, *Memoirs of a Labour Leader*, 207.

40. Roberts, *A Wandering Scholar*, 56.

41. Butler, *Narrative of Serjeant Butler*, 128–29.
42. Butler, *Narrative of Serjeant Butler*, 280.
43. Butler, *Narrative of Serjeant Butler*, 281.
44. Henry Holloway, *A Voice from the Convict Cell: or, Life and Conversation of Henry Holloway* (Manchester: John Heywood, 1877), 11, 18
45. Holloway, *Voice from the Convict Cell*, 33.
46. Holloway, *Voice from the Convict Cell*, 35, 90.
47. Thomas Carter, *Memoirs of a Working Man*, 111.
48. Newman Hall, ed., *Hope for the Hopeless: An Autobiography of John Vine Hall* (New York: American Tract Society), 1865), 17, 40
49. Hall, ed., *Hope for the Hopeless*, 48, 58.
50. Hall, ed., *Hope for the Hopeless*, 49.
51. Hall, ed., *Hope for the Hopeless*, 178, 114.
52. Teasdale, *Life and Adventures of Harvey Teasdale*, 95.
53. Teasdale, *Life and Adventures of Harvey Teasdale*, 99.
54. Charles Humphreys, *The Life of Charles Humphreys (Bookseller) of Paternoster Row, Told by Himself* (London: Wickliffe Press, 1928), 28.
55. Humphreys, *Life of Charles Humphreys*, 39.
56. Humphreys, *Life of Charles Humphreys*, 92.
57. Humphreys, *Life of Charles Humphreys*, 152, 173, 189, 221, 251.
58. Humphreys, *Life of Charles Humphreys*, 228.
59. Martin, *A Brief Sketch of the Life of the Late Sarah Martin*, 10.
60. William Bowcock, *The Life, Experience and Correspondence of William Bowcock, The Lincolnshire Driller* (London: Houlston and Stoneman, 1851), 84.
61. Dunn, *From Coal Mine Upwards*, 75.
62. Dunn, *From Coal Mine Upwards*, 81.
63. W. Edwards, ed., *My Life's History: The Autobiography of Rev. Thomas Lewis, Baptist Minister, Newport* (Newport: C. E. Lewis, 1902), 5–6.
64. Edwards, ed., *My Life's History*, 34, 41–42, 45, 47, 90, 130.
65. Pat Hudson and Lynette Hunter, eds., "The Autobiography of William Hart, Cooper, 1776–1857," *London Journal* 7, no. 2 (1981): 144–60.
66. Hudson and Hunter, eds., "The Autobiography of William Hart," 156.
67. Pat Hudson and Lynnette Hunter, eds., "The Autobiography of William Hart, Cooper, 1776–1857: A Respectable Artisan in the Industrial Revolution, Part II," *London Journal* 8, no. 1 (1982): 63–75.
68. Hudson and Hunter, eds., "The Autobiography of William Hart . . . Part II," 73–74.
69. Anderson, *The Sailor*, 66.
70. Henry Taylor, *Memoirs of the Principal Events in the Life of Henry Taylor of North Shields* (North Shields: T. Appleby, 1811), 37.
71. Mead, *Life Story of an Essex Lad*, 6.
72. Lax, *Lax, His Book*, 218.
73. William Huntington, *Memoirs of the Reverend William Huntington, S.S., Coal-Heaver, Late Minister of Providence Chapel, Grey's Inn Lane* (London: J. Bailey, 1813), 5.
74. Oliver, *Autobiography of a Cornish Miner*, 58.
75. Kenney, *Westering*, 32.
76. Farningham (Mary Ann Hearn), *A Working Woman's Life*, 18.
77. Farningham (Mary Ann Hearn), *A Working Woman's Life*, 32.

78. Farningham (Mary Ann Hearn), *A Working Woman's Life*, 92.
79. Farningham (Mary Ann Hearn), *A Working Woman's Life*, 113, 14.
80. Brown, *Death of Christian Britain*, 131.
81. Kirkwood, *My Life of Revolt*, 33.
82. Snell, *Men, Movements and Myself*, 34–36.
83. Lax, *Lax, His Book*, 44.
84. Lax, *Lax, His Book*, 61.
85. Brown, *Death of Christian Britain*, 41. On the political training of Chartists, see Emma Griffin, "The Making of the Chartists: Popular Politics and Working-Class Autobiography in Early Victorian Britain," *English Historical Review* 129, no. 538 (June 2014): 578–605.
86. Joseph Livesey, "Autobiography," in *The Life and Teachings of Joseph Livesey* ed. John Pearce (London: National Temperance Publication Depot, 1887), 88, 90.
87. Livesey, "Autobiography," 31.
88. Livesey, "Autobiography," 40.
89. Whittaker, *Life's Battles in Temperance Armour*, 69, 106
90. Whittaker, *Life's Battles in Temperance Armour*, 146, 153, 213.
91. McCurrey, *Life of James McCurrey*, 189.
92. Will Thorne, *My Life's Battles* (London: George Newnes, 1925), 78.
93. Thorne, *My Life's Battles*, 221.
94. John Hodge, *Workman's Cottage to Windsor Castle* (London: Sampson Low, Marston, 1931), 264.
95. Hodge, *Workman's Cottage to Windsor Castle*, 376.
96. Preston, *Life and Opinions of Thomas Preston*, 13.
97. Preston, *Life and Opinions of Thomas Preston*, 34, 37.
98. James Watson to Ellen Watson, September 12, 1834, reprinted in W. J. Linton, *James Watson: A Memoir* (New Haven: Appledore Private Press, 1879), 62.
99. Linton, *James Watson*, 69.
100. John James Bezer, "The Autobiography of One of the Chartist Rebels of 1848," in *Testaments of Radicalism: Memoirs of Working Class Politicians, 1790–1885*, ed. John Vincent, (London: Europa, 1977), 147–88.
101. Adams, *Memoirs of a Social Atom*, 261.
102. Adams, *Memoirs of a Social Atom*, 322.
103. Harrison and Hollis, eds., *Robert Lowery*, 198.
104. William Lovett, *The Life and Struggles of William Lovett, in His Pursuit of Bread, Knowledge, and Freedom* (London: Trubner, 1876), 257.
105. Lovett, *Life and Struggles of William Lovett*, 79.
106. Lovett, *Life and Struggles of William Lovett*, 125.
107. Leno, *The Aftermath*, 89.
108. Emanuel Lovekin, "Some Notes of My Life," Burnett Archive.
109. Graeme Osborne, "Mann, Thomas (Tom), 1856–1941," *Australian Dictionary of National Biography*, http://adb.anu.edu.au/biography/mann-thomas-tom-7475, accessed June 20, 2016.
110. Tom Mann, *Tom Mann's Memoirs* (London: MacGibbon and Kee, 1967 [1923]), 96.
111. Lansbury, *My Life*, 4, 122.
112. Lansbury, *My Life*, 265, 287.
113. Kitz, *Recollections and Reflections*, 4.

114. Jones, *Unfinished Journey*, 207.
115. John McAdam, *Autobiography of John McAdam, 1806–1883, with Selected Letters* (Edinburgh: Clark Constable, 1980), 93–4.
116. Joseph Arch, *The Story of His Life Told by Himself* (London: Hutchinson, 1898), 46–47.
117. Arch, *Story of His Life*, 389.
118. Arch, *Story of His Life*, 371.
119. Edwards, *Crow-Scaring to Westminster*, 110.
120. Collison, *Apostle of Free Labour*.
121. Collison, *Apostle of Free Labour*, 230, 233, 298–99.
122. Collison, *Apostle of Free Labour*, 326.
123. Collison, *Apostle of Free Labour*, 326.
124. Karen Chase Levenson, "'Happiness Is Not a Potato': The Victorian Cultivation of Happiness," *Nineteenth-Century Contexts* 33, no. 2 (May 2011): 161–69.
125. Ablett, *Reminiscences of an Old Draper*, 235.
126. George Mitchell, *The Skeleton at the Plough, or the Poor Farm Labourers of the West: With the Autobiography and Reminiscences of George Mitchell, 'One from the Plough'* (London: George Potter, 1875), 95–120.
127. "Memoir of a Working Man," *Kendal Mercury*, January 23, 1841, 4.
128. John Passmore Edwards, *A Few Footprints* (London: Watts, 1906), vi, 36.
129. Passmore Edwards, *A Few Footprints*, 48.
130. Passmore Edwards, *A Few Footprints*, 53.
131. Carter, *Memoirs of a Working Man*, 24.
132. Carter, *Memoirs of a Working Man*, 47.
133. Carter, *Memoirs of a Working Man*, 76, 95.
134. Carter, *Memoirs of a Working Man*, 233; Thomas Carter, *A Continuation of the Memoirs of a Working Man* (London: Charles Cox, 1850), 81.
135. Carter, *Continuation of the Memoirs of a Working Man*, 81–82.
136. Carter, *Continuation of the Memoirs of a Working Man*, 234.
137. Gabbitass, *Heart Melodies*, xl, xlviii.
138. Askham, *Sketches in Prose and Verse*, xv.

Chapter 8: Absent Happiness

1. Cf. Ahmed, *Promise of Happiness*, chap. 2.
2. Steedman, *Radical Soldier's Tale*, 77, 194.
3. Susan Broomhall, "Feeling in the Wynds: Media Representations of Affective Practices in Urban Scotland in the First Half of the Nineteenth Century," in Broomhall, ed., *Spaces for Feeling*, 202–22.
4. Avi Ohry, "Shake Me Up, Judy! On Dickens, Medicine, and Spinal Cord Disorders," *Ortopedia Traumatologia Rehabilitacja* 14, no. 5 (2012): 483–91, at 484.
5. Amanda Caleb, "Contested Spaces: The Heterotopias of the Victorian Sickroom," *Humanities* 80, no. 8 (2019): 1–9.
6. Elizabeth Storie, *Autobiography of Elizabeth Storie* (Glasgow: Richard Stobbs, 1859), 152, 2, 23, 83, 146.
7. On the strategic familial use of workhouses and other institutions for the poor, see Lydia Murdoch, *Imagined Orphans: Poor Families, Child Welfare and Contested Citizenship in London* (New Brunswick, NJ: Rutgers University Press, 2006), 67–91.

8. "Recollections of John Munday," in Reginald Blunt, *Red Anchor Pieces* (London: Mills and Boon, 1928), 111–21.

9. Josiah Bassett, *The Life of a Vagrant, or the Testimony of an Outcast to the Value and Truth of the Gospel* (London: Charles Gilpin, 1850), 3.

10. Bassett, *Life of a Vagrant*, 9.

11. Bassett, *Life of a Vagrant*, 83.

12. Thomas Jackson, *Narrative of the Eventful Life of Thomas Jackson* (Birmingham: Josiah Allen and Son, 1847), 123.

13. Jackson, *Narrative of the Eventful Life of Thomas Jackson*, 154.

14. Bronstein, *Caught in the Machinery*, 87; David M. Turner and Daniel Blackie, *Disability in the Industrial Revolution: Physical Impairment in British Coal-Mining, 1780–1880* (Manchester: Manchester University Press, 2018), 37, 72.

15. Kim Price, "'Where Is the Fault?' The Starvation of Edward Cooper in the Isle of Wight Workhouse in 1877," *Social History of Medicine* 26, no. 1 (2012): 21–37.

16. Turner and Blackie, *Disability in the Industrial Revolution*, 144–48, 151, 153.

17. Andrew, *Recorded Mercies*, 42.

18. Quoted in Martha Stoddard Holmes, *Fictions of Affliction: Physical Disability in Victorian Culture* (Ann Arbor: University of Michigan Press, 2004), 138, 147, et seq.

19. Leatherland, *Essays and Poems*, 35.

20. Christine Jones, "Disability in Herefordshire, 1851–1911," *Local Population Studies* 87 (Autumn 2011): 29–44.

21. John Kitto, *The Lost Senses* (London: Charles Knight, 1845), 91.

22. Kitto, *The Lost Senses*, 51, 54.

23. Although as Katie Barclay points out, social marginality could also be a potent spur to negative emotions and frustrated desires. See "Marginal Households and Their Emotions," 107.

24. Anna Davin, "Waif Stories in Late Nineteenth-Century England," *History Workshop Journal* 52 (Autumn 2001): 67–98; Murdoch, *Imagined Orphans*, 12–42.

25. Mark Sorrell, *The Peculiar People* (Greenwood, SC: Attic Press, 1979), 117.

26. George Atkins Brine, *King of the Beggars: The Life and Adventures of George Atkins Brine* (London: Ward, Lock, 1883), passim.

27. J. H. Crawford, *The Autobiography of a Tramp* (London: Longmans Green, 1900), passim.

28. William Marcroft, *The Marcroft Family* (London: John Heywood, 1886), passim.

29. J. G., *Prisoner Set Free: The Narrative of a Convict in the Preston House of Corrections, with a Few Remarks by the Reverend John Clay, B.D.* (Preston: L. Clarke, 1846), 8.

30. May, *Tiger-Woman*, 231–32.

31. Stephen Tunnicliffe, "A Newly Discovered Source for the Life of William Gifford," *Review of English Studies*, New Series, 16, no. 61 (1965): 25–34.

32. William Gifford, *Memoir of William Gifford, Written by Himself* (London: Hunt and Clarke, 1827), 16.

33. Gifford, *Memoir of William Gifford*, 23.

34. Hackett, "A Different Form of 'Self,'" 223.
35. Nathaniel Dale, *The Eventful Life of Nathaniel Dale* (printed by the author, n.d.), passim.
36. J. W. Horsley, "Autobiography of a Thief in Thieves' Language," *Macmillan's Magazine* (1879): 500–506.
37. "Autobiography of a Convict," in *Cheltenham Chronicle and Parish Register*, June 10, 1856.
38. David Prince Miller, *The Life of a Showman* (London: Lacy, 1849), passim.
39. William Cameron, *Hawkie*, 62, 118.
40. P. E. H. Hair, ed., *Coals on Rails, or the Reason of My Wrighting: The Autobiography of Anthony Errington* (Liverpool: Liverpool University Press, 1988), 222.
41. Kenney, *Westering*, 314–15.
42. Kenney, *Westering*, 319.
43. Kenney, *Westering*, 322.
44. Thorne, *My Life's Battles*, 35.
45. J. E. Patterson, *My Vagabondage: Being the Intimate Autobiography of a Nature's Nomad* (London: William Heinemann, 1911), 9, 16, 22, 87.
46. Patterson, *My Vagabondage*, 31.
47. Davin, "Waif Stories," 75, 85.

Chapter 9: Sadness, Fear, and Anger
1. See Griffin, *Bread Winner*, 250.
2. Joanne Begiato, "Punishing the Unregulated Manly Body and Emotions in Early Victorian England," in *The Victorian Male Body*, ed. Joanne Ella Parsons and Ruth Heholt (Edinburgh: Edinburgh University Press, 2018), 46–64.
3. Quoted in Burnett, *Annals of Labour*, 85.
4. Dixon, *Weeping Britannia*, 108.
5. David Fraser, ed., *The Christian Watt Papers* (Edinburgh: Paul Harris, 1983), 59.
6. Fraser, ed., *Christian Watt Papers*, 15, 38, 95–96.
7. Fraser, ed., *Christian Watt Papers*, 103.
8. Fraser, ed., *Christian Watt Papers*, 115.
9. Nor was she alone in this, as asylums in this period seemed to lack norms for complicated grief. See Strange, *Death, Grief, and Poverty in Britain*, 221–28.
10. Allan Beveridge and Fiona Watson, "The Psychiatrist, the Historian and the Christian Watt Papers," *History of Psychiatry* 17, no. 2 (2006): 205–21.
11. Thomas Buller Mitchell, "Tommy's Book," TS, Reference Library, Bradford, 17.
12. Roberts, *Wandering Scholar*, 306–7.
13. Roberts, *Wandering Scholar*, 389, 433.
14. Roberts, *Wandering Scholar*, 434–35.
15. Roberts, *Wandering Scholar*, xx.
16. Vincent, "Love and Death and the Nineteenth-Century Working Class," 245.
17. Sanger, *Seventy Years a Showman*, 170.
18. See Ross, *Love and Toil*, 190–92; Strange, "'She Cried a Very Little,'" 160.
19. "Autobiography of Samuel Fielden," in *The Autobiographies of the Haymarket Martyrs*, ed. Philip Foner (New York: Pathfinder, 1969), 175–213, at 180.
20. Wilson, *Memories of a Labour Leader*, 45–46.

21. Ashford, *Licensed Victualler's Daughter*, 18.
22. Pat Jalland, *Death and the Victorian Family* (Oxford: Oxford University Press, 1996), 120.
23. Dixon, *Weeping Britannia*, 161–62. On the denial of working-class grief by middle-class onlookers, see Lydia Murdoch, "'The Dead and the Living': Child Death, the Public Mortuary Movement, and the Spaces of Grief and Selfhood in Victorian London," *Journal of the History of Childhood and Youth* 8, no. 3 (Fall 2015): 378–402.
24. Strange, "'She Cried a Very Little,'" 154; *Death, Grief and Poverty in Britain*, chap. 8.
25. On differences in mourning practices as indicative of civilization versus barbarism, see Murdoch, "'The Dead and the Living,'" 381, 390.
26. Lauder, *Roamin' in the Gloamin'*, 200.
27. Lauder, *Roamin' in the Gloamin'*, 211.
28. Lauder, *Roamin' in the Gloamin'*, 236.
29. Jacques, "Glimpses," November 1, 1856, 3.
30. Jacques, "Glimpses," November 8, 1856, 3.
31. Stirrup, "Autobiography of a Journeyman Shoemaker," *Commonwealth* (Glasgow), December 6, 1856, 2–3.
32. Powell, *Life Lessons*, 28.
33. James D. Wright, *Steeple Jack's Adventures* (Aberdeen: W and W Lindsay, 1890), 73.
34. Wright, *Steeple Jack's Adventures*, 96.
35. Gammon, *Desire, Drink, and Death in English Folk and Vernacular Song*, 229.
36. Campbell, *Songs of My Pilgrimage*, xvii, 127–28.
37. Chancellor, ed., *Master and Artisan*, 224.
38. Rushton, *My Life*, 291.
39. Patterson, *My Vagabondage*, 58, 130.
40. Strange, *Death, Grief and Poverty in Britain*, 197–203.
41. John Thompson, *Memoir of John Thompson* (Sunderland: Forster, 1893), 30.
42. McCurrey, *Life of James McCurrey*, 182, 192.
43. Thale, ed., *Autobiography of Francis Place*, 254,
44. Holmes, *In Bed with the Victorians*, 83.
45. Barr, *Climbing the Ladder*, 117, 122.
46. "A Little of My Life," *London Mercury* 13, no. 76, November 1925–April 1926, reprinted in Burnett, *Annals of Labour*, 67–77.
47. Ireson, "Reminiscences," Burnett Archive, 49.
48. Gough, *Autobiography by John B. Gough*, part one.
49. Gough, *Autobiography by John B. Gough*, 42, 54, 57, 60.
50. Robert Flockhart, *The Street Preacher: Being the Autobiography of Robert Flockhart* (Edinburgh: Adam and Charles Black, 1858), 23, 24, 32.
51. John Shinn, "A Sketch of My Life and Times," Burnett Archive, 8.
52. Powell, *Life Lessons*, 53, 109.
53. Ruth Strong, ed., *Autobiography of Israel Roberts* (Pudsey: Civic Society, 2000), 34.
54. West, ed., *Autobiography of Robert Watchorn*, 16.
55. West, ed., *Autobiography of Robert Watchorn*, 17–18.
56. Meek, *George Meek*, 161,

57. Mitchell, *Hard Way Up*, 170.
58. Struthers, *Poetical Works*, xlii.
59. Struthers, *Poetical Works*, lxxxiii, cxli.
60. Roger J. Owen, "The Autobiography of Robert Spurr," *Baptist Quarterly* 26, no. 6 (1976): 282–288.
61. Butler, *Narrative of Serjeant B———*, 39.
62. Donaldson, *Recollections of an Eventful Life, Chiefly Passed in the Army*, 66–67.
63. Strange, *Death, Grief and Poverty in Britain*, 212. On masculinity and emotional display, see Frost, *Promises Broken*, 55.
64. Forrest, *Chapters in the Life of a Dundee Factory Boy*, 57.
65. Ashdown, *Gleanings by a Watchman*, 152.
66. Flockhart, *The Street Preacher*, 23, 42.
67. Martin Douglas, *The Life and Adventures of Martin Douglas, Sunderland Keelman and Celebrated Life Saver* (Stockton on Tees: R. Firth, 1848), 78.
68. Thomas Davies, *Short Sketches from the Life of Thomas Davies* (Haverfordwest: William Perkins, n.d.), 2.
69. Dunn, *From Coal-Mine Upwards*, 21, 66.
70. Rushton, *My Life*, 28.
71. Todd, *My Life as I Have Lived It*, 14–16. See also Younger, *Autobiography of John Younger*, 65.
72. Plamper, "History of Emotions," 259.
73. Thale, ed., *Autobiography of Francis Place*, 218.
74. Vincent, *Bread, Knowledge, and Freedom*, 168.
75. Charles Shaw, *When I Was a Child*, chap. 15, http://www.thepotteries.org/focus/011_15.htm, last accessed January 4, 2021.
76. Lax, *Lax, His Book*, 33.
77. Lax, *Lax, His Book*, 36.
78. Severn, *Life Story and Experiences of a Phrenologist*, 6.
79. Snell, *Men, Movements and Myself*, 4. See also Barr, *Climbing the Ladder*, 42–43.
80. Campbell, *Reminiscences and Reflections*, 3–4.
81. Vincent, *Literacy and Popular Culture*, 159.
82. Bewick, *Memoir of Thomas Bewick*, 30.
83. Harman, *Sketches of the Bucks Countryside*, 75.
84. John Sykes, *Slawit in the Sixties*, in *The Voices of Children, 1700–1914*, ed. Irina Strickland (New York: Barnes and Noble Books, 1973), 167, 171.
85. Hair, ed., *Coals on Rails*, 32–33.
86. Arnold, *Recollections of William Arnold*, 29.
87. J. Wardle, *The Story of My Life* (London: Epworth Press, 1924), 86.
88. Hamish [Mary Loughran], *Adventures of an Irish Girl*, 122.
89. On religious fears, see Brown, *Death of Christian Britain*, 122.
90. John Stradley, "John Stradley Memoir," PCmf4, Wake Forest University Library Special Collections, 23.
91. Andrew, *Recorded Mercies*, 8.
92. Love, *Life, Adventures and Experiences of David Love*, 88.
93. Henry Hughes, "Autobiography," Burnett Archive, 30.
94. Nye, *Small Account of My Travels*, 16.
95. Ward, *Memoirs of Jonathan Saville*, 24–25.

96. Ward, *Memoirs of Jonathan Saville*, 28.
97. Bullen, *Log of a Sea-Waif*, 192–93.
98. Patterson, *My Vagabondage*, 316.
99. Wilson, *Memories of a Labour Leader*, 149.
100. Saunders, *Reflections and Rhymes of an Old Miller*, 71.
101. Sanger, *Seventy Years a Showman*, 30.
102. Hunter, *Retrospect of an Artist's Life*, 100.
103. Joanne Begiato, "Between Poise and Power: Embodied Manliness in Eighteenth- and Nineteenth-Century British Culture," *Transactions of the Royal Historical Society* 26 (2016): 125–47; Begiato, "Punishing the Unregulated Manly Body," 60.
104. Nancy Tomes, "A 'Torrent of Abuse': Crimes of Violence between Working-Class Men and Women in London, 1840–1875," *Journal of Social History* 11, no. 3 (1978): 328–45; Holmes, *In Bed with the Victorians*, 57.
105. Lynn Abrams, "The Taming of Highland Masculinity: Inter-personal Violence and Shifting Codes of Manhood, c. 1760–1840," *Scottish Historical Review* 92, no. 233 (April 2013): 100–122.
106. Steedman, *An Everyday Life*, 83–88, 96–97.
107. Bewick, *Memoir of Thomas Bewick*, 46.
108. Todd, *My Life as I Have Lived It*, 32.
109. J. Middleton "The Cock of the School: A Cultural History of Playground Violence in Britain, 1880–1940," *Journal of British Studies* 52, no. 4 (2013): 887–907.
110. Edwards, *From Crow-Scaring to Westminster*, 28.
111. Dunn, *From Coal-Mine Upwards*, 14.
112. West, ed., *Autobiography of Robert Watchorn*, 53.
113. John Whale, "Daniel Mendoza's Contests of Identity: Masculinity, Ethnicity and Nation in Georgian Prize-Fighting," *Romanticism* 14, no. 3 (2008): 259–71.
114. Alex Joanides, ed., *Memoirs of the Life of Daniel Mendoza* (1816) (n.p.: Romeville Enterprises, 2011), 81.
115. Jem Mace, *Fifty Years a Fighter: The Life Story of Jem Mace* (London: Caestus Books, 1998), 31.
116. James M'Kaen, *The Life of James M'Kaen, Shoemaker in Glasgow* (Glasgow: Brath and Reid, 1797), 17, 50.
117. M'Kaen, *Life of James M'Kaen*, 60.
118. Strange, *Fatherhood and the British Working Class*, 186.
119. Thale, ed., *Autobiography of Francis Place*, 61–62, 115.
120. Rymer, *Martyrdom of the Mine*, 16.
121. Rymer, *Martyrdom of the Mine*, 17.
122. Rymer, *Martyrdom of the Mine*, 18.
123. Rymer, *Martyrdom of the Mine*, 28.
124. Fraser, ed., *Christian Watt Papers*, 53.
125. Jermy, *Memories of a Working Woman*, 57, 59.
126. Griffin, *Bread Winner*, 244.

Chapter 10: The Past and the Present Converse

1. A good review of modern concepts of happiness and subjective and objective well-being can be found in Jayawickreme et al., "The Engine of Well-Being."
2. Michael A. Cohn, Barbara Fredrickson, Stephanie L. Brown, Joseph A. Mikels, and Anne M. Conway, "Happiness Unpacked: Positive Emotions Increase Life Satisfaction by Building Resilience," *Emotion* 9, no. 3 (2009): 361–68.

3. Aleksandra Mindoljevic Drakulic, "A Phenomenological Perspective on Subjective Well-Being: From Myth to Science," *Psychiatra Danubina* 24, no. 1 (2012): 31–37.
4. Howell and Howell, "Relationship of Economic Status to Subjective Well-Being."
5. Amartya Sen, *The Idea of Justice* (Cambridge, MA: Belknap Press, 2009), 269–90.
6. Sen, *Idea of Justice*, 284.
7. Martha Nussbaum, *Frontiers of Justice: Disability, Nationality, Species Membership* (Cambridge, MA: Belknap Press, 2006), 76–78.
8. Robert L. Woolfolk and Rachel H. Wasserman, "Count No One Happy: Eudaimonia and Positive Psychology," *Journal of Theoretical and Philosophical Psychology* 25, no. 1 (2005): 81–90.
9. Waterman, "Relevance of Aristotle's Conception of Eudaimonia"; Matthew Cashen, "Happiness, Eudaimonia, and the Principle of Descriptive Adequacy," *Metaphilosophy* 43, no. 2 (2012): 619–35.
10. Kristján Kristjánsson, "Positive Psychology, Happiness, and Virtue: The Troublesome Conceptual Issues," *Review of General Psychology* 14, no. 4 (2010): 296–310.
11. Phil Withington, "The Invention of 'Happiness,'" in *Suffering and Happiness in England, 1550–1850*, ed. Michael J. Braddick and Joanna Innes (Oxford: Oxford University Press, 2017), 23–44.
12. Katie Barclay, "Happiness: Family and Nation in Nineteenth-Century Ireland," *Nineteenth-Century Contexts* 43, no. 2 (2021): 171–90.
13. Sarah Lloyd, "'The Wretch of To-day May Be Happy To-Morrow': Poverty and Happiness in England, c.1700–1840," in Braddick and Innes, eds., *Suffering and Happiness*, 190–207, at 193, 198.
14. Joanna Innes, "Happiness Contested: Happiness and Politics in the Eighteenth and Early-Nineteenth Centuries," in Braddick and Innes, eds., *Suffering and Happiness*, 87–110, at 91, 106; Lloyd, "'The Wretch of To-day,'" 196.
15. Kristján Kristjánsson points out that the definition of happiness used in "positive psychology" studies assumes the preeminence of the Enlightenment individual self, and that this self is both geographically and historically contextual. See "Positive Psychology, Happiness, and Virtue."
16. For discussion of emotional regimes and emotional communities, see Jan Plamper, "The History of Emotions: An Interview with William Reddy, Barbara Rosenwein, and Peter Stearns," *History and Theory* 49 (May 2010): 237–65; Boddice, *History of Emotions*, 76–80.
17. McKenzie, "Happiness vs. Contentment?"
18. Bruno Frey, *Happiness: A Revolution in Economics* (Cambridge, MA: MIT Press, 2008), 72.
19. Reverse causation is always a potential issue in these studies. It is not clear, for example, whether lives are improved by marriage, or whether people who have happier temperaments are more likely to marry. See Frey, *Happiness*, 88; David G. Myers, "The Funds, Friends, and Faith of Happy People," *American Psychologist* 55, no. 1 (January 2000): 56–67, at 63.
20. Calvo et al., "Well-Being and Social Capital on Planet Earth."
21. Myers, "Funds, Friends, and Faith," 64.

22. Carol Graham, *The Pursuit of Happiness: An Economy of Well-Being* (Washington, DC: Brookings Institution Press, 2011), 46.
23. Madhu S. Mohanty, "What Determines Happiness? Income or Attitude: Evidence from U.S. Longitudinal Data," *Journal of Neuroscience, Psychology, and Economics* 7, no. 2 (2014): 80–102. See also Kit Eaton, "Positive Thinking, with a Little Help from Your Phone," *New York Times*, October 15, 2014, http://www.nytimes.com/2014/10/16/business/positive-thinking-with-a-little-help-from-your-phone.html?module=Search&mabReward=relbias%3Ar, last accessed December 1, 2014.
24. Frey, *Happiness*, 124.
25. Lyubomirsky et al., "Benefits of Frequent Positive Affect," 841.
26. Cohn et al., "Happiness Unpacked," 361–68.
27. Daniel Haybron, "On Being Happy or Unhappy," *Philosophy and Phenomenological Research* 71, no. 2 (2005): 287–317.
28. Mark Walker, *Happy-People-Pills for All* (Oxford: Wiley-Blackwell, 2013).
29. Innes, "Happiness Contested," 92–93.
30. John Britton, *The Autobiography of John Britton, FSA, Honorary Member of Numerous English and Foreign Societies* (London: printed by the author, 1850), 22.
31. Lipton, *Leaves from the Lipton Logs*, 23. Of course, Lipton also invented retail advertising in late nineteenth-century Britain, so if anyone were going to create a persona . . . See "Life of Lipton, to a T.," *The Herald, Scotland*, February 26, 1998, at http://www.heraldscotland.com/sport/spl/aberdeen/life-of-lipton-to-a-t-1.352524, last accessed October 8, 2014.
32. Carnegie, *Autobiography of Andrew Carnegie*, 3, 162, 322.
33. Plummer, *Songs of Labour*, xviii.
34. Dixon, "Psychology of the Emotions in Britain and America," 317.
35. Keating, *My Struggle for Life*, 224.
36. Keating, *My Struggle for Life*, 190.
37. Campbell, *Memoir of Charles Campbell*, 27.
38. Campbell was judged not guilty by reason of insanity. See Campbell, *Memoir of Charles Campbell*, 48.
39. John Lee, *John Babbacombe Lee: The Man They Could Not Hang* (Exeter: Devon Press, 1985), 29–30.
40. [Leask], *Struggles for Life*, 100.
41. Joseph Barker, *The History and Confessions of a Man: As Put Forth by Himself; Showing How He Became a Methodist and a Methodist Preacher* (London: printed by the author, 1846), 23.
42. Barker, *History and Confessions*, 26.
43. Thomas Lidgett, *The Life of Thomas L. Lidgett* (Lincoln: W. K. Morton and Sons, 1908), 23–24.
44. Johanna Brooks, *A Handmaid of the Lord: Some Records of Johanna Brooks* (London: Ludgate and Chase, 1868), 33, 39.
45. John Savage, *Memoirs Containing some Particulars of the Life, Family, and Ancestors of John Savage* (Ipswich: S. & W. J. King, n.d.), 4.
46. Savage, *Memoirs Containing Some Particulars*, 42.
47. Thomas Wilkinson Wallis, *Autobiography of Thomas Wilkinson Wallis, Sculptor in Wood, and Extracts from His Sixty Years' Journal* (Louth: J. W. Goulding and Son, 1899), 56.

48. Charles Manby Smith, *The Working Man's Way in the World* (London: W. and F. G. Cash, 1857), 106–7.
49. Ellen Johnston, *Autobiography, Poems and Songs of Ellen Johnston, the Factory Girl* (Glasgow: William Love, 1867), 8, 9.
50. Harvey Teasdale, *The Life of Harvey Teasdale, the Converted Clown and Man Monkey* (Sheffield: C. Leonard and Son, 1870), 83.
51. [Leask], *Struggles for Life*, 351.
52. [Leask], *Struggles for Life*, 358.
53. Jocelyn Baty Goodman, ed., *Victorian Cabinet Maker: The Memoirs of James Hopkinson, 1819–1894* (New York: Augustus Kelley, 1968), 6.
54. Goodman, ed., *Victorian Cabinet Maker*, 39, 41.
55. Goodman, ed., *Victorian Cabinet Maker*, 10.
56. Goodman, ed., *Victorian Cabinet Maker*, 29, 40, 82.
57. Goodman, ed., *Victorian Cabinet Maker*, 82.
58. Goodman, ed., *Victorian Cabinet Maker*, 83.
59. Goodman, ed., *Victorian Cabinet Maker*, 85.
60. Goodman, ed., *Victorian Cabinet Maker*, 96.
61. Goodman, ed., *Victorian Cabinet Maker*, xiii.
62. Swan, *Journals of Two Poor Dissenters*, 23–24.
63. Swan, *Journals of Two Poor Dissenters*, 44.
64. Swan, *Journals of Two Poor Dissenters*, 49, 56, 71.
65. Swan, *Journals of Two Poor Dissenters*, 76.
66. Wilkinson Wallis, *Autobiography of Thomas Wilkinson Wallis*, 56, 58, 65.
67. Johnston, *Autobiographical Reminiscences of David Johnston*, 137–38. This superstition persists in many forms, including the compulsion to "knock wood."
68. Stanley, ed., *Diaries of Hannah Cullwick*, 182.
69. Stanley, ed., *Diaries of Hannah Cullwick*, 3.
70. Richard A. Easterlin, "Explaining Happiness," *PNAS* 100, no. 19 (September 2003): 11176–83.
71. Myers, "Funds, Friends, and Faith," 56–67.
72. Shmotkin, "Happiness in the Face of Adversity"; Ed Diener, Louis Tay, and Shigehiro Oishi, "Rising Incomes and the Subjective Well-Being of Nations," *Journal of Personality and Social Psychology* 104, no. 2 (2013): 267–76.
73. Robert H. Frank, "The Easterlin Paradox Revisited," *Emotion* 12, no. 6 (2012): 1188–91.
74. Frey, *Happiness*, 130–31.
75. Howell and Howell, "Relation of Economic Status to Subjective Well-Being," 540.
76. Frey, *Happiness*, 174.
77. Hutton, *Life of William Hutton*, 107.
78. Deborah Smith, *My Revelation* (London: Houghton, 1934), 25.
79. Burnett, *Useful Toil*, xiv.
80. Baldry, *Rabbit-Skin Cap*, 212.
81. P. A. S. Pool, ed., *The Life and Progress of Henry Quick of Zennor* (n.p.: Penzance, 1963), 20.
82. Plummer, *Northamptonshire Rambles*, 7.
83. Gammon, *Desire, Drink and Death in English Folk and Vernacular Song*, 117.

84. Burnett, *Annals of Labour*, 14; Vincent, *Bread, Knowledge, and Freedom*, 91.
85. Burnett, *Destiny Obscure*, 16.
86. Howell and Howell, "Relation of Economic Status to Subjective Well-Being," 538; Mohanty, "What Determines Happiness?"
87. *A Short Account of the Life and Hardships of a Glasgow Weaver, with His Opinion on the Question at Present in Hot Dispute, between Churchmen and Voluntaries* (Glasgow: David Maclure, 1834), 6.
88. Mitchell, *Skeleton at the Plough*, 98.
89. Stamper, *Less Than the Dust*, 59, 192, 278.
90. Buckmaster, ed., *A Village Politician*, 6, 8.
91. Mary Saxby, *Memoirs of a Female Vagrant, Written by Herself* (Dunstable: J. W. Morris, 1806), 5.
92. Saxby, *Memoirs of a Female Vagrant*, 18.
93. Saxby, *Memoirs of a Female Vagrant*, 34.
94. John Brown, *A Memoir of Robert Blincoe*, reprinted in Simmons, ed., *Factory Lives*, 1023–33.
95. "Penny-a-yard," *Liverpool Mercury*. The author, Edward Finlay, born in Ireland, was located in the 1851 census, living with his wife Susana. No children are listed living with them. Class: *HO107*; Piece: 2229; Folio: 304; Page: 7. Ancestry.com. *1851 England Census* [database on-line]. Provo, UT, USA: Ancestry.com Operations Inc., 2005.
96. Powell, *Life Incidents and Poetic Pictures*, 1.
97. Snell, *Men, Movements and Myself*, 39–40.
98. Howell and Howell, "The Relation of Economic Status to Subjective Well-Being," 555.
99. F. M. F. Skene, "Autobiography of a Tramp," *Belgravia: A London Magazine* 81 (May 1893): 168–79.
100. Rogers, *Labour, Life and Literature*, 102.
101. Forrest, *Chapters in the Life of a Dundee Factory Boy*, 28.
102. Ann Kussmaul, ed., *The Autobiography of Joseph Mayett of Quainton (1783–1839)* (Oxford: Buckinghamshire Record Society, 1986), 59.
103. Oliver, *Autobiography of a Cornish Miner*, 98.
104. William Green, *The Life and Adventures of a Cheap Jack* (London: Chatto and Windus, 1881), 143.
105. Thomas Barclay, *Memoirs and Medleys: The Autobiography of a Bottle Washer* (Leicester: Edgar Backus, 1934), 3.
106. See, for example, Paul Frijters and Tony Beatton, "The Mystery of the U-Shaped Relationship between Happiness and Age," *Journal of Economic Behavior and Organization* 82 (2012): 525–42; Nigel Hawkes, "Happiness Is U-Shaped, Highest in the Teens and 70s, Survey Shows," *BMJ: British Medical Journal* 344, no. 7836 (March 3, 2012): 1; Seppo Laaksonen, "A Research Note: Happiness by Age Is More Complex Than U-Shaped," *Journal of Happiness Studies* 19 (2018): 471–82. Arguing that the U-shaped curve is a methodological artifact that occurs due to inappropriate controls is Ottar Hellevik, "The U-Shaped Age-Happiness Relationship: Real or Methodological Artifact?" *Quality and Quantity* 51 (2017): 177–97.
107. Frijters and Beatton, "Mystery of the U-Shaped Relationship," 540; Hellevik, "U-Shaped Age-Happiness Relationship," 188.

108. Frijters and Beatton, "Mystery of the U-Shaped Relationship," 529.
109. Chancellor, *Master and Artisan in Victorian England*, 236.
110. Chancellor, *Master and Artisan in Victorian England*, 237.
111. Hunter, *Retrospect of an Artist's Life*, 315.
112. Sanger, *Seventy Years a Showman*, 60.
113. *Autobiography of a Scotch Lad*, 121–22.
114. Robson, *Autobiography of Joseph Philip Robson*, 17.
115. Mullin, *Story of a Toiler's Life*, 232.
116. Blatchford, *My Eighty Years*, 271.
117. Blatchford, *My Eighty Years*, 272.
118. Anthony Grundy, *My Fifty Years in Transport: The Life of a Pioneer in Passenger Travel* (London: Tramway and Railway World, 1944), 39.
119. Lax, *Lax, His Book*, 325.
120. Younger, *Autobiography of John Younger*, 70.
121. Alf Ireson, "Reminiscences," Burnett Archive, ii.
122. John Wilson, *Memories of a Labour Leader*, 141.
123. Mitchell, *Recollections of a Lifetime*, 98.
124. Rogers, *Labour, Life and Literature*, viii.
125. Rogers, *Labour, Life and Literature*, 320.
126. Griffin, *Liberty's Dawn*, passim; Walter Freer, *My Life and Memories* (Glasgow: Civic Press, 1929), 95.
127. James Houston, *Autobiography of Mr. James Houston, Scotch Comedian* (Glasgow: John Menzies, 1889), 102.
128. Dunn, *From Coal-Mine Upwards*, xi.
129. Fraser, *Sixty Years in Uniform*, 250.
130. White, *Record of My Life*, 179; Clare, "Sketches in the Life of John Clare," 1. See also Farish, *Autobiography of William Farish*, 54.

Conclusion

1. Friedrich Engels, *The Condition of the Working Class in England* (Stanford: Stanford University Press, 1968).
2. Some of the recent debates on the question are recapitulated in Charles H. Feinstein, "Pessimism Perpetuated: Real Wages and the Standard of Living in Britain during and after the Industrial Revolution," *Journal of Economic History* 58, no. 3 (September 1988): 625–58; Daniel Gallardo-Albarán and Herman De Jong, "Optimism or Pessimism: A Composite View on English Living Standards during the Industrial Revolution," *European Review of Economic History* 25 (2020): 1–19.
3. On factory workers in this period, see Cunningham, *Invention of Childhood*, 156–58.

BIBLIOGRAPHY

UNPUBLISHED SOURCES

Bradford Reference Library, Bradford
Mitchell, Thomas Buller. "Tommy's Book," TS.

Burnett Archive of Working-Class Autobiographies, Brunel University
Ashley, James. "Autobiography."
Castle, John. "The Diary of John Castle."
Forsdick, Stephen. "Untitled."
Goring, Jack. "Autobiographical Notes of Jack Goring."
Hobley, Frederick. "The Autobiography of Frederick Hobley, Written at the Special Request of His Children, October 1905."
Hughes, Henry. "Autobiography."
Ireson, Alf. "Reminiscences."
Lovekin, Emanuel. "Some Notes of My Life."
Lloyd, George. "The Autobiography of Georgie Brawd."
Marling, Frank George. "Reminiscences."
McKenzie, James H. "Strange Truth: The Autobiography of a Circus, Showman, Stage and Exhibition Man."
Mockford, George. "Wilderness Journeyings and Gracious Deliverances: The Autobiography of George Mockford."
Rayment, T. "Memories of an Octogenarian, 1864–1949."
Shinn, John. "A Sketch of My Life and Times."
Terry, Joseph. "Recollections of My Life."
Webb, William. "Reminiscences of an Ordinary Life."

Islington Local History Library
Price, Henry. "Memoir of Henry Price: The Diary of a Working Man Long Resident in Islington." GB 1032 S/HEP.

Wake Forest University Library Special Collections
Stradley, John. "John Stradley Memoir, 1757–1784." PCmf.4.

PUBLISHED SOURCES

Ablett, William H. J. *Reminiscences of an Old Draper*. London: Searle and Rivington, 1876.

Abrams, Lynn. "The Taming of Highland Masculinity: Inter-personal Violence and Shifting Codes of Manhood, c. 1760–1840." *Scottish Historical Review* 92, no. 233 (April 2013): 100–122.

Adams, Albert Charles. *The History of a Village Shopkeeper: An Autobiography*. Edinburgh: John Menzies, 1876.

Adams, William Edwin. *Memoirs of a Social Atom*. London: Hutchinson and Son, 1903.

"Adventures of an Author, Written by Himself." *Commonwealth* (Glasgow), January 3, 1857, 3.

Ahmed, Sarah. *The Promise of Happiness*. Durham, NC: Duke University Press, 2010.

Aird, Andrew. *Autobiography*. Glasgow: n.p., 1899.

Aknin, Lara B., Tanya Broesch, J. Kiley Hamlin, and Julia W. Van de Vondevoort. "Prosocial Behavior Leads to Happiness in a Small-Scale Rural Society." *Journal of Experimental Psychology* 144, no. 4 (2015): 788–95.

Alexander, Alec. *A Wayfarer's Log*. London: John Murray, 1919.

Allan, Blake A., Cassondra Batz-Barbarich, Haley M. Sterling, and Louis Tay. "Outcomes of Meaningful Work: A Meta-Analysis." *Journal of Management Studies* 56, no. 3 (2019): 500–528.

Allen, George. *The Machine-Breaker: Or, the Heart-Rending Confession of George Allen, Written by Himself*. London: J. Duncombe, 1831.

Allen, Rose. *The Autobiography of Rose Allen, Edited by a Lady*. London: Longman, Brown, Green and Longman, 1847.

Anderson, Edward. *The Sailor; a Poem. Description of His Going to Sea, through Various Scenes of Life* . . . Workington: printed by the author, 1792.

Anderson, Isaac. *The Life History of Isaac Anderson, A Member of the Peculiar People*. N.p., 1882.

Anderson, R. D. "Education and the State in Nineteenth-Century Scotland." *Economic History Review* 36, no. 4 (1983): 518–34.

Anderson, Robert. *The Poetical Works of Robert Anderson, Author of Cumberland Ballads*. Carlisle: B. Scott, 1820.

Andrew, Janes. *Recorded Mercies: Being the Autobiography of Jane Andrew*. London: E. Wilmshurst, 1890.

Arch, Joseph. *Joseph Arch, the Story of His Life, Told by Himself*. London: Hutchinson, 1898.

Armstrong, Chester. *Pilgrimage from Nenthead: An Autobiography*. London: Methuen, 1938.

Arnold, William. *Recollections of William Arnold*. Northampton: Privately printed, 1915.

Ashdown, Eli. *Gleanings by a Watchman on a Dark Corner of Zion's Walls . . . Being the Autobiography of Eli Ashdown*. London: Farncombe and Son, 1904.
Ashford, Mary Ann. *Life of a Licensed Victualler's Daughter, Written by Herself*. London: Saunders and Otley, 1844.
Askham, John. *Sketches in Prose and Verse*. Northampton: S. S. Campion, 1893.
Austin-Bolt, Caroline. "Sarah Ellis's *The Women of England*: Domestic Happiness and Gender Performance." *Nineteenth-Century Contexts* 37, no. 3 (2015): 183–95.
"Autobiography of a Blacksmith, Written by Himself." *Commonwealth* (Glasgow), January 17, 1857, 3.
"Autobiography of a Convict." *Cheltenham Chronicle and Parish Register*, June 10, 1856.
"Autobiography of a Miner." *Commonwealth* (Glasgow), October 25, 1856, 4.
The Autobiography of a Private Soldier, Showing the Danger of Rashly Enlisting. Sunderland: Williams and Binns, 1838.
Autobiography of a Scotch Lad; Being Reminiscences of Threescore Years and Ten. Glasgow: David Bryce and Son, 1887.
"Autobiography of a Thief in Thieves' Language." *MacMillan's Magazine* 40 (1879): 500–506.
"The Autobiography of Robert Spurr." *Baptist Quarterly* 26 (April 1976): 282–88.
Bain, Alexander. *Autobiography*. London: Longmans, Green, 1904.
Bain, John. *Life of a Scottish Sailor*. Nairn: George Bain, 1897.
Baldry, George. *The Rabbit Skin Cap: A Tale of a Norfolk Countryman's Youth*. London: Collins, 1939.
Bamford, Samuel. *The Autobiography of Samuel Bamford*. New York: Augustus Kelley, 1967.
———. *Early Days*. London: Simkins and Marshall, 1848.
———. *Early Days*. New York: Augustus Kelley, 1967.
Barca, Stefania. "Laboring the Earth: Transnational Reflections on the Environmental History of Work." *Environmental History* 19 (January 2014): 3–27.
Barclay, Katie. "Happiness: Family and Nation in Nineteenth-Century Ireland." *Nineteenth-Century Contexts* 43, no. 2 (2021): 171–90.
———. "Narrative, Law and Emotion: Husband-Killers in Early Nineteenth-Century Ireland." *Journal of Legal History* 38, no. 2 (2017): 203–27.
———. "Performing Emotion and Reading the Male Body in the Irish Court, c. 1800–1845." *Journal of Social History* 51, no. 2 (Winter 2017): 293–312.
Barclay, Thomas Patrick. *Memoirs and Medleys: The Autobiography of a Bottle-Washer*. Leicester: Edgar Backus, 1934.
Barker, Joseph. *The History and Confessions of a Man: As Put Forth by Himself; Showing How He Became a Methodist and a Methodist Preacher*. London: printed by the author, 1846.
Barnes, George Nicoll. *From Workshop to War Cabinet*. London: Herbert Jenkins, 1923.
Barnett, Richard. "The View from Below Deck: The British Navy, 1777–1781." *American Neptune* 38, no. 2 (1978): 92–100.
Barr, David. *Climbing the Ladder: The Struggles and Successes of a Village Lad*. London: Robert Culley, 1910.
Bassett, Josiah. *The Life of a Vagrant, or the Testimony of an Outcast to the Value and Truth of the Gospel*. London: Charles Gilpin, 1850.

Bastian, Brook, Peter Kuppens, Kim De Roover, and Ed Diener. "Is Valuing Positive Emotion Associated with Life Satisfaction?" *Emotion* 14, no. 4 (2014): 639–45.
Bathgate, Janet. *Aunt Janet's Legacy to Her Nieces: Recollections of Humble Life in Yarrow at the Beginning of the Century*. Selkirk: G. Lewis and Son, 1894.
Baynham, Henry. *From the Lower Deck: The Royal Navy, 1780–1840*. Barre, MA: Barre, 1970.
Begiato, Joanne. "Between Poise and Power: Embodied Manliness in Eighteenth and Nineteenth-Century British Culture." *Transactions of the Royal Historical Society* 26 (2016): 125–47.
———. "Selfhood and 'Nostalgia': Sensory and Material Memories of the Childhood Home in Late Georgian Britain." *Journal for Eighteenth-Century Studies* 42, no. 2 (2019): 229–46.
———. "Tears and the Manly Sailor in England, c. 1760–1860." *Journal for Maritime Research* 17, no. 2 (2015): 117–33.
Behlmer, George, and Fred Leventhal, eds., *Singular Continuities: Tradition, Nostalgia, and Identity in Modern British Culture*. Stanford: Stanford University Press, 2000.
Bennett, Roger. "Why Urban Poor Donate: A Study of Low-Income Charitable Giving in London." *Nonprofit and Voluntary Sector Quarterly* 41, no. 5 (2012): 870–91.
Bent, James. *Criminal Life: Remembrances of Forty-Two Years as a Police Officer*. London: n.p., 1891.
Bentham, Jeremy. *Rationale of Reward*. London: C. and W. Reynell, 1830.
Beveridge, Allan, and Fiona Watson. "The Psychiatrist, the Historian and the Christian Watt Papers." *History of Psychiatry* 17, no. 2 (2006): 205–21.
Blake, Jim. *Jim Blake's Tour from Clonave to London*. Dublin: MH Gill, 1867.
Blair, Kirstie. "'A Very Poetical Town': Newspaper Poetry and the Working-Class Poet in Victorian Dundee." *Victorian Poetry* 50, no. 1 (2014): 89–109.
Blatchford, Robert. *My Eighty Years*. London: Cassell, 1931.
Blunt, Reginald. *Red Anchor Pieces*. London: Mills and Boon, 1928.
Boddice, Rob. *The History of Emotions*. Manchester: Manchester University Press, 2018.
Bonwick, James. *An Octogenarian's Reminiscences*. London: J. Nichols, 1902.
Boos, Florence. "Collaboration and the Victorian Oral Narrative: The *Autobiography of a Charwoman*." *Forum for Modern Language Studies* 52, no. 2 (April 2016): 218–31.
———. "Introduction: The Literature of the Victorian Working Classes." *Philological Quarterly* 92, no. 2 (Spring 2013): 130–45.
———. *Memoirs of Working-Class Women: The Hard Way Up*. London: Palgrave, 2017.
———. "Under Physical Siege: Early Victorian Autobiographies of Working-Class Women." *Philological Quarterly* 92, no. 2 (2013): 251–68.
Bowcock, William. *The Life, Experience and Correspondence of William Bowcock, the Lincolnshire Drillman*. London: Houlston and Stoneman, 1851.
Bowd, James. "The Life of a Farm Worker." *Countryman* 51, no. 2 (1965): 293–300.
Braddick, Michael J., and Joanna Innes, eds. *Suffering and Happiness in England, 1550–1850*. Oxford: Oxford University Press, 2017.

Brierley, Ben. *Home Memories and Recollections of a Life*. Manchester: Abel Heywood, 1886.
Brine, George Atkins. *The King of the Beggars: The Life and Adventures of George Atkins Brine*. London: Ward, Lock, 1883.
Britton, John. *The Autobiography of John Britton, FSA, Honorary Member of Numerous English and Foreign Societies*. London: printed by the author, 1850.
———. *The Beauties of Wiltshire*. London: J. Noves, 1825.
Broadhurst, Henry. *Henry Broadhurst, MP: From the Stonemason's Bench to the Treasury Bench*. London: Hutchinson, 1901.
Bronstein, Jamie. *Caught in the Machinery: Workplace Accidents and Injured Workers in Nineteenth-Century Britain*. Stanford: Stanford University Press, 2008.
Brooks, Johanna. *A Handmaid of the Lord: Some Records of Johanna Brooks*. London: Ludgate and Chase, 1868.
Broomhall, Susan, ed. *Spaces for Feeling: Emotions and Sociabilities in Britain, 1650–1850*. London: Taylor and Francis, 2015.
Broughton, Trev Lynn, and Linda Anderson, eds. *Women's Lives / Women's Times: New Essays on Autobiography*. Albany: State University of New York Press, 1997.
Brown, Callum. *The Death of Christian Britain*. London: Routledge, 2001.
Buchanan, Thomas C. "Class Sentiments: Putting the Emotion Back in Working-Class History." *Journal of Social History* 48, no. 1 (2014): 72–87.
Buckmaster, John, ed. *A Village Politician: The Life of John A. Buckley*. London: T. Fisher Unwin, 1897.
Bullen, Frank. *Confessions of a Tradesman*. London: Hodder and Stoughton, 1908.
———. *The Log of a Sea-Waif*. London: Smith, Elder, 1899.
Burdon, James. *Reminiscences of Ruskin: By a St. George's Companion*. London: Burdon, 1919.
Burn, James. *The Autobiography of a Beggar Boy*. London: William Tweedie, 1855.
Burnett, John. *Annals of Labour: Autobiographies of British Working-Class People, 1820–1920*. Bloomington: Indiana University Press, 1974.
———. *Destiny Obscure: Autobiographies of Childhood, Education and Family from the 1820s to the 1920s*. London: Penguin Books, 1982.
———. *Useful Toil: Autobiographies of Working People from the 1820s to the 1920s*. London: Allen Lake, 1974.
———, David Vincent, and David Mayall, eds. *Autobiography of the Working Class: An Annotated Critical Bibliography, Vol. 1: 1790–1900*. New York: NYU Press, 1984.
Burstow, Henry. *Reminiscences of Horsham: Being Recollections of Henry Burstow*. Horsham: Free Church Book Society, 1911.
Burt, Thomas. *Thomas Burt, MP, DCL, Pitman and Privy Councillor, An Autobiography*. London: T. Fisher Unwin, 1924.
Butler, Serjeant Robert. *Narrative of the Life and Travels of Sergeant B———, Written by Himself*. Edinburgh: David Brown, 1823.
Bywater, James. *The Trio's Pilgrimage: Autobiography of James Bywater*. N.p.: Bywater Family Foundation, 1947.
Caine, Barbara. *Friendship: A History*. New York: Routledge, 2014.
Caleb, Amanda. "Contested Spaces: The Heterotopias of the Victorian Sickroom." *Humanities* 80, no. 8 (2019): 1–9.

Calvo, Rocio, Yuhui Zheng, Santosh Kumar, Analia Olgati, and Lisa Berkman. "Well-Being and Social Capital on Planet Earth: Cross-National Evidence from 142 Countries." *PLOS One* 5, no. 8 (August 2012): 1–9.
[Cameron, William]. *Hawkie: The Autobiography of a Gangrel*. Glasgow: Oliver and Boyd, 1888.
Campbell, Charles. *Memoir of Charles Campbell, at Present Prisoner in the Jail at Glasgow*. Glasgow: James Duncan, 1828.
Campbell, Duncan. *Reminiscences and Reflections of an Octogenarian Highlander*. Northern Counties Newspaper and Printing, 1910.
Campbell, Elizabeth. *Songs of My Pilgrimage*. Edinburgh: Andrew Eliot, 1875.
Campkin, James. *Struggles of a Village Lad*. London: Tweedie, 1858.
Candler, Ann. *Poetical Attempts by Ann Candler, a Suffolk Cottager, with a Short Narrative of Her Life*. Ipswich: John Raw, 1803.
Caprara, Vian Vittorio, and Patrizia Steca. "Affective and Social Self-Regularity Efficacy Beliefs as Determinants of Positive Thinking and Happiness." *European Psychologist* 10, no. 4 (2005): 275–86.
Caractacus [pseud.]. *Autobiography of a Poacher*. N.p.: John Macqueen, 1901.
Carnegie, Andrew. *Autobiography of Andrew Carnegie*. Boston: Houghton Mifflin, 1920.
Carter, Harry. *The Autobiography of a Cornish Smuggler*. Truro: Joseph Pollard, 1894.
Carter, Thomas. *Memoirs of a Working Man*. London: Charles Knight, 1845.
———. *A Continuation of the Memoirs of a Working Man*. London: Charles Cox, 1850.
Cashen, Matthew. "Happiness, Eudaimonia, and the Principle of Descriptive Adequacy." *Metaphilosophy* 43, no. 2 (2012): 619–35.
Cassial [Richard Gooch]. *Memories, Remarkable Vicissitudes, Military Career and Wanderings in Ireland, Mechanical and Astronomical Exercises, Scientific Researches, Incidents and Opinions of Cassial, the Norfolk Astrologer, Written by Himself*. Norwich: Thorndick, 1844.
Catling, Thomas Thurgood. *My Life's Pilgrimage*. London: John Murray, 1911.
Catton, Samuel. *A Short Sketch of the Long Life of Samuel Catton, Once a Suffolk Ploughboy*. London: Arpthorpe, 1863.
Chadwick, William. *Reminiscences of a Chief Constable*. Manchester: John Heywood, 1900.
Chancellor, Valerie, ed. *Master and Artisan in Victorian England: The Diary of William Andrews and the Autobiography of Joseph Gutteridge*. London: Evelyn, Adams and MacKay, 1969.
Chase, Malcolm, ed. *The Life and Literary Pursuits of Allen Davenport, with a Further Selection of the Author's Work*. London: Routledge, 1994.
[Chatterton, Daniel.] *Autobiography of Dan Chatterton, Atheist and Communist*. London: D. Chatterton, 1891.
Clark, Anna. *The Struggle for the Breeches: Gender and the Making of the British Working Class*. Berkeley: University of California Press, 1995.
Claxton, Timothy. *Hints to Mechanics on Self-Education and Mutual Instruction*. London: Taylor and Walton, 1836.
Cliff, James Henry. *Down to the Sea in Ships: The Memoirs of James Henry Treloar Cliff as Told to P. W. Birkbeck*. Redruth: Dyllansow Truran, 1983.
Clift, William. *Reminiscences of William Clift of Bramley*. Basingstoke: Bird Brothers, 1908.

Coe, Richard. *When the Grass Was Taller: Autobiography and the Experience of Childhood*. New Haven, CT: Yale University Press, 1984.
Cohn, Michael A., Barbara Fredrickson, Stephanie L. Brown, Joseph A. Mikels, and Anne M. Conway. "Happiness Unpacked: Positive Emotions Increase Life Satisfaction by Building Resilience." *Emotion* 9, no. 3 (2009): 361–68.
Collison, William. *The Apostle of Free Labour: The Life Story of William Collison, Founder and General Secretary of the National Free Labour Association*. London: Hurst and Blackett, 1913.
Constantine, Joseph. *Fifty Years of the Water Cure*. London: John Heywood, 1892.
Cook, Richard. *The Memoirs of Richard Cook: South Ferriby in the Mid-19th Century*. Brigg: John Nelthorpe School, 1977.
Coombs, Mabel Frances. *The Early Recollections of Moses Horler*. Radstock: n.p., 1900.
Cooper, Frank. *The Life of Francis Cooper, Written by Himself*. Nottingham: the author, 1856.
Cooper, Thomas. *Life of Thomas Cooper*. London: Hodder and Staughton, 1872.
Coward, Sir Henry. *Reminiscences of Henry Coward*. London: J. Curwen and Sons, 1919.
Crawford, J. H. *The Autobiography of a Tramp*. London: Longmans Green, 1900.
Crispin [Barnabas Britten]. *Woodyard to Palace*. Bradford: Broadacre Books, 1958.
Crittall, F. H. *Fifty Years of Work and Play*. London: Constable, 1934.
Crimmins, James E. "Jeremy Bentham." In *The Stanford Encyclopedia of Philosophy* (summer 2020 edition), ed. Edward N. Zalta, available at https://plato.stanford.edu/archives/sum2020/entries/bentham.
Croll, James. *Autobiographical Sketch of James Croll, with a Memoir of His Life and Work*. London: Stanford, 1896.
Cropazano, Russell, and Thomas Wright. "Is a 'Happy' Worker Really a 'Productive' Worker? A Review and Further Refinement of the Happy-Productive Worker Thesis." *Consulting Psychology Journal: Practice and Research* 53, no. 3 (2001): 182–99.
Crowe, Robert. *Reminiscences of Robert Crowe, the Octogenarian Tailor*. New York: 1901.
Csíkszentmihályi, Mihály. *Flow: The Psychology of Optimal Experience*. New York: Harper and Row, 1990.
———. "Happiness, Flow, and Economic Equality." *American Psychologist* 55, no. 10 (2000): 1163–64.
———. "If We Are So Rich, Why Aren't We Happy?" *American Psychologist* 54, no. 10 (1999): 821–27.
Cunningham, Hugh. *The Invention of Childhood*. London: BBC Books, 2006.
Dale, Nathaniel. *The Eventful Life of Nathaniel Dale*. Kimbolton: printed by the author, 1871.
Darnton, Robert. "The Pursuit of Happiness." *Wilson Quarterly* 19, no. 4 (1995): 42–53.
Davies, Margaret Llewellyn, ed. *Life as We Have Known It*. London: W. W. Norton, 1975.
Davies, Thomas. *Short Sketches from the Life of Thomas Davies*. Harverfordwest: William Perkins, n.d.
Davies, William Henry. *Autobiography of a Super-Tramp*. London: A. C. Field, 1920.

Davin, Anna. *Growing Up Poor: Home, School and Street in London, 1870–1914.* London: Rivers Oram Press, 1996.

———. "The Jigsaw Strategy: Sources in the History of Childhood in Nineteenth-Century London." *History of Education Review* 15, no. 2 (1986): 2–17.

———. "Waif Stories in Late Nineteenth-Century England." *History Workshop Journal* 52 (Autumn 2001): 67–98.

Dickson, David. *Memorials of a Faithful Servant, William Innes.* Edinburgh: Lorimer and Gillies, 1876.

Diener, Ed, Louis Tay, and Shigehiro Oishi. "Rising Incomes and the Subjective Well-Being of Nations." *Journal of Personality and Social Psychology* 104, no. 2 (2013): 267–76.

Dixon, Thomas. "The Psychology of the Emotions in Britain and America in the Nineteenth Century: The Role of Religious and Antireligious Commitments." *Osiris* 16 (2001): 288–320.

———. *Weeping Britannia: Portrait of a Nation in Tears.* Oxford: Oxford University Press, 2015.

Dodd, William. *The Factory System Illustrated.* Edited by W. H. Chaloner. New York: Augustus Kelley, 1968.

Dodgson, Joshua. "Diary of Joshua Dodgson, Founder of an Elland Dyeworks in 1832." *Halifax Guardian*, May 19 and 26, 1856, J. F. C. Harrison Collection, Brigham Young University.

Donaldson, Joseph. *The War in the Peninsula: A Continuation of the Recollections of the Eventful Life of a Soldier.* Glasgow: W. R. McPhun, 1825.

———. *Recollections of an Eventful Life, Chiefly Passed in the Army.* Glasgow: W. R. McPhun, 1825.

Dottie, Robert. *The Rambles and Recollections of "R'Dick".* Manchester: Albert Sutton, 1898.

Douglas, Martin. *The Life and Adventures of Martin Douglas, Sunderland Keelman and Celebrated Life Saver.* Stockton-on-Tees: R. Firth, 1848.

Drakulic, Aleksandra Mindoljevic. "A Phenomenological Perspective on Subjective Well-Being: From Myth to Science." *Psychiatra Danubina* 24, no. 1 (2012): 31–37.

Dunn, James. *From Coal-Mine Upwards: or, Seventy Years of an Eventful Life.* London: W. Green, 1910.

Easterlin, Richard A. "Explaining Happiness." *PNAS* 100, no. 19 (September 2003): 11176–83.

Easterlin, Richard A., Laura Angelescu McVey, Malgorzata Switek, Onnicha Sawangfa, and Jacqueline Smith Zweig. "The Happiness–Income Paradox Revisited." *Proceedings of the National Academy of Sciences* 107, no. 52 (December 28, 2010): 22463–68.

Eaton, Kit. "Positive Thinking, with a Little Help from Your Phone." *New York Times*, October 15, 2014. http://www.nytimes.com/2014/10/16/business/positive-thinking-with-a-little-help-from-your-phone.html?module=Search&mabReward=relbias%3Ar, last accessed December 1, 2014.

Eden, Eleanor, ed. *The Autobiography of a Working Man.* London: Richard Bentley, 1862.

Edwards, George. *From Crow-Scaring to Westminster: An Autobiography.* London: Labour, 1922.

Edwards, John Passmore. *A Few Footprints.* London: Watts, 1906.

Edwards, W., ed. *My Life's History: The Autobiography of Rev. Thomas Lewis, Baptist Minister, Newport.* Newport: C. E. Lewis, 1902.
Elson, George. *The Last of the Climbing Boys: An Autobiography.* London: John Long, 1900.
Engels, Friedrich. *The Condition of the Working Class in England.* Stanford: Stanford University Press, 1968.
Eustace, Nicole, Eugenia Lean, Julie Livingston, Jan Plamper, William Reddy, and Barbara Rosenwein. "AHR Conversations: The Historical Study of Emotions." *American Historical Review* 115, no. 5 (December 2012): 1487–530.
Exell, A. W., and N. M. Marshall, eds. *Autobiography of Richard Boswell Belcher of Banbury and Blockley.* Blockley: Blockley Antiquarian Society, 1976.
Falke, Cassandra. *Literature by the Working Class: English Autobiographies, 1820–1848.* Amherst, MA: Cambria Press, 2013.
Farish, William. *The Autobiography of William Farish: The Struggle of a Handloom Weaver.* London: Caliban Books, 1996.
Farningham, Marianne [Mary Ann Hearn]. *A Working Woman's Life.* London: James Clarke, 1907.
Farrar, Major, ed. *The Diary of Colour-Sergeant George Calladine, 19th Foot, 1793–1837.* London: E. Fisher, 1922.
Featherstone, Peter. *Reminiscences of a Long Life.* London: Charles H. Kelly, 1905.
Feinstein, Charles H. "Pessimism Perpetuated: Real Wages and the Standard of Living in Britain during and after the Industrial Revolution." *Journal of Economic History* 58, no. 3 (September 1988): 625–58.
Feldman, Fred. *What Is This Thing Called Happiness?* Oxford: Oxford University Press, 2010.
Finney, John. *Sixty Years' Reminiscences of an Etruscan.* Stoke-upon-Trent: J. P. Fenn, 1902.
Fleishman, Avrom. *Figures of Autobiography: The Language of Self-Writing in Victorian and Modern England.* Berkeley: University of California Press, 1983.
Flockhart, Robert. *The Street Preacher: Being the Autobiography of Robert Flockhart.* Edinburgh: Adam and Charles Black, 1858.
Foner, Philip S. *The Autobiographies of the Haymarket Martyrs.* New York: Pathfinder, 1969.
Forrest, Frank. *Chapters in the Life of a Dundee Factory Boy: An Autobiography.* Dundee: James Myles, 1850.
Frank, Robert H. "The Easterlin Paradox Revisited." *Emotion* 12, no. 6 (2012): 1188–91.
Fraser, David, ed. *The Christian Watt Papers.* Edinburgh: Paul Harris, 1983.
Fraser, John. *Sixty Years in Uniform.* London: Stanley Paul, 1939.
Freer, Walter. *My Life and Memories.* Glasgow: Civic Press, 1929.
French, G. S. "Marsden, Joshua." In *Dictionary of Canadian Biography*, vol. 7, University of Toronto/Université Laval, 2003. http://www.biographi.ca/en/bio/marsden_joshua_7E.html, accessed September 11, 2016.
Frey, Bruno. *Happiness: A Revolution in Economics.* Cambridge, MA: MIT Press, 2008.
Frijters, Paul, and Tony Beatton. "The Mystery of the U-Shaped Relationship between Happiness and Age." *Journal of Economic Behavior and Organization* 82 (2012): 525–42.

Frost, Ginger. *Illegitimacy in English Law and Society, 1860–1930*. Manchester: Manchester University Press, 2016.

———. *Promises Broken: Courtship, Class, and Gender in Victorian England*. Charlottesville: University Press of Virginia, 1995.

Frost, Thomas. *Forty Years' Recollections*. London: Sampson Low, Marston, Searle and Rivington, 1880.

Frow, Edmund, and Ruth Frow, eds. *The Dark Satanic Mills: Child Apprentices in Derbyshire Spinning Factories*. Manchester: Working Class Library, 1980.

G., J. *Prisoner Set Free: The Narrative of a Convict in the Preston House of Corrections*. Preston: L. Clarke, 1846.

Gabbitass, Peter. *Heart Melodies: For Storm and Sunshine*. Bristol: n.p., 1885.

Gagnier, Regenia. *Subjectivities: A History of Self-Representation in Britain, 1832–1920*. New York: Oxford University Press, 1991.

[Gallagher, Patrick]. *My Story: By Paddy the Cope*. New York: Devin-Adair, 1942.

Gallardo-Albarán, Daniel, and Herman De Jong. "Optimism or Pessimism: A Composite View on English Living Standards during the Industrial Revolution." *European Review of Economic History* 25 (2020): 1–19.

Gammage, Robert. *Reminiscences of a Chartist*. Edited by W. H. Maehl. Manchester: Manchester Free Press, 1983.

Gammon, Vic. *Desire, Drink and Death in English Folk and Vernacular Song, 1600–1900*. Burlington, VT: Ashgate Press, 2008.

Gaskell, S. Martin. "Gardens for the Working Class: Victorian Practical Pleasures." *Victorian Studies* 23, no. 4 (1980): 479–501.

Geary, William. *Autobiography of Captain William Geary*. South Shields: Greenwood and Sons, 1924.

Gergen, Kenneth J. "History and Psychology: Three Weddings and a Future." In *An Emotional History of the United States*, edited by Peter Stearns and Jan Lewis, 15–29. New York: NYU Press, 1998.

Gifford, William. *Memoir of William Gifford, Written by Himself*. London: Hunt and Clarke, 1827.

Goldman, Alan H. "Happiness Is an Emotion." *Journal of Ethics* 27 (2017): 1–16.

Gompers, Samuel. *Seventy Years of Life and Labor*. New York: E. P. Dutton, 1957.

Goodman, Jocelyn Baty, ed. *Victorian Cabinet Maker: The Memoirs of James Hopkinson, 1819–1894*. New York: Augustus Kelley, 1968.

Goodwyn, E. A., and J. C. Baxter, eds. *East Anglian Reminiscences*. Ipswich: Boydell Press, 1976.

Gosling, Harry. *Up and Down Stream*. London: Methuen, 1927.

Goss, Fred. *Memories of a Stag Harbourer: A Record of Twenty-Eight Years with the Devon and Somerset Stag-Hounds, 1894–1921*. London: H. F. and G. Witherby, 1931.

Gough, John B. *An Autobiography of John B. Gough*. Boston: printed by the author, 1845.

Gould, F. J. *The Life-Story of a Humanist*. London: Watts, 1923.

Graham, Carol. *The Pursuit of Happiness: An Economy of Well-Being*. Washington, DC: Brookings Institution Press, 2011.

Gray, Robert. *The Factory Question and Industrial England, 1830–1860*. Cambridge: Cambridge University Press, 1996.

Green, William. *The Life and Adventures of a Cheap-Jack*. London: Chatto and Windus, 1881.

Greenland, William Kingscote, ed. *Raymond Preston, British and Australian Evangelist: Life Story and Personal Reminiscences.* London: Epworth Press, 1930.
Griffin, Emma. *Bread Winner: An Intimate History of the Victorian Economy.* New Haven, CT: Yale University Press, 2020.
———. "Diets, Hunger and Living Standards during the British Industrial Revolution." *Past & Present* 239, no. 1 (May 2018) 71–111.
———. "The Emotions of Motherhood: Love, Culture and Poverty in Victorian Britain." *American Historical Review* 123, no. 1 (February 2018): 60–80.
———. *Liberty's Dawn: A People's History of the Industrial Revolution.* New Haven, CT: Yale University Press, 2013.
———. "The Making of the Chartists: Popular Politics and Working-Class Autobiography in Early Victorian Britain." *English Historical Review* 129, no. 538 (2014): 578–605.
Grundy, A. G. *My Fifty Years in Transport: The Life Story of a Pioneer in Passenger Travel.* London: Tramway and Railway World, 1944.
Gwyer, Joseph. *Sketches in the Life of Joseph Gwyer, (Potato Salesman) with His Poems.* Penge: printed by the author, 1877.
Hackett, Nan. *XIX-Century British Working-Class Autobiographies: An Annotated Bibliography.* London: AMS Studies in Social History No. 5, 1985.
———. "A Different Form of 'Self': Narrative Style in British Nineteenth-Century Working-Class Autobiography." *Biography* 12, no. 3 (Summer 1989): 208–26.
Haddow, William Martin. *My Seventy Years.* Glasgow: Robert Gibson and Sons, 1943.
Haggard, Lilias Rider, ed. *I Walked by Night: Being the Life and History of the King of the Norfolk Poachers.* New York: E. P. Dutton, 1936.
Haggart, David. *The Life of David Haggart, alias John Wilson, alias John Morison, alias Barney M'Coul, alias John M'Colgan, alias Daniel O'Brien, alias the Switcher.* Edinburgh: W. and C. Tait, 1821.
Hair, P. E. H., ed. *Coals on Rails, or the Reason of My Wrighting: The Autobiography of Anthony Errington.* Liverpool: Liverpool University Press, 1988.
Hall, Newman, ed. *Hope for the Hopeless: An Autobiography of John Vine Hall.* New York: American Tract Society, 1865.
Hall, Robert G., and Stephen Roberts, eds. *William Aitken: The Writings of a Nineteenth-Century Working Man.* Tameside: Tameside Leisure Services, 1996.
Hamish, Maureen [Mary Loughran]. *Adventures of an Irish Girl at Home and Abroad.* Dublin: J. K. Mitchell, 1906.
Hammond, William. *Recollections of William Hammond, a Glasgow Handloom Weaver.* Glasgow: Citizen Press, 1904.
Hampton, Richard. *Foolish Dick: An Autobiography of Richard Hampton, the Cornish Pilgrim Preacher.* London: A. Trengove, 1873.
Hard Times in the Forest. Coleford: Forest of Dean Newspapers, 1971.
Harman, Horace. *Sketches of the Bucks Countryside.* London: Blandford Press, 1934.
Harris, John. *My Autobiography.* London: Hamilton, Adams, 1882.
Harris, Samuel. *The History and Conversion of Samuel Harris, A Polish Jew.* Bradford: printed by the author, 1833.
Harrison, Brian, and Patricia Hollis, eds. *Robert Lowery, Radical and Chartist.* London: Europa, 1979.
Harte, Liam. *The Literature of the Irish in Britain: Autobiography and Memoir, 1725–2001.* Basingstoke: Palgrave Macmillan, 2009.

Hawkes, Nigel. "Happiness Is U-Shaped, Highest in the Teens and 70s, Survey Shows." *BMJ: British Medical Journal* 344, no. 7836 (March 3, 2012): 1.
Haybron, Daniel. "Do We Know How Happy We Are? On Some Limits of Affective Introspection and Recall." *Noûs* 41, no. 3 (2007): 394–428.
———. "On Being Happy or Unhappy." *Philosophy and Phenomenological Research* 71, no. 2 (2005): 287–317.
Heaton, William. *The Old Soldier, The Wandering Lover, and Other Poems*. London: Simpkin, Marshall, 1857.
Hellevik, Ottar. "The U-Shaped Age-Happiness Relationship: Real or Methodological Artifact?" *Quality and Quantity* 51 (2017): 177–97.
Herbert, George. *Shoemaker's Window: Recollections of Banbury before the Railway Age*. Chichester: Phillmore, 1971.
Herbert, Henry. *Autobiography of Henry Herbert, a Gloucestershire Shoemaker and Native of Fairford*. Gloucester: printed by the author, 1876.
Hillocks, James. *Life Story: A Prize Autobiography*. London: Houlston and Wright, 1860.
Hobbs, Andrew. "Five Million Poems, or the Local Press as Poetry Publisher, 1800–1900." *Victorian Periodicals Review* 45, no. 4 (Winter 2012): 488–92.
Hobley, Frederick. "From the Autobiography of Frederick Hobley, a Nineteenth-Century Schoolteacher." *Alta: The University of Birmingham Review* 6 (Summer 1968): 331–39.
Hodge, John. *Workman's Cottage to Windsor Castle*. London: Sampson Low, Marston, 1931.
Hogg, James. *The Mountain Bard, with a Memoir of the Author's Life, Written by Himself*. Edinburgh: Oliver and Boyd, 1821.
Holcroft, Thomas. *Memoirs of the Late Thomas Holcroft*. London: Longman, Hurst, Rees, Orme and Brown, 1816.
Holkinson, Jacob. "The Life of Jacob Holkinson, Tailor and Poet, Written by Himself." *Commonwealth* (Glasgow), January 24 and 31, 1857, 3.
Holmes, Martha Stoddard. *Fictions of Affliction: Physical Disability in Victorian Culture*. Ann Arbor: University of Michigan Press, 2004.
Holmes, Vicky. *In Bed with the Victorians: The Life-Cycle of Working-Class Marriage*. London: Palgrave Macmillan, 2017.
Holyoake, George Jacob. *Sixty Years of an Agitator's Life*, vol. 1. London: T. Fisher Unwin, 1893.
Hooper, Edith Sophia. "George Huntington." In *Dictionary of National Biography, 1912 Supplement*, available at https://en.wikisource.org/wiki/Huntington,_George_(DNB12), last accessed October 12, 2018.
Hopwood, D. Caroline. *An Account of the Life and Religious Experiences of D. Caroline Hopwood*. Leeds: E. Baines, 1801.
Horn, Pamela. *Ladies of the Manor: Wives and Daughters in Country-house Society, 1830–1918*. Phoenix Mills: Alan Sutton, 1991.
———. *The Rural World: Social Changes in the English Countryside, 1780–1850*. New York: St. Martin's Press, 1980.
Horne, Eric. *What the Butler Winked At*. New York: John Seltzer, 1924.
Horsley, J. W. "Autobiography of a Thief in Thieves' Language." *Macmillan's Magazine* (1879): 500–506.
Houston, James. *Autobiography of Mr. James Houston, Scotch Comedian*. Glasgow: John Menzies, 1889.

Howell, Ryan T., and Colleen Howell. "The Relationship of Economic Status to Subjective Well-Being in Developing Countries: A Meta-Analysis." *Psychological Bulletin* 134, no. 4 (2008): 536–60.
Hudson, Pat, and Lynette Hunter, eds. "The Autobiography of William Hart, Cooper, 1776–1857: A Respectable Artisan in the Industrial Revolution." *London Journal* 7, no. 2 (Winter 1981): 144–60.
———. "The Autobiography of William Hart, Cooper, 1776–1857: A Respectable Artisan in the Industrial Revolution, Part II." *London Journal* 8, no. 1 (1982): 63–75.
Humphreys, Charles. *The Life of Charles Humphreys (Bookseller) of Paternoster Row, Told by Himself.* London: Wickliffe Press, 1928.
Humphries, Jane. "Care and Cruelty in the Workhouse: Children's Experiences of Residential Poor Relief in Eighteenth- and Nineteenth-Century England." In *Childhood and Child Labour in Industrial England: Diversity and Agency, 1750–1914,* edited by Katrina Honeyman and Nigel Goose, 115–34. Farnham: Routledge, 2013.
———. *Childhood and Child Labour in the British Industrial Revolution.* Cambridge: Cambridge University Press, 2010.
———. "Childhood and Child Labour in the British Industrial Revolution." *Economic History Review* 66, no. 2 (May 2013): 395–418.
Hunter, John Kelso. *The Retrospect of an Artist's Life.* Greenock: Orr, Pollock, 1868.
Huntington, George. *The Autobiography of John Brown, Cordwainer.* London: A. R. Mowbray, 1867.
Huntington, William. *Memoirs of the Reverend William Huntington, S.S., Coalheaver, Late Minister of Providence Chapel, Grey's Inn Lane.* London: J. Bailey, 1813.
Hutton, William. *The Life of William Hutton, FASS.* London: Baldwin, 1817.
Ince, Thomas. *Beggar Manuscripts: An Original Miscellany in Verse and Prose.* Blackburn: North-East Lancashire Printing, 1888.
Jackson, Thomas. *Narrative of the Eventful Life of Thomas Jackson, Late Sergeant of the Coldstream Guards.* Birmingham: Joseph Allen and Son, 1847.
Jacques. "Glimpses of a Chequered Life." *Commonwealth* (Glasgow), November 1, 8, and 15, 1856, 3.
Jalland, Pat. *Death and the Victorian Family.* Oxford: Oxford University Press, 1996.
Jayawickreme, Eranda, Marie J. C. Forgeard, and Martin E. P. Seligman. "The Engine of Well-Being." *Review of General Psychology* 16, no. 4 (2012): 327–42.
Jeal, Tim. *Stanley: The Impossible Life of Africa's Greatest Explorer.* New York: Faber and Faber, 2007.
Jermy, Louise. *Memories of a Working Woman.* Norwich: Goose and Son, 1934.
Joanides, Alex, ed. *Memoirs of the Life of Daniel Mendoza (1816).* London: Romeville Enterprises, 2011.
Johnston, David. *Autobiographical Reminiscences of David Johnston, an Octogenarian Scotchman.* Chicago: n.p., 1885.
Johnston, Ellen. *Autobiography, Poems and Songs of Ellen Johnston, the Factory Girl.* Glasgow: William Love, 1867.
Johnston, William. *The Life and Times of William Johnston.* Peterhead: William Taylor, 1859.

Jones, Christine. "Disability in Herefordshire, 1851–1911." *Local Population Studies* 87 (Autumn 2011): 29–44.
Jones, Henry. *Old Memories*. New York: George H. Doran, 1922.
Jones, Jack. *Unfinished Journey*. New York: Oxford University Press, 1937.
Jones, Thomas. *Rhymney Memories*. Llandysul: Gomerian Press, 1970.
Joyce, Patrick. *Democratic Subjects: The Self and the Social in Nineteenth-Century England*. Cambridge: Cambridge University Press, 1994.
Keating, Joseph. *My Struggle for Life*. Dublin: University College Press, 2005 [1916].
Kelly, Alfred. *The German Worker: Working-Class Autobiographies from the Age of Industrialization*. Berkeley: University of California Press, 1987.
Kennerly, David. "Strikes and Singing Classes: Chartist Culture, 'Rational Recreation' and the Politics of Music after 1842." *English Historical Review* 576 (October 2020): 1165–94.
Kenney, Annie. *Memories of a Militant*. London: Butler and Tanner, 1924.
Kenney, Rowland. *Westering: An Autobiography*. London: J.M. Dent, 1939.
King, Laura A., and Joshua A. Hicks. "Whatever Happened to 'What Might Have Been?': Regrets, Happiness and Maturity." *American Psychologist* 62, no. 7 (2007): 625–36.
Kirkwood, David. *My Life of Revolt*. London: George Harrap, 1935.
Kitto, John. *The Lost Senses*. London: Charles Knight, 1845.
Kitz, Frank. *Recollections and Reflections*. London: Carl Slienger, 1976.
Kotchemidova, Christina. "From Good Cheer to 'Drive-by Smiling': A Social History of Cheerfulness." *Journal of Social History* 39, no. 1 (2005): 5–37.
Krishnamurthy, Aruna, ed. *The Working-Class Intellectual in Eighteenth- and Nineteenth-Century Britain*. Farnham: Ashgate, 2009.
Kristjánsson, Kristján. "Positive Psychology, Happiness, and Virtue: The Troublesome Conceptual Issues." *Review of General Psychology* 14, no. 4 (2010): 296–310.
Kussmaul, Ann, ed. *The Autobiography of Joseph Mayett of Quainton (1783–1839)*. Oxford: Buckinghamshire Record Society, 1986.
Laaksonen, Seppo. "A Research Note: Happiness by Age Is More Complex Than U-Shaped." *Journal of Happiness Studies* 19 (2018) 471–82.
Langhamer, Claire. *The English in Love: The Intimate Story of an Emotional Revolution*. Oxford: Oxford University Press, 2013.
Lansbury, George. *My Life*. London: Constable and Co., 1928.
Lauder, Sir Harry. *Roamin' in the Gloamin'*. London: J. Lippicott, 1928.
Lax, William Henry. *Lax, His Book: The Autobiography of Lax of Poplar*. London: Epworth Press, 1937.
[Leask, W.] *Struggles for Life: The Autobiography of a Dissenting Minister*. London: W. and F. G. Cash, 1864.
Leatherland, J. A. *Essays and Poems, with a Brief Autobiographical Memoir*. London: W. Tweedie, 1862.
Lee, John. *John Babbacombe Lee: The Man They Could Not Hang*. Exeter: Devon Press, 1985.
Leech, Samuel. *Thirty Years from Home; or a Voice from the Main Deck*. London: H. G. Collins, 1851.
Leno, John Bedford. *The Aftermath; with Autobiography of the Author*. London: Reeves and Turner, 1892.

Levenson, Karen Chase. "'Happiness Is Not a Potato: The Victorian Cultivation of Happiness." *Nineteenth-Century Contexts* 33, no. 2 (May 2011): 161–69.
Lewis, Thomas. *These Seventy Years*. London: Carey Press, 1930.
Lidgett, Thomas L. *The Life of Thomas L. Lidgett*. Lincoln: W. K. Morton and Sons, 1908.
"The Life of a Cotton Spinner, Written by Himself." *Commonwealth* (Glasgow), December 27, 1856, 3.
"The Life of a Handloom Weaver, Written by Himself." *Commonwealth* (Glasgow), April 25, 1857, 1.
"The Life of a Journeyman Baker, Written by Himself." *Commonwealth* (Glasgow), December 13 and 20, 1856, 3.
"The Life of a Journeyman Baker, Written by Himself." *Commonwealth* (Glasgow), May 2, 1857, 3.
"The Life of a Letterpress Printer, Written by Himself." *Commonwealth* (Glasgow), February 7, 1857, 3.
"Life of Lipton, to a T." *The Herald, Scotland*, February 26, 1998. http://www.heraldscotland.com/sport/spl/aberdeen/life-of-lipton-to-a-t-1.352524, last accessed October 8, 2014.
Lindquist, Kristin, Suzanne Oosterwijk, Maria Gendron, and Lisa Feldman Barrett. "Do People Essentialize Emotions? Individual Differences in Emotion Essentialism and Emotional Experience." *Emotion* 13, no. 4 (2013): 629–44.
Lindquist, Kristen, Karen S. Quigley, Erika H. Siegel, and Lisa Feldman Barrett. "The Hundred-Year Emotion War: Are Emotions Natural Kinds or Psychological Constructions? Comment on Lench, Flores, and Bench (2011)." *Psychological Bulletin* 139, no. 1 (2013): 255–63.
Linton, W. J. *James Watson: A Memoir*. New Haven, CT: Appledore Private Press, 1879.
Lipton, Thomas. *Leaves from the Lipton Logs*. London: Hutchinson, 1930.
Livesey, Joseph. "Autobiography." In *The Life and Teachings of Joseph Livesey*, edited by John Pearce. London: National Temperance Publication Depot, 1887.
Love, David. *The Life, Adventures and Experience of David Love*. Nottingham: Sutton and Son, 1823.
Lovett, William. *The Life and Struggles of William Lovett, in His Pursuit of Bread, Knowledge, and Freedom*. London: Trubner, 1876.
Lyons, Albert Michael Neil. *Robert Blatchford: The Sketch of a Personality*. London: Clarion Press, 1910.
Lyubomirsky, Sonja, Laura King, and Ed Diener. "The Benefits of Frequent Positive Affect: Does Happiness Lead to Success?" *Psychological Bulletin* 131, no. 6 (2005): 803–55.
M'Kaen, James. *The Life of James M'Kaen, Shoemaker in Glasgow*. Glasgow: Brath and Reid, 1797.
Mace, Jem. *Fifty Years a Fighter: The Life Story of Jem Mace*. London: Caestus Books, 1998.
Maidment, Brian. *The Poorhouse Fugitives: Self-taught Poets and Poetry in Victorian Britain*. Manchester: Carcanet Press, 1987.
Manby Smith, Charles. *The Working Man's Way in the World*. London: W. and F. G. Cash, 1857.
Mann, Tom. *Tom Mann's Memoirs*. London: MacGibbon and Kee, 1967.
Manton, Henry. "Alderman Manton's Reminiscences." *Birmingham Weekly Mer-*

cury, November 15, 22, and 29, December 6, 13, 20, and 27, 1902; January 10, 17, 24, and 21, and February 7, 14, and 21, 1903, all p. 1.

Marcroft, William. *The Marcroft Family*. London: John Heywood, 1886.

Marsden, Joshua. *Sketches in the Early Life of a Sailor*. Hull: William Ross, n.d.

Martin, J., ed. *Incidents in the Life of Robert Henderson, or Extracts from the Autobiography of 'Newcassle Bob.'* Carlisle: Halstead and Beaty, 1869.

Martin, Jonathan. *The Life of Jonathan Martin, of Darlington, Tanner*. Darlington: Thomas Thompson, 1825.

Martin, Sarah. *A Brief Sketch of the Life of the Late Sarah Martin of Great Yarmouth*. Yarmouth: n.p., 1844.

Marx, Karl. "Estranged Labour." *Economic and Social Manuscripts of 1844*, available at https://www.marxists.org/archive/marx/works/1844/manuscripts/labour.htm, last accessed January 21, 2021.

Matt, Susan J., and Peter Stearns, eds. *Doing Emotions History*. Urbana-Champaign: University of Illinois Press, 2013.

Mauss, Iris, Maya Tamir, Craig Anderson, and Nicole Savino. "Can Seeking Happiness Make People Unhappy? Paradoxical Effects of Valuing Happiness." *Emotion* 11, no. 4 (2011): 807–15.

Mauss, Iris B., Nicole S. Savino, Max Weisbuch, Craig Anderson, Maya Tamir, and Mark Laudenslager. "The Pursuit of Happiness Can Be Lonely." *Emotion* 12, no. 5 (2012): 908–12.

May, Betty. *Tiger-Woman*. London: Duckworth, 1929.

Mays, Kelly J. "Domestic Spaces, Readerly Acts: Reading, Gender and Class in Working-Class Autobiography." *Nineteenth-Century Contexts* 30, no. 4 (2008): 343–68.

McAdam, John. *Autobiography of John McAdam, 1806–1883, with Selected Letters*. Edinburgh: Clark Constable, 1980.

McCurrey, James. *The Life of James McCurrey (from 1801 to 1876), Containing Thirty Nine Years' Experience as a Temperance Advocate and Missionary, Collated from His Personal Narrative, Journals Etc*. London: S. W. Partridge and Son, 1876.

McDermid, Jane. "The Making of a 'Domestic' Life: Memories of a Working Woman." *Labour History Review* 73, no. 3 (December 2008): 253–68.

McKenzie, Jordan. "Happiness vs. Contentment? A Case for a Sociology of the Good Life." *Journal of the Theory of Social Behavior* 46, no. 3 (2015): 252–67.

McMahon, Darrin. *Happiness: A History*. New York: Atlantic Monthly Press, 2006.

McNaughton, John Donkin. *The Life and Happy Experience of John Donkin McNaughton*. Stokesley: W. Pratt, 1810.

Mead, Isaac. *The Life Story of an Essex Lad, Written by Himself*. Chelmsford: A. Driver and Sons, 1923.

Meek, George. *George Meek, Bath-Chair Man, by Himself*. New York: E. P. Dutton, 1910.

Memoirs of a Smuggler, Compiled from His Diary and Journal. Sidmouth: J. Harvey, 1837.

Middleton, J. "The Cock of the School: A Cultural History of Playground Violence in Britain, 1880–1940." *Journal of British Studies* 52, no. 4 (2013): 887–907.

Mill, John Stuart. *Utilitarianism*. London: Longmans Green, 1879.

Miller, David Prince. *The Life of a Showman*. London: Lacy, 1849.

Miller, Hugh. *My Schools and Schoolmasters; or, the Story of My Education.* Edinburgh: Johnstone and Hunter, 1854.
Millim, Anne-Marie. *The Victorian Diary: Authorship and Emotional Labour.* Burlington, VT: Routledge, 2013.
Milne, William. *Reminiscences of an Old Boy: Being Autobiographical Sketches of Scottish Rural Life from 1832 to 1856.* Forfar: John McDonald, 1901.
Mitchell, Alexander. *The Recollections of a Lifetime.* Edinburgh: n.p., 1911.
Mitchell, George. *The Skeleton at the Plough, or the Poor Farm Labourers of the West: With the Autobiography and Reminiscences of George Mitchell, 'One from the Plough.'* London: George Potter, 1875.
Mitchell, Hanna Maria. *The Hard Way Up: The Autobiography of Hannah Mitchell, Suffragette and Rebel.* London: Faber and Faber, 1968.
Mockford, George. *Wilderness Journeyings and Gracious Deliverances: The Autobiography of George Mockford.* Oxford: J. C. Pembrey, 1901.
Mohanty, Madhu S. "What Determines Happiness? Income or Attitude: Evidence from U.S. Longitudinal Data." *Journal of Neuroscience, Psychology, and Economics* 7, no. 2 (2014): 80–102.
Morton, William. *I Remember.* Hull: Goddard, Walker and Brown, 1934.
Mullin, James. *The Story of a Toiler's Life.* Dublin: University College Dublin Press, 2000.
Murdoch, Lydia. *Imagined Orphans: Poor Families, Child Welfare, and Contested Citizenship in London.* New Brunswick, NJ: Rutgers University Press, 2006.
———. "'The Dead and the Living': Child Death, the Public Mortuary Movement, and the Spaces of Grief and Selfhood in Victorian London." *Journal of the History of Childhood and Youth* 8, no. 3 (Fall 2015): 378–402.
Murison, Alexander. *Memoirs of 88 Years (1847–1934): Being the Autobiography of Alexander Falconer Murison.* Aberdeen: University of Aberdeen Press, 1935.
Myers, David G. "The Funds, Friends, and Faith of Happy People." *American Psychologist* 55, no. 1 (January 2000): 56–67.
Navickas, Katrina. "'God's Earth Will Be Sacred': Religion, Theology and the Open Space Movement in Victorian England." *Rural History* 22, no. 1 (2011): 31–58.
———. "Moors, Fields, and Popular Protest in South Lancashire and the West Riding of Yorkshire, 1800–1848." *Northern History* 46, no. 1 (March 2009): 93–111.
Nicholson, Hamlet. *An Autobiographical and Full Historical Account of the Persecution of Hamlet Nicholson.* Manchester: Barber and Farnsworth, 1892.
Nicol, James. *The Life and Adventures of James Nicol, Mariner.* Edited by John Howell. Edinburgh: W. Blackwell, 1822.
Nightingale, Elizabeth, ed. *A Bible Woman's Story: Being the Autobiography of Mrs. Collier of Birmingham.* London: Religious Tract Society, 1882.
Nussbaum, Martha. *Frontiers of Justice: Disability, Nationality, Species Membership.* Cambridge, MA: Belknap Press, 2006.
Nye, James. *A Small Account of My Travels through the Wilderness.* Edited by Vic Gammon. Brighton: Queens Park Press, 1981.
Oakley, Elizabeth. "Autobiography of Elizabeth Oakley." *Norfolk Record Society* 56 (1991): 113–50.
Offer, Avner. *In Pursuit of the Quality of Life.* Oxford: Oxford University Press, 1996.
Ohry, Avi. "Shake Me Up, Judy! On Dickens, Medicine, and Spinal Cord Disorders." *Ortopedia Traumatologia Rehabilitacja* 14, no. 5 (2012): 483–91.

Okey, Thomas. *A Basketful of Memories: An Autobiographical Sketch.* London: J. M. Dent and Sons, 1930.

Oliver, Thomas. *Autobiography of a Cornish Miner.* Camborne: Camborne Printing and Stationery, 1914.

O'Neill, Elizabeth. *Extraordinary Confessions of a Female Pickpocket.* Preston: J. Drummond, 1850.

Osborn, Matthew. "The Weirdest of All Undertakings: The Land and the Early Industrial Revolution in Oldham, England." *Environmental History* 8 (April 2003): 246–69.

Osborne, Graeme. "Mann, Thomas (Tom), 1856–1941." In *Australian Dictionary of National Biography*, available at http://adb.anu.edu.au/biography/mann-thomas-tom-7475, last accessed June 20, 2016.

Parkinson, George. *True Stories of Durham Pit-Life.* London: Charles H. Kelly, 1912.

Parsons, Joanne Ella, and Ruth Heholt, eds. *The Victorian Male Body.* Edinburgh: Edinburgh University Press, 2018.

Parsons, S. *Poetical Trifles: Being a Collection of Songs, and Fugitive Pieces.* York: R. Johnson, 1822.

Paterson, James. *Autobiographical Reminiscences.* Glasgow: Maurice Ogle and Son, 1871.

Patterson, J. E. *My Vagabondage: Being the Intimate Autobiography of a Nature's Nomad.* London: William Heinemann, 1911.

Pavord, Anna. *Landskipping: Painters, Ploughmen and Places.* London: Bloomsbury, 2016.

"Penny-a-Yard: or the Autobiography of a Liverpool Beggar." *Liverpool Mercury*, August 4, 1854.

Plamper, Jan. "The History of Emotions: An Interview with William Reddy, Barbara Rosenwein, and Peter Stearns." *History and Theory* 49 (May 2010): 217–65.

———. *The History of Emotions: An Introduction.* New York: Oxford University Press, 2015.

Plummer, John. *Songs of Labour: Northamptonshire Rambles and Other Poems.* London: W. Tweedie, 1860.

Pool, P. A. S., ed. *The Life and Progress of Henry Quick of Zennor.* Penzance: n.p., 1963.

Porter, Roy. "Happy Hedonists." *British Medical Journal* 321, no. 7276 (December 23–30, 2000): 1572–75.

Potkay, Adam. *The Story of Joy: From the Bible to Late Romanticism.* Cambridge: Cambridge University Press, 2007.

Powell, J. H. *Life Incidents and Poetic Pictures.* London: Trubner, 1865.

Presto, Jonathan. *Five Years of Colliery Life.* Manchester: John Heywood, 1884.

Preston, Thomas. *Life and Opinions of Thomas Preston, Patriot and Shoemaker.* London: A. Seale, 1817.

Price, Kim. "'Where Is the Fault?' The Starvation of Edward Cooper in the Isle of Wight Workhouse in 1877." *Social History of Medicine* 26, no. 1 (2012): 21–37.

Pugh, Albert. "I Helped to Build Railroads." *Pilot Papers* 1, no. 4 (1946): 75–98.

Rann, John. *The Life and Times of John Rann.* London: n.p., 1816.

Ratcliffe, George. *Sixty Years of It: Being the Story of My Life and Public Career.* London: A. Brown and Sons, n.d.

Reddy, William M. *The Navigation of Feeling: A Framework for the History of Emotions.* New York: Cambridge University Press, 2001.

Rediker, Marcus. *Between the Devil and the Deep Blue Sea: Merchant Seamen, Pirates and the Anglo-American Maritime World, 1700–1750*. Cambridge: Cambridge University Press, 1989.
Reiss, Steven. "Human Individuality, Happiness, and Flow." *American Psychologist* 55, no. 10 (2000): 1161–62.
Ricketts, Joseph. "Notes on the Life of Joseph Ricketts, Written by Himself." *Wiltshire Archaeological and Natural History Magazine* 60 (1965): 120–26.
Riddell, Henry Scott. *Poetical Works of Henry Scott Riddell*. Edited by James Bryson. Glasgow: Maurice Ogle, 1871.
Roberts, Robert. *A Wandering Scholar: The Life and Opinions of Robert Roberts*. Cardiff: University of Wales Press, 1991.
Robson, Joseph Philip. *The Autobiography of Joseph Philip Robson*. Newcastle upon Tyne: John Clark, 1870.
———. *The Life and Adventures of the Far-Famed Billy Purvis*. Newcastle upon Tyne: John Clarke, 1849.
Robinson, Eric, ed. *John Clare's Autobiographical Writings*. Oxford: Oxford University Press, 1983.
Rogers, Frederick. *Labour, Life and Literature: Some Memories of Sixty Years*. Edited by David Rubinstein. Brighton: Harvester Press, 1973.
Rogers, Helen, and Emily Cuming. "Revealing Fragments: Close and Distant Reading of Working-Class Autobiography." *Family and Community History* 21, no. 3 (October 2018): 180–201.
Rolfe, Frederick. *I Walked by Night: Being the Life and History of the King of Norfolk Poachers*. London: Ivor Nicholson and Watson, 1935.
Rose, Jonathan. *The Intellectual Life of the British Working Classes*. New Haven, CT: Yale University Press, 2001.
Rosenwein, Barbara. *Emotional Communities in the Early Middle Ages*. Ithaca, NY: Cornell University Press, 2006.
———. "Worrying about Emotions in History." *American Historical Review* 107, no. 3 (June 2002): 821–45.
Rosenwein, Barbara, and Riccardo Cristiani. *What Is the History of Emotions?* Cambridge: Polity Press, 2018.
Ross, Ellen. *Love and Toil: Motherhood in Outcast London, 1870–1914*. New York: Oxford University Press, 1993.
Rossi, Mauro. "Happiness, Pleasure, and Emotions." *Philosophical Psychology* 31, no. 6 (2018): 898–919.
Rushton, Adam. *My Life as a Farmer's Boy, Factory Lad, Teacher and Preacher*. Manchester: S. Clarke, 1909.
Russell, James A. "Culture and the Categorization of Emotions." *Psychological Bulletin* 110, no. 3 (1991): 426–50.
Rutherford, John. *Indoor Paupers, by One of Them*. London: Workhouse Press, 2013.
Rymer, Edward. *The Martyrdom of the Mine*. Middlesbrough: Jordison, 1898.
Sachse, William L., ed. *The Diary of Roger Lowe of Ashton-in-Makerfield, Lancashire, 1663–74*. New Haven, CT: Yale University Press, 1938.
Safdar, Saba, David Matsumoto, Katherine T. Kwantes, Wolfgang Friedlmeier, Seung Hee Yoo, Hisako Kakai, and Eri Shigemasu. "Variations of Emotional Display Rules within and across Cultures: A Comparison between Canada, USA, and Japan." *Canadian Journal of Behavioral Science* 41, no. 1 (2009): 1–10.

Sanderson, Thomas. *Chips and Shavings of an Old Shipwright: Or the Life, Poems and Adventures of Thomas Sanderson.* Darlington: Bragg, 1873.

Sanderson, Thomas, ed. *The Poetical Works of Robert Anderson, Author of 'Cumberland Ballads,' etc., To Which Is Prefixed the Life of the Author, Written by Himself.* Carlisle: B. Scott, 1820.

Sanger, "Lord" George. *Seventy Years a Showman.* New York: E. P. Dutton, 1926.

Saunders, James Edwin. *The Reflections and Rhymes of an Old Miller.* London: Hodder and Staughton, 1938.

Savage, John. *Memoirs Containing Some Particulars of the Life, Family, and Ancestors of John Savage, Miller, of St. Mary Stoke, Ipswich.* Ipswich: S. & W. J. King, 1900.

Saville, R. J., ed. *A Langton Quarryman's Apprentice: James Corben's Autobiography.* Langton Maltravers Local History Society, 1996.

Saxby, Mary. *Memoirs of a Female Vagrant, Written by Herself.* Dunstable: J. W. Morris, 1806.

Scott, Robert. *The Life of Robert Scott, Journeyman Wright.* Dundee: T. Colville and Son, 1801.

Secord, Anne. "'Be What You Would Seem to Be': Samuel Smiles, Thomas Edward, and the Making of a Working-Class Scientific Hero." *Science in Context* 16 no. 1/2 (2003): 147–73.

———. "Botany on a Plate: Pleasure and the Power of Pictures in Promoting Early Nineteenth-Century Scientific Knowledge." *Isis* 93, no. 1 (March 2002): 28–57.

Sen, Amartya. *The Idea of Justice.* Cambridge, MA: Belknap Press, 2009.

Severn, Joseph Millott. *The Life and Experiences of a Phrenologist.* Brighton: Severn, 1929.

Shaw, Charles. *When I Was a Child: Growing Up in the Potteries in the 1840s.* Dormouse Press, 2013 [1903].

Shipp, John. *The Path of Glory: Being the Memoirs of the Extraordinary Military Career of John Shipp, Written by Himself.* London: Chatto and Windus, 1969 [1834].

Shmotkin, Dov. "Happiness in the Face of Adversity: Reformulating the Dynamic and Modular Bases of Subjective Well-Being." *Review of General Psychology* 9, no. 4 (2005): 291–325.

A Short Account of the Life and Hardships of a Glasgow Weaver with His Opinion upon the Question at Present in Hot Dispute between Churchmen and Voluntaries. Glasgow: W. R. McPhun, 1834.

Sigsworth, Michael, and Michael Worboys. "The Public's View of Public Health in Mid-Victorian Britain." *Urban History* 21, no. 2 (1994): 237–50.

Simmons, H. *Ernest Struggles: Or the Comic Incidents and Anxious Moments in Connection with the Life of a Station Master.* Reading: J. J. Beecroft, 1879.

Simmons, James R., Jr., ed. *Factory Lives: Four Nineteenth-Century Working-Class Autobiographies.* Peterborough: Broadview Press, 2007.

Skeen, Robert. *Robert Skeen's Autobiography.* London: Wyman and Sons, 1876.

Skene, F. M. F. "Autobiography of a Tramp." *Belgravia: A London Magazine* 81 (May 1893): 168–79.

Smiles, Samuel. *Self-Help.* London: John Murray, 1860.

———. *Self-Help.* Oxford: Oxford University Press, 2002.

Smith, Deborah. *My Revelation.* London: Houghton, 1934.

Smith, George. *From Gipsy Tent to Pulpit: The Story of My Life.* London: Thomas Law, n.d.

———. *Incidents in a Gipsy's Life*. Leicester: Wales Printing Works, n.d.
Smith, Mary Ann. *The Autobiography of Mary Smith, Schoolmistress and Nonconformist*. London: Bemrose and Sons, 1892.
Smyth, Adam ed., *A History of English Autobiography*. Cambridge: Cambridge University Press, 2016.
Smyth, Edward. *The Extraordinary Life and Christian Experience of Margaret Davidson (as Dictated by Herself)*. Dublin: The Editor, 1802.
Snell, Henry. *Men, Movements and Myself*. London: J. M. Dent and Sons, 1936.
Snell, K. D. M. "Belonging and Community: Understandings of 'Home' and 'Friends' among the English Poor, 1750–1850." *Economic History Review* 65, no. 1 (2012): 1–25.
Snowden, Rita. *Prodigal of the Seven Seas*. London: Epworth Press, 1942.
Somerville, Alexander. *The Autobiography of a Working Man*. London: Charles Gilpin, 1848.
Sorrell, Mark. *The Peculiar People*. Greenwood, SC: Attic Press, 1979.
Southey, Robert. *The Lives and Works of the Uneducated Poets*. London: Humphrey Milford, 1925.
Spacks, Patricia Meyer. "Stages of Self: Notes on Autobiography and the Life Cycle." *Boston University Journal* 25, no. 2 (1977): 7–17.
Spencer, Frederick H. *An Inspector's Testament*. London: English Universities Press, 1937.
Spiegel, Alix. "Changing Social Norms Can Save Your Life." *Invisibilia* Podcast, National Public Radio. https://www.npr.org/2016/06/17/482443233/listen-to-the-episode.
Stamper, Joseph. *Less Than the Dust: The Autobiography of a Tramp*. London: Hutchinson, n.d.
Stanley, Henry Morton. *The Autobiography of Henry Morton Stanley*. New York: Houghton Mifflin, 1909.
Stanley, Liz, ed. *The Diaries of Hannah Cullwick, Victorian Maidservant*. New Brunswick, NJ: Rutgers University Press, 1984.
Stearns, Peter. *American Cool: Constructing a 20th-Century Emotional Style*. New York: NYU Press, 1994.
———. *American Fear: The Causes and Consequences of High Anxiety*. New York: Routledge, 2006.
———. *Battleground of Desire: The Struggle for Self-Control in Modern America*. New York: NYU Press, 1999.
———. *Jealousy: The Evolution of an Emotion in American History*. New York: NYU Press, 1989.
Stearns, Peter, and Carol Stearns. *Anger: The Struggle for Emotional Control in America's History*. Chicago: University of Chicago Press, 1987.
———. "Emotionology: Clarifying the History of Emotions and Emotional Standards." *American Historical Review* 90 (1985): 813–36.
Steedman, Carolyn. *An Everyday Life of the British Working Class: Work, Self and Sociability in the Early Nineteenth Century*. Cambridge: Cambridge University Press, 2014.
———. *The Radical Soldier's Tale: John Pearman, 1819–1908*. New York: Routledge, 1988.
Stevens, William. *A Memoir of Thomas Martin Wheeler*. London: J. B. Leno, 1862.

Stevenson, Jane. *Homely Musings from a Rustic Maiden*. Kilmarnock: printed by the author, 1870.
Stewart, Alexander. *The Life of Alexander Stewart, Prisoner of Napoleon and Preacher of the Gospel*. London: George Allen and Unwin, 1948.
Stewart, Bruce, ed. *The Irish Book Lover: An Irish Studies Reader*. Monaco: Princess Grace Irish Library, 2004.
Stewart, Donald. *The Life of an Agitator*. Hull: Elson, 1921.
Stirrup. "Autobiography of a Journeyman Shoemaker." *Commonwealth*, November 22 and 29, 1856, and December 6, 1857, 3.
Stone, Arthur A., and Christopher Mackie, eds. *Subjective Well-Being: Measuring Happiness, Suffering, and Other Dimensions of Experience*. Washington, DC: National Academies Press, 2013.
Storie, Elizabeth. *The Autobiography of Elizabeth Storie*. Glasgow: Richard Stobbs, 1859.
Story, Robert. *The Poetical Works of Robert Story*. Newcastle upon Tyne: Thomas and James Figg, 1856.
Strack, Fritz, Norbert Schwarz, and Elisabeth Gcshnedinger. "Happiness and Reminiscing: The Role of Time Perspective, Affect, and Mode of Thinking." *Journal of Personality and Social Psychology* 49, no. 6 (1985): 1460–69.
Strange, Julie-Marie. *Death, Grief, and Poverty in Britain, 1870–1914*. Cambridge: Cambridge University Press, 2005.
——. *Fatherhood and the British Working Class, 1865–1914*. Cambridge: Cambridge University Press, 2015.
——. "'She Cried a Very Little': Death, Grief and Mourning in Working-Class Culture, c. 1880–1914." *Social History* 27, no. 2 (May 2002): 143–61.
Strickland, Irina, ed. *The Voices of Children, 1700–1914*. New York: Barnes and Noble Books, 1973.
Strong, Ruth, ed. *Autobiography of Israel Roberts*. Pudsey: Civic Society, 2000.
Struthers, John. *The Poetical Works of John Struthers*. London: A. Fullerton, 1850.
Sturrock, John. *The Language of Autobiography: Studies in the First Person Singular*. Cambridge: Cambridge University Press, 1993.
Sutton, William. *Multum in Parvo: Of the Ups and Downs of a Village Gardener*. Kenilworth: Robertson and Gray, 1903.
Swan, William. *The Journals of Two Poor Dissenters, 1786–1880*. London: Routledge and Kegan Paul, 1970.
Swift, Anne, ed. *The Story of George Cooper, Stockport's Last Town Crier, 1824–1895*. Stockport: Anne Swift, 1975.
Sykes, John. *Slawit in the 'Sixties: Reminiscences of the Moral, Social and Industrial Life of Slaithwaite and District in and about the Year 1860*. London: Schofield and Sims, 1926.
Tandler, Nancy, Annette Krauss, and René T. Proyer. "Authentic Happiness at Work: Self- and Peer-Rated Orientations to Happiness, Work Satisfaction, and Stress Coping." *Frontiers in Psychology* 11 (2020): 1–16.
Taylor, Henry. *Memoirs of the Principal Events in the Life of Henry Taylor of North Shields*. North Shields: T. Appleby, 1811.
Taylor, Peter. *Autobiography of Peter Taylor*. Paisley: Alexander Gardiner, 1903.
Taylor, Samuel. *Records of an Active Life*. London: Simpson, Marshall, 1886.
Taylor, William. *The Life and Work of the Late William Taylor, the Navvy*.

Glasgow: John Rae, 1892.
Teasdale, Harvey. *The Life of Harvey Teasdale, the Converted Clown and Man Monkey*. Sheffield: C. Leonard and Son, 1870.
Teer, John. *Silent Musings*. Manchester: Ainsworth and Cheetham, 1869.
Terry, Stephen. *Glasgow Almanac: An A–Z of the City and Its People*. Glasgow: Neil Wilson, 2005.
Thale, Mary, ed. *The Autobiography of Francis Place*. Cambridge: The University Press, 1972.
Thomas Hardy Society. "Negotiating the Emotional Habitus of the Middle Classes in *The Mayor of Casterbridge*." *Thomas Hardy Journal* 28 (2011): 44–67.
Thompson, Dorothy, ed. *Chartist Biographies and Autobiographies*. New York: Garland, 1986.
Thompson, John. *Memoir of Mr. John Thompson*. Sunderland: Forster, 1893.
Thompson, Laurence. *Robert Blatchford: Portrait of an Englishman*. London: Victor Gollancz, 1951.
Thomson, Christopher. *Autobiography of an Artisan*. Nottingham: J. Shaw, 1847.
Thorne, Will. *My Life's Battles*. London: George Newnes, 1925.
Tibble, J. W., and Ann Tibble, eds. *The Prose of John Clare*. London: Routledge and Kegan Paul, 1951.
Timney, Meagan Birchmore. "Working-Class Women's Writing in the Nineteenth-Century Radical Periodical Press: Chartist Threads." *Philological Quarterly* 92, no. 2 (2013): 177–97.
Todd, Thomas. *My Life as I Have Lived It*. Leeds: Thomas Todd, 1935.
Tomes, Nancy. "A 'Torrent of Abuse': Crimes of Violence between Working-Class Men and Women in London, 1840–1875." *Journal of Social History* 11, no. 3 (1978): 328–45.
Tomkins, Alannah. "Poor Law Institutions through Working-Class Eyes: Autobiography, Emotion, and Family Context, 1834–1914." *Journal of British Studies* 60 (April 2021): 285–309.
Trinder, B. A., ed. "The Memoir of William Smith." *Transactions of the Shropshire Archaeological Society* 58, no. 2 (1965): 178–85.
Tunnicliffe, Stephen. "A Newly Discovered Source for the Life of William Gifford." *Review of English Studies*, New Series, 16, no. 61 (1965): 25–34.
Turner, David M., and Daniel Blackie. *Disability in the Industrial Revolution: Physical Impairment in British Coal-Mining, 1780–1880*. Manchester: Manchester University Press, 2018.
Turner, J. Arthur, ed. [George Lewin, author]. *The Life of a Chimney Boy, Written by Himself*. London: Charles H. Kelly, 1901.
Urie, John. *Reminiscences of Eighty Years*. Paisley: Alexander Gardner, 1908.
Veder, Robin. "The Gardener's Exercise: Rational Recreation in Early Nineteenth-Century Britain." *Proteus* 25, no. 2 (2008): 53–59.
Vincent, David. *Bread, Knowledge and Freedom: A Study of Nineteenth-Century Working-Class Autobiography*. London: Europa, 1981.
———. *Literacy and Popular Culture, England 1750–1914*. Cambridge: Cambridge University Press, 2011.
———. "Love and Death and the Nineteenth-Century Working Class." *Social History* 5, no. 2 (1980): 223–47.
———. *Testaments of Radicalism: Memoirs of Working Class Politicians, 1790–1885*. London: Europa, 1977.

Wakeman, Annie. *Autobiography of a Charwoman*. London: John Macqueen, 1900.
Walker, Mark. *Happy-People-Pills for All*. Oxford: Wiley-Blackwell, 2013.
Wallis, Thomas Wilkinson. *Autobiography of Thomas Wilkinson Wallis, Sculptor in Wood, and Extracts from his Sixty Years' Journal*. Louth: J. W. Goulding and Son, 1899.
Wardle, Joseph. *The Story of My Life*. London: Epworth Press, 1924.
Waterman, Alan S. "The Relevance of Aristotle's Conception of Eudaimonia for the Psychological Study of Happiness." *Theory and Philosophy of Psychology* 10, no. 1 (1990): 39–44.
West, Francis A. *Memoirs of Jonathan Saville of Halifax*. London: Hamilton, Adams, 1843.
West, Herbert Faulkner. *The Autobiography of Robert Watchorn*. Oklahoma: Robert Watchorn Charities, 1958.
Weston, Mary. *The Story of Our Sunday Trip to Hastings, as Related by One of the Party*. London: Working Men's Lord's Day Rest Association, 1890.
Whale, John. "Daniel Mendoza's Contests of Identity: Masculinity, Ethnicity and Nation in Georgian Prize-Fighting." *Romanticism* 14, no. 3 (2008): 259–71.
White, Henry. *The Record of My Life: An Autobiography*. Cheltenham: n.p., 1889.
White, Nicholas P. *A Brief History of Happiness*. Oxford: Blackwell, 2006.
White, Robert. *Autobiographical Notes*. Newcastle: Privately printed, 1966.
Whittaker, Thomas. *Life's Battles in Temperance Armour*. London: Hodder and Stoughton, 1884.
Wickberg, Daniel. "What Is the History of Sensibilities? On Cultural Histories, Old and New." *American Historical Review* 112, no. 3 (2007): 661–84.
Wilkins, John. *The Autobiography of an English Gamekeeper*. New York: Macmillan, 1892.
Wilkinson, Dyke. *A Wasted Life*. London: Grant Richards, 1902.
Willes, Margaret. *The Gardens of the British Working Class*. New Haven, CT: Yale University Press, 2014.
Williams, Heather A. *Help Me to Find My People: The African American Search for Family Lost in Slavery*. Chapel Hill: University of North Carolina Press, 2012.
Williams, Henry Willey. *Some Reminiscences, 1838–1918*. Penzance: J. A. D. Bridger, 1918.
Wilson, John. *Memories of a Labour Leader*. London: T. Fisher Unwin, 1910.
Wiwad, Dylan, and Lara B. Aknin. "Motives Matter: The Emotional Consequences of Recalled Self- and Other-Focused Prosocial Acts." *Motivation and Emotion* 41 (2017): 730–40.
Womack, Elizabeth Coggin. "Window Gardening and the Regulation of the Home in Victorian Periodicals." *Victorian Periodicals Review* 51, no. 2 (Summer 2018): 269–88.
Woolfolk, Robert L., and Rachel H. Wasserman. "Count No One Happy: Eudaimonia and Positive Psychology." *Journal of Theoretical and Philosophical Psychology* 25, no. 1 (2005): 81–90.
Working Man, A. *Reminiscences of a Stonemason*. London: John Murray, 1908.
Working Man, A. *Scenes from My Life, by a Working Man*. London: Seeley's, 1858.
Wright, James D. *Steeple Jack's Adventures*. Aberdeen: W. and W. Lindsay, 1890.

Wright, William. *From Chimney-Boy to Councillor: The Story of My Life.* Medstead: Azania Press, n.d.
Younger, John. *Autobiography of John Younger.* Edited by William Brockie. Kelso: J. & J. H. Rutherfurd, 1881.
Zborowski, Mark. *Life Is with People: The Culture of the Shtetl.* New York: Schocken Books, 1952.

INDEX

Ablett, William, 46, 144
Adams, William E., 49–50, 82, 117, 139
Ahmed, Sarah, 148
Allen, Rose, 39, 119
Anderson, Edward, 32, 88, 134
Anderson, Isaac, 153
Anderson, Robert, 103
Andrew, Jane, 86–87, 151–52, 176–77
Andrews, William, 49
anger, 2, 3, 9, 155, 158–59, 179–84; boxing and, 180–81; masculinity and 179–82, 184; women and, 183
anxiety, 72, 125, 128, 151, 161, 174, 177, 181–82, 190, 204. *See also* fear
Arch, Dick, 200
Arch, Joseph, 142–43
Aristotle, 8, 186
Armstrong, Chester, 48, 67, 112
Arnold, William, 38–39, 176
Ashdown, Eli, 127, 172
Ashford, Mary Ann, 62–63, 163
Ashley, James, 93, 121
Askham, Robert, 82, 94, 145
autobiography, 6–7, 11–26; and audience expectations, 19, 159; and *Bildungsroman*, 157–58; and childhood, 27, 202–3; and emotional display, 19, 22–23; 101, 129–30, 145, 148, 158–61, 171–72, 183, 187; epistemic properties of, 12–15, 25–26, 209; evolution of, 156–59; and genre conventions, 17, 93, 125–26, 148, 156–57, 167–68, 174; and introspectiveness, 24, 155–59; and memory, 23, 205–6; and old age, 203–5; purposes of, 15–17; representativeness of, 23–24; and respectability, 107, 121; self-censorship of, 22–23, 162, 171–73, 180; of women, 19–22, 160–61, 183–84

Baker, Ottilie, 43
Baldry, George, 50, 82, 196
Bamford, Samuel, 33, 99, 109
Barca, Stefania, 93–94
Barclay, Katie, 22
Barclay, Tom, 201
Berker, Joseph, 190–91
Barr, David, 16, 167–68
Bassett, Josiah, 150
Bathgate, Janet, 33
Begiato, Joanne, 53, 159
Belcher, Richard Boswell, 39

281

Bent, James, 57
Bent, Robert, 88
Bentham, Jeremy, 4, 106, 123
Bergg, Franz, 60
Beveridge, Alan, 161
Bewick, Thomas, 175, 179–80
Bezer, John James, 139
Blackie, Daniel, 151
Blake, Jim, 77
Blatchford, Robert, 14–15, 70, 81, 89, 109, 111, 204
Blincoe, Robert, 17, 198–200
Boos, Florence, 13
Bowd, James, 66
Brierley, Benjamin, 35, 83, 84,
Brine, George Atkins, 153
Britten, Barnabas, 50
Britton, John, 1–2, 189
Broadhurst, Henry, 55, 85–86, 98–99, 101
Brodie, Mark, 78
Brooks, Johanna, 191
Broomhall, Susan, 65
Brown, Callum, 88, 125
Bryant, John Frederick, 118
Buckley, John, 38, 59, 87, 198
Buckley, Joseph, 55
Bullen, Frank, 51, 53, 56, 79, 111, 119, 177–78
Burn, James Dawson, 74, 76, 84–85, 90
Burnett, John, 11–12, 24, 43–44, 107, 125, 151, 196
Burt, Thomas, 31–32, 69, 109
Burstow, Henry, 44, 81, 120
Butler, Serjeant Robert, 52, 88–89, 120, 130, 171
Bywater, James, 76

Caine, Barbara, 78
Calladine, George, 51–52, 89–90
Cameron, William, 85, 156
Campbell, Charles, 106–7, 190
Campbell, Duncan, 55, 175
Campbell, Elizabeth, 33, 166
Campkin, James, 49, 74, 95, 109
Candler, Anne, 21
Carnegie, Andrew, 22, 45–46, 70, 90, 108, 112, 189
Carter, Henry, 76, 127–28

Carter, Thomas, 82, 103, 131, 145–46
charity. *See* prosocial behavior
Chartist Co-Operative Land Company, 98
Chartism, 8, 29, 36, 46, 49, 78, 80, 82, 95, 98, 104, 116–117, 119, 139–41, 147, 186, 211
childhood, 6–7, 27–41, 209–10; and abuse, 197–200; and fear, 174–75; and food, 34–35, 197; and freedom, 32; grandparents and, 7, 21, 29–30, 34; and imagination, 33, 110–11; and music, 34; and nature, 98–100, 113; nostalgia for, 28, 35–36; parents and, 28, 30–31, 33–34, 205, 207; reading and, 108–11, 115; Sundays and, 7; 38–39; tears and, 173; transition to adulthood, 39–40; work during, 7, 30, 32, 35–39, 44–45, 101–5, 210; workhouses, 29–30
children. *See* childhood
Christianity. *See* religion
Clare, John, 35, 51, 58, 68, 90, 99, 116
Claxton, Timothy, 43
Clift, William, 120
Coe, Richard, 15–16
Collison, William, 39–40, 143–44
Commons Preservation Society, 96
Cooper, George, 47
Cooper, Thomas, 29, 78, 99, 109, 119
Corben, James, 38
Crawford, J.H., 153
Crittall, F.H., 67
Croll, James, 101
Csikszentmihalyi, Mihaly, 5, 7, 42–43
Cullwick, Hannah, 61, 71–72, 194–95

Dagley, Will, 35
Dale, Nathaniel, 155
Davenport, Allen, 50, 77, 118
Davidson, Margaret, 126
Davies, Thomas, 120, 173
Davin, Anna, 28
deafness, 152–153
depression. *See* sadness
despair. *See* sadness
Diener, Ed, 189
dignity, 148, 153–154, 198, 201, 207

disability, 8, 120, 126, 134, 138–39, 149–58, 182–83
Dixon, Thomas, 160, 164
Dobbs, Betty. *See* Grimes, Martha
Dodd, William, 111
Donaldson, Joseph, 16, 53, 110, 171–72
Dottie, Robert, 16, 87
Douglas, Martin, 172–73
Dunn, James, 85, 86, 133, 173, 180, 206
Dunn, William, 38.
duty, 124–47, 210–11; Chartism as, 138–41; conversion narratives and, 125–26, 177, 211; family and, 142; fatalism and, 133, 147; righteousness and, 132–33; as self-sufficiency, 144–45

Easterlin, Richard, 5, 195
education. *See* self-cultivation
Edward, Thomas, 113
Edwards, George, 37–38, 90–91, 97, 143, 180
Elias, Norbert, 3
emotions: catharsis and, 125; communities of, 4, 187; display of, 19, 22–23; 101, 129–30, 145, 148, 158–61, 171–72, 187; history of, 2–4; memory and, 6, 182; nature of, 2–3; regimes of, 3. *See also* anger; anxiety; fear; happiness; shame
Engels, Friedrich, 209
environment. *See* nature
Errington, Anthony, 156–57, 175–76
eudaimonia, 8, 43, 124, 186. *See also* duty
evangelicalism, 88, 136–37

Farish, William, 97
Farningham, Marianne. *See* Mary Ann Hearn
fear, 9, 78, 128, 159, 173–79; and bodily integrity, 177–78; in childhood, 174–75; physiology of, 178–79; and religion, 176–77; and rusticity, 175–76
Febvre, Lucien, 3
Fielden, Samuel, 163

Finlay, Edward, 17, 199–200
Finney, John, 92–93, 95
Flockhart, Robert, 169, 172
Forrest, Frank, 38–39, 109, 172, 200–201
Fraser, John, 98, 116–17, 206
Freer, Walter, 206
Frost, Ginger, 66

Gabbitass, Peter, 71, 145
Gammage, Robert, 49
Gammon, Vic, 15, 82, 197
Gifford, William, 154–55
Gompers, Samuel, 34
Goring, Jack, 117
Gough, John Bartholomew, 45, 168–69
Graham, Carol, 188
Green, William, 201
Griffin, Emma, 11, 19–20, 25, 34, 61, 183, 206, 211
Grimes, Martha, 13–14, 73, 97–98
Grundy, Anthony, 204
Gutteridge, Joseph, 6, 85, 113–14, 127, 166, 202–3

Hackett, Nan, 125
Hall, John Vine, 131
Hamish, Maureen. *See* Loughran, Mary
Hammond, William, 31
Hampton, Richard, 80
happiness: absence of, 2, 8–9; 148–158, 197–200; and adaptation, 151–153, 185–186, 194–197, 200–202, 207; in childhood, 27–41, 202, 207 (*see also* childhood); and class, 4–5, 197, 207; community traditions and, 81–83; consumption and, 4–5; definitions of, 1–2, 4, 185–87, 194–95; fatherhood and, 73–74; as flourishing, 185–86; friendships in, 56, 74, 78–81; and inequality, 188, 195–96; and memory, 205–6; and mental framing, 193–94; as moods, 9; 125, 185, 189–92, 207, 211; and music, 119–121, 126; and nature, 7–8, 32, 92–105, 113–15, 183, 210–11 (*see also* nature); and play, 31–32, 56; poverty and, 8–9, 85–91, 148–49,

happiness (*cont.*)
  153–155, 195, 197, 200–202; prosocial behavior and, 84–91, 124, 138; religion and, 8, 88–89, 129–32, 145–46, 192 (*see also* religion); resilience in, 154–55, 189, 191–93, 211–12; self-cultivation and, 8, 106–23 (*see also* self-cultivation); social ties and, 7, 54–57, 65–91, 210 (*see also* personal relationships); work and, 7, 31–32, 37, 42–64 (*see also* work); U-shaped curve and, 9, 202–07; women and, 5, 19–21, 41, 195, 211
happiness studies, 5, 84, 184, 188–207, 211
Harman, Horace, 175
Harris, John, 16, 29, 33–34, 81, 109, 111–12, 118–19
Hart, William, 133–34
Haybron, Daniel, 189
Hearn, Mary Ann, 21–22, 94, 118, 121, 135
Heaton, William, 98, 109, 118, 120
hedonic treadmill, 5, 201, 207, 212
Hedonism, 2, 43, 56, 129, 203
Herbert, George, 79, 100
Herbert, Henry, 80
Hill, Octavia, 95
Hillocks, James, 57, 109
Hobbs, Andrew, 117
Hodge, John, 138–139
Holcombe, John, 60
Holcroft, Thomas, 28, 58
Holloway, Henry, 131
Holkinson, Jacob, 33, 109–10
Holmes, Vicky, 167
Holyoake, George Jacob, 50
Hopkinson, James, 192–193
Hopwood, Caroline, 125
Horler, Moses, 83
Horne, Eric, 57–58, 61–62
Houston, James, 206
Hughes, Henry, 177
Humphreys, Charles, 132
Humphries, Jane, 29, 34–36, 71
Huntington, George, 12
Huntington, William, 134
Hunter, John Kelso, 51, 86, 179, 203
Hutton, William, 1–2, 70, 81, 83, 196

illness, 149–158; 160–61
India, 52, 58, 89, 116, 130, 169, 171–72, 206
Innes, Joanna, 186–87, 189
Ireland, 22, 31, 62, 77, 88
Ireson, Alfred, 32, 75, 168, 205

Jackson, Thomas, 150–51
"Jacques," 19, 68, 165
Jermy, Louise, 20–21, 72, 183
Johnston, David, 70, 194
Johnston, Ellen, 20, 192
Jones, Henry, 31, 115–16
Jones, Jack, 80–81, 83, 142
Jones, John, 117–18
Jones, Thomas, 33, 99

Keating, Joseph, 45, 114–15, 190
Kenney, Annie, 63
Kenney, Rowland, 111, 135, 157
King, Laura, 189
Kirkwood, David, 22, 32, 40, 135–36
Kitto, John, 101, 152–53
Kitz, Frank, 141–142
Kotchemidova, Christina, 3

Lansbury, George, 58, 141
Lauder, Harry, 31, 48, 56, 164–65
Layton, Elizabeth, 97, 100
Lax, William Henry, 35, 44–45, 48, 93, 134, 136, 174, 204–5
Leatherland, John, 56, 109, 152
Lee, Charles Babbacombe, 190
Leech, Samuel, 53–54
Leno, John, 59–60, 140
Levenson, Karen Chase, 144
Lewin, George, 89
Lewis, Thomas, 48–49, 76, 132
Lidgett, Joseph, 191
Lipton, Joseph, 80
Lipton, Thomas, 28, 37
Livesey, Joseph, 69, 136
Lloyd, George, 30
Lloyd, Sarah, 186–87
London Working Men's Association, 140
Loughran, Mary, 19, 30, 62, 176
Love, David, 101, 177
Lovekin, Emmanuel, 140

Lovett, William, 121, 140
Lowery, Robert, 36, 67, 139
Luck, Lucy, 168
Lyubomirsky, Sonja, 189

Mace, Jem, 181
MacMahon, Darrin, 3
Mann, Tom, 141
Marcroft, William, 153–54
Marling, Frank George, 110
marriage, 66–73, 91, 187. *See also* personal relationships
Marsden, Joshua, 30, 128
Martin, Jonathan, 125
Martin, Sarah, 89
May, Betty, 100, 154
Mayett, Joseph, 201
Mays, Kelly, 108, 122
McAdam, John, 142
McCurrey, James, 67, 77, 137, 167
McKenzie, Jordan, 187
McPherson, Charles, 54
Mead, Isaac, 49, 134
Meek, George, 39, 56, 80, 112, 114, 170
memory, 23, 92, 165, 182, 193, 205–6
Mendoza, Daniel, 180–81
Mill, John Stuart, 4, 106, 121, 123
Miller, David Prince, 156
Miller, Hugh, 50, 95–96
Milne, William, 59, 81–82, 97, 105
Mitchell, Alexander, 54–55, 74, 102, 205
Mitchell, George, 144, 197–98
Mitchell, Hannah Maria, 62, 72–73, 170
Mitchell, Tommy Buller, 161
M'Kaen, James, 181
Mockford, George, 104, 126–27
Mockford, Mary, 72
Mullin, James, 55, 75, 95, 115, 204
Munday, John, 150
Murison, Alexander, 32, 69, 93
mutual aid. *See* prosocial behavior

National Free Labour Association, 143
nature, 7–8, 32–33, 92–105, 152; allotments and, 96–98; commodification of, 103–4; discomfort and, 104–5; environmentalism and, 93, 105; flowers and, 97–98; freedom and, 94; gardening, 96–98; and noise, 101; resources, 94, 98–99, 103, 210–11; pollution in, 95; solitude of, 93, 100–101
Navickas, Katrina, 96, 103–4
Nicholson, Hamlet, 95, 100
Nicol, James, 44
Nussbaum, Martha, 185–86
Nye, James, 85, 120, 126, 177

Oakley, Elizabeth, 29, 54, 104, 109
Ohry, Avi, 149
Okey, Thomas, 88
Oliver, Thomas, 76, 83, 101, 114, 134–35, 201
O'Neill, John Ward, 159
Osborn, Matthew, 92

Parkinson, George, 16, 22–23, 29, 38, 45, 77–78
Parsons, Samuel, 16–17,
Passmore Edwards, John, 144–45
Patterson, J.E., 158, 166–67, 178
Pearman, John, 52, 95, 148
personal relationships, 65–91; community and, 81–83, 210; family and, 74–78; fatherhood and, 73–74; friends and, 78–81; marriage, 66–73; 91, 167–68, 205, 210; prosocial behavior and, 84–91, 188; reunions and, 74–77, 210; siblings and, 76–77, 166–67
Place, Francis, 112, 167, 174, 182
Plummer, John, 116, 189, 196–97
poetry, 116–19, 122,
Powell, J. H., 44, 87, 98, 110, 164, 169–70, 199–200
Preston, Raymond, 77, 89
Preston, Thomas, 73–74, 138
Price, Henry, 29–30, 68, 113
Prince, Mary, 17
prosocial behavior, 84–91, 124, 138
Pugh, Albert, 85
Purvis, Billy. *See* Joseph Robson

Quick, Henry, 196

Ratcliffe, George, 79, 97
Rattenbury, John, 53
Reddy, William, 3
religion, 124–36; aesthetic pleasures of, 135, 210; and conversion narratives, 125–26, 145, 190; envy in 134; fatalism of, 133; fear and, 176–77; moods and, 124–29, 190–91; and poverty, 134–35; and righteousness, 132–33; sin in, 125–27; sociability of, 135, 188
Riddell, Henry Scott, 60, 117
Roberts, Israel, 170
Roberts, Robert, 60, 75, 108, 130, 161–62
Robson, Joseph, 30–33, 83, 87–88, 203–4
Rogers, Frederick, 47, 87, 94, 116, 200, 205–6
Rolfe, Frederick, 30, 60
Rose, Jonathan, 107–8
Rosenwein, Barbara, 3–5, 174
Ross, Ellen, 39
Rowlands, John, 12–13
Rushton, Adam, 75, 108, 166, 173
Russell, Mrs., 122
Rymer, Edward, 98, 182–83

sadness, 9, 125–26, 154, 159–73; grief, 163–68; homesickness, 168; poverty and, 169–70; tears, 9, 129–30, 164, 167–68, 172–73, 183–84, 198
Sanger, George, 37, 163, 178–79, 203
Saunders, James Edwin, 16, 99, 102–3, 178
Savage, John, 191
Saville, Jonathan, 14, 30, 177
Saxby, Mary, 198
Scotland, 22–23, 26, 30–31, 33, 54, 56, 62, 77, 84, 89, 93, 102, 107, 150, 179.
Scott, Mrs., 60, 122
Scott, Robert, 40–41
Secord, Anne, 113
self-cultivation, 8, 106–23, 210; and authorship, 110; and book-borrowing, 111–13, 122, 210; imagination, 110–111; music, 119–121; *Pilgrim's Progress* and, 109; and poetry, 116–119, 210; reading, 108–110, 115, 122; schools, 107–111, 115, 118, 211; self-directed research, 110, 113–15, 122; women and, 122
Self-Help, 107
Sen, Amartya, 185–86
Severn, Joseph, 32, 37, 71, 83, 95, 102, 114, 174
shame, 3, 12, 129, 168–69, 171, 173, 182
Shaw, Charles, 28, 38, 56–57, 99–100, 174
Shinn, John, 120–21, 169
Shipp, John, 52–53
Smiles, Samuel, 107, 144
Smith, Charles Manby, 67–68, 76, 191–92
Smith, Deborah, 20, 72, 99, 111, 196
Smith, George, 122
Smith, Mary, 31, 36, 108, 118
Snell, Henry, 80, 103, 104, 136, 174, 199–200
Socialism, 8, 14, 138, 141, 157, 201
Somerville, Alexander, 35, 119
Southey, Robert, 117
Spencer, Frederick Herbert, 33, 79
Spurr, Robert, 57, 171
Stamper, Joseph, 104, 198
Standard-of-living debate, 209
Stanley, Henry Morton. *See* Rowlands, John
Stearns, Peter, 3
Stearns, Carol, 3
Steedman, Carolyn, 25, 43, 78
Stewart, Alexander, 76
Stewart, Donald, 74
"Stirrup", 165
Storie, Elizabeth, 17, 149–51
Story, Robert, 116
Stradley, W. John, 54, 176
Strange, Julie-Marie, 11, 24–25, 50, 74, 159, 164, 167, 182
Struthers, John, 85, 170–71
Swan, William (b. 1819), 193–94
Swan, William Thomas (b. 1786), 89, 193
Sykes, John, 175

Tayler, William, 100–101

Taylor, Henry, 134
Taylor, John, 118
Taylor, Peter, 55–56
Taylor, Samuel, 114
Teasdale, Harvey, 132
temperance, 8, 124, 131, 136–37, 169, 210–11
Terry, Joseph, 32, 46–47, 69–70, 86, 98
Thomas, John Birch, 46
Thompson, John, 167
Thomson, Christopher, 28, 82
Thorne, Will, 137, 157–58
Todd, Thomas, 98, 173, 180
Tomkins, Alannah, 29
trade unions, 8, 124, 137–38, 142–43, 147, 157, 180
Turner, David, 151

Urie, John, 94–95

Vincent, David, 11, 18, 22, 24, 43–44, 57, 66, 78, 108, 110, 162–63, 173, 197
volunteerism. *See* prosocial behavior

Wales, 21, 76, 83, 128, 133, 142, 150, 161–62, 177
Wallis, Thomas Wilkinson, 191, 194
Walker, Mark, 189
Wardle, Joseph, 176
Watchorn, Robert, 79, 170, 180
Watson, Fiona, 161
Watson, James, 138–39
Watt, Christian, 160–61, 183
Waugh, Edwin, 71, 98

West, Frank. *See* Campkin, James
Weston, Mary, 41
Wheeler, Thomas Martin, 98
White, Henry, 35, 68, 77, 102
White, Robert, 112
Whittaker, Thomas, 67, 110, 136–37
whole-life satisfaction, 2, 84, 185, 203
Willes, Margaret, 96
Williams, H.G., 162
Williams, Heather A., 25
Wilkins, John, 60
Wilkinson, Dyke, 67
Wilson, John, 19, 109, 114, 163, 178, 205
women: and autobiography, 19–21; in marriage, 66–73; and religion, 135; and sadness, 160–61; and work, 61–63, 210
work, 42–64, 210; and adventure, 43, 51–54; and autonomy, 43, 46, 54, 187; and creativity, 50–51, 210; and domestic service, 57–58, 61–62; farm labor and, 58–61, 101–5; "fit" and, 43, 46, 47–50, 210; "flow", 43–44, 53, 210; skill transfer, 55–56; social ties in, 43, 54–57, 65–91, 187 (*see also* personal relationships); women and, 61–63, 210; workplace conditions, 43, 58–6, 102–5
Woolley, Joseph, 43, 179
Wright, James D., 165–66

Yearsley, Ann, 118
Younger, John 28, 36, 113, 205

The authorized representative in the EU for product safety and compliance is:
Mare Nostrum Group
B.V Doelen 72
4831 GR Breda
The Netherlands